THE TRANSATLANTIC HISPANIC BAROQUE

The Transatlantic Hispanic Baroque

Complex Identities in the Atlantic World

Edited by

HARALD E. BRAUN
University of Liverpool, UK

JESÚS PÉREZ-MAGALLÓN
McGill University, Canada

LONDON AND NEW YORK

First published 2014 by Ashgate Publishing

Published 2016 by Routledge
2 Park Square, Milton Park, Abingdon, Oxon OX14 4RN
711 Third Avenue, New York, NY 10017, USA

Routledge is an imprint of the Taylor & Francis Group, an informa business

Copyright © 2014 Harald E. Braun and Jesús Pérez-Magallón

Harald E. Braun and Jesús Pérez-Magallón have asserted their right under the Copyright, Designs and Patents Act, 1988, to be identified as the editors of this work.

All rights reserved. No part of this book may be reprinted or reproduced or utilised in any form or by any electronic, mechanical, or other means, now known or hereafter invented, including photocopying and recording, or in any information storage or retrieval system, without permission in writing from the publishers.

Notice:

Product or corporate names may be trademarks or registered trademarks, and are used only for identification and explanation without intent to infringe.

British Library Cataloguing in Publication Data
A catalogue record for this book is available from the British Library

The Library of Congress has cataloged the printed edition as follows:
The Transatlantic Hispanic Baroque: Complex Identities in the Atlantic World / edited by
   Harald E. Braun and Jesús Pérez-Magallón.
      pages   cm
   Includes bibliographical references and index.
   1. Civilization, Hispanic – History. 2. Civilization, Baroque – Spain – History.
   3. Civilization, Baroque – Latin America – History. 4. Identity (Psychology) – Spain –
   History. 5. Identity (Psychology) – Latin America – History. 6. Cultural pluralism – Spain
   – History. 7. Cultural pluralism – Latin America – History. 8. Catholic Church – Spain
   – History. 9. Catholic Church – Latin America – History. 10. Spain – Colonies – America
   – Social conditions. I. Braun, Harald (Harald Ernst) II. Pérez Magallón, Jesús, 1952-
   DP48.T674 2014
   909'.097246–dc23   2014017431

ISBN 9781472427502 (hbk)

Contents

List of Figures	*vii*
List of Tables	*ix*
Notes on Contributors	*xi*

Introduction		1
Harald E. Braun and Jesús Pérez-Magallón		

PART I: THE CONSTITUTION OF IDENTITIES IN THE HISPANIC BAROQUE

1	Person and Individual: Baroque Identities in Theology and Law *Bartolomé Clavero*	17
2	Towards a Constructionist Essentialism: Critical Race Studies and the Baroque *Ruth Hill*	35
3	Higher Education, "Soft Power," and Catholic Identity: A Case Study from Early Modern Salamanca *Harald E. Braun*	55
4	"The People of the King": Autonomy and Collective Identity in Coyaima *Renée Soulodre-La France*	75

PART II: HISPANIC BAROQUE: RELIGION, POLITICS, SOCIETY

5	Baroque Religion in Spain: Spanish or European? *Henry Kamen*	95
6	The Baroque and the Influence of the Spanish Monarchy in Europe (1580–1648) *José Javier Ruiz Ibáñez*	113

vi   *The Transatlantic Hispanic Baroque*

7   Rethinking Identity: Crisis of Rule and Reconstruction of
      Identity in the Monarchy of Spain   129
      Pablo Fernández Albaladejo

8   The Preacher Feeds and the Sermon Soothes: Body and
      Metaphor in Jesuit Preaching   151
      Carlos-Urani Montiel and Shiddarta Vásquez Córdoba

PART III: THE URBAN WORLD AND THE HISPANIC BAROQUE

9   The Creole Metropolis   171
      Manuel Lucena Giraldo

10   Foreign Communities in the Cities of the Catholic Monarchy: A
      Comparative Perspective between the Overseas Dominions and
      the Crown of Castile   187
      Manuel Herrero Sánchez

11   Writing Madrid, Writing Identity: A Spatial Dialogue between
      the Seventeenth and Eighteenth Centuries   205
      Jesús Pérez-Magallón

12   The City and the Phoenix: Earthquakes, Royal Obsequies, and
      Urban Rivalries in Mid-Eighteenth-Century Peru   219
      José R. Jouve Martín

13   The Imagery of Jerusalem in the Colonial City   237
      Patricia Saldarriaga

PART IV: NEO-BAROQUE APPROACHES TO IDENTITY

14   Elegies for a Homeland: A Baroque Chronicle, a Marxist
      Critique, and Conflicting Identities in Colonial Guatemala   255
      W. George Lovell

15   Neo-Baroque Catholic Evangelism in Post-Secular Mexico   273
      Kristin Norget

16   La Fiesta de Santo Tomás as a Technology of Culture: Memory,
      Carnival, and Syncretism in the Modern Guatemalan Identity   291
      Anabel Quan-Haase and Kim Martin

Index   *307*

List of Figures

2.1 Frontispiece depicting Della Porta and the various topics of natural philosophy addressed in his treatises. Giambattista Della Porta. *De humana physiognomonia*. Rouen: Jean Berthelin, 1650. By kind permission of Brown University Library.   44

2.2 Frontispiece. Woodcut by Daniel Widman visually distills Della Porta's doctrine as abridged by Stelluti. Giambattista Della Porta. *Della fisonomia di tutto il corpo humano. Libri Quattro. Hora brevemente in tavole sinottiche ridotta et ordinata da Francesco Stelluti*. Ed. Francesco Stelluti. Rome: Vitale Mascardi, 1637. By kind permission of Brown University Library.   45

2.3 Types of nose and lips signal virtues and vices in humans and brutes. Man with pig's snout and man with dog's snout. Giambattista Della Porta. *De humana physiognomonia*. Rouen: Jean Berthelin, 1650. By kind permission of Brown University Library.   47

14.1 The "Corregimiento de Totonicapán y Huehuetenango," as rendered in the late seventeenth century by Francisco Antonio de Fuentes y Guzmán (private collection).   257

List of Tables

8.1   Mapping between different conceptual domains
(THE PREACHER FEEDS)   156

8.2   Mapping between different conceptual domains
(THE SERMON SOOTHES)   157

Notes on Contributors

Harald E. Braun is Senior Lecturer in European History (1300–1700) at the University of Liverpool. He is the author of *Juan de Mariana and Early Modern Spanish Political Thought* (2007). He co-edited *Contexts of Conscience in Early Modern Europe* (2004), *The Renaissance Conscience* (2011), and *Theorising the Ibero-American Atlantic* (2013), and has published articles and chapters on early modern intellectual history, especially the history of early modern Spanish political thought, culture, and communication.

Bartolomé Clavero is Professor of Legal History at the University of Seville. He is the author of numerous books, chapters and articles on legal and cultural history. More recently, his work has focused on the relationship between Latin American constitutional culture, human rights, international law, and the claims of indigenous peoples. His books include *La grâce du don. Anthropologie catholique de l'économie modern* (1996), *Genocide or Ethnocide, 1933–2007: How to Make, Unmake, and Remake Law with Words* (2008), and *Derecho Global: Por una historia verosímil de los derechos humanos* (2014).

Pablo Fernández Albaladejo is Professor of Early Modern Spanish History at the Universidad Autónoma de Madrid. He works on the political and constitutional history of the Ançien Regime, including the relationship between historical writing and identity building in Early Modern Spain. His most recent publications include *Materia de España. Cultura política e identidad en la España moderna* (2007) and *La crisis de la Monarquía*, the fourth volume of the *Historia de España* edited by J. Fontana and R. Villares (2009).

Manuel Herrero Sánchez is Associate Professor in Early Modern History at the Universidad Pablo de Olavide. He has published extensively on international relations and the central role of the mercantile republics of Genoa and the United Provinces in early modern Europe, the diffusion of European knowledge in the early modern world, and the role of foreign communities in the Spanish monarchy. He is the author of *El acercamiento hispano-neerlandés (1648–1678)* (2000), and co-editor of several volumes including *Génova y la Monarquía Hispánica (1528–1713)* (2011), *El arte de la prudencia. La Tregua de los Doce Años en la Europa de los pacificadores* (2012), and *La España de los Austrias. La actividad política* (2011).

Ruth Hill is Professor of Spanish and Andrew W. Mellon Chair of the Humanities at Vanderbilt University. She is the author of *Sceptres and Sciences in the Spains: Four Humanists and the New Philosophy* (2000), *Hierarchy, Commerce, and Fraud in Bourbon Spanish America* (2005), and many articles on race in colonial Spanish America. She is currently working on a history of Aryanism in the Americas entitled *Incas, Aztecs, and Other White Men: A Hemispheric History of Hate*, as well as a study of whitening called *Race and the Transnational South from Simón Bolívar to Hinton Rowan Helper*.

José R. Jouve Martín is Associate Professor of Hispanic Studies in the Department of Languages, Literatures, and Cultures, and Chair of the Latin American and Caribbean Studies interdisciplinary programme at McGill University. His research concentrates on the role of writing, science, and music in the constitution on colonial identities in Latin America. He is the author of *Esclavos de la ciudad letrada* (2005) and *The Black Doctors of Colonial Lima: Science, Race, and Writing in Colonial and Early Republican Peru* (2014). He co-edited *La Constitución del Barroco Hispano-Transatlántico* (2008), *Del Barroco al Neo-Barroco: Realidades y Transferencias Culturales* (2011), and *Contemporary Debates in Ecology, Culture, and Society in Latin America* (2011).

Henry Kamen is a British historian who held academic positions at the University of Warwick, the University of Wisconsin–Madison, and the Higher Council for Scientific Research in Barcelona until his retirement in 2002. He has published extensively on the Baroque, the Enlightenment and the Spanish Inquisition, as well as individual figures such as Philip II, Charles II of Spain, and the Duke of Alba.

W. George Lovell, Fellow of the Royal Society of Canada, is Professor of Geography at Queen's University, Kingston, and Visiting Professor in Latin American History at the Universidad Pablo de Olavide. His scholarly interests relate primarily to colonial experiences, race mixture, and patterns of indigenous survival in Central America, where the fate of Maya peoples in Guatemala has consumed much of his attention. He has 13 book titles to his credit, among them *A Beauty That Hurts: Life and Death in Guatemala* (2010) and (with Christopher H. Lutz) *"Strange Lands and Different Peoples": Spaniards and Indians in Colonial Guatemala* (2013). The recipient of the Carl O. Sauer Distinguished Scholarship Award from the Conference of Latin Americanist Geographers, he is president-elect of the American Society for Ethnohistory (2014–2017).

Manuel Lucena Giraldo is Senior Research Fellow at the Spanish Council for Scientific Research, a member of the Advisory Committee of *National Geographic* in Global History, and Education Attaché at the Spanish Embassy in Colombia. His publications include a number of books on travel, scientific expeditions and cities, as well as nation, empire and globalization in the public imagination. His most recent books are *Naciones de rebeldes. Las revoluciones de independencia latinoamericanas* (2010) and *Francisco de Miranda. La aventura de la política* (2011).

Kim Martin is a PhD candidate in Library and Information Science at Western University. Her research interests include the use of e-books in the humanities, the role of serendipity in historical research, and the information habits of digital humanists. Her academic background is in the areas of English Literature and History, and she is working to keep an interdisciplinary approach throughout her doctoral work by participating in the growing world of the Digital Humanities.

Carlos-Urani Montiel is Professor in the Department of Humanities at the Universidad Autónoma de Ciudad Juarez. He completed his PhD in Hispanic Studies at Western University, where he was part of the project *The Hispanic Baroque: Complexity in the First Atlantic Culture*. He has published several articles on Jesuit history and Latin American and Spanish literature, culture and theatre in a number of academic journals.

Kristin Norget is an Associate Professor of Anthropology at McGill University. Her research examines the relation between religiosity, the Catholic Church, political violence, and the complexity of identity formation in contemporary Latin American society. She is the author of articles and book chapters as well as the monograph *Days of Death, Days of Life: Ritual in the Popular Culture of Oaxaca* (2006). She co-edited a special issue of the journal *Postscripts* entitled *Economies of Sanctity: The Trans-local Roman Catholic Church in Latin America* (2011). Her current projects are a co-edited volume, *The Anthropology of Catholicism*, and a monograph, *Between a Cross and a Hard Place: Practicing Indigenous Theology in Mexico*.

Jesús Pérez-Magallón is Professor of Hispanic Studies at McGill University. His principal areas of research is the origins of modernity, particularly the transition from the Baroque to the Enlightenment and nineteenth-century intellectual history. Other research areas are the Hispanic Baroque, Golden Age Drama, and Textuality and Nationalism. He has published extensively, including *Construyendo la modernidad. La cultura española en el tiempo de los novatores (1675–1725)* (2002), and *Calderón. Icono cultural e identitario del conservadurismo político* (2010). He was awarded the *Encomienda de la Orden del Mérito Civil* by the Spanish government (2009), and is a recipient of the McGill University Faculty of Arts Award for High Distinction in Research (2000).

Anabel Quan-Haase is Associate Professor in the Department of Sociology, Western University, and runs the Socio Digital Lab at Western. She investigates questions around digital technologies and social media – their use, implementation, and social consequences. She currently holds a five-year SSHRC Insight Grant to study how electronic resources and digital tools are changing the nature of scholarship in the digital humanities. She is the author of *Technology and Society: Inequality, Power, and Social Networks* (2013).

José Javier Ruiz Ibáñez is Professor of History at the University of Murcia. His work centres on the formation of the Spanish Monarchy as a global power, especially the local meaning and effects of Spanish imperial hegemony, Spain's allies, and the projection of the country's image beyond its boundaries through military presence, exiles, and the emergence of a discourse of hispanophilia. His many publications include *Felipe II y Cambrai, el consenso del pueblo. La soberanía entre la práctica y la teoría política (1595–1677)* (2003), and, as editor, *Las Milicias del rey de España. Política, Sociedad e Identidad en las Monarquías Ibéricas* (2009).

Patricia Saldarriaga is Professor of Spanish at Middlebury College. She is the author of *Los espacios del Primero Sueño de Sor Juana Inés de la Cruz* (2006) and several articles on early modern Spanish literature and culture. She is currently working on two book projects: *The Virgin of Guadalupe in Contemporary Mexico* and *Geometrization of Power: The Use of Spheres in Baroque Imagery*.

Renée Soulodre-La France is Associate Professor of History at King's University College, Western University, and Affiliate Scholar with the Harriet Tubman Research Institute for Research on the Global Migrations of African Peoples at York University, Toronto. She is the author of *Región e imperio. El Tolima Grande y las Reformas Borbónicas en el siglo XVIII* (2004) and co-edited *Africa and the Americas: Interconnections during the Slave Trade* (2004). Her more recent work focuses on the social and cultural history of the enslaved in Latin America and the interracial relationships that developed within the colonial world when Indigenous, African and European populations were brought together.

Shiddarta Vásquez Córdoba is Assistant Professor at the Universidad Popular Autónoma de Veracruz. He recently completed his PhD, entitled *La crónica de Potosí y sus milagros: complejidad cultural y modelación de relaciones simbólicas*, at Western University.

Introduction

Harald E. Braun and Jesús Pérez-Magallón

Our volume investigates the Hispanic Baroque, the first transatlantic cultural formation, through the prism of identity. Contributors examine complex processes of identity formation in the Hispanic world during the early modern period, and, in some instances, relate these earlier processes and formations to Neo-Baroque and postmodern conceptualizations of identity.

It would require several volumes to cover the many attempts to synthesize an understanding, interpretation, and definition of the Baroque. We have opted for a pragmatic and operational notion of the Baroque. For the purpose of this volume, the Hispanic Baroque extends from the beginning of the seventeenth century until the end of the eighteenth and the beginning of the nineteenth century. Contrary to José Antonio Maravall's view, however, we do not view this cultural formation as simply monolithic and hermetic or propagandistic and manipulative—although we readily acknowledge that these features can be used to describe its hegemonic expressions. Instead, we understand the Baroque as a formation that features breaks, interstices, and cracks through which—alongside hegemonic politics, ideologies and aesthetics—other alternatives constantly emerge, develop, and reach a highly prominent position within the overall formation. The Hispanic Baroque, moreover, is characterized by the development and increase of specific cultural technologies which originated in humanism and became fundamental parts of this complex and enduring cultural formation. The Hispanic Baroque, consequently, shows an unrivaled capacity to adapt and reproduce—a capacity illustrated, for instance, by the "unfinished series of aesthetic accounts" defining Latin American Baroque and Neo-Baroque culture today (Moraña, "Baroque/Neobaroque/Ultrabaroque" 251).

This Baroque capacity to adapt, reproduce, and transform is reflected in the failure of many and varied scholarly attempts to provide a stringent definition. The majority of "defining" approaches chose to employ and contain the Baroque within aesthetic, identitarian, or cultural paradigms of interpretation, and chose to root it firmly in the early modern period. When discussing the Baroque in terms of an aesthetic (or stylistic/artistic) paradigm inspired by the history of art, for instance, many critics (Wölfflin, D'Ors, Weisbach; also Hatzfeld, Orozco, Rousset) have been caught up in classifications and points that are clearly insufficient in order to understand the Baroque as a whole. Both Wölfflin and D'Ors allude to supra-temporal notions, transcendent criteria that do not grasp the historical contexts and conditioning of each concrete cultural formation. Weisbach, on the other hand, links the Baroque to a specific cultural product, the Counter-Reformation. He thus closes the doors to a wider understanding and invites narrow confessional interpretation and propaganda. Without a doubt the most productive contribution in terms of cultural paradigms of interpretation is Maravall's. Within the framework of an early modern social, economic, and political crisis, he views the Baroque as a cultural instrument of aristocratic elites and a mouthpiece for hegemonic values. His Baroque comprises the entire "mobilization of technical resources" (124) that elites in power will use, along with physical repression, in order to define the terms and strengthen the means of social integration. In other words—and closer to Maravall's own words—the Baroque is a directed, mass, urban and conservative culture. Though Maravall may explain Baroque *hegemonic* discourse, he does not cover the *concurrent multitude* of Baroque political, cultural, and social discourses (following Marc Angenot)—since he rigidly elides and invalidates contradictions and ambiguities. Critics of Maravall's rigid interpretation have pointed out the limitations of his research. Fernando R. de la Flor recently suggested that we re-introduce an "openness to represent a death impulse and a principle to go beyond all determinations, including those of the very reason, call it practical reason, experimental reason or even *reason of state*" (19) into Baroque research. The editors and authors contributing to this volume go even further than de la Flor in highlighting the plurality of Baroque discourses—which Maravall and others only read and interpret unequivocally, mono-logically and mono-discursively—as the only way to explore the genesis of modernity in the Hispanic Baroque.

The contributions to this volume also recognize the reality of the Hispanic Baroque as transatlantic reality—existing within contexts discussed and established by David Armitage, Bernard Bailyn, Jorge Cañizares-Esguerra, and José C. Moya, among others. Though we may still want to discuss manifestations of the Renaissance or the Baroque within the confines of a specific European territory, therefore, this is simply not possible in the case of Spain. Juan Luis Suárez has pointed out that part of the difficulty of theorizing about the Hispanic Baroque stems from this transatlantic aspect and the fact that it makes the Hispanic Baroque the first global cultural formation (35). As noted by Carlos Fuentes long ago, the Atlantic Ocean did not act as a separation, barrier or border between Europe and the Americas, or between Spain and its Latin American viceroyalties, but rather as a bridge, a metaphoric highway, on which goods, people, ideas and cultural objects circulated in both directions. Julio Ortega, too, quite rightly emphasized the Atlantic's unifying aspect with regard to the institutional and political reality as well as the economic and cultural reality of the Spanish Monarchy and Hispanic Empire.

Introduction   3

The imposition of chronological boundaries on the Baroque raises obvious questions—whether it be placed within the parentheses of one century (1580–1680) as Fernando R. de la Flor suggests, or extending it from the sixteenth century to the period of the *novatores* and the beginning of the Spanish Enlightenment as Jesús Pérez-Magallón proposes. Here, the contribution of Claude-Gilbert Dubois is helpful and illustrative. According to Dubois, the historic and political Baroque began as a reaction to sixteenth-century reforms that lasted until the end of the eighteenth century. What characterizes the Baroque age, then, at the political level, is the tension between the theory and propaganda of absolute or divine right monarchy, on the one hand, and its actual reality and practice on the other. Enlightened despotism is only one actualization of an invented tradition and imagination of power that was constantly forced to steep low and adapt to varying circumstances in distant and culturally and geographically diverse regions. The observations of Dubois and others concerning the constant tension in the political sphere are of wider significance for our understanding of the Hispanic Baroque. This Hispanic Baroque is defined by—and its cultural dynamic and longevity rooted in—contradictory aspects that have been marginalized or considered mutually exclusive in previous attempts at periodization and chronology. A willingness to accept the impossibility of resolving contradictions and courage to turn complexity into a dynamic of interpretation and cultural practice characterizes the Hispanic Baroque In contrast to Renaissance ideals of harmony, the Hispanic Baroque often consciously synergizes and disperses the flow of imagination. Ultimately, it could be defined as a utopia of impossible diversity and unity—unitary and binary, authoritarian and schizoid at the same time.

For the purposes of this volume, then, the Hispanic Baroque is defined, following Juan Luis Suárez, as a cultural system characterized by forms of expression that are extremely charged with meaning, whose interactions follow a certain model through the effective and technically oriented combination of a variety of information codes (visual, linguistic and imaginative) coalescing in the same individual representation—the same cultural object—through the use of imaginative, non-linear techniques. Insofar as we are referring to a complex system, the cultural formation of the Baroque can be defined as "one made up of a large number of parts that have many interactions" (Simon 183–4). In the words of Yaneer Bar-Yam, this methodology for approaching the Baroque "deals with the description of a complex reality and, simultaneously, the elements that, in its interactions, provoke this complexity" (5–6). The adaptive ability of this cultural system and its survival depend on a sustained balance between forces such as social diversity, religious variations, and physical distance on the one hand, and the tendency to impose unilateral and uniform perceptions, values, and structures (for instance in terms of government) on an extremely diverse reality. In the case of a cultural and political system as complex as the Hispanic

Monarchy, Suárez identifies three factors capable of working towards a state of dynamic equilibrium: modes of representation, forms of domination, and systems of information (Suárez, "Hispanic Baroque" 41). These three factors enabled the political and cultural expansion of the territories of the Spanish Monarchy or Hispanic Empire, the first wave of global capitalism in the Western world. They allowed, for instance, for the development of a series of common codes of representation, which we call Baroque style in art, music, and literature, with regional variations and diachronic appearances, from the beginning of the seventeenth to the beginning of the nineteenth century. The result of cultural developments that took place in the regions of Europe and the Americas colonized by the Spanish Monarchy, the Hispanic Empire not only became the model for subsequent European expansion and colonization, but gave rise to the first complex and transcontinental cultural system of modernity (Suárez, "Hispanic Baroque" 38).

The editors and contributors to this volume—while bearing in mind the issues raised by Handler, Brubaker, Cooper, Melo, and others—still make use of the concept of national identity (or identities). We follow Tim Edensor's suggestion that "[n]ational identity persists in a globalising world, and perhaps the nation remains the pre-eminent entity around which identity is shaped" (iv). The resultant dilemma is perhaps best summed up by the Spanish political cartoonist "El Roto," who in a cartoon published in *El País* 22 May 2013 suggests that "[i]dentities are established in the vacuum of what we are." Arguably, the very notion of identity, national identity not least, already subject to postmodern deconstructions, could be abandoned altogether. However, there would still be a space to be filled with the characteristics of communities, groups and individuals constituting themselves and inviting exploration. In the wake of Edward Said, Homi K. Bhabha, Eric Hobsbawm, Benedict Anderson and Anthony D. Smith, this volume, therefore, continues to explore challenges to essentialist, transcendent and static notions of national identity which constitute the conceptual sublimation or reduction of a certain perception of the country's history and reality.

We prefer a flexible, open and immanent conception. Like Foster, we posit that "[n]either the nation-as-community nor, therefore, national culture has any essential properties [...] Nations, and national cultures are artifacts" (252). The same can be said of identities that are built on, exist within, or concur with nations and national cultures. With Amaryll Chanady, we hold that "[a]ny investigation of collective identity today, if it is not to become an essentialist quest for a national spirit of soul, must necessarily bear in mind that knowledge is constructed, and that this construction is endlessly renewed" (x). Several contributions reflect Stuart Hall's assertion that "[i]dentities are never unified and, in late modern times, increasingly fragmented and fractured; never singular but multiply constructed across different, often intersecting and antagonistic

Introduction

discourses, practices and positions" (4). We apply the notion of identities as cultural creations rooted in historical and social processes to manifestations of identities—nation, race, individual—from the early modern to the modern period. New forms of written, iconographic or cybernetic representation of identity remind us of Benedict Anderson's and Eric Hobsbawm's point that any identity is an ideological construct, an invented tradition or series of cultural practices and re-workings of memory.

In the case of the Hispanic Monarchy, from the nineteenth century onwards, essentialist perspectives determined "Spanish" as Catholic, monarchist and romantic. Hispanic America in turn was considered essentially Baroque (a concept that the Frenchman Yves Bottineau also applied to the Spanish). Whatever did not conform to this paradigm was seen as the "Other," within and yet outside the national community, and thus a threat to its identity. This notion of otherness, and others based on gender, race or religious difference, reflect ideological and political difference and can be referred to as *internal otherness* (José Antonio Giménez Micó). Whether the Hispanic (Spanish or Latin American) is defined a monarchist or Catholic, Baroque or romantic, always depends on a biased reading of the nation's history and cultural practice that imposes the suppression or repression of everything that does not fit into it. If we must accept the existence of a so-called "collective identity," then it should without a doubt be a dialectical and flexible concept that incorporates various explicit and frequently conflicting expressions of nationhood.

Is it at all possible, then, to speak of national identity or identities when referring to the transatlantic Hispanic Baroque? This is a crucial question, since if we accept that national identity is a social and cultural construct, as already stated above, we can assume that *collective* (community) identity is the result of a similar process. Montserrat Guibernau (11–25) suggests that we break down and analyze national identity in terms of five components: psychological, cultural, historical, territorial and political. The question is not one of investigating what constitutes the essence of identity or identities, but instead of concurrently approaching those factors that influenced, helped shape or reflect on a particular identity. There is still the question whether we can consider "one" national identity, especially if we take into account contact with other nations in the peninsula and in the European and Latin American viceroyalties. The fact is that Spanish identity as a collective identity does not seem to be firmly established at any point anywhere during the sixteenth and seventeenth centuries. Castile sought to monopolize the representation of territory-based identity. However, this assumed identity monopoly—accompanied by what Antoni Jutglar describes as a "pluralistic mechanism" of political management—was challenged and eroded by Catalonia and Portugal in the middle of the seventeenth century. Their challenge did not originate solely in cultural causes; rather, it had economic and political reasons in the form of a power struggle. The marginalization that

Castile sought to impose on other territories of the peninsula, too, encouraged increasingly strong reactions to the exercise of imperial power (see the work of John H. Elliott or Eva Serra).

The arrival of the Bourbons, while further opening up trade to other territories of the monarchy, did not really mark a watershed in this respect. The Bourbons, too, tried to exclude Creoles and aristocrats from positions of power and control. Eventually, popular resistance encouraged and stimulated increasingly strong nationalism, whose emergence may be counted among the causes of the articulation of new American nations. Emerging Latin American interpretations of identity included a plethora of ethnic and racial aspects, as highlighted by García Canclini or Gloria Anzaldúa, for example, whose work suggests mixing and hybridization to be the dominant trait in the construction of Latin American identities. Their approach is reflected in almost all subsequent contributions to scholarship. The fact that many nations or tribes have preserved their racial specificity makes the picture even more complex than might be immediately apparent. Past attempts to establish a national genealogy (in the sense that this word can or could be applied to Latin America) through the role of Creoles and Creole identity reflect this complexity. This process of establishing and critiquing national genealogies—a process in which many intellectuals, including Roggiano, Moraña and Hill, have participated—bore the unmistakable signs of differences within the context of a shared world.

Contributions in this volume explore this shared world as one thriving with hybrid, complex, and competing notions, practices, and realities of identity, and offering viewpoints from the sixteenth to the twenty-first century. For a long time, the very structure of the Spanish Monarchy facilitated a strategic coexistence between nations and communities. This coexistence later fed into the monarchy's attempts to build a single national identity corresponding to a single nation. What is significant is that this process took place in both the peninsula and in the viceroyalties, initiating a process that would eventually give rise to new independent nations.

***

We have divided our volume into four parts because we believe that it is an appropriate way to approach the complexity of the issues explored here. Thus, Part I addresses the transatlantic Hispanic Baroque in theoretical and practical terms. Part II explores the role of religion in the development of notions of identity. Part III deals with urban space as a point from which to investigate the relationship between the city and the complex representation of identities. Finally, within a framework of the cultural transfer of the Hispanic Baroque into twentieth and twenty-first century societies, contributors analyze practical expressions of cultural technologies and notions of identity in three contemporary locations and contexts, and using three different approaches.

Introduction 7

Since we do not intend to deal with the complexity and conflict of collective identities from an essentialist or a nationalist perspective, the question then arises: What various elements make up the identities within the framework of the transatlantic Hispanic Baroque? In other words, what elements do we need to consider in order to try to understand these complex and conflicting identities? In the first section, we offer reflections on when and how a person could become an individual in Europe, a protagonist in political and national, social and cultural transformations of identity that continued beyond the early modern period. The first to examine this issue is Bartolomé Clavero. He develops his argument not only within the Hispanic transatlantic framework, but also within the broader framework of Western Europe during this period, and with particular attention to the central role played by English authors. Thus, beginning with Sebastián de Covarrubias, then moving on to John Locke, and concluding with William Blackstone, Clavero seeks to establish a Western European genealogy of the articulation of individual rights and, consequently, individual identity as the very basis of a political being. Recent research, for example the contributions in the volume published by Danna Levin and Federico Navarrete, *Indios, mestizos y españoles* (2007), or the collection of essays published by Andrew B. Fisher and Matthew D. O'Hara, *Imperial Subjects: Race and Identity in Colonial Latin America* (2009), make clear that any reflection on communities in Latin America is inconceivable without accepting the ethnic component. Contributions in this volume highlight this concern, particularly the chapter by Ruth Hill. In dialogue and debate with writers such as Bruno Latour, Peter Wade and Michael Root, Hill reiterates the contributions and positions of the Hispanic Baroque on the modalities of race and, in particular, the biological variations linked to the concept of race. She concludes that "baroque alterity was cognitively and conceptually derived from a constructionist essentialism." Harald E. Braun then presents a case study from early modern Salamanca, analyzing the ways in which elite transnational communities and networks could establish themselves through shared education as well as social and cultural practice. Braun explores the University of Salamanca, the center providing most of the future officials and leaders of the Spanish Monarchy, as a hub or "open space" where individuals could furnish the complex and many-layered identity needed to succeed in early modern European politics and society. Renée Soulodre-La France in turn focuses on the survival of non-hybrid ethnic communities, and allows us to follow the varying fortunes of the Coyaima and their strategies of establishing identity in conflict and cooperation with colonial authorities and indigenous neighbors from the sixteenth to the twenty-first century.

The second section explores the religious component in Hispanic identity or identities. Contributors acknowledge that attempts at religious homogenization formed a central part of the Spanish Monarchy's colonizing plan. At the same time, these attempts occurred in a political world characterized by diversity and a high degree of autonomy available to various viceroys. While the Spanish language was central to the process of evangelization and colonization, it was by no means its sole or exclusive vehicle—aspects not usually considered need to be included. Henry Kamen sets out to do so in terms of a reflection on the nature of religion, the basis of colonization, and by attempting to answer the question of the origin of the religiosity that marked the monarchy's Latin American venture and ended up being a determining, albeit modified factor in shaping the Baroque. José Javier Ruiz Ibáñez then goes on to explore the role religion played in the Hispanic Empire's political and military ventures, especially in Europe. In fact, in his chapter, Ruiz Ibáñez traces the instrumentalization of religion back to the sixteenth century, noting its expansion in the next century and, most importantly, pointing out the ambivalent effects of this instrumentalization, particularly in relation to France and Flanders. Next, Pablo Fernández Albaladejo analyzes the self-reflection that took place in the second half of the seventeenth century—reflection on what could be understood as the identity of the country and how to deal with a collective crisis of conscience in the entire Western European region. According to Fernández Albaladejo, in the last third of the seventeenth century, "*Spain* had simply ceased to be what it had once been. At the beginning of the reign of Charles II, *Spain* was experiencing an identity crisis, an upheaval so profound that the party concerned seemed not to recognise its own reflection." Finally, Carlos-Urani Montiel and Shiddarta Vásquez Córdoba investigate one of the crucial processes in colonial evangelization: the role of Jesuit sermons. More specifically, the authors examine the function of images and metaphors of food as a vehicle through which the Spanish colonizers' homogenizing and evangelistic message was recorded and conveyed in terms of religion and identity.

In Part III, the city takes center stage. We take our cue from Claude Lefort, who, following Marc Bloch, writes about Europe as a field of urban culture in which the city is the place of a particular humanity. The city, however, is not, and was not, only European. In the Spanish Monarchy and her various viceroyalties, cities became "natural" centers of power, culture, arts and social life. In Europe, the capital cities competed with one another in order to become the paradigm and the model to be emulated by others. In the Americas, however, the picture was somewhat different. There were relatively few, but very significant, great cities in the pre-Hispanic cultures. Located in Mexico and Peru, Tenochtitlán and Ciudad de los Reyes emulated and surpassed European cities. From this perspective, Manuel Lucena Giraldo presents the role of Lima and Mexico as cities where Spaniards and Creoles promoted a vitality comparable, if not superior, to the metropolis. Manuel Herrero Sánchez then explores the presence and development of "foreign" communities in the cities of the Hispanic Empire and shows the ease with which these communities—despite their religious, cultural and identity differences—settled and marked the identity of Hispanic

Introduction 9

cities with their presence. Jesús Pérez-Magallón looks at the city of Madrid, contemplating the marks of identity that various social sectors and cultural groups left on the imperial capital's architecture and urban development, and, in particular, how some designs of Baroque origin were superimposed with different programmatic designs that were clearly linked with neoclassical and Enlightenment considerations. José R. Jouve Martín discusses the funeral rituals performed in far-off places such as Peru after the death of the monarch in Madrid. These funerals became a stage to convey social differences and to confront sectors that wanted to adopt such obsequies as a mechanism to express a marked and different identity. Finally, Patricia Saldarriaga investigates the role of a utopian reading of Jerusalem in the configuration of the urban landscapes, arts and urban life of Mexico City. Saldarriaga explores the specific way in which the indigenous, *mestizo*, *criollo*, and Spanish discourses coexisted with their different religious, ritual, psychological, hierarchical, and cultural obligations, and how they came to transform their urban labyrinths into places where indigenous peoples were able to inscribe their own culture and, thus, include some of their signs of identity.

Not only did the Baroque establish itself as a hegemonic culture in the early modern Hispanic Atlantic, two main factors ensured its transfer into the twentieth and twenty-first century world: first, the vitality of the Baroque cultural system and the malleability of its technologies; and secondly, a certain overlap in the characteristic features of the international situation, which led to a cultural evolution some authors have defined as the emergence of postmodernity. The fourth and final section of our volume, therefore, engages with a number of—conflicting and competing—vantage points on the transfer of the Baroque into the twenty-first century.

One is Bolívar Echeverría's critique of postmodernism as a cultural system ideologically subjugated by the political hegemony of conservatism. He theorizes about the Baroque position within the context of what he considers to be a civilizatory crisis extending for more than a century. Echeverría describes this crisis as "the project of modernity that was imposed on human civilization's modernization process: the capitalist project in its puritanical and Northern European form, which was slowly asserted and perfected to prevail over other alternatives" (15). In response, Echeverría constitutes a Baroque *ethos* that perceives post-capitalist modernity as an "attainable utopia" (17). This Baroque *ethos* is a "distant way [...] to view the transcendent need of the capitalist reality. However, it does not accept or appropriate it, but instead always regards it as unacceptable and alien" (20). Ultimately, the Baroque serves Echeverría as a reference for a future alternative to the dominance of capitalism. His ideas, that the Baroque is equivalent to a "conflicting combination of conservatism and non-conformity" and that "Baroque behaviour begins with despair and ends with vertigo" (26), illustrate the difficulty of establishing a simplistic and seemingly coherent connection between the Baroque and modernity.

In this vein, Alfredo Roggiano and Mabel Moraña posit that Baroque poetics arrived in the New World against the will of authorities, and attribute it to a marginal, transgressive and subversive reality that is related to Severo Sarduy's "Baroque of the Revolution" (184) and diametrically opposed to what John Beverley described as the "Baroque of the State." According to Roggiano, the Baroque in the Americas is not a creation of the Spanish Monarchy, and, in the words of Lezama Lima, can in fact be seen as a "counter-conquest." In this view, the Baroque was a cultural weapon *against* the colonizers. Neo-Baroque embodiment, in turn, brings hope and the militant and instrumental value of utopian thought.

Contributions to Part IV of the volume prefer to approach the problem of the Neo-Baroque from another angle instead. Like Nicholas Spadaccini and Luis Martín-Estudillo, contributors start from the premise that the Hispanic Baroque is open to and characterized first and foremost by "recyclings and permutations" (ix). The chapters in this section thus revisit the notion of cultural transfer and argue that the reappearance of the Baroque—like the Neo-Baroque and/or Ultra-Baroque at the end of the twentieth century and early twenty-first century, and within the Hispanic as well as other geographical and cultural contexts—confirms the cultural strength of the Baroque system. This analysis is rooted in the work of Calabrese, Chiampi and Ndalianis—among others—and more recently Monika Kaup, who "reconceptualizes the Baroque's transhistorical and transnational continuities, explaining why it has experienced such a surprising resurgence over the last century and why it could manifest itself far beyond its traditionally-conceived geographical and temporal limits" (Austin 394). However, it is not simply a reappearance—contrary to a conservative idea of postmodernism. Rather, the Neo-Baroque established itself as a militant but in no way ideologically coherent system engaging with political, social and cultural realities, and as a political instrument that gives a voice to marginalized silence. This actualization of the Neo-Baroque is superbly examined by Katherine A. Austin in her analysis of the performances by Gómez-Peña and La Pocha Nostra, Amalia Mesa-Bains' installations, and Ana Castillo's writings (all of whom are located in the border-culture between the United States and Mexico). According to Austin, the Neo-Baroque "serves as a paradigm for understanding yet another period of transculturation—globalization" (394).

Three very different essays explore this resurgence and transformation of the Baroque in terms of a politically *engagé* Neo-Baroque. Each pays special attention to the ways in which the Neo-Baroque links into the articulation of complex identities. First, W. George Lovell explores the intellectual and imaginary mechanisms that enabled Severo Martínez Peláez, the Guatemalan author of *La patria del criollo*, to find an "indisputable reference" to *criollo* identity in the

Introduction 11

characteristically Baroque work of Francisco Antonio de Fuentes and Guzmán, *Recordación florida* (written at the end of the seventeenth century). The work of Fuentes and Guzmán allows Martínez Peláez to articulate his own thoughts on the contemporary reality of Guatemala and, in particular, its highly specific identity and racial structure. In what seems to be a paradox, if not an antinomy, the Marxist author refers time and again to the Baroque text in order to understand and facilitate the understanding of colonial society, the framework within which Guatemala's present-day society developed. Kristin Norget then examines Neo-Baroque strategies of the Catholic Church in contemporary Mexico. She emphasizes how these strategies work in Oaxaca in the church's evangelistic efforts to incorporate indigenous forms in what is essentially a metropolitan discourse. Catholic evangelistic strategies acquire a very powerful value in relation to the Virgin of Guadalupe, a key part in the articulation of Mexican identity. At the same time, the Virgin is an icon of collective identity that undoubtedly and deliberately refers to the Baroque. Finally, Anabel Quan-Haase and Kim Martin specifically examine the Fiesta Santo Tomás of Chichicastenango, Guatemala, as an excellent example of the ways in which different forms of representation reflect modes of domination. What the Fiesta de Santo Tomás also allows us to trace and assess is the process of syncretism and cultural parallelism between various social and ethnic groups in modern Guatemala. Quan-Haase and Martin thus provide an up-to-date understanding of collective identity and its religious component, and a fascinating example of how the complex societies of the transatlantic Hispanic Baroque facilitated cultural interaction that resulted in hybrid forms of identity maintained to the present day.

***

This volume brings together significant, though not necessarily concordant voices from a wide range of disciplines, including contributions from scholars in law, geography, history, political theory, anthropology, and literature. It aims to offer the reader diverse vantage points on the same, challenging problem: how identity or identities in the Hispanic world may be analyzed and interpreted. Though contributors approach the Baroque from different disciplinary and theoretical angles, they share a sense of the Hispanic Baroque as a complex and global culture, as a culture that encapsulates the ways in which a great number of communities—communities characterized by striking differences in culture, race, religion, and language—were and to this day remain in vital contact and intensive interaction. In more than one sense, in fact, this volume reflects the results of such contacts and their effect on the construction of identity/identities in the early modern Hispanic Empire and the Hispanic world since the eighteenth century.

The Introduction and chapters by Pérez-Magallón, Jouve Martín and Saldarriaga have been translated by Myles McKelvey. Chapters by Clavero, Ruiz Ibáñez, Montiel and Vásquez Córdoba, Lucena Giraldo, and Herrero Sánchez have been translated by Judy Kerry. Spanish quotations in Kamen's chapter have been translated by Meredith Richard. We thank all of them for their invaluable help.

We would like to thank the Social Sciences and Humanities Research Council of Canada for the generous grant they provided us under the program of Major Collaborative Research Initiatives.

Bibliography

Anderson, Perry. *The Origins of Postmodernism*. London: Verso, 1998.

Armitage, David. "Tres conceptos de historia atlántica." *Revista de Occidente* 281 (2004): 7–28.

Austin, Katherine A. *"Review of Neobaroque in the Americas: Alternative Modernities in Literature, Visual Art, and Film*. Charlottesville: University of Virginia Press. 2012. 378 pp." *Revista Canadiense de Estudios Hispánicos* 37.2 (2013): 392–4.

Bar-Yam, Yaneer. *Dynamics of Complex Systems*. Reading, MA: Addison-Wesley, 1997.

Beverley, John. "Nuevas vacilaciones sobre el Barroco." *Revista de Crítica Literaria Latinoamericana* 14.28 (1988): 215–27.

Brading, David A. *The First America: The Spanish Monarchy, Creole Patriots, and the Liberal State 1492–1867*. Cambridge: Cambridge University Press, 1991.

Brubaker, Rogers, and Frederick Cooper. "Beyond Identity." *Theory and Society* 29 (2000): 1–47.

Canny, Nicholas and Anthony Pagden, eds. *Colonial Identity in the Atlantic World, 1500–1800*. Princeton: Princeton University Press, 1987.

Chanady, Amaryll. "Introduction: Latin American Imagined Communities and the Postmodern Challenge." *Latin American Identity and Constructions of Difference*. Ed. Amaryll Chanady. Minneapolis, MN: University of Minnesota Press, 1994. ix–xlvi.

Compagnon, Antoine. *Les cinq paradoxes de la modernité*. Paris: Seuil, 1990.

de la Flor, Fernando R. *Barroco. Representación e ideología en el mundo hispánico (1580–1680)*. Madrid: Cátedra, 2002.

D'Ors, Eugenio. *Lo barroco*. Madrid: Aguilar, 1944.

Dubois, Claude-Gilbert. *Le baroque. Profondeurs de l'apparence*. Paris: Larousse, 1973.

Echeverría, Bolívar. "El *ethos* barroco." *Modernidad, mestizaje cultural, "ethos" barroco*. Ed. Bolívar Echeverría. Mexico, DF: Universidad Nacional Autónoma de México; El Equilibrista, 1994. 13–36.

Edensor, Tim. *National Identity, Popular Culture and Everyday Life*. Oxford: Berg Publishers, 2002.

Fisher, Andrew B. and Matthew D. O'Hara, eds. *Imperial Subjects: Race and Identity in Colonial Latin America*. Durham, NC: Duke University Press, 2009.

Foster, Robert J. "Making National Cultures in the Global Ecumene." *Annual Review of Anthropology* 20 (1991): 235–60.

Giménez Micó, José Antonio. "*Biografía de un cimarrón*, de Miguel Barnet/ Esteban Montejo." *Memorias y olvidos: autos y biografías (reales, ficticias) en la cultura hispánica*. Ed. J. Pérez-Magallón, R. de la Fuente Ballesteros and K.M. Sibbald. Valladolid: Universitas Castellae, 2003. 129–46.

Guibernau, Montserrat. *The Identity of Nations*. Cambridge: Polity, 2007.

Hall, Stuart. "Introduction: Who Needs Identity?" *Questions of Cultural Identity*. Ed. S. Hall and P. du Gay. London: Sage, 1996. 1–17.

Handler, Richard. "Is 'Identity' a Useful Cross-Cultural Concept?" *Commemorations: The Politics of National Identity*. Ed. John R. Gillis. Princeton, NJ: Princeton University Press, 1994. 27–40.

Hatzfeld, Helmut A. *Estudios sobre el barroco*. Madrid: Gredos, 1964.

Jutglar, Antoni. *La España que no pudo ser*. Barcelona: Anthropos, 1971.

Kaup, Monika. *Neobaroque in the Americas: Alternative Modernities in Literature, Visual Art, and Film*. Charlottesville, VA: University of Virginia Press, 2012.

Levin, Danna and Federico Navarrete, eds. *Indios, mestizos y españoles. Interculturalidad e historiografía en la Nueva España*. Mexico, DF: Universidad Autónoma Metropolitana Azcapotzalco and Universidad Nacional Autónoma de México, 2007.

Lezama Lima, José. "La curiosidad barroca." *Confluencias. Selección de ensayos*. Ed. and Prologue by Abel E. Prieto. Havana: Letras Cubanas, 1988. 229–46.

Maravall, José Antonio. *La cultura del barroco*. 2nd edition. Barcelona: Ariel, 1981.

Melo, Jorge Orlando. "Contra la identidad." *El Malpensante* 74 (2006): 85–94.

Moraña, Mabel. "Baroque/Neobaroque/Ultrabaroque: Disruptive Readings of Modernity." *Hispanic Baroques: Reading Cultures in Context*. Ed. Nicholas Spadaccini and Luis Martín-Estudillo. Nashville, TN: Vanderbilt University Press, 2005. 241–81.

———. "Barroco y conciencia criolla en Hispanoamérica." *Revista de Crítica Literaria Latinoamericana* 14.28 (1988): 229–51.

Moser, Walter. "Le recyclage culturel." *Recyclages. Économies de l'apprpriation culturelle*. Ed. Claude Dionne, Silvestra Marinello and Walter Moser. Montreal: Les Éditions Balzac, 1996. 23–53.

Orozco, Emilio. *Manierismo y barroco*. Salamanca: Anaya, 1970.

Pagden, Anthony. *Spanish Imperialism and the Political Imagination: Studies in European and Spanish-American Social and Political Theory 1513–1830*. New Haven, CT: Yale University Press, 1990.

Parkinson Zamora, Lois. *The Inordinate Eye: New World Baroque and Latin American Fiction*. Chicago: University of Chicago Press, 2006.

Pérez-Magallón, Jesús. *Construyendo la modernidad: la cultura española en el "tiempo de los novatores" (1675–1725)*. Madrid: Consejo Superior de Investigaciones Científicas, 2002.

———. "The Baroque: The Intellectual and Geopolitical Reasons for a Historiographical Erasure." 3 May 2012. <http://dossiersgrihl.revues.org/5197>.

Pratt, Mary-Louise. *Imperial Eyes: Travel Writing and Transculturation*. London: Routledge, 1992.

Roggiano, Alfredo A. "Para una teoría de un Barroco hispanoamericano." *Relecturas del Barroco de Indias*. Ed. Mabel Moraña. Hanover: Ediciones del Norte, 1994. 1–11.

"El Roto." Cartoon. *El País* 22 May 2013.

Rousset, Jean. *Dernier regard sur le baroque*. Paris: Éditions Corti, 1998.

Sarduy, Severo. "El barroco y el neobarroco." *América Latina en su literatura*. Coordination and Introduction by César Fernández Moreno. Mexico, DF: Siglo Veintiuno, 1977. 167–84.

Simon, Herbert. *The Sciences of the Artificial*. London and Cambridge: MIT Press, 1996.

Spadaccini, Nicholas, and Luis Martín-Estudillo. "Introduction: The Baroque and the Cultures of Crises." *Hispanic Baroques: Reading Cultures in Context*. Ed. Nicholas Spadaccini and Luis Martín-Estudillo. Nashville, TN: Vanderbilt University Press, 2005. ix–xxxvii.

Suárez, Juan Luis. "Hispanic Baroque: A Model for the Study of Cultural Complexity in the Atlantic World." *South Atlantic Review* 72.1 (2007): 31–47.

———. "Complejidad y barroco." *Revista de Occidente* 323 (2008): 58–74.

Weisbach, Werner. *El barroco, arte de la contrarreforma*. Trans. and Introduction by Enrique Lafuente Ferrari. Madrid: Espasa-Calpe, 1942.

Wölfflin, Heinrich. *Conceptos fundamentales en la historia del arte*. Trans. José Moreno Villa. Madrid: Espasa, 1936.

———. *Renacimiento y barroco*. Madrid: Alberto Corazón, 1976.

PART I
The Constitution of Identities in the Hispanic Baroque

Chapter 1

Person and Individual: Baroque Identities in Theology and Law

Bartolomé Clavero

[R]eperta personae est definitio: naturae rationabilis indiuidua substantia.

A.M.S. Boethius, c. 515.

Persona est is qui suo vel alieno nomine res agit: si suo, persona propria sive naturalis est; si alieno, persona est ejus, cujus nomine agit, repraesentativa.

Th. Hobbes, 1668.

Person, s[ubstantive] a man or woman. Personal, a[djective] proper to him or her. Personality, s[ubstantive] the individuality of any one.

W. Perry, 1775.

Person and Individual

The place is Madrid; the year, 1611; the occasion, the publication of the *Tesoro de la lengua castellana o española* [*Treasures of the Castilian or Spanish Language*] by Sebastián de Covarruvias y Orozco. Among the jewels in this treasure trove is the definition of the term *person*: "according to the philosophers, *persona est naturae rationalis indiuidua substantia*," thus, an individual being with a rational nature, as we might translate this formulaic expression from the original Latin. It is a meaning presented in philosophical terms and is not followed by any other definitions for use other than in philosophy. No legal sense is given. What does this definition of *person* entail? Is only the philosophical relevant? Does it really have no relation to law?[1]

A different place: Edinburgh; the year, 1775; the occasion, the appearance of *The Royal Standard English Dictionary* by William Perry. *Person* here is defined

---

[1]   My thanks go to Laura Beck Varela and Jesús Vallejo for reading the text and for their suggestions.

18 *The Transatlantic Hispanic Baroque*

in a much simpler fashion: "a man or woman," that is, a human being. There is a synonym, *individual*: "every single person," however, this dictionary never uses this second term, *individual*, but always the first one, *person*, as the noun identifying the subject, and only employs the term *individual* as an adjective, to signify the particular. In every case, *individuality* is the equivalent of *personality*, the distinction of every one in particular. So why are there two words, *person* and *individual*, and their derivatives for the same concept, but each with such different usage? Was it a question of philosophical terminology? Or does all this have something—or perhaps a great deal—to do with the law? And, if so, what might be the legal implications?

But enough of such opening statements and initial questions. The object here is not to point to a history of the term *person*, but to reflect on when this concept was the subject of creative polemic or, better yet, when the notions of *person* and *individual* were considered as equal in meaning and scope. This is the moment—the Baroque—when the anthropological keys to the earlier classification of the subject of law were translated into the various languages of Western Europe, and became the predominant vehicles of communication for most of mankind. The reference to anthropology is made here to highlight from the outset the differences in historical culture with regard to the vicissitudes in the meaning of *person* that will be considered here. If reference were made only to history, a mistaken idea of the genesis of the usage might occur (see Clavero, *Antidora*).

Person as a Theological Hypostasis and as Social Class

The first historical moment when productive debate surrounding *person* occurred was that which resulted in the definition recorded by the above-mentioned seventeenth-century publication *Tesoro de la lengua*: "Persona est naturae rationalis indiuidua substantia." "According to the philosophers," is how the definition appeared in the *Tesoro*, itself the work of a philosopher, albeit a philosopher who became a theologian. The issue of the *person* as a subject of controversy is thus between the original philosophical definition and theology, with no other implications than those pertaining to theology.

The context in which the definition was given form was in fact a theological one, and one repeated over time and in many instances such as that of the *Tesoro de la lengua*. This was a very old definition, as old in the seventeenth century as it is today. At that time, there was no need for a dictionary to record the source in order to document precedence in usage. The definition was originally produced by Anicius Manlius Severinus Boethius in the early sixth century, concretely ,between the middle and the last years of the second decade.

Person and Individual 19

The definition is contained in a passage of the work by Boethius entitled *De Persona et Duabus Naturis contra Eutychen et Nestorium*, in his reflection on Christ as both man and God at the same time. Boethius attributed to Him a single *person* with two natures as opposed to the dual nature, divine and human, preached by Nestorius, Patriarch of Constantinople (now, of course, Istanbul in Turkey), and also as opposed to the fusion of the two natures into one, as advocated by Eutyches, the Archimandrite in the same metropolis. This is the key passage by Boethius:

> Quocirca si persona in solis substantiis est atque in his rationabilibus substantiaque omnis natura est nec in uniuersalibus sed in indiuiduis constat, reperta personae est definitio: naturae rationabilis indiuidua substantia. [...] Hoc interim constet quod inter naturam personamque differre praediximus, quoniam natura est cuiuslibet substantiae specificata proprietas, persona uero rationabilis naturae indiuidua substantia.

> [Wherefore if Person belongs to substances alone, and these rational, and if every nature is a substance, existing not in universals but in individuals, we have found the definition of Person, viz.: "The individual substance of a rational creature." [...] For the time being [until the Church determines otherwise] let that distinction between Nature, and Person hold which I have affirmed, viz. that Nature is the specific property of any substance, and Person the individual substance of a rational nature].

Here is a formula, of a somewhat improvised and temporary (*interim*) nature, which has enjoyed great success over the centuries. The *Tesoro de la lengua castellana* itself is an indication of this reiteration of Boethius's definition word for word over a very long period of time. In fact, it was the canonical definition for centuries. According to Stanley J. Grenz, "the concept of *individual* that lies at the heart of Boethius's definition of person [...] is not identical to the modern idea. Nevertheless, it opened the way for the development of its modern counterpart. [Boethius] opened the door to the modern *inner self* as the seat of unique personal identity" (66–7). It is precisely the advent of the individual thanks to Boethius that I am going to begin questioning here. Charles Taylor takes us on a journey through prehistory from Plato to Descartes, passing through Augustine, but not through Boethius, and arriving at Locke, rather than Blackstone, as we shall do here.

Not only was there originally a certain degree of temporality in the definition, but also a sense of uncertainty. Given that *De Persona et Duabus Naturis* considers a Trinity where the one person is included in the dual nature of Christ, the vocabulary he uses is less than dogmatic. Indeed, Galonnier notes that in Boethius the theological use of the term *person* "manque de fermeté" (Boethius,

20   *The Transatlantic Hispanic Baroque*

Opuscula 281), that is, lacks firmness. In *De Persona et Duabus Naturis* it is clearly acknowledged that the notion of *person* appropriate for theological purposes does not correspond to the idea commonly evoked by the Latin word, and was also difficult to extend outside of the determination of nature and person which, according to theology, are joined together in Christ, man and at the same time one of the persons of the divinity considered to be a Trinity:

> Sed nos hac definitione eam quam Graeci hypostasin dicunt terminauimus. Nomen enim personae uidetur aliunde traductum, ex his scilicet personis quae in comoediis tragoediisque eos quorum interest homines repraesentabant.

> [Now by this definition (the individual substance of a rational creature) we have described what the Greeks call *hypostasis*. For the word person seems to be borrowed from a different source, namely from the masks which used to signify the different subjects of representation in comedies and tragedies].

Artificial faces superimposed on to real faces (see Frontisi-Ducroux). Thus this *person* in the theological context came to be used, not just for any mask, but for the specific hypostasis, in the heart of a god as the Trinity, with a dual nature, divine and human, in one single *person*, Christ—precisely the effect that Nestorius and his followers considered impossible. Outside of the theological context, if the person could be made singular, it would be between human beings and between animals. There was nothing specifically and exclusively human in such classifications (Törönen 55–6; Tisserand 11).

To summarise, neither the term *person* nor, of course, the term *hypostasis*, bore any connotation of singling out or identifying beings that are human alone. Theologically the human being could not be a *person*, an individual entity, as it was considered to consist of a soul of divine provenance and a body of human provenance. If any relationship did exist, it was not with the human being himself, but with the *personae* or masks that were customarily used for the dramatic or comedic representation of his life story. This was how it was in the sixth century and how it would continue to be for centuries. To use terms that are anachronistic for those times: *person* neither meant nor could mean *individual* in the sense of a human being (see Picasso Muñoz 20).

In Boethius's time, the term *person*, with its meaning of mask, had been extended to other uses which were not as contentious as the theological use. And this was indeed the case in law. The mask of Boethius also became the way of legal presentation or representation. Two decades after the *De Persona et Duabus Naturis* came the compilation in Byzantium of the *Codex Iustiniani*, which begins with the *Summa Trinitas*, the treatise on the divine Trinity. The figure of Christ in the *Codex* corresponds to Boethius's version and, in short, the orthodox Byzantine version corresponded to the orthodox Roman version established at the Council of Nicaea (now Iznik in Turkey), almost two centuries earlier than the *De Persona et Duabus Naturis*, without the *Codex* making use of the term *person* either for Christ or for any other member of the Trinity. The debate surrounding the person of a dual nature, divine and human, did not, however, wane after Justinian, or for some time after, although this was only due to the power of the Nestorian Church itself, a fact which tends to be forgotten (see Jenkins).

In the field of law, one of the sections of the Byzantine *Codex* provides nothing new at this point as can be seen in the following quotation: "Qui legitimam personam in iudiciis habent vel non," i.e. he who has or has not *personhood* by law to act before the courts, that is, he who can and he who cannot legitimately wear the mask that gives access to justice, is he who has or has not the necessary capacity in this regard. In the Byzantine compilation, *De Personis* or *De Iure Personarum* is the main part of the first book of the *Institutiones* or the *Instituta*, the basic elements of law; *de personis* or *de iure personarum*, i.e., concerning the capacities or legal status of individuals rather than the individual as such. It is always a case of *habere personam*, of there being a determined capacity or a particular dignity as a direct result and strictly in accordance with the prevailing order of social or political hierarchies. The continuity of this use may be seen in Charles du Cange's *Glossarium*.

In legal terms, then, *personhood* is something that is possessed, that does not "be." Personhood is having, not being. Personhood is put on and taken off, just like a mask. This would also be the case for centuries in law. Thus, in law, no one *was* a person and everyone could have or not have *personhood*, the latter in the case of slavery since a slave was not considered to be a person. Those who have personhood are free, but in accordance with a diverse range of capacities, i.e. a number of free persons, that constitute and form a hierarchical order within freedom that is clearly dependent on events, on social standing and status (Clavero, "Almas y cuerpos" 153–71).

Person as a Human Entity

Let us now go to the seventeenth century, to England at the middle of that century, during the height of the Baroque period, when Thomas Hobbes published his *Leviathan or the Matter, Forme, and Power of a Common Wealth, Ecclesiasticall and Civil*, a work written during the 1640s, when he was living abroad, keeping his distance from civil war and reflecting upon it. *Leviathan* is the well-known product of his thoughts on the bloody breakdown of order in England (see Tuck). It was here that the specifically legal issues emerged surrounding the *person* as a subject of law and meaning a human being (Tomaselli 185–205).

22   *The Transatlantic Hispanic Baroque*

Prior to Hobbes, the meaning of *person* was unproblematic, and with no particular issues outside of the realm of religion, a mask, a theatrical or, in a similar sense, legal representation. The issues, and there were, indeed, some, were theological and practically insurmountable among Christian churches in very different parts of the world. The legal interpretation was introduced by Hobbes to the lands of Western Europe. Here with regard to his *Leviathan* we are only interested in what relates to the *person*, and it is clear that there is something new here. First, let us look at the first part, "De Homine," "Of Man" or "Of the Human Condition," since the innovation here is the appearance of the human being in the singular, and in the legal sense only in the final chapter and not at the beginning. Specifically, what interests us is the sixteenth and final chapter, "Of Persons, Authors, and Things Personated, De Personis et Authoribus," which begins as follows:

> Persona est is qui suo vel alieno nomine res agit: si suo, persona propria sive naturalis est; si alieno, persona est ejus, cujus nomine agit, repraesentativa.
>
> [A person, is he whose words or actions are considered, either as his own, or as representing the words or actions of another man, or of any other thing to whom they are attributed, whether Truly or by Fiction. When they are considered as his owne, then is he called a Naturall Person: And when they are considered as representing the words and actions of another, then is he a Feigned or Artificiall person].

The innovation lies in this very beginning: *the person is he who or whose*—he who or of whom, pertaining to an identifiable human being. Such is the *own and natural person*, the true person, whatever theology says and whatever the established law might say.

Here we have the human being as a *person* in the legal sense. Here we also have the mask, seemingly the same mask of Boethius and of so many who, before and after, have referred to the theatrical meaning of the word. Except that it is no longer exactly the same mask. The same metaphorical figure is another. The mask is no longer a disguise to cover the face. By being evoked following the new definition of person, and only by this, it would now become a human face. And so it is in fact:

> The word Person is latine: instead whereof the Greeks have Prosopon, which signifies the Face, as Persona in latine signifies the Disguise, or Outward Appearance of a man, counterfeited on the Stage; and somtimes more particularly that part of it, which disguiseth the face, as a Mask or Visard: And from the Stage, hath been translated to any Representer of speech and action, as well in Tribunalls, as Theaters. So that a Person, is the same that an Actor is, both on the Stage and

Person and Individual 23

in common Conversation; and to Personate, is to Act, or Represent himselfe, or an other; and he that acteth another, is said to beare his Person, or act in his name (in which sence Cicero useth it where he saies, "Unus Sustineo Tres Personas; Mei, Adversarii, et Judicis, I beare three Persons; my own, my Adversaries, and the Judges").

To summarise, the human face represents the genuine sense (Napier 8). The mask is no longer a disguise that hides the true features in order to represent a different face. A trinity also appears in this context, but neither is it that of Boethius or that of the Most Sacred Emperor Justinian. It is that of human persons who converge and represent themselves in different positions in law.

In order to clarify his concept of person, Hobbes addresses the question of hypostasis to which it was linked theologically. He does not do so in the chapter "Of Persons," but in another, "Of Darkness from Vain Philosophy, and Vain Traditions," the 26th chapter, belonging to the fourth and final part, "Of the Kingdom of Darkness." Hobbes links the Greek term *hypostases* to the Latin term *substantia* to disassociate it from *persona*. And he reaffirms the concept of *person* whereby his concept of a person is associated with *man*, "a living body," something which is, or exists, by itself:

When we say, a Man, is, a living Body, we mean not that the Man is one thing, the Living Body another, and the Is, or Beeing a third; but that the Man, and the Living Body, is the same thing: because the Consequence, if hee bee a Man, hee is a living Body, is a true Consequence, signified by that word Is.

Hobbes must have deemed important this distancing from the theology of the person in order to establish the law of the person, as he takes advantage of the Latin edition of the *Leviathan* to add a long appendix "De Symbolo Niceno," on the Nicene Creed, the creed of the Trinity of the Byzantine Council established in this city around two centuries before Boethius began his defence with his work *De Persona et Duabus Naturis contra Eutychen et Nestorium*. The key to the categorical difference between the theological person and the legal person was still being elucidated in discussions being held between both camps in order to succeed in identifying the latter, the person in law, in a human form.

With regard to the legal terms and their meaning, Hobbes would change their sense not by whim or by instinct, but in accordance with the requirements of a legal order that was based on the human capacity to restore peace, rather than on the religious debates that were staining Europe red with blood. Thus, he decided that *right* or *ius* should mean freedom, and *law* or *lex* regulation—a distinct definition, not usual at the time and not easily accepted as he postulated a new meaning of *person*, not as a mask that is put on and taken off, covering the face, but as a human presence of clean or made-up features; human faces, in

24   *The Transatlantic Hispanic Baroque*

other words. Here is a strict origin of the conception of the *person* as a human entity in law which was shocking in its time and is not usually appreciated today, as Quentin Skinner demonstrates (157, 158).

In other words, a human *individual* in accordance with *right-ius*-freedom, rather than legal capacity in accordance with *law-lex*-regulation, had to be the subject of law. Except that Hobbes did not consider the term *individual* as a noun. *Individua* was an adjective that qualified the entity of the *person* in Boethius's definition, the definition which, given its theological context and sense, was in fact of no use; the new scenario of Hobbes's work of necessity dismissed it.

Person as a Legal Term

Words do not change their meaning due to the persistence of the speaker alone. It is even less likely for such a change to occur in the case of practical concepts such as those of a legal nature. The news of Hobbes's linguistic idea was spreading among jurists, but they tended not to make a point of discussing it because, apart from the risk of contact with heresies that were not even that contagious, the very reality of the established order rejected it. In law, the association of the person with a human being was a "vulgare axioma." The evidence is provided by the law itself whereby more than one person may converge in a single human being, in a single entity. There can be "personarum differentiam et duplicitatem in eodem subiecto," as Larrea states in his *Allegationes fiscales*. We continue with the scenario of the masks that may thus be considered in the plural, according to the different capacities that correspond to an entity in accordance with the established order, and nowhere above or beyond those who were considered persons (see the classic Kantorowicz; Clavero, *Tantas personas*).

Subsequent to *Leviathan*, it was not difficult to publish a treatise, for example, on *De Pluralitate Hominis Legali et Unitate Plurium Formali* or, as the title itself outlines, on *reduplicationem personae et unitatem plurium personarum*, that is, on the legal plurality of a single man and the formal unity of many men, or of the reduplication of the person and the unity of many persons, as in this work by Carlo Antonio de Luca from which I quote. This explains that "unus et idem homo numero iuxta Phisicos et Theologos" [the man considers himself as one and the same only among physicians and theologians, not among jurists]; that "in una persona materiali in iure datur multiplicatio" [in a material person is the multiplication of persons in law]; that "plures personae formales in una materiale" [many formal persons in a single material or physical one] can be accumulated; that there can thus be "tot personae quot feuda" or "tot personae quot status" [as many persons as political or social statuses]. Persons are therefore represented "in comediis vel tragediis" [in law as in the theatre]. "Is qui habet duos status aut dignitates aut etiam diversa officia, duas etiam ipsemet repraesentat personas, et

Person and Individual

diversas ac separatas aenigmatice" [he who has two statuses, ranks or functions, represents two persons himself, enigmatically diverse and separate]. "In eadem persona duae et diversae personae considerantur ex diversis iuris et qualitatibus" [in the same person two or more persons are considered according to the diversity of law and of the qualities].

The person may, of course, be perceived as a human being: *persona materialis* or physical, but this is never relevant in law. In law, persons are represented or are always the object of *repraesentatio*. They are never associated with the actor, whether he acts on his own behalf or through representation. Hobbes's notion thus makes no sense at all. No real distinction can be made between the real person and the represented person. Given that the human being is not a person himself, fictitious persons may be even more real than physical beings (Clavero, "Hispanus"). The *person* is always *ficta, repraesentata, immaginaria, intellectualis*. The *homo legalis* is unfailingly *homo fictus* as opposed to the *homo verus*, something different and something that is never associated with him. In law, the first is the second by virtue of the *veritas fictionis vel ex repraesentatione*. All persons are, in short, legally immaterial, even if they can and must act in one way or another through the material support of the human being, that *homo verus* without fiction or representation. Law was built on fiction and representation, not from natural or factual evidence, and even less so from physical or, as we would say today, psychological signs (see Hofmann, Todescan).

Person signifies human being in the singular, in theology in terms of the soul, and in medicine in terms of the body, but not in law. Given the physical and spiritual evidence of the singularity of every human being, of this being that is not individual, but made up of body and soul, *person* may now have even acquired the sense of human being in the singular for ordinary language, but not for specialised or technical legal language. And this being is not a person simply because of its components. The same evidence of singularity was not subject to question legally. In the field of law, it began to be called into question when collective persons were represented as perfectly ordinary persons or when resorting to the merging of persons, as between husband and wife, annulling the capacity of the latter, or between the head of the family and his successor, strengthening social or political dynasties. In such cases the argument was made according to the usual likeness between father and son, but only to strengthen the argument, not to lay its foundations, as the physical resemblance did not merge person in other cases, not even between brothers and, even less so, between brothers and sisters. When all was said and done, the artificial *person* was always the legal entity, never the physical being (Clavero, *Mayorazgo*). Every human being in the singular was a combination of body and soul in medicine and in theology, but not in the law under any circumstance.

What *person* as a human being in regard to the law is appropriate in those other compositions that may be set against Hobbes? The continuity between

De Corpore, De Homine and *De Cive* already excluded the division of the human being into body and soul, and allowed the said human being to be conceived as a person. Nevertheless, Boethius's definition still fails to take in the law with its different reasons, either through Hobbes's definition or the definition of those who maintained the most traditional conception. Also, the notion of *person* as a human being in the singular was then lost at that point in the literature on the plurality of persons, which in turn continues to be lost today, even in the history of law with respect to times which are now considered to be modern, as if it were something outside of medieval times. The loss may still be seen today, including in the specialised historiography.

Apart from in law, the specialised use for which the word *person* is mostly retained from this point onwards, as is the traditional use of characters in drama or comedy, *dramatis personae*, that is, masks (although masks were no longer customary on stage). In English, *persona* in its Latin form is used in the context of the theatre, while *person* in its vernacular derivation is now used in law. In other languages, there may, of course, be contemporary derivations of the word, but with no distinction of meaning. *Personne*, for example, in French meant the same then in law as *persona* in Latin (Marion does not include it). In Castilian Spanish, *persona* means person, also still the same in terms of its legal meaning.

Person as a Legal Term and Individual as a Human Entity.

Let us return to England, this time to the year 1765, when William Blackstone published the definitive version of the first book of his *Commentaries on the Laws of England*, a work that would become one of the century's bestsellers (Prest). These commentaries officially belong to the institutionist genre, based on the model of the Byzantine *Institutiones* with their first work *De Personis*, on person as terms. In accordance not only with the genre, but with the whole system of traditional tracts, this is what *person* continues to mean. Hobbes's issues do not yet pertain to the term *person* even in law. What happens next comes in the neologism, *individual*.

The first book of Blackstone's *Commentaries* in fact relates to persons, not *de iure personarum* [to the law of persons] but to *The Rights of Persons*, with an initial connotation which now may add to the meaning. Here, in this genre as with any other legal usage of the time, the meaning of *personae* initially did not nor could refer to human beings, but the role played in society, in the same way as roles are performed in a play, i.e., the term corresponded to political, social or family status, the latter also meaning at that time *economic* status. No other meanings are used initially in Blackstone's *Commentaries*, although these would be followed immediately by the fundamentally new development of the category of a subject in law.

Person and Individual 27

In the second chapter of the first book of the tome on the "Rights of Persons," Blackstone addresses the person still in the sense of a legal position, with the set of rights and duties that corresponds to every one according to their position in society: "We are next to treat of the rights and duties of persons, as they are members of society, and stand in various relations to each other." *Person* makes reference to the subject but is immediately qualified by his position in society as a determining factor of his own being, and is, in short, still the deciding factor in usage.

Following the consideration over twelve chapters, from the second to the thirteenth, of the various positions or *persons* of a political and social nature, from the fourteenth chapter (still of the same first book) concerning the "Rights of Persons," the objective or non-subjective significance of person is accentuated. This is the point when there is a shift from the position in society to the position in the family, to the set of rights and duties corresponding to everyone "in private oeconomical relations," i.e. those of a family nature. The fourteenth chapter is dedicated to the "master and servant" relationship, the latter in the sense of an employed worker of any kind, including those hired or under contract, strongly emphasising the state of subjection. The next chapter, the fifteenth, deals with the "husband and wife" relationship, equally or perhaps to an even greater extent underlining the *economic* status of the latter, namely, the wife.

I have not begun with the first chapter because this is where the innovation is to be found. The first chapter of the *Rights of Persons* relates to "the absolute rights of the individuals," absolute in the sense of above and beyond the legislation or obligations for the same:

> By the absolute rights of individuals we mean those which are so in their primary and strictest sense; such as would belong to their persons merely in a state of nature, and which every man is intitled to enjoy whether out of society or in it.

The concept of absolute rights generates the new subject of the *individual, every man*, to whose *person* the rights of such status, the absolute, correspond. *Person* continues to refer to the capacity of possessing both absolute and also relative rights—these other, relative, rights in accordance with legislation and neither above nor beyond:

> The rights of persons considered in their natural capacities are also of two sorts, absolute, and relative. Absolute, which are such as appertain and belong to particular men, merely as individuals or single persons: relative, which are incident to them as members of society, and standing in various relations to each other.

Both are *rights*. Both constitute *persons*. Such is the language given and the order established. This scope of rights as absolute liberties and as relative capacities "is the more popular acceptation of rights or jura," rights only partly in the sense that Hobbes intended, with this outcome. Along these lines, those of Hobbes, as already cited, "by the absolute rights of individuals we mean those which are so in their primary and strictest sense; such as would belong to their persons," whereby, as opposed to Hobbes himself, *persons* must continue to represent the traditional sense even in the case of absolute rights and with which the neologism of *individuals*, which was lacking in Hobbes, must therefore be coined for its subject. This now being a "popular acceptation" for Blackstone, it was evidently not he who coined this term. Its use had been accepted within just a few decades.

From where does it originate? I have no proof, but there are certainly some signs, namely in Boethius's definition of *person*. To recapitulate: "naturae rationabilis indiuidua substantia"; translated into English: "the individual substance of a rational nature" or, if no longer singularised in the hypostasis of Christ, "an individual substance of a rational nature," the man then, the *individual*. All of the signs indicate that the term appeared in English before passing into other languages, and that it also comes directly from Boethius's definition. Contrary to the norm, the adjective for *individual* does not come from the noun in English, but the reverse: the noun for *individual* comes directly from the adjective, and it was the adjective itself, *individual*, that was very apparent in Boethius's definition. There is no need to proceed with lexicological and bibliographical research to find this illustrative clue.

And who is the *individual*? Is it truly *every man*? This is how Blackstone presents it, and the question may also be asked in the form of: who is *the man*, in relation to the subject of law identified as *individual*? Albeit not complete, but sufficient for our purposes, we have already received an answer by way of exclusion. Confined within the *economic* spaces of strong subjection, neither the wife nor the employed worker may qualify as individuals. The masculine concept of *man* has the meaning not only of man but also of autonomous owner. With the exception of the wife and the worker, and by this we have already excluded more than half of society, we have a society in which there are only *persons*, termed in accordance with the constituted order, and not *individuals*, subjects of fundamental rights or, as they were known, absolute rights.

Individual and *person* are not incompatible classifications. As we have seen, the *individual* constitutes a singular class of *person*, the absolute, which may also assume other *Persons*, the relative persons in accordance with legislation. There are many who may only be *persons* in this other sense, the traditional sense, and have no access to the status of *individual*. With the wish for *person* to mean what is now referred to as *individual*, Hobbes had deprived the established legal system of a key category. Blackstone, on the other hand, fits the pieces together. Taking all of this into consideration, *individual* as a subject in law does not replace *person* as a legal term, but is placed within the same scenario. An individual is therefore a qualified person among ordinary persons. At that time and under these conditions the *individual* was born in society, and in doing so became a qualified form of *person* (see Coleman).

Duplicate Equivalence between Person and Individual

Once introduced to the world of law from the second half of the eighteenth century onwards, the success of the concept of *individual* may seem spectacular, certainly at the time it appeared to be. The best testimony is provided in the same genre of institutionist literature to which Blackstone's *Commentaries* belong. Humankind found a way of giving the mask of person a human face. In Castilian Spanish, this was the renewed definition for which there was, in fact, no need for the influence of the English jurist: "The person is the man (or the individual) considered in his state," with the insistence that: "there can be no person without his being considered in one state or another," both the civil or social state and the political or citizen's state. Individual and person might finally be considered to have the same meaning, but in the old terrain of persons, not in the new terrain of individuals, of subjects of absolute or fundamental rights. Even without incorporating the definition, this was also to be the composition of the person of civil codification from the *Code Napoléon* onwards, and so success was truly ensured (Clavero, *Happy Constitution*).

The terminology was already present in Castilian Spanish from the first half of the eighteenth century. The *Diccionario de Autoridades* (*Dictionary of Authorities*), dating back to that time, offers as a first acceptation of *Person* that of "individual of an intellectual nature, or of a human nature" and of *Individual*, that of "the entity of each species, whose reason is appropriate to all singularly." What has been said over the centuries can be said in the short period of decades. If it is amazing that the constant presence over many centuries of Boethius's definition had not produced an idea, and I do not mean a formed concept, of the *person* as an *individual*, it may seem equally surprising that the most accredited dictionary definitions of the time do not act as a source of an equation between person and individual. This is only conceived in the neutralising terms that have just been outlined. The same might of course be said of the old voice of Covarrubias in his *Tesoro de la lengua*. The concept had been around for a century or longer with no effect whatsoever in law.

From the second half of the eighteenth century, *person* and *individual* were able to coexist, even live parallel lives for some time. *Person* continued to be the term used in civil law, and restated in the nineteenth century by codification, to mean subject according to status, the institutionist concept with all of its implications. *Individual* would enter the area of constitutionality to mean the subject in law, with fundamental rights or otherwise, as premises of regulation. Thus, an unequal coexistence was maintained, whose essential composition

30   *The Transatlantic Hispanic Baroque*

coincided with that constructed by Blackstone. The equivalence is relative, but there will be no separation. The language is by now, in any event, subjective, concerning the subject in law or in rights. Person and individual as a rule complement each other and are often interchangeable, particularly in the field of the constitution. The rights of individuals are rights of persons, although, as we know, not of all persons, but of certain qualified persons among ordinary persons. And these others also include humankind from outside Europe or human beings who adopt the culture of Europe. Initially based on the *ius gentium*, the traditional law of nations, and without the need for codification, nineteenth-century international law gives these human beings the status of the least capable persons, and thus in need of European protection, in matters concerning the control of their land and resources. The *individuals*, the same constitutional individuals, also thereby dominate the *persons* in the colonies.

We now have the explanation for these phenomena in language and in the practice of law. The logic behind this history or, if you will, the story of law alone, is not exactly the logic of ideas. A system of social compartmentalisation, resulting in profound discrimination, began to block the very possibility that "naturae rationabilis individua substantia" may refer to the human being in society. Even when the human being began to be conceived of as a person, as "he whose words or actions are considered," "is qui [...] res agit," not even the use excluding the male facilitates the change of paradigm. This is never in force in this history, or only occurs in a controlled manner through the conception of the *individual* as a particular class of *person*, of the person which did not or could not simply mean the human being. This is as far as our outline goes. The equation between person and individual is mediated by status, both civil and political. Both words now have the same meaning, a human being, but not in the same way or for the same purposes, and thus both were kept in play. The juggling of words (not always consciously) may of course be key to the law and its most crucial concerns.

The relative equation between person and individual is not the end of the story, but of that particular evolution it is. A change in anthropology has, in fact, occurred at this stage, because other factors come into play. Today we can point to a consummate equation between person and individual, which is not the first one mediated by the civil or political status that involve exclusions, overlaps and discriminations. The individual and the person, every individual and every person, may now be deemed to be subjects in law, both terms meaning one and the same thing, the human being. The rights of individuals and the rights of persons now coincide. Whatever difficulties this composition may still have in gathering strength and taking hold, such is the equation evident today. It is often said that it comes from the past that we have seen, and there are even those who date it back to Boethius himself, but this is not the case. The same fiction of history may still be used today to maintain all the masks placed over

Person and Individual 31

the human face. In ordinary historiography, however, there is no need to pursue this objective in order for it to be achieved.

The new anthropology does not come from history. This, if still present, constitutes a serious obstacle to anthropological change itself. The new anthropology from which it has emerged has access to a common right in terms of shared rights, the rights of the said human beings, of sectors of European society and of human beings outside of Europe; access which was unthinkable for the tradition originating from the Most Sacred Emperor Justinian and his *Summa Trinitas* and which is made much more difficult by those who maintain the umbilical connection with history; access, in fact, advocated among the *persons* subjected to this legal tradition, literally forced by the determination for emancipation of the victims of the system. To put this more directly, the history outlined came to an end, or should have begun to come to an end, when human rights were formulated and adopted, that is, the rights of the human individual, and rights which have been adopted and which survive in spite of the tradition that stretches from Justinian's *Codex* to the *Code Napoléon*, passing through stages such as that of Hobbes's *Leviathan* and that of Blackstone's *Commentaries*.

For legal purposes, the equivalence between person and individual, individual and person, is virtually complete, but never in fact absolute. History is significant in language and its possibilities. *Individual* is, in short, the term most attached to the human being in the singular, whereas *person*, now based on its significance as individual, may be better extended to also denote collective bodies such as associations or foundations, which is naturally more difficult than when person did not mean individual. And it is not the only relative dissociation of course. The fact is that *individual* made its entrance in the field of constitutional law and *person* held out longer in the area of civil law or, rather, of a type of law from which constitutional law tends to distinguish or even separate itself; nonetheless, it can still achieve some kind of effect that is to a greater or lesser extent substantive or more or less still equivocal, although now always secondary in comparison with what has occurred in the past in any consideration of these two terms. There are certain differentiations which in any event retain a relationship with history seen at least as far as human issues are concerned. If we move away from this field, there are further differences. *Individual* and not *person* may be said of an animal or *individuals* used for a number of animals. Animals would find it difficult to wear a mask.

Not only in Castilian Spanish are *individual* rights understood to be all the rights of the individual, whereas by *personal* rights, we understand only some; the *personal* right to freedom which is now also constitutional, or the right of disposition, or the right to guarantees of privacy. Similar effects may occur with the derivations. Individualism and personalism are not the same thing; nor is individuality exactly the same as personality. Yet even when these terms were coined they might mean the same, as we saw in *The Royal Standard English*

32 *The Transatlantic Hispanic Baroque*

Dictionary. All of this is, of course, secondary. As it is in comparison with the doctrinal inertia that still links the *person* with social *status(es)* or masks, making it difficult for these same *personal* rights to be effective with respect to all subjects, both male and female, without discrimination. For the avoidance of ambiguity and manipulation, it would obviously be better today to abandon the term *person* and to adopt the term *individual* for all purposes, as they have, or should have, the same meaning. However, as we know, from the experience of Hobbes, language does not change that easily. Perhaps the most expedite way of dealing with this would be to put an end to ambiguous equivalencies, such as that still present in the *Diccionario de la lengua española* in its definitions of *person* and *individual*.

As things stand, the equivalencies may be controlled by due distinction. Those between person and individual, the partial equation that still overlaps with a lack of equivalence and the now complete equation for certain practical purposes, have no genetic or logical relation. One story has come to an end with the former and a different one has begun with the latter. One weighs upon the other and contaminates it, but does not reduce or penetrate it. They are in fact different, however much we try to invent tradition through one, the European story of the eighteenth and nineteenth centuries, or by allowing the other, the cosmopolitan story of the twentieth and twenty-first centuries, to dominate. As far as person is concerned, religion concurs and even competes with law when it comes to inventing tradition. There is no need to illustrate this here; it is quite clear to see if one really wishes to look hard enough.

Bibliography

Blackstone, William. *Commentaries on the Laws of England*. Philadelphia: William Young Birch and Abraham Small. Printed by Robert Carr, 1803. 4 April 2013. <http://www.constitution.org>.

Boethius. *De Persona et Duabus Naturis contra Eutychen et Nestorium*. [*A Treatise against Eutyches and Nestorius*]. London: W. Heinemann; New York: G.P. Putnam's Sons, 1918. 4 April 2013. <http://www.documentacatholicaomnia.eu/03d/04800524,_Boethius,_The_Theological_Tractates,_EN.pdf>.

———. *Opuscula Sacra*. Vol. 1. Ed. Alain Galonnier. Louvain and Paris: Peeters, 2007.

Clavero, Bartolomé. "Hispanus fiscus, persona ficta. Concepción del sujeto político en el Ius Commune europeo." *Quaderni Fiorentini* 11–12 (1982–1983): 95–167.

———. *Tantas personas como estados: por una antropología política de la historia europea*. Madrid: Fundación Cultural Enrique Luna Pena, 1986.

———. *Mayorazgo: propiedad feudal en Castilla, 1369–1836.* Madrid: Siglo XXI, 1974; expanded edition, 1989.

———. "Almas y cuerpos: sujetos del derecho en la edad moderna." *Studi in Memoria di Giovanni Tarello.* Vol. 1. Milan: Giuffrè, 1990. 153–71.

———. *Antidora: Antropología católica de la economía moderna.* Milan: Giuffrè, 1991.

———. *Happy Constitution. Cultura y Lengua Constitucionales.* Madrid: Trotta, 1997.

Coleman, Janet, ed. *The Individual in Political Theory and Practice.* Oxford: Oxford University Press, 1996.

Corpus Iuris Civilis. Vol. 2: *Codex Iustinianus.* Ed. Paul Krüger. Berlin: Weidmann, 1877. 4 April 2013. <http://www.archive.org/stream/codexiustinianu00kruegoog#page/n8/mode/2up>.

Covarrubias y Orozco, Sebastián. *Tesoro de la lengua castellana o española.* Madrid: Luis Sánchez, 1611. 4 April 2013. <http://www.cervantesvirtual.com>.

De Luca, Carlo Antonio. *Tractatus de Pluralitate Hominis Legali et Unitate Plurium Formali Agens.* Naples: Franciscus Mollo, 1723.

Diccionario de la lengua castellana, en que se explica el verdadero sentido de las voces, su naturaleza y calidad, con las phrases o modos de hablar, los proverbios o refranes, y otras cosas convenientes al uso de la lengua [*Diccionario de Autoridades*]. Madrid: Real Academía Española, 1726–1739.

Diccionario de la lengua española. 22nd edition. Madrid: Real Academía Española, 2001. 4 April 2013. <http://www.rae.es>.

Du Cange, Charles. *Glossarium ad Scriptores Mediae et Infimae Latinitatis.* Frankfurt: Ex Officina Zunneriana, apud Johannem Adamum Jungium, 1710. 4 April 2013. <http://www.uni-mannheim.de/mateo/camenaref/ducange.html>.

Frontisi-Ducroux, Françoise. *Du Masque au Visage. Aspects de l'identité en Grèce ancienne.* Paris: Flammarion, 1995.

Galonnier, Alain, ed. *Anecdoton Holderi ou Ordo Generis Cassiodororum: Éléments pour une étude de l>authenticité boécienne des "Opuscula Sacra."* Louvain and Paris: Peeters, 1997.

Grenz, Stanley J. *The Social God and the Relational Self: A Trinitarian Theology of the Imago Dei.* Louisville, KY: Westminster John Knox, 2001.

Hobbes, Thomas. *Leviathan or the Matter, Forme, and Power of a Common Wealth, Ecclesiasticall and Civil.* London: Andrew Crooke, 1651. 4 April 2013. <http://www.gutenberg.org>.

Hofmann, Hasso. *Räpresentation: Studien zur Wort- und Begriffsgeschichte von der Antike bis ins 19. Jahrhundert.* Berlin: Duncker und Humblot, 1974.

Jenkins, Philip. *The Lost History of Christianity: The Thousand-Year Golden Age of the Church in the Middle East, Africa, and Asia – And How it Died*. New York: HarperOne, 2008.

Kantorowicz, Ernst H. *The King's Two Bodies: A Study in Mediaeval Political Theology*. Princeton: Princeton University Press, 1957.

Larrea, Juan. *Allegationes Fiscales*. Lugduni: Philippi Borde, Laurentii Arnaud, Petri Borde et Guill Barbier, 1699.

Marion, Marcel. *Dictionnaires des Institutions de la France aux XVIIe et XVIIIe siècles*. Paris: A. et J. Picard, 1969.

Napier, A. David. *Masks, Transformation, and Paradox*. Berkeley and Los Angeles, CA: University of California Press, 1986.

Perry, William. *The Royal Standard English Dictionary*. Edinburgh: David Willison, 1775.

Picasso Muñoz, Julio. "Introducción General." *Boecio: Cinco Opúsculos Teológicos (Opuscula Sacra)*. Lima: Pontificia Universidad Católica del Perú, 2002. 11–20.

Prest, Wilfrid. "Reconstructing the Blackstone's Archive, or Blundering after Blackstone." *Archives* 31.115 (2006): 108–118.

Skinner, Quentin. "Hobbes on Persons, Authors and Representatives." *The Cambridge Companion to Hobbes's Leviathan*. Ed. P. Springborg. Cambridge: Cambridge University Press, 2007. 157–79.

Taylor, Charles. *Sources of the Self: The Making of the Modern Identity*. Cambridge: Cambridge University Press, 1992.

Tisserand, Axel. *Pars Theologica: Logique et Théologique chez Boèce*. Paris: J. Vrin, 2008.

Todescan, Franco. *Diritto e realtà: Storia e teoría della fictio iuris*. Padua: Cedam, 1979.

Tomaselli, Sylvana. "The First Person: Descartes, Locke and Mind–Body Dualism." *History of Science* 22.2 (1984): 185–205.

Törönen, Melchisedec. *Union and Distinction in the Thought of St Maximus the Confessor*. Oxford: Oxford University Press, 2007.

Tuck, Richard. *Philosophy and Government, 1572-1651*. Cambridge: Cambridge University Press, 1993.

Chapter 2

Towards a Constructionist Essentialism: Critical Race Studies and the Baroque

Ruth Hill

Contemporary scholars of race collapse myriad explanations for biological variation in humans into a singular and overarching biological essentialism or biological race concept, shirking Stuart Hall's call for historical specificity.[1] They do not recognize the alterity of pre-Darwinian essentialism—"constructionist essentialism," I call it—without which, it is difficult to grasp alternative griddings of biological variation. This reductive approach to the history of the race construct obfuscates what I call the "plant-animal-human continuum" (not the human-animal divide) of the early modern mind. In broad terms, the semantic and cognitive mappings of alterity during the Baroque were quite different from those of the post-Darwinian nineteenth century. Specifically, Spanish approaches to human diversity (commonly known today as ethnicity or race), in the Iberian Atlantic and Pacific, allowed for changes in heritable traits such as hair texture and skin color that dispute Western modernity's *apparent* distinction between permanent and non-permanent characteristics.

In *We Have Never Been Modern*, anthropologist Bruno Latour asserts that people in the West have never truly distinguished between permanent and non-permanent traits while defining identities, though they have frequently invoked that distinction. Following on from Latour, Peter Wade has noted "a shifting tension between ideas of permanence/continuity and change/instability" (*Race, Nature* 10), which to me recalls baroque notions of alterity. "In Western ideas about people," he observes, "how they come to be as they are and how they are related to others, [...] it is not clear what is permanent and what is not: [...] the two realms interact and become mutually constitutive" (10). In other words, the natural/biological and the environmental/social overlap: "nurture can constitute (human) nature" (10–11). In the early modern Spanish world, this shifting line revealed itself in discussions and theories of sub-Saharan African

---

[1] In Hall's historical analysis of racial and class structures, African slavery was not legitimated by the biological race concept prior to the second half of the nineteenth century. Gunnar Myrdal and Louis Dumont have placed the origins of the biological race concept in the postbellum US.

and Indian hair types, facial features, body types, and fluids which are today commonly assumed to be phenotypical markers of an underlying genetic race/ethnicity.

Within critical race studies, however, baroque modalities of race are ignored or misrepresented as if alternative ways of thinking about biological variation—notions opposite to nineteenth-century biological determinism—had not existed prior to contemporary notions of biological essentialism. One of the most acute and widely anthologized theorists of race, Michael Root, exemplifies the problem that I wish to address here. In an influential essay penned for the *Philosophy of Anthropology and Sociology* (a volume of the standard reference work, *Handbook of the Philosophy of Science*), Root defined the biological race concept in the following terms:

> For many years, race was taken to be biological race. People believed that blacks and whites differ in genes as much as males and females differ in a chromosome. The biological conception that prevailed until recently included the following two tenets: (A) people of different races differ with respect to many genetic traits and (B) the populations identified as different races, at some point, were reproductively isolated, genetic differences developed between them, and the differences passed from one generation to the next and to the present day. On the biological conception of race, the races are natural kinds, and members of each race share some underlying property or essence that causes each members to look or act more or less like every other. (735–6)

Root's social-scientific understanding of the biological race concept is flawed on two accounts, both of which call into question the academic assumption that eliminating the biological race concept will limit or eradicate racism (see Andreasen).

First, Root reduces to one the multiple biological or natural explanations for variation in plants, animals, and humans that existed before Darwin's theory of evolution (if one wishes to call those explanations for human variation *biological race concepts*, so be it.) In actuality, the biological race concept to which Root refers dates from the second half of the nineteenth century and surfaces from an epistemology that is radically different from that of the Baroque. Second, Root ignores that the essentialism underpinning those explanations was not the essentialism against which he is writing, but, rather, from the perspective of today, a *constructionist* or *anti-essentialist essentialism*. The explanations (or biological race concepts) themselves are not only biological or natural, but also constructed or social—they are *biocultural*—in two senses: first, as explanations themselves they entail environmental as well as biological elements; and, second, the explainers and the explained are themselves historically situated, part of an interactive feedback loop (Hacking; Frank 1981). Hence, Atran and Medin's phrase: "the cultural construction of nature". I shall address a handful of baroque explanations for biological variation in the course of this chapter, but, first, I wish to elaborate on constructionist essentialism.

Scott Atran's *Cognitive Foundations of Natural History: Towards an Anthropology of Science* reconstructed the development of biological classification, or systematics, while highlighting the significance of folkbiology to both modern botany and zoology. Folk taxonomy of plants and brutes is rooted in appearance and a presumed essence or nature causally linked to that appearance: it is essentialist through and through. Folk perceive and reason from the known to the unknown, Atran explains, scrutinizing and reasoning about the organic world *analogically* and *essentially*, as Aristotle himself did. However, Atran rejects the uncomplicated notion of essentialism embraced by Michel Foucault and other postmodernists. Before Darwin's theory of evolution, "the notions traditionally attributed to essentialism, such as the idea of eternally fixed species and the belief that variation within species does not constitute a legitimate object of study," did not hold sway over what we today call the life and social sciences (Atran, *Cognitive* 7). According to Aristotle (and to the Thomistic Aristotelians who dominated the schools and colleges of Europe and the Americas well into the eighteenth century), heritage and milieu had to be examined in order to understand how organisms become essentially like others.[2] This constructionist essentialism was the foundation of the biocultural explanations of human diversity that I survey.[3]

---

[2]   Biologist Carol Kaesuk Yoon recently presented a cognitive framework similar to Atran's which guides human classification of brutes, plants, and humans: the *umwelt*, or *perceived world* (15). "It is the umwelt that gives us our stereotyped, hard-wired way of perceiving the order in living things. [...] The umwelt [is] the explanation for the similarity in ordering from Africa to Asia to the Americas, across different languages, cultures, societies, and habitats. We all have the same umwelt, so no wonder then that [...] we would make the same kinds of folk taxonomies, again and again and again" (15–16). Like Atran, Yoon contends that this pre-modern, pre-theoretical *umwelt* struggled against evolutionary science, or modern biology and zoology (16–17).

[3]   Atran's work has generated intense and protracted dialogue around essentialism and natural kinds. See, e.g., Dupré. Perhaps the most heated debate revolves around the relationship between Aristotelian and folk essentialism, as he defines it in *Cognitive Foundations*, and racial categorization—specifically, the question of whether races are or are not natural kinds to the human mind (race as immanence, I will call it). See Cosmides, Tooby, and Kurzban; Gelman and Hirschfeld ; Hirschfeld, "On a Folk Theory"; Hirschfeld, "Conceptual Politics"; Gil-White, "Are Ethnic Groups"; Gil-White, "How Thick Is Blood?"; Machery and Faucher; Kelly, Faucher, and Machery; Schulman and Glasgow. Atran's comments on this issue are brief but provocative: "The idea of underlying essence, which seems to be universally and spontaneously available to people for hierarchically classifying and understanding living kinds according to type, might be variously extended to other domains. For instance, apparent morphological distinctions between human groups are

38   *The Transatlantic Hispanic Baroque*

None of the pre-theoretical or pre-Darwinian concepts of biological variation demonstrates constructionist essentialism more lucidly than humoral theory, the basis of not only medicine since Hippocrates but also astronomy, husbandry, and animal husbandry. In the late sixteenth century, it is not difficult to find Spanish physicians and philosophers who wrote "books of secrets" (Eamon; Kavey) in which they attributed different "complexions" (color differences and moral and intellectual dispositions) to humors, which were influenced by the stars, air, water, and other climatic factors (Wheeler).[4] In *Secretos de filosofía y astrología y medicina y de las cuatro matemáticas ciencias* [*Secrets of Philosophy, Astrology, Medicine, and the Four Mathematical Sciences*], the Spanish physician Alonso López de Corella relied on the Arab philosophers Avicenna and Hali Abas to explain "the variation in looks that is caused by region" (379). People in lowlands had poor coloring because vapors bad for their complexion became trapped there. In contrast, people in highlands had a bright and healthy look, due to the favorable winds in such regions (379–80).

To put a finer point on it, the Spaniard's recycling of the ancient geographical concept was not about distance from the Equator; it was about altitude. It had been used by the Ancients to explain *intra-European* differences, rather than intercontinental ones. The Spaniard underscores: "And it is important to note that [...] there is this difference among Europeans, for those who live up in the mountains have a sturdy build, a great complexion, and are cruel by nature, whereas those who live in very low-lying lands where there is more heat than cold, are not built strong nor suited to hard labor, nor of good complexion" (378). It was this very sort of geographical thinking around biological variation, admittedly in a non-Spanish context, that led Michael Banton to assert the intra-

---

readily (but not necessarily) conceived as apparent morphological distinctions between animal species—that is, in accordance with presumptions about underlying physical natures. [...] Yet, no necessary or inevitable pattern of domain-crossing appears when the basic cognitive disposition, to conceive of living kinds as material essences with underlying natures, is further elaborated and transferred to such 'nearby' empirical domains as HUMANS and SUBSTANCES" (*Cognitive*: 78). This is a distinction between first-order cognitive disposition ("to conceive of species essentially") and second-order cognitive susceptibilities ("to further elaborate, transfer and integrate such conceptions") (*Cognitive*: 79).

4   Cañizares-Esguerra argues for a "patriotic astrology" and "a science of the racialized body" that marginalized Indians and sub-Saharan African slaves. He confuses astronomy, which concerned the planets and other elements of the natural environment, with astrology, which was akin to fortune-telling and dismissed by elites as 'vana astrologia judiciaria'. On the other hand, he backs away from his second claim, arguing that environmental forces were believed to change natural constitutions (94). On astronomy and alterity, see López Beltrán, "Hippocratic Bodies," and his brilliant *El sesgo hereditario* (which should have been translated into English years ago), in which he elucidates the different notions of heredity, and the Aristotelian concepts of accident and species, that Cañizares-Esguerra grapples with.

European origins of race, over three decades ago. Here we have a pre-theoretical foreshadowing of what biologist Robin Andreasen terms the "geographical" race concept, which was to characterize post-Darwinian racial thinking. At the same time, this baroque sketch of the geographical notion of biological race is offset by the precursor to what Andreasen terms the "typological" race concept. The latter assumes the existence of non-accidental properties that are intrinsic to all and only members of an identified human or nonhuman kind, group, or type (456). It was displaced by the concept of geographical race, which is actually made up of several populations who breed or have bred with each other, and is usually (but not always) an allopatric population, i.e., it is separated from others by some geographic barrier or other—plain, mountain, river, etc. (460–61).

The baroque alternation of typological and geographical concepts of race had another, defining dimension: analogical conceptualization of types of men, brutes, and plants. Whether racial categorization is immanent and does not rely on perception, or is, instead, the possible result of analogical transfer from "plant" and "animal" domains to the "human" domain, it is indisputable that analogical thinking around humans and animals is both ancient (Li Causi; Newmyer) and modern: "the comparison of man to animal [...] is [...] theory-constitutive: it is meant to lead, and in fact did lead, to a comparative zoology; just as the analogy between plant and animal would lay the foundation for a unified biology" (Atran, *Cognitive* 115). Apart from Archimboldo's paintings, there is no more vivid representation of the plant-animal-human continuum central to constructionist essentialism than books of secrets. Following Hippocrates, Aristotle confirmed for López de Corella that animals raised in the mountains were more robust and spirited than their counterparts raised in the plains, due to the superior mountain air and winds (378–9).

Books of holy secrets, if I may, of the Catholic Mysteries, also evinced analogical thinking. A mestizo priest in Lima, Francisco Dávila, resorted to animal analogies to defend the biblical accounts of the Creation in his 1648 catechism: "I ask you, my son, all of the horses in the world, where do they come from? [...] All of the dogs and sheep in the world, where do they come from? [...] From those very first animals that God created they have gone multiplying throughout the world. Well, then, in like manner, my sons, from the first man and the first woman that God created they have gone multiplying throughout the world" (104v). Such analogies are pervasive in baroque treatments of alterity, and they resurface later in this chapter.

Returning to the physician López de Corella, I note his assertion that skin color was determined by the amount of moisture in the skin, which itself was caused by the dryness or humidity of the place where an individual or group lived. Those who live in humid lands are very good-looking and their skin is very thin and soft, whereas those who live in dry lands have very dark-colored faces, according to Avicenna, "because with the dryness, whiteness of the face is lost

40 *The Transatlantic Hispanic Baroque*

and the skin becomes tough" (379). This also explained a difference between the sexes, that is, why women in general were whiter than men: "being more humid than men, they must have a softer skin, and being colder in complexion, they must be whiter" (379). However, and contradictorily, brown-skinned women had better breast milk, according to Aristotle, Conciliator, and Italian humanists (403–404). In López de Corella it is evident that biological variation is not, from the perspective of today, wholly biological. Rather, his biocultural explanation of human variation is rooted in the constructionist essentialism of Aristotelian and folk taxonomies that predate Darwin's theory of evolution. Physical appearance and disposition (intellectual, moral, behavioral) are determined by humors, themselves shaped by *both* heritage and environment (Cañizares-Esguerra).

More broadly, humoral theory and the relationships that it takes for granted between cosmos and microcosmos (man, animal, or plant) represent a path to knowledge about humans and the organic world different from that taken by modern science (i.e. evolutionary theory). On Atran's account, the late French anthropologist Foucault's epistemic understanding of natural history (primarily of early modern physiognomy) overlooks a fundamental distinction: "The epistemological aim of lay taxonomy differs from that of [modern] scientific taxonomy. Both provide a classification that is a key to nature, but they have different presumptions about what nature is. For folk, nature can never be completely 'hidden,' the presumption being that at least some of the typical features of a kind are necessary, rather than incidental, to its nature" (78). Contemporary race theory's dependence on the Foucauldian paradigm sidesteps an intrinsic and defining difference between Baroque and post-Darwinian ways of knowing, as Atran allows us to infer:

> [W]hatever scientific epistemology is adopted, there is a methodological presupposition to the effect that [modern] science seeks to decompose and explain the known in terms of the unknown. Common sense distinguished itself from science by aiming principally to maintain the familiar composition of the world and, if necessary, to assimilate the unknown to the known. [...] Science and common sense thus do not presuppose the same ontologies, and their respective semantic frameworks deal, as it were, with 'different' worlds. (79)

Constructionist essentialism and analogical thinking were not unidirectional in the Baroque, as the case of Spanish humanist Jerónimo Cortés attests. The Valencian savant published works on mathematics, astronomy, natural history, agriculture, and popular medicine that were translated into all of the European languages and republished well into the eighteenth century. In *El non plus ultra del lunario* (1594), he noted the folk and learned practice of totemism—i.e., transferring human properties to brutes, plants, and other elements of Nature. Mars was red and fiery, like humans with this complexion; Saturn was dark and gray (230). Why did astronomers depict planets with human aspects and dispositions? "[T]he reason that they depict the planets with such figures is because of the effects that they cause and influence in men" (230). In 1617, writing of fields best suited for growing wheat, Friar Miguel Agustín explained in his book of farming secrets: "Just as we weigh the variety of complexions in men from different provinces and regions according to the air and disposition of the heavens, so we do likewise in agricultural fields, which have different complexions, because some are strong and others weak; some dry, others humid; the soil is heavy in some, and thin in others; some rocky, others even; and, finally, some sandy and others fat [...]" (167). By what grew on top of the soil, one judged the humor that was in the ground underneath (168). Here, as Atran proposes, we see that folk and Aristotelians alike made assumptions and assertions about nature based on morphology or appearances: they "assimilate[d] the unknown to the known."

In the second part of his *Monarquía Indiana* (1615), Fray Juan de Torquemada recalled that Greek, Roman, and Arab philosophers and historians had attributed the origins of different skin colors in humans to geography—concretely, to a region's distance from or proximity to the Equator—before he speculated about the causes of different skin colors in Amerindians (609–611; bk 14, ch. 18). In black men, "hot complexion overcomes their bodies and thereafter the form and the color of their hair accord with the nature from which they spring, and because the complexion of their nature is very hot, they are perforce black, and because the pores of their bodies are clogged due to the dryness of the body on which they are found, they are perforce to a great degree kinky" (610). In lands with cool summers and cold winters, "the cold overcomes heat and traps the humidities and vapors in bodies, blocking or narrowing the surface or skin of bodies, which is why human bodies are white, and due to the trapping of the humidities the hair is blond, white, and straight" (610). "Indians lived in a temperate climate and were therefore neither black nor white, but, instead, saffron-colored or tan; their hair was soft, straight, and black for the most part, although some Indian women's hair was blondish" (610). To detractors who noted that Spaniards in the New World did not change color or engender children who looked like Indians, Torquemada suggested that this biological explanation could nonetheless be true if divine intervention supplemented climate (611). He did not ultimately accept this biological explanation; he instead subscribed to the Curse of Ham, which began as an anti-Semitic exegesis before it was transferred to Black African slaves, and, eventually, Indians in the New World (Hill, "Entering and Exiting").

In Father Alonso de Sandoval's *Un tratado sobre la esclavitud* [*A Treatise on African Slavery*], the most important treatise on sub-Saharan Africans published before the nineteenth century (Franklin; Bénassy-Berling), he addresses climate and complexion as potential causes of biological alterity. He explained that many philosophers tied skin colors in humans to the complexions of the lands that they inhabited (73). This is what we know today as geographical differentiation. The Jesuit missionary and historian was interested not only in blackness and whiteness; thus he writes of Canton, where Chinese merchants travel frequently, and whose population is of many different colors: "those who are born in Canton and its coast are brown like people in Fez or Barbary [...], and those in the other provinces inland are white, some whiter than others, the further they go into cold land. For there are some people who are like people in Spain, and others blonder, up to the point that they become blond and ruddy like Germans" (74). Africans possibly had kinky hair due to the heat, "for hair like everything else bends, rolls up, and twists just as we see in an animal skin that is burnt" (75). Another possible cause, one already seen in Torquemada's *Monarquía Indiana*, was derived from the first: humors. But Sandoval was not convinced by that ancient theory, either: "because we know that inland, within the city of Brava and Mogadishu, [...] there lived a community of Ethiopians as black as ebony, [...] who have straight hair and very good and aristocratic facial features" (76). If heat, or a combination of heat and humors, produced the facial features and hair textures commonly associated with Black slaves, the same effects would be recorded for all members of the group living in that geographical region.

Nonetheless, some two decades after Father Sandoval's account, the mestizo priest Fernando de Avendaño explained the different appearances but same underlying essence of humans by resorting to grains and vegetables grown in specific geographic environments:

> When you plant four seeds of white corn, tell me, doesn't a stalk come up? And on that stalk are there not white, black, and brown kernels? Don't we see this everyday? [...] The wheat in the highlands makes sweet bread, and here in the hot lowlands, (even) when they plant wheat from the highlands, it doesn't make sweet bread like in the highlands. [...] Well, then, in like manner in Guinea, because the earth is hot and dry and there is a burning sun, men are black [...]. (107r)

Climate, soil, and air—geography, in short—produced biological diversity in plants as well as peoples, for this mestizo priest trained in Thomistic Aristotelianism by Schoolmen in Peru. Constructionist essentialism in the Baroque epoch encompassed the entire organic world, including the environment, unlike modern and postmodern biological essentialisms.

Although physiognomy apparently sorted men and brutes into types, its reliance on humoral theory and its baroque essentialism reveal it to be more geographical than typological in regard to biological race. In Cortés's late-sixteenth-century *Fisonomía y varios secretos de naturaleza* [*Physiognomy and Sundry Natural Secrets*], he explained how physiognomy, or the doctrine of signs, worked. Nature expressed her wisdom "in the natural physiognomy of man, in the part of him that is animal, signifying as if with a finger the bad or good composition, [the] natural inclination, of each one, and even kindness or malice of the soul often tracks the good or bad complexion of the body" (*Fisonomía* 243). In aligning men with their animal prototypes, physiognomy consistently resorted to humoral theory, producing interpretations of skin color, facial features, body frames, limbs, and members that cannot be ignored in a survey of biological alterity concepts from the Baroque. Cortés explains: "So, one discovers the good or bad inclination from the disposition of limbs and the features of the face, for Nature at the time of conception of the human animal disposes all of the parts and limbs of the human body, according to whether she finds the qualities of the four humors restrained or exuberant" (243). Again, we see an Aristotelian episteme that consistently attempts to correlate the unseen and unknown to the perceptible and known, in contradistinction to the episteme of modern science.

No physiognomer was more famous or successful than Giambattista Della Porta, an amateur scientist and dramatist in Spanish Naples. The influence of his many treatises on physiognomy, especially *De humana physiognomonia* (first published in 1586), was enormous in the Hispanic Baroque. Doubtless most Spanish authors (whether armchair scientists or academics) knew Della Porta's recipes, interpretations, and discoveries through his published works. His *Natural Magic* went through many editions and translations in the Baroque and beyond.[5] Even if they did not, however, they would have had the opportunity to come across them through Sebastián de Covarrubias's 1611 *Tesoro de la lengua castellana* (the first Spanish dictionary of hard words), who lauds Della Porta in his dismissive entry on physiognomy (597–8) and plagiarizes the Neapolitan's works in many others, or through Cortés's *Fisonomía* and other treatises. I shall limit myself to a handful of examples.

"Those who have a prominent mouth, and have round and thick lips," the Italian explained, "are of piggish works and customs. [...] [T]he protruding mouth, round and folded under with thick lips, as if it were a steep hill, indicates a filthy, gluttonous, stupid man [...]" (312; bk 2, ch. 13). This pig prototype also applies to the man with a thick and flattened nose. Such men were by nature ignorant and coarse like swine, just as the man with a sharp nose talked like a dog barking and was quick to anger. Similarly, Cortés's *Fisonomía* read lips as signs, without invoking geography or race. "Those who have thick and protruding lips," he affirmed, "show that they are of scant judgment and of great simplicity, and will believe anything" (17). Della Porta argued later that people with frizzy or kinky hair tended to be fearful, harsh, gullible, hateful, and fraudulent (*Della*

---

[5]   On physiognomy in early modern European culture, see Porter's magisterial *Windows of the Soul*. On Della Porta's influence and popularity, see Getrevi, especially 60–72; Bianchi, 90–92.

Figure 2.1 Frontispiece depicting Della Porta and the various topics of natural philosophy addressed in his treatises. Giambattista Della Porta. *De humana physiognomonia*. Rouen: Jean Berthelin, 1650. By kind permission of Brown University Library.

Figure 2.2 Frontispiece. Woodcut by Daniel Widman visually distills Della Porta's doctrine as abridged by Stelluti. Giambattista Della Porta. *Della fisonomia di tutto il corpo humano. Libri Quattro. Hora brevemente in tavole sinottiche ridotta et ordinata da Francesco Stelluti*. Ed. Francesco Stelluti. Rome: Vitale Mascardi, 1637. By kind permission of Brown University Library.

fisonomia dell'uomo 637). Cortés, for his part, wrote: "Kinky locks denote a coarseness of wits and simplemindedness in a man, and in a woman shamelessness and brass" (9). Neither Della Porta nor Cortés, who mentioned the Neapolitan in his own treatise, limited this hair type to people born in a specific region or of a specific ancestry. Della Porta noted that the Greek Ulysses had this type of hair and he was fearful and deceitful. So had a duke of Poland in the early twelfth century, who was timid and an imbecile (*Della fisonomia dell'uomo* 637–8).[6]

In Covarrubias's dictionary, such signs and their exegesis played out differently. He did not carry forth the humoral segment of physiognomy; he crudely copied Della Porta's intellectual, moral, and behavioral profiles for phenotypes of humans and brutes and applied them narrowly. At his entry on *bezo* (literally, "biglip"), for instance, we read:

> BEZO is the lip when it is thick like that of blacks; *buza* was derived from *buca*, and *bezo*, from *buza*. Its origins might be the Hebrew word [...] for "to scorn," because those who mock and scorn make a certain snub with their mouth by stretching out their lips and expressing scorn with them and with their nose. And those who write about physiognomy say that those who have thick lips, which we calls *bezos*, are scornful and slanderous [...]. (214)

Similarly, the entry on *labio* ("lip") mentions, "Thick and misshapen lips we call *bezos*, like those of blacks" (746). Moreover, Covarrubias's prototypical pig man has a long snout with protruding lips, but, unlike Della Porta, the Spanish humanist specifies that *hocicudo* (literally, "long-snouted") applies to black or Moorish women (*negras*) as well as to pigs, dogs, and other brutes (248). Covarrubias applied to sub-Saharan African and Moorish slaves—of which there was no shortage in his Spain—what Della Porta had written about specific facial "signs" or features distributed across many populations and regions (Hill, "*Casta* as Culture" 248–51).

Because humoral theory was rooted in ancient ideas about plants, brutes, and humans, it did not encompass the complexions and humors of the various peoples in sub-Saharan Africa (Lower Ethiopia, or "New Africa," as the Baroque knew it [Hill, "Entering and Exiting"]). This limited circumference, I am convinced, would eventually consign humoral theory to oblivion. By the mid-seventeenth century, protracted Spanish, British, and French experience with Indians and African slaves in the New World rendered unconvincing the

---

6   In Stelluti's abridged handbook, laid out in charts, he listed Ethiopians as the group to which the sign of kinky or frizzy hair was associated, making them timid and deceitful, whereas the man with straight hair was judged to be merely timid (65). The problem, of course, lies in the use of *Etiopi* for the "Ethiopia," or Africa, known to Della Porta's ancient sources primarily as North Africa.

Figure 2.3   Types of nose and lips signal virtues and vices in humans and brutes. Man with pig's snout and man with dog's snout. Giambattista Della Porta. *De humana physiognomonia*. Rouen: Jean Berthelin, 1650. By kind permission of Brown University Library.

correspondence of brown or black skin with melancholy (dark humor in the body) and therefore with poetic and philosophical gifts, or the assignment of a coleric disposition to persons with a ruddy complexion caused by Mars. Likewise, Spanish authorities on veterinary matters and agriculture in the seventeenth century began to question the merits of physiognomy, finding that the colors, tails, tongues, feet, and shapes of horses, dogs, sheep, and so forth, did not reveal consistent patterns of behavior, much less their inner virtues and vices. In the late Baroque era, authors such as Father Benito Feijoo dismissed physiognomy (and its handmaiden, humoral theory) outright as a means of knowing humans, while horse doctors ridiculed its contradictory advice to horse breeders and horse traders.

There is one more biocultural explanation for biological variation in brutes and humans that deserves a brief analysis: maternal impression, or the power of the maternal imagination to imprint and shape the foetus. In his book of secrets, the physician López de Corella reported that in Sicily a white woman slept with

48   *The Transatlantic Hispanic Baroque*

a black man and then gave birth to a white girl, who in turn gave birth to a black boy who resembled his grandfather. This atavism he supported with Aristotle, Galen, and Avicenna (308). He also included anecdotes from Savonarola (that go back at least to St Augustine) about a white woman who looked at a black man (or painting of a black man) when she was having sex with her white husband, and subsequently gave birth to a black child (309).

The missionary Sandoval recalled Aristotle's explanation for biological variation in the offspring of humans and brutes: the maternal imagination (69). Experience appeared to confirm Aristotle's theory, "since, we so often see ugly children born to beautiful parents, and the contrary, beautiful children born to ugly parents; and brown and even very black children born to white parents, and to black parents, children who are very white, blond, with light blue and violet eyes; and to a very good mare of prized breed and a stallion to match, a colt similar to his parents is born, and then another that is not; the truth of which is recognized by all [...]" (69). All of this confirmed the Old Testament tale of Jacob, who placed sticks of many colors in the watering holes where the sheep gathered so that those colors would imprint themselves on the imagination of the sheep during conception and would result in lambs of many colors for Jacob's coat (69–70). He trots out numerous cases in world history, ancient and modern, of white women who gave birth to black babies, and black women who gave birth to white babies. (71).

After dismissing the notion that Black Africans were black because of Ham's Curse, the mestizo priest Avendaño presented a different theological possibility. Blackness was not a divine punishment, but, instead, a biological variation caused by maternal impression:

> Other very wise authorities state that the reason why Cush was born black could be because his mother was thinking about some black thing when she was conceiving him, and due to this vehement imagination Cush was born black. Likewise, sometimes a very white boy with hair like snow is born among Indians, about whom you all usually say that he is the son of the Sun, and the cause of this is that his mother was thinking vehemently about some white thing when she was conceiving him, and that's why he was born so white. Many times you all must have seen a mottled child, more than one color, and the reason is because when she was carrying the child in her womb she got a craving for some thing of the color of those spots that the child got, and since she couldn't eat what she was craving, that's why the child was born with those spots, as we see everyday. [...] This Cush married a white woman and had many children and grandchildren, of whom some were born black because they took after their father, and others were born white because they took after their mother, and we see these things everyday, for mestizos—children of a Spanish man and an Indian woman—sometimes look

like their father, and are very white, and other times they look like their mother, and are brown-colored like their mother. (106)

Amidst a very complex and persuasive argument about the fabrication of whiteness in the United States, Matthew Frye Jacobson notes the paradox that a white woman can give birth to a black child, but a black woman cannot give birth to a white child (Jacobson; Wade, *Race, Nature*; Zack). It should be clear from the foregoing passages on maternal impression that this paradox did not exist in the ancient world, nor in the Spanish world of the Baroque. Its very absence proves that a different cognitive framework—a different conceptual grid—was engaged when early moderns approached alterity in general and human variation (especially hair type and skin color) in particular. The buttress of baroque alterity was, to put it in contemporary terms, a constructionist (or anti-essentialist) essentialism. This has been overlooked by scholars in critical race studies largely due to the fact that we still lack a critical language for tackling folkbiology or Aristotelian science in non-racialized terms. Indeed, we can scarcely even conceive of any essentialism involving the organic world (plants, animals, and humans) that is *not* racial, much less a concept of biological race that is *not* essentialist, in the postmodern sense. Given that anti-essentialism is "a kind of theoretical *Rashomon* [...] within critical race discourse" (Valdés, Culp, and Harris 3), the notion of constructionist essentialism not only illuminates the alterity of baroque griddings of alterity, but might also prove useful to the anti-racist pedagogy and research program of the Critical Race Theory movement (CRT, as legal scholars call it) and critical race studies in general.

Let us return to Root's race-as-social-category definition, which is steeped in the very sort of essentialism that his anti-racist scholarship and pedagogy repudiate. First, he writes that race, though not biological, is "biologically rather than culturally transmitted" (737), which flies in the face of race as a construct or social category, reducing it to physical and heritable traits. Second, while contrasting race with citizenship, Root claims that "passing is not being" (738), as if race were a biological essence that racial passing in society could temporarily mask but never hope to permanently alter. Indeed, Root confirms my reading: "There is a difference between race and perceived race, for a person who passes for black or white only passes. Were being and being perceived the same, race would not be real but simply a matter of appearance. That is, race would not be real if to be black were simply to be seen as black, since 'real' implies a contrast and, in particular, a difference between being and seeming to be" (738).

The second proposition is particularly vexing for scholars of baroque philosophy, history, and literature who cut their teeth on *engaño* versus *desengaño*, appearances versus essences, and other staples of the Baroque. Root's debts here are (like Foucault's) thoroughly rationalist to spite himself. Let us recall that Descartes and Cartesian rationalists abhorred appearances and complained repeatedly that Aristotelians (the neo-scholastics who dominated the colleges and universities not only in Spain but in France itself) were, like folk, contented with appearances rather than with reality. In philosophical terms, they mistook accidental properties for essential or specific properties, according to Descartes and his disciples. This takes us back to Atran's distinction between pre-theoretical (Aristotelian, folk) essentialism and scientific (post-Darwinian) epistemologies, including the sort of biological essentialism that was to produce the biological race concept discussed by Root. The latter argues that acting/appearing is not being, but this does not hold for pre-theoretical essentialism, which is a constructionist essentialism: you are what you perform or appear to be. In the Baroque this essentialism is taken to new heights, but it already existed in the sixteenth century, being particularly visible in the arena of self-fashioning for social climbing. I believe, though I cannot explore here, that the new philosophy or new science provoked a crisis of constructionist essentialism, i.e. that Aristotelian and folk essentialism were weakened when Cartesians and Baconians butted heads with the Schoolmen. It was only after Aristotelianism was vanquished, and traditional folk beliefs discredited, that biological essentialism of the sort that Root describes could emerge in the nineteenth century.

All of the texts that I have surveyed touch on the fraught relationship between heredity and environment, between essence and appearance, between—in today's vernacular—genotype and phenotype. Their authors—monks, missionaries, physicians in the Old World and the New—contended that heritable traits such as skin color might change over the lifespan of an individual or of his/her offspring, and, over the course of several generations, in an entire group. As Wade has stated regarding the relationship between lived experience and somatic characteristics: "What is needed here is an appreciation of the difficult tension between permanence and change: social processes become congealed into the body to create forms that are not immediately changeable; yet in principle such forms are changeable because they are themselves in process" (Wade, *Race, Nature* 120–21). Not heritage alone but also environmental conditions—food, exposure to air, sun, water, relations with other humans—altered the essence and appearance of individuals and groups. Baroque authors who defended biological (as opposed to supernatural) explanations often disagreed (as their ancient sources had before them) about *how* that change had occurred in the past and might occur in the future: some presented geography and humors as possible causes, whereas others invoked maternal impression. In either case, baroque alterity was cognitively and conceptually derived from a constructionist essentialism. It is only by recognizing this fact that we can begin to write the critical history of biological race, whose prologue was as cultural as it was biological.

Bibliography

Agustín, Miguel. *Libro de los secretos de agricultura, casa de campo y pastoril.* Facsimile edition. Valladolid: Editorial Maxtor, 2001.

Andreasen, Robin O. "Biological Conceptions of Race." *Handbook of the Philosophy of Science: Philosophy of Biology.* Ed. Mohan Matthen and Christopher Stephens. Amsterdam and Boston: Elsevier, 2007. 455–81.

Atran, Scott. *Cognitive Foundations of Natural History: Towards an Anthropology of Science.* Cambridge and New York: Cambridge University Press, 1990.

Atran, Scott and Douglas Medin. *The Native Mind and the Social Construction of Nature.* London and Cambridge: MIT Press, 2008.

Avendaño, Fernando de. *Sermones de los misterios de nuestra santa Fe católica.* Lima: Jorge López de Herrera, 1649.

Banton, Michael. *The Idea of Race.* London: Tavistock Publications, 1977.

Bénassy-Berling, Marie-Cécile. "Alonso de Sandoval, les jésuites et la descendance de Cham." Études sur l'impact culturel du Nouveau Monde. Paris: Editions L'Harmattan, 1981. 49–60.

Bianchi, Massimo Luigi. *Signatura rerum: Segni, magia e conoscenza da Paracelso a Leibniz.* Rome: Edizioni dell'Ateneo, 1987.

Cañizares-Esguerra, Jorge. "New World, New Stars: Patriotic Astrology and the Invention of Amerindian and Creole Bodies in Colonial Spanish America, 1600–1650." *Nature, Empire, and Nation: Explorations of the History of Science in the Iberian World.* Stanford, CA: Stanford University Press, 2006. 64–95.

Correas, Gonzalo. *Vocabulario de refranes y frases proverbiales.* Prologue by Miguel Mir. Ed. Víctor Infantes. Madrid: Visor Libros, 1992.

Cortés, Jerónimo. *El non plus ultra del lunario y prognóstico perpetuo, general y particular.* Facsimile edition. Valencia: Librerías París-Valencia [1992].

———. *Fisonomía y varios secretos de Naturaleza.* Facsimile of 1741 expurgated edition. Valencia: Librerías París-Valencia, 1992.

Cosmides, Leda, John Tooby and Robert Kurzban. "Perceptions of Race." *Trends in Cognitive Sciences* 7.4 (April 2003): 173–9.

Covarrubias, Sebastián de. *Tesoro de la lengua castellana o española según la impresión de 1611, con las adiciones de Benito Remigio Noydens publicadas en la de 1674.* Ed. Martín de Riquer. Barcelona: S.A. Horta, 1943.

Dávila [de Ávila], Francisco. *Tratado de los Evangelios.* Lima: n.p., 1648.

Della Porta, Giambattista. *Della fisonomia di tutto il corpo humano. Libri Quattro. Hora brevemente in tavole sinottiche ridotta et ordinata da Francesco Stelluti.* Rome: Vitale Mascardi, 1637.

———. *De humana physiognomonia.* Rouen: Jean Berthelin, 1650.

———. *Della magia naturale.* Naples: Bulifon, 1677.

―――. *Natural Magick by John Baptista Porta, A Neapolitane, in Twenty Books Wherein are set forth All the Riches and Delights of the Natural Sciences.* Facsimile of 1658 edition. Ed. Derek J. Price. New York: Basic Books, 1957.

―――. *Della fisonomia dell'uomo.* Ed. Mario Cicognani. Milan: Longanesi & C., 1971.

Dumont, Louis. *Homo Hierarchicus: The Caste System and Its Implications.* Revised edition. London: Paladin, 1972.

―――. *Homo aequalis: genèse et épanouissement de l'idéologie économique.* Paris: Gallimard, 1977.

Dupré, John. *The Disorder of Things: Metaphysical Foundations of the Disunity of Science.* London and Cambridge: Harvard University Press, 1993.

Eamon, William. *Science and the Secrets of Nature: Books of Secrets in Medieval and Early Modern Culture.* Princeton: Princeton University Press, 1994.

Feijoo, Benito Jerónimo. "Color etiópico." *Teatro crítico universal.* Vol. 7: 66–93. Proyecto Filosofía en Español. Biblioteca Feijooniana 1–14. Madrid: Real Compañía de Impresores y Libreros, 1778. November 8, 2009. <www.filosofía.org>.

Foucault, Michel. *The Order of Things: An Archaeology of the Human Sciences.* New York: Vintage, 1994.

Frank, Reanne. "What to Make of It? The (Re)emergence of a Biological Conceptualization of Race in Health Disparities Research." *Social Science & Medicine* 64 (2007): 1977–1983.

Franklin, Vincent P. "Bibliographical Essay: Alonso de Sandoval and the Jesuit Conception of the Negro." *The Journal of Negro History* 58.3 (1973): 349–60.

Gelman, Susan A. and Lawrence A. Hirschfeld. "How Biological Is Essentialism?" *Folkbiology.* Ed. Douglas L. Medin and Scott Atran. London and Cambridge: MIT Press, 1999. 403–446.

Getrevi, Paolo. *Le Scritture del Volto: Fisiognomica e modelli culturali dal medioevo ad oggi.* Milan: Franco Angeli, 1991.

Gil-White, Francisco J. "How Thick is Blood? The Plot Thickens...: If Ethnic Actors are Primordialists, What Remains of the Circumstantialist/Primordialist Controversy?" *Ethnic and Racial Studies* 22.5 (September 1999): 789–820.

―――. "Are Ethnic Groups Biological 'Species' to the Human Brain? Essentialism in Our Cognition of Some Social Categories." *Current Anthropology* 42.4 (August–October 2001): 515–54.

Goldberg, David Theo. *Racist Culture: Philosophy and the Politics of Meaning.* Oxford: Blackwell, 1993.

Hacking, Ian. *The Social Construction of What?* London and Cambridge: Harvard University Press, 1999.

Hall, Stuart. "Race, Articulation, and Societies Structured in Dominance." *Race Critical Theories: Text and Context.* Ed. David Theo Goldberg and Philomena Essed. Oxford: Blackwell, 2001. 38–68.

Herrera, Gabriel Alonso de. *Obra de Agricultura.* Biblioteca de Autores Españoles CCXXXV. Ed. and Introduction by José Urbano Martínez Carreras. Madrid: Atlas, 1970.

Hill, Ruth. "*Casta* as Culture and the *Sociedad de Castas* as Literature." *Interpreting Colonialism.* Ed. Byron Wells and Philip Stewart. Oxford: Voltaire Foundation, 2004. 231–59.

———. "Introduction." *Categories and Crossings: Critical Race Studies and the Spanish World.* Ed. Ruth Hill. Special issue of *Journal of Spanish Cultural Studies* 10.1 (March 2009): 1–6.

———. "Entering and Exiting Blackness: A Color Controversy in Eighteenth-Century Spain." *Categories and Crossings: Critical Race Studies and the Spanish World.* Ed. Ruth Hill. Special issue of *Journal of Spanish Cultural Studies* 10.1 (March 2009): 43–58.

Hirschfeld, Lawrence A. "The Conceptual Politics of Race: Lessons from Our Children." *Ethos* 25.1 (1997): 63–92.

———. "On a Folk Theory of Society: Children, Evolution, and Mental Representations of Social Groups." *Personality and Social Psychology Review* 5.2 (2001): 107–117.

Jacobson, Matthew Frye. *Whiteness of a Different Color: European Immigrants and the Alchemy of Race.* London and Cambridge: Harvard University Press, 1998.

Kavey, Allison. *Books of Secrets: Natural Philosophy in England, 1550–1600.* Urbana and Chicago: University of Illinois Press, 2007.

Kelly, Daniel, Luc Faucher and Edouard Machery. "Getting Rid of Racism: Assessing Three Proposals in Light of Psychological Evidence." *Journal of Social Philosophy* 41.3 (Fall 2010): 293–322.

Li Causi, Pietro. *Generare in comune. Teorie e rappresentazioni dell'ibrido nel sapere zoologico dei Greci dei Romani.* Palermo: Palumbo, 2008.

López Beltrán, Carlos. *El sesgo hereditario: ámbitos históricos del concepto de herencia biológica.* Mexico, DF: Universidad Nacional Autónoma de México, 2004.

———. "Hippocratic Bodies: Temperament and Castas in Spanish America (1570–1820)." *Science in Translation: The Commerce of Facts and Artifacts in the Transatlantic Spanish World.* Ed. Miruna Achim. Special issue of *Journal of Spanish Cultural Studies* 8.2 (July 2007): 253–89.

López de Corella, Alonso. *Secretos de filosofía y astrología y medicina y de las cuatro matemáticas ciencias.* Ed. Juan Cruz Cruz. Pamplona: Departamento de Educación y Cultura, 2001.

Machery, Edouard and Luc Faucher. "Social Construction and the Concept of Race." *Philosophy of Science* 72 (December 2005): 1208–1219.

Newmyer, Stephen T. *Animals in Greek and Roman Thought: A Sourcebook.* London and New York: Routledge, 2011.

Porter, Martin. *Windows of the Soul: Physiognomy in Early Modern Culture.* Oxford: Clarendon, 2005.

Robbins, Jeremy. *The Challenges of Uncertainty: An Introduction to Seventeenth-Century Spanish Literature.* Lanham, MD: Rowman & Littlefield Publishers, Inc., 1998.

Root, Michael. "Race in the Social Sciences." *The Philosophy of Anthropology and Sociology.* Ed. Stephen P. Turner and Mark W. Risjord. Amsterdam and Boston: Elsevier, 2007. 735–53.

Sandoval, Alonso de. *Un tratado sobre la esclavitud (Tractatus de instauranda aethiopum salute, 1627).* Introduction, transcription and translation by Enriqueta Vila Vilar. Madrid: Alianza Universidad, 1987.

Shulman, Julia L. and Joshua Glasgow. "Is Race-Thinking Biological or Social, and Does It Matter for Racism? An Exploratory Essay." *Journal of Social Philosophy* 41.3 (Fall 2010): 244–59.

Torquemada, Juan de. *Segunda parte de los veinte y un libros rituales y Monarchia Indiana. Con el Origen y guerras de los Yndias Occidentales [sic]. De sus Poblaçones, Descubrimiento, Conquista, Conversion y otras cosas maravillosas de la mesma tierra distribuydos en tres tomos.* Madrid: Matthias Clavijo, 1615. 3 vols.

Valdés, Francisco, Culp, Jerome McCristal and Harris, Angela P. *Crossroads, Directions, and a New Critical Race Theory.* Philadelphia, PA: Temple University Press, 2002.

Wade, Peter. *Race and Ethnicity in Latin America.* London: Pluto Press, 1997.

———. *Race, Nature and Culture: An Anthropological Perspective.* London: Pluto Press, 2002.

Wheeler, Roxann. *The Complexion of Race: Categories of Difference in Eighteenth-Century British Culture.* Philadelphia, PA: University of Pennsylvania Press, 2000.

Yoon, Carol Kaesuk. *Naming Nature: The Clash Between Instinct and Science.* New York: W.W. Norton & Company, 2009.

Zack, Naomi. *Race and Mixed Race.* Philadelphia, PA: Temple University Press, 1993.

Chapter 3

Higher Education, "Soft Power," and Catholic Identity: A Case Study from Early Modern Salamanca

Harald E. Braun

In a letter from 20 August 1605, Gil González Dávila, historian and man of letters, praises Salamanca as "la ciudad imperial de las lettras" (209).[1] His words capture local pride in Salamanca as not just the foremost place of higher learning in the Spanish Habsburg monarchy and one of the great European universities at the time, but as a busy centre of intellectual production, cultural exchange and political communication.[2] González Dávila celebrates the "university-city" as a hub where diverse and sometimes conflicting cultures of knowledge and learning could meet and complement one another. In the view of the future *cronista mayor de las Indias*, Salamanca was a place where excellence in formal legal or theological instruction mingled with a vibrant and anything but provincial humanist culture. This "city of letters" existed within and at the same time transcended the actual *universitas* or corporate body of students and teachers both in terms of the opportunities it offered and of the traces it left on students' memory and later lives.[3] It was a place of intellectual endeavour, discovery and friendship as much as a place of formal instruction. What distinguished Salamanca even more in González Dávila's eyes, though, was the imperial reach of this particularly happy union of *estudios* and *letras*. Salamanca was not only the place where future careers in state and church were forged.

---

[1]   Gil González Dávila (1578–1658)—*racionero* of Salamanca cathedral and latterly *cronista mayor de las Indias* (1617)—used his historiographical expertise to exult university and city, for instance in his antiquarian polemic *Declaración de la antigüedad del toro del puente de Salamanca* (1596), or his history of Salamanca *Historia de las antigüedades de la ciudad de Salamanca* (Salamanca: Taberniel, 1606). On early modern Spanish historiography see Richard L. Kagan, *Clio & the Crown*.

[2]   On the University of Salamanca during the later sixteenth and early seventeenth century, see Luis Enrique Rodríguez-San Pedro Bezares; also the illuminating study by Andrew Hegarty. On Iberian universities during the early modern period more widely, see the contributions in Luis E. Rodríguez-San Pedro Bezares and Juan Luis Polo Rodríguez.

[3]   For early modern Leiden as a useful comparison see Daniela Prögler.

56 *The Transatlantic Hispanic Baroque*

González Dávila regarded Salamanca rather than Madrid as the intellectual and cultural showcase of the Spanish monarchy, and as the place where cultural and intellectual capital would turn into political currency. Salamanca, in other words, might have exerted something like "soft power"—through various forms of cultural and intellectual exchange, communication, and networks—on foreign students and visitors.[4]

Recent scholarship tends to substantiate this impression of sixteenth- and seventeenth-century Salamanca as a Catholic, Spanish, and imperial space and "lecture hall of the Catholic monarchy."[5] While students from the Iberian Peninsula and Castile in particular clearly dominated matriculation throughout the period, the student body to some degree at least reflected the political geography of the *monarquía española*.[6] There was a regular and notable presence of students from the Italian territories under Spanish Habsburg rule (especially Milan and the viceroyalty of Naples) and the Americas (especially the viceroyalties of New Spain and Peru). Salamanca also attracted students from territories not directly under Spanish Habsburg rule but within the Spanish imperial or hegemonic sphere—especially Portugal and, again, Italy (Genoa, Florence, Naples, also the papal lands).[7] A smaller number of students came to Salamanca from territories outside the Spanish hemisphere, mostly from France, but also the Holy Roman Empire, and Ireland. If matriculations at Salamanca did reflect a general trend towards "regionalisation" of universities during the early modern period, then the city and university retained cosmopolitan colour and appeal nonetheless.[8]

---

[4] For a working definition of soft power and a comparative approach to culture as a significant element in (contemporary) public diplomacy and strategic communication see, for instance, Craig Hayden. I do not suggest that monarchy or university consciously pursued a rhetoric or strategy of soft power exploiting Salamanca's status as an international centre of Higher Education and humanist endeavour. At the same time, much of what happened "on the ground"—in practical terms of education, cultural interaction, exchange and network building—can, arguably, be described as a convergence of cultural and political influence. The problem of evaluating or measuring such influence does, of course, remain.

[5] For an overview and summary analysis see Ángel Weruaga Prieto.

[6] For the relative size of the foreign contingents at Salamanca during the early modern period, see Rodríguez-San Pedro Bezares and Polo Rodríguez, *Historia de la universidad* 2: 607–64. Weruaga Prieto provides a revised statistical profile of the provenance of students from outside the Iberian Peninsula.

[7] For Italians in Salamanca, see the brief survey by Antonio Pérez Martin, and Rodríguez-San Pedro Bezares, *La universidad salmantina* 3: 185–334, especially 195–8, 209–211.

[8] See the general discussion in Hilde de Ridder-Symoens, especially 439–46; also Michel Bideaux and Marie-Madeleine Fragonard. For Salamanca and Spanish universities, see Rodríguez-San Pedro Bezares and Polo Rodríguez. Rodríguez-San Pedro Bezares, *La universidad salmantina* 3: 195–6, estimates that non-peninsular students accounted for just

Higher Education, "Soft Power," and Catholic Identity

This picture is differentiated further by the fact that the Salamancan student body cannot easily be divided up and described in terms of "natives" and "foreigners." Students from the crowns of Castile and Aragon, the heartlands of the Spanish monarchy, did not share anything resembling a single cohesive notion of *patria* or *nación*.[9] Students from Spanish Flanders, Milan, and the kingdom of Naples, on the other hand, did not even necessarily speak Spanish as their first language, yet would be likely to entertain a complex and varied sense of being part of the *monarquía española*. Students, again, who arrived in Salamanca from territories within the Spanish hegemonic sphere but not under direct Spanish Habsburg rule brought with them connections, expectations and affinities that facilitated integration and interaction with a predominantly Castilian student body.

The Irish at Salamanca provide a useful point of reference in this respect. The foundation of the *Real Colegio de San Patricio de Nobles Irlandeses* in 1592 established Salamanca as one of several educational and ideological centres of the Irish secular and clerical elite well into the seventeenth century.[10] One of the more prominent members of the European network of Irish Colleges, the *Real Colegio* provided a focal point for Irish Catholic identity during turbulent periods in that country's history—first as a seminary and bolthole for resistance to the Tudor state, and subsequently as a hub for exiles and migrants making home somewhere in the Iberian world. The Irish came to Salamanca in the later sixteenth century in order to study, make useful contacts, and to ensure that the monarchy would continue to champion their cause. Their situation, though, was specific in several respects—they were political and religious exiles—and they are just one example for why young men of social standing who did not live under the rule of the Spanish Habsburgs came to Salamanca. Other members of

---

over one per cent of total matriculations between 1598 and 1625, but for about ten per cent of the "nobles-generosos" that matriculated during that same period. He arrives at his estimate on the basis of snapshots of matriculations in the years 1604/5, 1614/15, and 1624/25. In the case of the Italians, he only counts students from families of a status comparable to that of Spanish grandees—the sons of the Medici, Spinola, or Gonzaga—among the "nobles-generosos." Lower nobility and quasi-noble patricians like Da Sommaia are not included. Rodríguez-San Pedro Bezares himself points out that "nobles-generosos" is a flexible category, and he explains how recalcitrant sources make it difficult to arrive at precise figures; *La universidad salmantina* 3: 72–184, 256–71.

9   On the long, uneven and unfinished road from regional, fragmented and multi-layered early modern notions of *patria* to the crystallisation of a Spanish national identity in eighteenth-century courtly Madrid, see I.A.A. Thompson; also Tamar Herzog or Veronika Ryjik.

10   On the Irish colleges in the peninsula see, for instance, Patricia O'Connell; on the early modern Irish diaspora more widely, see the contributions in Thomas O'Connor and Mary Ann Lyons.

58 *The Transatlantic Hispanic Baroque*

the early modern European Catholic elite—such as the sons of leading families of Genoa or Milan—had less overtly political and pressing grounds to study at the university.

The different, often related reasons that brought foreigners to Salamanca are reflected in the ways and the degree to which these students interacted not just with fellow students and the institution, but with Spanish culture and people more widely. Looking at such interactions, in turn, leads on to the closely related question of whether and how a period of study in Salamanca might have affected these students' view of themselves as well as their view of Spain and the Spanish monarchy. In other words, is González Dávila's praise mere hyperbole, or did the university-city inadvertently exert a degree of soft power? Did study at Salamanca foster something akin to a shared sense of elite cultural identity—Catholic, Baroque, and imperial—in some of its foreign *alumni* at least? Could time spent in Salamanca encourage a sense of a "republic of letters" predicated upon Hispanic culture and intellectual life even in students from outside the monarchy? The question of how far study abroad lastingly affected the cultural identity, sense of self and political outlook of the non-Iberian, non-Habsburg Salamanca *alumnus* is extremely challenging. It is difficult to produce satisfying answers not least because of the relative paucity of life-writing and other autobiographical material that would allow the historian to reconstruct possible connections between study abroad and early modern identity.

In the following, I try and make a small window into the experience of *estudiantes extranjeros* in early modern Salamanca—their many acts of communication and their decisions to engage with, embrace or reject a foreign environment. I gather and assemble impressions, observations and reflexions from the personal records of one foreign student in particular—the Florentine patrician Girolamo da Sommaia (1573–1635).[11] The young Italian left us with a unique record of his time in Spain and of the features that characterised Salamanca as a place to experience and explore many facets of Hispanic life, culture and politics. His experience was one of a university and a city at the crucible of early modern Hispanic empire and culture.

***

Da Sommaia arrived in Salamanca in 1599 in order to study civil and canon law, a young man of 21 years, and one possessed of a lively intellect. He left the university and the country in 1607 a *bachiller utroque iuri*, after a comparatively long period of study. The young Florentine recommends himself as a witness for a number of reasons. While in Salamanca, he consciously and persistently sought to make use of what the place had to offer in terms of learning beyond the

---

[11] The best source for information on Da Sommaia's life is still George Haley, "Introducción" 9–35.

Higher Education, "Soft Power," and Catholic Identity   59

lecture hall and the textbook. Libraries, learned conversations, and many other kinds of intellectual endeavour took up a good part of his time. He returned to Italy a loyal connoisseur of Spanish thought and letters. We know this because Girolamo left us with a good number of excerpts from his Salamanca reading list and also with an extraordinary and possibly unique record: his diary covering the latter years of his stay (1602–1607).[12] The *Diario* helps flesh out our knowledge of what brought well-connected and well-off foreigners to Salamanca in the first instance, what more or less tangible benefits they expected from their stay, and how they experienced Salamanca and let it shape their perceptions and memories of Spain.

Girolamo Da Sommaia's *Diario* suggests that Salamanca appealed to some born and bred in the lap of Italian humanist culture and polities not least because of its "extra-curriculum."[13] Much of what Da Sommaia learned and much of what left a Hispanic imprint on his likes and dislikes happened outside the lecture hall and was not included in the official syllabus. Some of it occurred in a kind of twilight zone, more or less removed from official and institutional control. This extracurricular formation happened during private tutorials, regular visits to the theatre, in conversations, or over a bottle of wine and playing cards and talking politics and literature well into the small hours. Reading was a crucial part of it. Girolamo was a voracious reader and a compiler of substantial personal anthologies with excerpt from works of Spanish history and politics, prose and poetry. In today's parlance, what was particularly attractive to a student like Girolamo Da Sommaia was what Salamanca offered in terms of "added value"—education and opportunity in terms of cultural and political capital beyond or on top of the degree as such. The ambitious, sociable and scholarly student could combine the acquisition of specific expertise and professional qualification with the freedom to satisfy intellectual curiosity and ample opportunities to build or expand political and social networks. Salamanca offered the prospect of learning about Spanish culture and mentality and a means to strike friendships and establish networks relevant to a future career in Italian courts and states often firmly situated within the Hispanic sphere of influence.[14]

The decision to attend Salamanca rather than one of the Italian universities—the Medici *studium* in nearby Pisa would have been an obvious

---

[12] *Diario* is George Haley's summary title for the two autograph manuscripts with almost daily entries in Da Sommaia's *fondo* in the Biblioteca Nazionale Centrale Florencia (BNCF): MS. Magliabechi VIII, 29 and VIII, 30. For a brief description, Haley, "Introducción" 1 n.1.

[13] I borrow this fortunate term from Richard Kagan, "La Salamanca del Siglo de Oro." See also Manuel Fernández Álvarez. Useful in terms of context is Kagan, *Students and Society*.

[14] Humanist networks and politics of friendship are the subject of a rich and growing literature. See, for instance, the essay by Peter Burke. On the many variations and conceptualisations of friendship, see the contributions in Albrecht Classen and Marilyn Sandidge.

60 *The Transatlantic Hispanic Baroque*

choice—would have involved not only Girolamo and his parents, but the social and family networks into which he had been born. The *consorteria* or kin community allowed individuals like Girolamo access to shared resources—human and financial, material and symbolic—on the understanding that their success would in turn replenish and enhance these resources and create opportunities for other members of the collective. Sending a young man to study at Salamanca was such a decision affecting communal resources—in terms of funds, contacts, and reputation, for instance—and therefore required the consent of the *consorteria* as a whole or its significant parts.[15] It is not possible to reconstruct the process of consultation and discussion that brought Girolamo to Spain and Salamanca in any detail. Circumstantial evidence, however, indicates that this was a deployment of a member of the kin community grounded in hard-nosed political and social opportunism coupled with a sense of know-how concerning all things Spanish. In a nutshell, the motivation for sending the young man to Salamanca was to help secure his family's future as functionaries of the Medici ducal government, open up new opportunities of patronage and employment, and enhance the cultural and material capital of the collective that way.

Girolamo Da Sommaia was the scion of a patrician family already established in Medici Florence at the time of his birth. On his father's side, the family hailed from old Lombard nobility and had been part of the elite pool of patrician families providing high officials or *priori* for the Republic during the fifteenth and early sixteenth century.[16] More importantly, the Da Sommaia were among the minority of patrician houses who successfully negotiated the transition from republic to Medici principate.[17] Girolamo's paternal grandfather and namesake held important positions in government and was made a senator by Cosimo I Medici in 1554. His son, Giovanni de Sommaia, was awarded the same honour in 1588 by the new grand-duke Ferdinando I. Though the Da Sommaia could not quite compete with the leading patrician clans in terms of wealth, glory and political influence, their rank and status allowed them to intermarry with the *grandi*. In 1567, Giovanni Da Sommaia raised his family's profile and

---

[15] Concerning the role of family and kinship in early modern Italian politics and commerce, see, for instance, Paul D. McLean. The ways in which families in the upper echelons of early modern Italian society sought to use diplomatic service and networks across Europe in the hope for collective profit serve as a good case in point. See the helpful article by Catherine Fletcher and Jennifer Mara DeSilva.

[16] For Da Sommaia genealogy, see Haley "Introducción" 9–14.

[17] On the transformation of Florentine patrician houses into nobility and functionaries of Medici government see Robert Burr Litchfield, especially 24–51, 63–126. The Da Sommaia were among the limited number of families who made up the political and administrative core of the Medici court – gathered in the Senate and Order of St Stephen. Unlike the wealthier and more powerful Guicciardini, the Da Sommaia never secured a fiefdom; see Appendix B, 362, 381.

Higher Education, "Soft Power," and Catholic Identity

consolidated their access to lucrative office and opportunities at the Medici court by marrying Costanza Guicciardini.

The match closely aligned the Da Sommaia with one of the wealthiest and most high-profile families in Florentine history and long-standing supporters of the Medici.[18] It also opened the doors to the Guicciardini family archive. Managed by Costanza's father Agnolo Guicciardini,[19] the archive included the works and correspondence of Francesco Guicciardini (1483–1540), famous Florentine diplomat and historian, contemporary and critic of Machiavelli. Francesco's first diplomatic mission, at the age of only 23 years, had taken him to Spain and the court of Ferdinand of Aragon at Logroño (1512).[20] His *Diario del viaggio in Spagna*, completed in the same year, reflects less on the mission itself as on the thrill and adventure of travel. In subsequent reports and letters as well as in his *Relazione di Spagna* (1514), on the other hand, Guicciardini repeatedly analyses the complex, fluid, and always seminal relationships between the Spanish monarchs and the Italian powers. While he is no friend of Spain or Spanish culture, Guicciardini is a remarkably sober and analytical observer of the politics of power and a quiet admirer-cum-critic of King Ferdinand I of Aragon's political nous and cunning.[21]

His father's fortunate marriage made the writings of his illustrious maternal ancestor—and in fact the extensive record of Guicciardini expertise in business, politics and diplomacy generally—an integral part of Girolamo's upbringing. Such instruction became immediately relevant when Girolamo's uncle, Francesco di Agnolo Guicciardini, was made Medici ambassador to the Madrid court in 1593.[22] The appointment of a close relative to the political and administrative centre of the European hegemon represented an opportunity not just for the individual, but for kith and kin as well. With Spain yet again a particularly prominent and promising feature in the career trajectory of a Guicciardini, the mentally agile Girolamo was chosen and provided with ample funds to build on the revival of his family's "Spanish connection."

In the first instance, then, Girolamo Da Sommaia's time in Salamanca was to build his career in a way that would best serve and further family interests. Study abroad was to continue and build on a process of grooming that had begun long before he actually went to Spain. The Guicciardini archive, family

---

[18] See Richard A. Goldthwaite on the Guicciardini, especially 109–56.

[19] Employed in high office by the Medici and a very successful businessman, Agnolo Guicciardini still found time to pursue humanist projects. He prepared the first edition of his famous uncle's *Storia d'Italia* (Amberes, 1561).

[20] On Francesco Guicciardini's experience as a diplomat, see Douglas Biow 128–54.

[21] See, for instance, Guicciardini, Francesco, *Considerazioni* 1.29.

[22] Francesco di Agnolo Guicciardini, Medici ambassador to the Madrid court from 1593 to his death in 1602. His responsibilities included arrangements such as the import of Tuscan art and luxury goods discussed in Edward L. Goldberg.

62   *The Transatlantic Hispanic Baroque*

lore, and Florentine intellectual practice and tradition is likely to have framed the ways in which the young man would engage with the experience of Spain and things Spanish to some degree. This frame of mind included Italian and Florentine traditions of life-writing.[23] During much of his time in Salamanca, Girolamo kept an increasingly detailed and wide-ranging record of his activities and contacts.[24] Though originally conceived and used as an account book or "liber rationorum," he significantly expanded its function and content during the latter half of his stay, especially from around the year 1605. Girolamo now conceived of it as "liber ad formam Ephimerides": while still using it to keep his accounts, he also sought to provide himself with a future record of "omnia acta diurna" while at Salamanca (307). The *Diario* became the place where he gave himself factual, often detailed accounts of his daily life—events witnessed, activities undertaken, and observations made, and encompassing his physical, political, intellectual and spiritual experience. The *Diario* is a meticulous account of official lectures, private tutorials, social gatherings, debts paid and alms given, as well as books bought, lent, borrowed, and read. Also, and with matching accuracy, it records transgressions of flesh and mind. This post-1605 diary is a tool aimed at enabling and facilitating accurate recollection at a much later date rather than self-analysis. It serves as a register of activities, experiences and contacts the diarist wanted to be able to remember and utilise in years to come. On these terms, it allows the modern reader a degree of access to the complex layers of exposure and experience that prompted Da Sommaia to record his Salamanca years in the first instance.

One lasting legacy of the Salamanca years was his discovery of Seneca. Reading the Stoic profoundly influenced Girolamo's view of life, and in fact initiated the expansion and transformation of the *Diario* in the first instance. Maxims drawn from the Senecan oeuvre, especially from the *Epistulae morales ad Lucilium*, trigger and steer the thought process that brought him to turn the diary from a *libro de caja* into an account of his personal conduct. In early 1605, Girolamo makes Seneca the authority defining his personal ethics of time. He adopts the maxim 'nulla dies sine linea' as his motto, and from then on subjects himself to daily, painstaking scrutiny of how he uses his time.[25] It is possible, of course, that Girolamo read Seneca prior to his arrival in Spain, and perhaps he had done so. Undoubtedly though, it was in the context of his study abroad, as a result of ever more calls on his time, concentration, curiosity and conscience,

---

[23]   See the overview by Martin McLaughlin; also Nicholas Spadaccini and Jenaro Talens. On the constitution of the early modern self in reading and writing, see the wide-ranging discussion in Kevin Sharpe.

[24]   The autograph manuscript is in the Biblioteca Nazionale Centrale, Florence: MS Magliabechi VIII, 29 (1603–1605) and MS Magliabechi VIII, 30 (1605–1608). See Haley, "Introducción," especially 37–8; and María Teresa Cacho.

[25]   Seneca, *Epistolae morales*, VIII, 28, 2.

Higher Education, "Soft Power," and Catholic Identity

and in the light of his reading and discussion of Seneca's works that the Stoic became his silent teacher in life.

The "Seneca-experience" highlights an important facet of Da Sommaia's experience and its record. The *Diario* is a composite source that mixes genres and objectives to a considerable degree. Entries range from the trivial to the deeply personal, encompassing personal hygiene, superstitious habits, health scares, frequent sexual encounters, and the meticulous listing of daily expenses. They also bear witness to the constitution of the self through reading, writing and the frequent debate and discussion of humanist matters. The *Diario*, in other words, defies easy categorisation in terms of literary as well as historiographical analysis. It is, of course, the expression and record of a number of more or less discernible discourses and languages. Yet perhaps its most valuable characteristic for the intellectual and cultural historian of early modern Europe is that it is removed from the immediate need to perform and appeal politically or socially. It was meant only ever to have one reader. Though constructed and regulated by contemporary conventions concerning the perception and writing of the self, it is still less likely to anticipate and respond directly to public expectations—unlike ambassadorial reports and official or even private letters, for instance. With the element of performance much reduced, and information recorded primarily as *aide-mémoire*, the diary is also less bound by conventions—not least specifically Italian conventions of constructing and describing the Spanish monarchy and the Spanish.

Once in Salamanca, Girolamo had many opportunities to meet people and to make friends using family connections, in lectures and tutorials, or through student organisations like the *cofradía de Aragon*.[26] The latter was one of several student corporations providing spiritual and charitable support as well as social and networking opportunities for students from outside Castile. In 1604, his fellow students and members of the confraternity elected him as one of its four officials. Girolamo's membership and involvement with the *cofradía* is just one example for his social success. The *Diario* provides ample evidence to suggest that the young man quickly became a well-liked and respected member of the many intersecting communities and circles within the university. The composition of his body of friends and acquaintances, in turn, reflected the position of Salamanca as a cultural and political hub of the Hispanic monarchy as well as Catholic Europe more widely.

---

[26] The *cofradía de Aragon* had its own statutes and was run by four elected officials or *mayordomos*, one each representing students from the Kingdom of Aragon, the principalities of Catalonia and Valencia, and the Balearic Isles. Da Sommaia was *mayordomo* for Aragon from 1604–1606. The *Diario* suggests that the *cofradía's* reach extended well beyond the territories of the crown of Aragon and that its membership included students from across northern Italy. There is little substantive research on the *cofradías*. See the brief remarks in Rodríguez-San Pedro Bezares, *La universidad salmantina* 3: 436–9.

64 *The Transatlantic Hispanic Baroque*

His friends among local academics included intellectual luminaries like the grammarian Baltasar de Céspedes, the jurist Juan de Solórzano Pereira, and the Jesuits Gil González Dávila—whose eulogy opened this chapter—and Martín Antonio del Rio. Céspedes is a frequent partner in conversation and nurtured Girolamo's understanding of Stoic philosophy, for instance through his 1605 lectures on Seneca. This passion for Seneca's works also inspired his friendship with Del Rio. Bonding over humanist and literary interests in turn led to other shared activities. Girolamo not only attended Del Rio's lectures on Scripture at the Jesuit *colegio*, but volunteered to serve as his unpaid assistant and helped prepare and deliver his friend's teaching. His noticeable affinity for academic life included enjoyment of academic pomp and circumstance, too, partly because it interrupted the routine of lectures, partly because it provided him with an opportunity to understand the political workings of the university and gauge the status of individuals and groups. From the outset, the young Florentine is interested and active in university politics. The *Diario* is filled with observations and notes concerning the votes he and his friends canvassed and cast in the election of chairs. In December 1605, for instance, he notes his vote for his teacher and friend Juan de Solórzano Pereira, who was indeed elected as *catedrático de Digesto Viejo* (439).[27]

Girolamo's acquaintances and friends among fellow students come from different nations and are attached to different *colegios*, convents, and faculties. Italian contacts include Fray Filippo Visconti, member of one of the most prominent Italian ruling families and future general of the Augustinian order, Ascanio Sforza, latterly Count of Borgonuevo, Fray Jacinto Petronio, the future general of the Neapolitan inquisition, as well as members of the Irish, English, and German Catholic nobility. Among the Spaniards we find many members of the *colegios mayores* such as Juan Chumacero y Carrillo, a future president of the Council of Castile, Juan de Salas y Valdés, a future *oidor* at the Real Chancillería de Granada, and Baltasar Navarro Arroyta, another man of letters and future bishop of Tarragona. A particularly close associate—feverish bibliophilia initiating a strong bond between them—is Lorenzo Ramírez de Prado.[28] The two young men admire and discuss the works of Lipsius and other Stoic and neo-Stoic authors; they often dine together and talk into the small hours. Together they visit bullfights, plays, and the houses of their many friends

---

[27] Juan de Solórzano Pereira (1575–1668), humanist, professor of law in Salamanca, the leading Spanish jurisprudent of his generation, and distinguished servant of the crown of Castile in the peninsula and the Americas. See the political and intellectual biography by Enrique García Hernán.

[28] On the life and career of Lorenzo Ramírez de Prado, politician and official of the Holy Inquisition, humanist, friend of Lope de Vega and Luis de Góngora, and great collector of books and art, see Joaquín de Entrambasaguas.

Higher Education, "Soft Power," and Catholic Identity 65

and acquaintances. Yet churches, convents, and especially libraries also form a frequent and firm part of the two friends' Salamancan itinerary.

The *Diario* makes plain that much of what Girolamo wanted to remember about his time in Salamanca had to do with reading and with the mostly literary and political debate that inspired his reading and was in turn inspired by what he read. Reading and everything to do with books was clearly of immense importance to the young Florentine. Books, reading, and discussion were at the heart of his social and cultural activities and networks. He always carefully catalogues his library, and cataloguing techniques form a staple of his conversations with fellow bibliophiles. He befriends and regularly visits prominent Salamancan booksellers like the Frenchman Guillaume Pesnot. At times, the *Diario* resembles the catalogue of a private lending library and reading-room, with systematic entries on books and manuscripts received and read, taken out and returned by friends, on books bought, sold, or given as a present. What Girolamo read, how he came into possession of specific books and manuscripts, and with whom he shared his reading and his thoughts highlights Salamanca as a place of cultural exchange, and a place able to shape foreigners' perceptions of early modern Spanish learning, culture and politics. Reading in private and exchanges in tutorials and over dinner with friends contributed as much and possibly more than academic study to his formation both as a connoisseur of things Spanish and as a Medici servant able to operate successfully across the Italo-Hispanic political sphere.

Much of what Girolamo read while in Spain was common currency in the European republic of letters, of course, in terms of genre and languages as well as authors. Works of history are particularly prominent on his reading list—or history and politics rather, given the close relation between these two fields of inquiry in early modern learning and perception of the world. Girolamo ploughs his way through the Greeks and Romans, with particular attention to Plutarch, Dio Cassius, and Sextus Aurelius Victor. He frequently and enthusiastically returns to Tacitus—who would remain a major point of reference in terms of political nous—and "Tacitist" authors more generally. Among the *moderni*, Italians and especially contemporary Florentine historians feature prominently. For instance, he reads and carefully compares Scipione Ammirato's *Istorie fiorentine* with other works on Florentine history, and with particular regard to his family's portrayal and reputation.[29] His taste for historiography as the condensation of experience in public service is tangible. Much of what he reads, unsurprisingly, betrays a concern with future employ in government.

In late 1606, for instance, he explores, and presumably discusses with his friends and acquaintances, some texts very much at the core of sixteenth-century political debate. They include Machiavelli's *Il Principe*, Bodin's *Six livres de la*

---

[29] This entry in the Miscellánea: BNCF MS. Magliabechi, VIII, 27, 212v.

66   *The Transatlantic Hispanic Baroque*

République, and a range of publications produced as a result of the war of words between the Republic of Venice and the papacy following the papal interdict (568).[30] He compares these works—*Il Principe* already on both the Roman and the Spanish *Index librorum prohibitorum*, Bodin's *République* a candidate for future inclusion—in order to learn about the zones of conflict and boundaries defining the relationship between secular and spiritual government.[31]

The young Italian felt obliged to report this particular set of texts—albeit in a cursory and summary fashion—to his Spanish confessor. There is no indication whatsoever that he incurred any spiritual penalty as a result. Attitudes towards heterodox or controversial texts—including Machiavelli's infamous political manual—varied considerably among Spanish clergy and laity, just as they did in Italy and elsewhere in Europe.[32] Though Girolamo made this particular reading experience part of a confession, he did so by his own volition, possibly moved by his conscience, but not in obvious violation of laws and guidelines. He was not expected to seek a licence for reading *Il Principe* in the first instance—which is what he would have been expected to do back home in Florence. Likewise, he noted in his *Diario* that he had obtained and read a copy of Antonio Pérez's *Relaciones*, printed in Paris in 1598. The ferocious, incriminating polemic of the disgraced and exiled secretary of Philip II was among the texts most offensive to Spanish officialdom.[33] This in no way deterred Girolamo. In fact, as his autograph anthology testifies, he made Pérez a mainstay of his largely extracurricular and self-motivated exploration of the processes and gambits of early modern European politics.[34] Censorship, mild reproach even, appear absent from the young Italian's Salamancan experience, regardless of where his curiosity or desire took him. In the view of the Florentine patrician as well as his teachers and fellow students, and possibly that of his confessor, too, Girolamo simply availed himself of the opportunity to widen his intellectual and moral

---

[30]   On the Interdict of 1606–1607 as a crisis of the Venetian political system and crisis of communication, see Filippo De Vivo, especially Chapters 5 and 6.

[31]   For the complex reception of Bodin in Italy and Spain, see Michaela Valente, Harald E. Braun. *Il Principe* was widely discussed and circulated in Spain, even after being put on the Roman (1559) and Spanish (1584/84) *Indices*; see Helena Puigdomenech; and the brief comparative survey by Humfrey C. Butters 75–87, especially 80–83, and Appendices.

[32]   In 1596, the Roman Inquisition intervened to prevent the publication of expurgated versions of *Il Principe* and Boccacio's *Decameron* spearheaded by Grand Duke Ferdinando de Medici. The incident illustrates the prevailing atmosphere of intellectual inquiry and literary taste at the Medici court at the time. See Peter Godman 327–9.

[33]   On the scandal, exile and subsequent polemic revolving around the person of Antonio Pérez, see the classic study by Gregorio Marañon.

[34]   There is a copious amount of material from Pérez's works in Da Sommaia's anthology of Spanish, mainly historical and political authors: MS Magliabechi VIII, 26, especially 148–82v, 185–94, 204–210.

Higher Education, "Soft Power," and Catholic Identity   67

horizon while at university. He clearly did his utmost to exploit the liberty to read whatever he thought might provide him with useful instruction and feed into fecund political debate.

If history and law are staples on Da Sommaia's bookshelves, so is literature. Latin and Italian vernacular prose and poetry attract him – namely Dante and Petrarch, Poliziano and Bembo. The *Diario*, however, also testifies to his growing taste and lasting interest in Spanish life and letters. Again, historical and political literature features prominently. Lodovici Guicciardini's description of the Low Countries and don Diego Hurtado de Mendoza's *Guerra de Granada* show Girolamo's intention to gain better knowledge and understanding of the history and current affairs of the Spanish Habsburg monarchy.[35] He worked his way through some standard works, such as Juan de Mariana's multi-volume *Historiae de rebus Hispaniae*, Alfonso de Ullua's *vita* of emperor Charles V, or Pero López de Ayala's *Crónica del rey don Pedro*. Concerning the Americas, Peru and the accounts by Zárate and Inca Garcilaso de la Vega appear to have been of particular interest to him.

In terms of literary prose and poetry, Góngora and Lope de Vega are his favourites by some distance. The interest in a spiritual exposition of the world is another constant, and attracts him to the neo-Platonic verse of Francesco Aldana and the conceptual poetry of Alonso de Ledesma. Spiritual literature, though, is always balanced by more wordly letters, such as Mateo Alemán's *Guzman de Alfarache* or Francisco López de Úbeda's *La Picara Justina*. The extent and quality of his connections and the extent of the trust and esteem he enjoyed is reflected in that he got his hands on many manuscripts that would take a while to make it to the printing press, such as Diego Hurtado de Mendoza's or Fray Luis de León's poetry (432, 434).[36] With his teacher and friend Solórzano Pereira—soon to be widely acknowledged as one of the leading legal thinkers of the seventeenth century—he debates juridical issues and sources, of course, but also literature. During private tutorials they work their way through *Las Siete Partidas* or the *Nueva Recopilación*—both legal compilations crucial to understanding how the Spanish monarchy actually worked, and neither of them part of the official syllabus. They then turn to the latest literary sensations such as a manuscript version of the first of Quevedo's satirical sueños, *El Sueño del Juicio Final* (first published in 1627). Girolamo generally excelled in getting his hands on the latest literary sensation and disseminating it among his friends.

Reading in early modern Salamanca, Girolamo combined private pleasure and conversation with humanist endeavour, conversation and network-

---

[35] *Descrittione di tutti I Paesi Bassi* (Antwerp: Willem Silvius, 1567). Girolamo read Hurtado de Mendoza's work—first published in Lisbon in 1627—in manuscript.

[36] For a critical edition and analysis of Spanish poetry in Girolamo's autograph anthology, see Francesca De Santis.

68 *The Transatlantic Hispanic Baroque*

building. His reading involved the exchange of books and manuscripts as well as regular and extensive discussions with a wide circle of friends of similar outlook and inclination. This was one way of cementing friendships and establishing connections for the future. His practice and experience of reading in Salamanca identify him as a passive member of the European "Republic of Letters," yet also suggest that a period of study at Salamanca could stimulate a Hispanophile sense of intellectual and cultural belonging among members of the European Catholic elite.

Girolamo Da Sommaia's reading experience and the ways in which he made his reading an experience for others are manifold and diverse. They were not restricted to fellow students and tutors. He mentions, for instance, that he gifted his copy of Francisco López de Úbeda's *La Pícara Justina* to a young woman called Maricca. The *Diario* leaves readers in little doubt that Maricca made a living by offering sexual favours in exchange for money or other gifts, and that Girolamo was a regular customer over a lengthy period of time. Did he read particularly entertaining and revealing passages from the book to his lover? Did they both enjoy the sarcasm and often vicious exposure of the vices and corruption of Spanish society? And did they reflect on their own lust and vice as well as that of their friends, acquaintances, and neighbours while doing so in the privacy of their room? Girolamo Da Sommaia surely read with passion, and he brought some passion to his reading of Spain. He even took his reading from gown to town.

***

Sommaia had arrived in Salamanca in order to study civil and canon law, and to immerse himself in Spanish culture, politics and networks. This he achieved. He was successful academically, too, and he left Salamanca a member of a network of future high-ranking, mostly Spanish and Italian civil servants and humanist men of letters. After a brief interlude as a legal practitioner in Florence and a disillusioning spell at the apostolic chancery, he entered Medici service in 1612 and was made *provveditore* or governor of the *studium* in Pisa in 1614. The member of a family distinguished in Medici service, a person trusted and esteemed by the Grand Duke and an intellectual and humanist sympathetic to university life and matters he must have recommended himself for this position. As the Grand Duke's man in Pisa, Da Sommaia kept the university in line with Medici politics, fought for funding from Medici coffers and defended its liberties against incursions, especially interventions on the part of episcopal or papal authority. His curiosity, maturity and the independence of mind—nurtured and evident already during his time at university—would determine the way in

Higher Education, "Soft Power," and Catholic Identity

which he handled the critique of the Medici court and the University of Pisa for keeping Galileo Galilei and his pupils in employ.[37]

Girolamo Da Sommaia's diary provides the reader with a near-kaleidoscopic view of academic, social and cultural, not least literary life in turn-of-the-century Salamanca. It helps explain why Catholic noble and aristocratic families from other parts of Europe might decide to send their offspring to Spain rather than a university nearer to home. The university-city emerges as a place of learning and letters as well as a place to mix and mingle with other members of the European Catholic elite on a daily basis, a place to build career networks and hone the intellectual, social and political skills so eminently important for success in European princely courts and courts of law. Salamanca was a place to fathom the mechanics of power more generally and the mechanics of Hispanic empire in particular. The *Diario* identifies Salamanca as a place where the Spanish monarchy—this patchwork of European, American, and Asian polities, possibly the most complex and Baroque of early modern body politics—appeared rooted and in fact able to transcend some of the challenges intrinsic to its structure.[38] Many *estudiantes extranjeros* travelled long distances—certainly by early modern standards—to study and meet their like in Salamanca. Each and every one of them—arriving, learning, socialising, and finally returning home—helped shorten and improve the empire's internal and external lines of communication, at least to some degree and for some time. Each and every one of them represented an opportunity to build, maintain or expand the networks of friendship and kinship connecting the different parts of the monarchy with one another and with the early modern Catholic world more widely.

Da Sommaia's experience of Salamanca was one of an imperial space open, busy, and exciting in terms of intellectual, social and sexual adventure. The *Diario* testifies that he absorbed the culture and established friendships with many members of the Spanish political, academic and cultural elite. Girolamo's perceptiveness and respect for Spain, her people and culture contradicts the notion that '[n]o sixteenth-century Italian could be expected to forgive Spain for having conquered and for ruling over his country' (Hillgarth 128). Spain was well entrenched as the hegemon of Europe and dominated Italian political affairs in the late 1500s and early 1600s. Many Italians lived under one form or other of Spanish rule, often mediated through native rulers and officials. If this state of affairs continued to cause chagrin among many Italian observers, it also kept interest in all things Spanish on the boil. For the aspiring noble or patrician

---

[37] On Da Sommaia's involvement with Galileo and the "Galileo affair" still Haley, "Introduccion" 25–37.

[38] On the *monarquía española* and empire see the work of John H. Elliott, for example "A Europe of Composite Monarchies.

70 *The Transatlantic Hispanic Baroque*

of Milanese, Genoese, Florentine or Neapolitan birth, first-hand knowledge of things Spanish was likely to be an asset.

The young Florentine certainly appears to have arrived in Spain already in a more than forgiving mood. On the evidence before us, the years of study and encounter only confirmed and expanded this attitude. Girolamo neither arrived in 1599, nor left Spain in 1607, with a view of his hosts as inferior to Italian culture and letters and in dire need of Italian "civilising" influence so common earlier in the century.[39] His response to Spanish letters, libraries and theatre indicates that by the late 1600s at least, educated Italians no longer necessarily regarded their Spanish counterparts as "mere emulators of Italy." He became and remained deeply interested in Spanish letters and culture more generally. Though difficult to gauge or quantify, it is clear that Spanish culture, as experienced in Salamanca, inadvertently exercised something like soft power on the Florentine.

If Da Sommaia stood out for his curiosity and for the open mind to go with it, the many layers of interaction and exchange between Spaniards, Italians and other Europeans suggest that he can have hardly been alone in his appreciation of Spain and Spanish letters. By the late sixteenth and early seventeenth century, an Italian possessed of a pragmatic view of European political affairs and confident of his specific cultural and political heritage—Florentine, Genoese, or Neapolitan—was not necessarily compelled to approach Spain on dismissive and defensive terms. For Girolamo Da Sommaia, the *sacco di Roma* was not a point of reference in terms of cultural and political identity and memory. A curious and discriminating individual, he disregarded or overcame the stereotypes familiar from hostile ambassadorial reports, anti-Hispanic propaganda and the pan-European construct of the "black legend."[40] Girolamo returned to Florence with a cherished trove of memories, Spanish literature, and many friends.

---

[39] On Italian perceptions of Spain and the Spanish during the first half of the sixteenth century—with the *Sacco di Roma* a watershed—see Catherine Fletcher; also Hillgarth, especially 209–308. Hillgarth 205 n.154, refers to Da Sommaia only once and in passing as "this not particularly perceptive traveller." His remarks may reflect the fact that Sommaia rarely if ever offers punchy value judgements—arguably, the sign of a good head and balance of judgement rather than lack of perceptiveness.

[40] On the "black legend" see Margaret R. Greer, Walter D. Mignolo and Maureen Quilligan. What we now know about the circulation of scholars and students between Spain and Italy and the presence of Spanish scholars in European intellectual networks disowns Ortega y Gasset's dictum that sixteenth century Spanish academic and intellectual life was subject to a process of "tibetización" in the wake of Philip II's 1559 decision to limit Spanish students' options for studying abroad. Philip merely exacerbated or more likely consolidated existing trends in international academic experience and exchange in an age of confessional conflict.

Bibliography

Ayala, Francisco. *Ideas políticas de Juan de Solórzano*. Sevilla: Publicaciones de la Escuela de Estudios Hispano-Americanos de la Universidad de Sevilla, 1946.

Bideaux, Michel and Fragonard, Marie-Madeleine, eds. *Les échanges entre les Universités européennes à la Renaissance*. Geneva: Libraire Droz, 2003.

Biow, Douglas. *Doctors, Ambassadors, Secretaries: Humanism and Professions in Renaissance Italy*. Chicago: Chicago University Press, 2002.

Braun, H.E. "Making the Canon?: The Early Reception of the *République* in Castilian Political Thought." *The Reception of Bodin*. Ed. Howell A. Lloyd. Leiden: Brill, 2013. 257–92.

Burke, Peter. "Humanism and Friendship in Sixteenth-Century Europe." *Friendship in Medieval Europe*. Ed. Julian Haseldine. Stroud: Sutton, 1999. 262–74.

Butters, Humfrey C. "Conflicting Attitudes towards Machiavelli's Works in Sixteenth-Century Spain, Rome, and Florence." *Communes and Despots in Medieval and Renaissance Italy*. Ed. John E. Law and Bernadette Paton. Farnham: Ashgate, 2010. 75–87.

Cacho, María Teresa. *Manuscritos hispánicos en las bibliotecas de Florencia*. 2 vols. Florence: Alinea Editrice, 2001.

Cirot, George. *Mariana historien: études sur l'historiographie espagnole*. Bordeaux: Feret et Fils, 1905.

Classen, Albrecht, and Marilyn Sandidge, eds. *Friendship in the Middle Ages and Early Modern Age: Explorations of a Fundamental Ethical Discourse*. Berlin and New York: Walter de Gruyter, 2010.

Da Sommaia, Girolamo. *Diario de un estudiante de Salamanca. La crónica inédita de Girolamo de Sommaia*. Ed. and Introduction by George Haley. Salamanca: Ediciones Universidad de Salamanca, 1977.

———. "Miscellanea Spagnola." An anthology of Spanish, mainly historical and political authors. MS Magliabechi VIII, 26.

De Santis, Francesca. "Manoscritto Magliabechiano VII-353. Edizione dei testi e studio." PhD thesis. University of Pisa, 2005–2006.

De Vivo, Filippo. *Information and Communication in Venice: Rethinking Early Modern Politics*. Oxford: Oxford University Press, 2007.

Elliott, John H. "A Europe of Composite Monarchies." *Past and Present* 137 (1992): 48–71.

Entrambasaguas, Joaquín de. *Una familia de ingenios: los Ramírez de Prado*. Madrid: Consejo Superior de Investigaciones Científicas, 1943.

Fernández Álvarez, Manuel. "El diario de un estudiante: la Salamanca del Barroco." *La sociedad española en el Siglo de Oro*. Ed. Conrad Kent. 2 vols. Madrid: Gredos, 1989. 2: 818–47.

Fletcher, Catherine. "Mere Emulators of Italy: The Spanish in Italian Diplomatic Discourse, 1492–1550." *Renaissance Italy and the Idea of Spain*. Ed. Piers Baker-Bates and Miles Pattenden. Farnham: Ashgate, forthcoming.

———, and Jennifer Mara DeSilva. "Italian Ambassadorial Networks in Early Modern Europe – An Introduction." *Journal of Early Modern History* 14.6 (2010): 505–512.

García Hernán, Enrique. *Consejero de ambos mundos. Vida y obra de Juan Solórzano Pereira (1575-1655)*. Madrid: Fundación Mapfre, 2007.

Godman, Peter. *From Poliziano to Machiavelli: Florentine Humanism in the High Renaissance*. Princeton: Princeton University Press, 1998.

Goldberg, Edward L. "Artistic Relations between the Medici and the Spanish Courts, 1587–1621." *The Burlington Magazine* 138.1115 (1996): 105–114; 138.1121 (1996): 529–40.

Goldthwaite, Richard A. *Private Wealth in Renaissance Florence: A Study of Four Families*. Princeton: Princeton University Press, 1968.

González Dávila, Gil. Letter to Juan de Mariana SJ. British Library. Egerton MSS. 1875. Fol. 209.

Greer, Margaret R., Walter D. Mignolo and Maureen Quilligan, eds. *Rereading the Black Legend: The Discourses of Religious and Racial Difference in the Renaissance Empires*. Chicago: University of Chicago Press, 2007.

Guicciardini, Francesco. *Discorsi sopra la prima deca Tito Livio, [di] Niccolò Machiavelli, seguiti dalle "Considerazioni intorno ai Discorsi del Machiavelli" di Francesco Guicciardini*. Ed. Corrado Vivanti. Turin: Einaudi, 1983.

Guicciardini, Ludovico. *Descrittione di tutti I Paesi Bassi*. Antwerp: Willem Silvius, 1567.

Haley, George. "Introducción." *Diario de un estudiante de Salamanca. La crónica inédita de Girolamo de Sommaia*. Salamanca: Ediciones Universidad de Salamanca, 1977. 9–96.

Hayden, Craig. *The Rhetoric of Soft Power: Public Diplomacy in Global Contexts*. Lanham, MD: Lexington Books, 2012.

Hegarty, Andrew. "The Corporate University in the Age of Olivares: Salamanca c. 1620–1640." DPhil thesis. University of Oxford, 1998.

Herzog, Tamar. *Defining Nations: Immigrants and Citizens in Early Modern Spain and Spanish America*. London and New Haven: Yale University Press, 2003.

Hillgarth, Jocelyn. *The Mirror of Spain, 1500–1700. The Formation of a Myth*. Ann Arbor: University of Michigan Press, 2000.

Kagan, Richard L. "La Salamanca del Siglo de Oro: el extracurriculum y el declive español." *Salamanca en la edad de oro*. Ed. Conrad Kent. Salamanca: Librería Cervantes, 1970. 287–305.

———. *Students and Society in Early Modern Spain*. Baltimore: Johns Hopkins Press, 1974.

Higher Education, "Soft Power," and Catholic Identity 73

————. *Clio & the Crown: The Politics of History in Medieval and Early Modern Spain*. Baltimore: Johns Hopkins University Press, 2009.

————, and Geoffrey Parker, eds. *Spain, Europe and the Atlantic World: Essays in Honour of John H. Elliott*. Cambridge: Cambridge University Press, 1995.

Litchfield, Robert Burr. *Emergence of a Bureaucracy: The Florentine Patricians, 1530–1790*. Princeton: Princeton University Press, 1986.

Marañon, Gregorio. *Antonio Pérez*. 2 vols. Madrid: Espasa Calpe, 1947.

McLean, Paul D. *The Art of the Network: Strategic Interaction and Patronage in Renaissance Florence*. Durham: Duke University Press, 2007.

McLaughlin, Martin. "Biography and Autobiography in the Italian Renaissance." *Mapping Lives: The Uses of Biography*. Ed. Peter France and William St Clair. Oxford: Oxford University Press, 2002. 137–66.

O'Connell, Patricia. "The Early Modern Irish College Network in Iberia, 1590–1800." *The Irish in Europe, 1580–1815*. Ed. Thomas O'Connor. Dublin: Four Courts Press, 2001. 49–64.

O'Connor, Thomas and Lyons, Mary Ann, eds. *Irish Communities in Early Modern Europe*. Dublin: Four Courts Press, 2006.

Pérez Martin, Antonio. "Salamanca y las Italias, etapas medieval y renacentista." *Historia de la universidad de Salamanca*. Coord. Luis Enrique Rodríguez-San Pedro Bezares. Salamanca: Ediciones Universidad de Salamanca, 2004. 3.2: 1163–73.

Prögler, Daniela. *English Students at Leiden University, 1575–1650*. Farnham: Ashgate, 2013.

Puigdomenech, Helena. *Maquiavelo en España. Presencia de sus obras en los siglos XVI y XVII*. Madrid: Fundación Universitaria Española, 1988.

Ridder-Symoens, Hilde de. "Mobility." *A History of the University in Europe, Vol. 2: Universities in Early Modern Europe (1500–1800)*. Ed. Hilde de Ridder-Symoens. Cambridge: Cambridge University Press, 1996. 416–48.

Rodríguez-San Pedro Bezares, Luis Enrique. *La universidad salmantina del Barroco, período 1598–1625*. 3 vols. Salamanca: Ediciones Universidad de Salamanca, 1986.

————, coord. *Historia de la universidad de Salamanca*. 4 vols. Salamanca: Ediciones Universidad de Salamanca, 2002–2006.

————, and Polo Rodríguez, Juan Luis, eds. *Historiografía y líneas de investigación en historia de las universidades Europa Mediterránea e Iberoamérica. Miscelánea Alfonso IX*. Salamanca: Ediciones Universidad de Salamanca, 2012.

Ryjik, Veronika. *Lope de Vega en la invención de España. El drama histórico y la formación de la conciencia nacional*. Woodbridge: Tamesis, 2011.

Seneca, Lucius Annaeus. *Epistolae morales. Recognovit et adnotatione critica instruxit L.D. Reynolds*. Oxford: Clarendon Press, 1965.

74 *The Transatlantic Hispanic Baroque*

Sharpe, Kevin. *Reading Revolutions: The Politics of Reading in Early Modern England*. London and New Haven: Yale University Press, 2000.

Spadaccini, Nicholas, and Jenaro Talens, eds. *Autobiography in Early Modern Spain*. Minneapolis, MN: Prisma Institute, 1988.

Thompson, I.A.A "Castile, Spain and the Monarchy: The Political Community from *patria natural* to *patria nacional*." *Spain, Europe and the Atlantic World: Essays in Honour of John H. Elliott*. Ed. Richard L. Kagan and Geoffrey Parker. Cambridge: Cambridge University Press, 1995. 125–59.

Valente, Michaela. "The Works of Bodin under the Lens of Roman Theologians and Inquisitors." *The Reception of Bodin*. Ed. Howell A. Lloyd. Leiden: Brill. 2013. 219–35.

Weruaga Prieto, Ángel. "Aulas de la Monarquía Católica. Internacionalización y nobleza en la matrícula universitaria salmantina (siglos XVI–XVII)." *Historiografía y líneas de investigación en Historia de las Universidades: Europa Mediterrána E Iberoamérica, Miscelánea Alfonso IX, 2011*. Ed. Luis Enrique Rodríguez-San Pedro Bezares and Juan Luis Polo Rodríguez. Salamanca: Ediciones Universidad de Salamanca, 2012. 299–343.

Acknowledgement

The author gratefully acknowledges the support of the Social Sciences and Humanities Research Council of Canada as well as the research project *Afinidad, violencia y representación: el impacto exterior de la Monarquía Hispánica*, Ministerio de Economía y Competitividad (España). HAR2011-29859-C02-02.

Chapter 4

"The People of the King": Autonomy and Collective Identity in Coyaima[1]

Renée Soulodre-La France

On August 25, 2004, a member of the Pijao Cheche Tunarco indigenous group from the town of Coyaima, Jairo Vega Sogamoso, was shot to death in the center of town as he went about his work organizing indigenous responses to the violence in the Colombian department of Tolima ("Colombia").[2] This event is one of the latest in the long history of the often deadly identity politics that have swirled around and through Coyaima since the coming of the Spaniards. Emerging through the violence of the sixteenth-century conquest of this central Colombian region, the Coyaima experienced a cycle of identity creation/transformation/re-creation that evokes the processes of conquest, colonization, de-colonization and nationalization. The struggle for stability through colonial and national impositions has shaped the history of Coyaima and those people who have become identified through the centuries as the "Coyaima." It is that narrative that reflected and helped create an image of the indomitable and indefatigable nature of the Coyaima as they became intertwined with the cultural system brought to the New World by the Spanish. Arriving simultaneously with the Spanish military, political and economic imperial project, the Hispanic Baroque provided the cultural context through which Spanish imperialism sought to function. This examination of the historical path of the Coyaima will explore the classifications and categories that framed colonial identities against that Hispanic Baroque background, to assess the parameters for the expression of subaltern, especially indigenous, identities in colonial Nueva Granada.

The Hispanic Baroque has been theorized as a cultural system that serves as an explanatory model for Hispanic society as a whole by José Antonio Maravall. In his formulation, this system was controlled by the monarchical, aristocratic structure of Hispanic society and projected a spirit that was firmly grounded in urbanism and conservatism (Jouve Martín and Soulodre-La France 2).

---

[1] I owe this title to the work of John Leddy Phelan, especially his remarkable *The People and the King. The Comunero Revolution in Colombia, 1781*.

[2] In 1964 the Ministerio del Gobierno listed the Coyaima as numbering 11,503, although now without a *resguardo* (Rubio Orbe 1108).

Meanwhile the known complexities of the colonial setting challenged New World thinkers to re-imagine the Baroque as a site of counter-conquest, to imbue the Baroque with subversive possibilities that could more readily accommodate the dense intricacies of the colonial system. Authors such as Carpentier, Lezama Lima and Sarduy sought to apply the analytical categories created within the Hispanic Baroque as a means to explain the dynamics of colonialism while simultaneously recognizing the expression of power by subalterns within that Baroque culture (Jouve Martín and Soulodre-La France 3). The utility of the Hispanic Baroque for the historian is that it allows one to trace historical processes and the expression of power through the cultural system, because it is both a colonial and post-colonial instrument that frames historical and contemporary cultural production and concrete intersections with cultural institutions (Parkinson Zamora and Kaup 2). The Baroque is an arrangement constantly seeking to adjust for contradictions and dissonance because it is such a porous and ample system, but this very state creates the possibility for its appropriation. As Parkinson Zamora and Kaup write "it is one of the few satisfying ironies of European imperial domination worldwide that the Baroque worked poorly as a colonizing instrument" (3). The validity of this statement is contingent upon an understanding of the "colonizing" project as a cultural imposition. Historian John Leddy Phelan, in his examination of Hispanic political culture and its colonial instruments, theorized decades ago that the very contradictory, flexible and expansive nature of the Spanish colonial system helped achieve its longevity, serving as an effective mechanism of exploitation. This understanding of the Baroque character (though these authors did not use that term) of Spanish colonialism also underpinned Charles Cutter's later examination of the colonial legal system in northern New Spain (Cutter; Phelan, "Authority"; *The People*).

The construction of identities is an apt sphere through which to test the theoretical understandings of the Baroque as a cultural system that could allow for a de-centering of social, cultural and political space. The identities of co-opted indigenous groups were subjected to the Baroque gaze, especially through two institutions, the church and the Spanish legal system. Both of those institutions imposed specific codes upon the Coyaima, however indigenous survival depended upon their ability to translate those codes into their own cultural and social idioms. The Hispanic Baroque's de-centered elliptical application to identity politics through the utopian idea of the Two Republics had an ambivalent impact. While it provided indigenous people with the Baroque forms to which they had to conform, it also afforded them the range of movement needed to continuously shape and reshape their identity. Historian Jamie Robertson argues that we can view identity formation through what he calls "cultural tremors" over a sustained period, rather than "a single tumultuous rupture with the past" (Robertson 466). The identities through which indigenous people imagined their communities during colonialism, and afterwards is a process that is nudged by different events and so it is relatively undefined; it is not a primordial character but "a fluid, layered and continually evolving belief structure" (Robertson 466). Its pathways are shaped by intersections rather than a linear trajectory. This conceptualization helps us understand the counter-intuitive result of the Coyaima's identity creation process in their relationship to the Pijao, Yanacona, and other indigenous groups they identified as Ladinos, as well as to the various ethnicities that were developing around them in the colonial period. A further paradoxical twist to these processes is that they allowed the Coyaima to protect their indigenous identity against the Ladinos' interests even while the latter had become more firmly assimilated into the Hispanic Baroque cultural system.

Yet another complicating feature of identity creation is proposed by Anthropologist Lee M. Panich in his study of the Paipai indigenous group of Baja California. Panich argues that "the cultural persistence of this group of native Californians was in part the result of the social world of the colonial period." He warns that we should beware of equating "authentic native identity with the retention of cultural practices that predate the arrival of Europeans" (227–8). Beyond this, Panich cautions against essentialist understandings of cultural survivals and suggests that "constructivist theories of identity" might be more appropriate for understanding the resilience of indigenous people since "they do not treat cultures as bounded entities." If we "understand identities to be socially constructed," then the processes by which they are created "through a constant tension between external categorization and internal self-identification can be more thoroughly explored" (Panich 229–30). This approach to grasping indigenous identity is particularly critical for dissecting the impact of the Hispanic Baroque since it associates identity less with ethnicity and culture and more with the social exigencies that draw people into an identity. As we will see, this was partially the case for the Coyaima.

To follow the tortuous path of identity formation among the Coyaima we will explore their early history as they were incorporated into the Hispanic colonial and Baroque system and along their peregrinations through the colonial and post-colonial periods. We will examine how the Coyaima were situated early on in this relationship and seek out those "cultural tremors" that shaped their identity and their relationship to the Hispanic Baroque society that grew around them. One of the constants to that identity was their distinctive attachment to a place known as the royal town, *Coyaima de la Real Corona*. The significance of this designation would be a critical element in the shaping of Coyaima identity within colonialism. After examining Coyaima's foundational moments we will explore centuries-old conceptualizations of the Coyaima's place, both figuratively and literally, in Nueva Granada. The major source of insight into these domains can be found in their interactions with Baroque Catholicism and the Spanish legal system. Within these frameworks they claimed to be ardent Christians—a

78 *The Transatlantic Hispanic Baroque*

claim often disputed by their clergy, and they made good use of the legal system to protect what would become the defining feature of their identity—their land. In the historical moments reflected in colonial documents we can untangle the special meaning that was encompassed in an indigenous town that belonged to the Crown. The symbiotic relations revealed through that exploration uncover even more the inconsistencies and paradoxes inherent to the Hispanic Baroque.

It was not by accident that the Coyaima came to be particularly important historical actors in the region of Tolima Grande. According to the early history of the colony, it was the decision of a group of captains who became identified as the Coyaima to ally themselves with the Spanish against the Pijao of the Sierra in the early seventeenth century that led to the establishment of the town under the auspices of the President of the *Audiencia* of Santa Fe, Juan de Borja. This was part of a concerted effort by the crown to deal with the aggressively recalcitrant indigenous populations that it sought to "pacify," as well as a bid to undermine the economic and political power of the Spanish *encomenderos* as a class. These goals were achieved by the negotiation of an alliance between the Spanish and the Coyaima and Natagaima (yet another indigenous group that agreed to live in a royal town) against the Pijao on one hand, and, on the other hand, the creation of *resguardos* (reserves) for both these groups; indigenous communities that would pay tribute to the crown, not to an *encomendero* (Clavijo Ocampo 49; Colmenares 88; Triana Antorveza, *La colonización* 15). Furthermore, the early-seventeenth-century alliance between the Spanish and the Coyaima against the Pijao of the Sierra was absolutely necessary for the survival of the town of Ibagué according to its *vecinos* (residents). Thus a special relation placing the Coyaima directly under the jurisdiction of the Crown was organized by Borja in 1606. The strategy led to a weakening of local administration that was manifest in the fact that the Coyaima themselves determined the amount of tribute in gold that they would pay, and they paid it directly to the King (Triana Antorveza, *La colonización* 257, 224; Pineda 7). The combination of factors that came together to shape the town of Coyaima and its economic and political configuration made it one of the most jealously autonomous institutions in the colony (Salinas Leal 86).[3] Their lands were measured out in 1621 and those limits of the *resguardo* would serve as the notarial basis for future disputes as the Indians tenaciously fought to preserve their territory against encroachment.

When indigenous populations proved too powerful to overcome militarily a common strategy was to gain indigenous allies to help overwhelm those who rebuffed Spanish advances (see Restall, Ch. 3). Such decisions were sometimes made for reasons contingent upon native ethnic differences, but in this case the

---

[3] Also, part of the logic behind the foundations was the Hispanic preoccupation with imposing order and space upon both the physical and mental landscape of the indigenous population. See Herrera Ángel 99, 113–14.

Coyaima and Pijao shared many kinship relations. In fact, according to Adolfo Triana Antorveza, even by the end of the war those relationships between the Coyaima and the Pijaos of the Sierra were still in place. The Pijao of the Sierra were punished for their resistance by subjection to enslavement if they were captured. Even when acting as Spanish allies the Coyaima absorbed those Pijao survivors who were not enslaved or sent to other regions (see Triana Antorveza, *La colonización* 166).[4] Many of the victims of these wars, especially women and children, were integrated into the Coyaima to avoid enslavement. Some escaped into the jungles of Caquetá and others were given in *encomiendas*. The Spaniards' failure to dominate the Pijao during the sixteenth century led Borja to recognize that he needed Coyaima assistance to win against other natives.[5] In order to convince the Coyaima to side with the Spaniards, Borja offered *capitulaciones* (terms) to their captains, assuring them of direct relations with the crown and removing them from those *encomenderos* who had managed to gain control of their labor (Triana Antorveza, *La colonización* 158, 162).

Essentially then, the creation of Coyaima identity in the early seventeenth century was based on a double irony. Firstly, they became distinguished from their kinfolk the Pijao through the alliance with the Spanish even while they were willing to absorb those Pijao who managed to survive the war of extinction to which they were subjected. The second irony inherent to these processes of town foundation and a collective identity linked directly to land within this indigenous group is that the Coyaima's social organization and economic base defied their alignment into a centralized population center. They were traditionally clustered in small groups under a captain and their agricultural system depended on a rotational system of land use that required dispersal of population (Triana Antorveza, *La colonización* 57–8; see Reichel-Dolmatoff 31–2). Their ongoing resistance to being gathered together in a traditional Spanish urban setting became the bane of their priests and *corregidores*.

Perhaps because of their special status and identification as direct vassals of the Crown, the Coyaima have always been reputed to be proud, haughty and intransigent, those characteristics summed up by the Spanish phrase "gran altivez." This typical characterization is manifest for example in the Tolimense song *Dulce Coyaima Indiana*, by Miguel Antonio Ospina Gómez: "Porque soy hijo de Coy, Pijao de gran altivez, / dulce Coyaima indiana, remanso fresco de mi niñez." The song was adopted by the municipality of Coyaima as its patriotic hymn, highlighting the process of identity formation from the 1930s that led

---

[4]   "Las relaciones de parentesco entre estos grupos Coyaimas, los Toamos y los Pijaos de la Sierra mantuvieron, aún al finalizar la Guerra, y los sobrevivientes que no fueron esclavizados y trasladados a otros regions fueron mezclados con los Natagaimas y Coyaimas" (Triana Antorveza 171).

[5]   There had been 48 expeditions against the Pijao by 1611. See Hernández de Alba 956.

80 *The Transatlantic Hispanic Baroque*

the Coyaima to re-identify with the Pijao from whom they had earlier sought to distinguish themselves (see Espinosa Arango).

A defining feature of many of the cases involving the Coyaima in colonial documents is the defence of land and agrarian conflict. The size of the *resguardos* granted to Coyaima and Natagaima would have an important impact on landholding in this area. According to Hernán Clavijo Ocampo, Natagaima was granted 55,000 hectares. Coyaima retained somewhat less, although the exact amount of land is unknown, but still the *resguardo* was of a substantial size. Comparing these land grants to other *resguardos* in the province of Santa Fe, which were between 900 and 3,500 hectares, it becomes evident that Natagaima and Coyaima would serve to severely limit the number of landholders that could establish themselves in the region during the seventeenth and eighteenth centuries (Clavijo Ocampo 110).

The major economic activity that developed in this region of southern Tolima was cattle ranching and so, combined with the autonomy created by its direct link to the crown, and its extensive *resguardo* lands, this served to assure the economic independence of the Indian town and the subsequent attempts by non-indigenous populations to gain access to those same lands. Even relatively early on in the seventeenth century the majority of Coyaima were involved in cattle ranching and they also developed an important trade in agricultural products to the mines in Mariquita (Triana Antorveza, *La colonización* 198, 212). Beyond this they had access to the alluvial gold of the Saldaña River with which they paid their tribute, helping solidify their autonomy (Salinas Leal 89).

The relatively ambiguous position of Coyaima, as part of the *República de Indios* but also firmly entrenched within the colonial economy, would lead to ongoing pressures upon the *resguardo* by growing *mestizo* populations as well as an expansionist *hacendado* class. The practical reality of the Indigenous population's integration into the colonial economy made it difficult to uphold the segregationist ideal of the dual republic, however, the symbolic distinction between the two was one which the Coyaima sought to preserve and exploit. This ambiguity was exacerbated through the eighteenth century as Spanish notions about the benefits of maintaining the separation and isolation of Indigenous groups were challenged (see Safford). Thus Coyaima relations with local authorities, whether secular or ecclesiastical, were often troubled and there was a constant need to renegotiate the way in which the Coyaima fit into their physical and social colonial landscape. For example, in 1740 a petition was brought forward by the protector of Indians for Salvador Yache, "Indio natural del Pueblo de Coyaima de Vuestra Real Corona," in which Yache, who was an *alcalde* (councilman), complained that the non-indigenous colonists from around the *resguardo* were robbing Indians and that their officials could not deal with these outrages because the criminals could easily escape out of their jurisdiction. To remedy this, the crown extended the *corregidor*'s jurisdiction in such cases (AGN Colonia, Vol. 33, ff. 956–959). The peculiar nature of the Indian republic then could supersede traditional jurisdictions to allow for the special circumstances that arose because of the *resguardo*'s existence.

That peculiar nature also had a direct impact to the Coyaima's situation within the Spanish legal system. Their identity as "indios de la Real Corona" allowed them to claim a unique legal identity and category that differentiated them from other corporate groups within colonial society. Beyond the special juridical characteristics applied to the classification "indio", in practice it was also the case that each town could hold a distinctive status before the law, depending upon the historical circumstances of its foundation, loyalty, rebellions, etc.[6] This specialized differentiation applied to the town of Coyaima based on its negotiated relationship with the Spanish Crown (Ceballos-Bedoya 229–30). The legal system also distinguished between "types" of Indians, and thus the Coyaima were able to establish their identity in consonance with the Crown's expectations regarding their willingness to subject themselves to royal authority, their acceptance of Christianity, and their gradual movement towards Hispanization. However, that course was juxtaposed upon the contrary Spanish legal impulse to preserve traditional indigenous mores within the *resguardo* system and specialized town jurisdictional setting (Ceballos-Bedoya 227, 230).

In the second half of the eighteenth century the Coyaima litigated against their priests, their *corregidores*, and against their neighbors. They sought to demonstrate their adherence to the forms of Hispanic cultural norms by pursuing their interests within specific Hispanic institutions like the Catholic *cofradías*. They purported to be good Christians and they expressed their Catholicism through the forms provided by Baroque counter-reformation patterns of behaviour. They also used the political possibilities provided by the *audiencia*'s *Protector de Naturales* to thwart intrusions upon their local politics and to protect their land. The instruments they applied to achieve these goals were often their own ever-shifting categorizations of what it meant to be an "indio de Coyaima" and thus they continuously challenged the Hispanic cultural discourse imposed upon them even while they adjusted to it for their own ends.

When the limits of the *resguardo* were established in 1621 the archbishop of Santa Fe questioned whether the priest could tend to both the Coyaima and the Natagaima. They were too dispersed and to maintain their congregation as one flock was complicated because they were "diferentes naciones." Also, they refused to leave their lands to facilitate indoctrination (AGN Colonia, Fábricas, ff. 143–160). Don Fernando de Saavedra responded from the field that it would be best to keep the two "nations" separate because of their aggressive

---

[6] For other corporate groups that developed collective identities because of their special relationship to the crown see Soulodre-La France, "*Los esclavos de su majestad*" 175–209.

relations. Each town should have its own church and priest so as to indoctrinate and acculturate the Coyaima more effectively. For example, he explained that they still did not use draught animals in their agricultural work and so much of their material culture as well as their faith culture had to be adjusted (AGN Colonia, Fábricas, ff. 146v–147r). In his opinion, the matter of their spiritual well-being hinged very much upon their productive technologies and the first would be achieved only through drastic changes in the latter. In 1620 then the Spanish decided to found two separate parishes in the towns which were little more than a collection of *bohíos* grouped around a church made of *bahareque* (wood and mud) with a palm roof. The indigenous resided in the town only intermittently as they often left to tend their land and animals. The church of Coyaima was consecrated in the name of *Nuestra Señora de la Asunción*, and in grand Baroque style, an oil painting of the patron was commissioned by the president of the *audiencia*, Borja. The artists contracted to produce the painting, for the price of 90 silver pesos, were Diego de Orlas and Gaspar de Figueroa. Historian Adolfo Triana Antorveza adds that the family of Gaspar de Figueroa belonged to one of the most well-known schools of painting in New Granada (AGN Colonia, Fábricas, f. 159r; see Triana Antorveza, *La colonización* 280). Borja's willingness to finance the ornamentation of the church in appropriate Baroque style suggests that the Coyaima were expected to conform quickly to Hispanic Catholic forms of worship including the physical representations of that worship. Such priorities also reflected the prevailing understanding that the spectacle of Baroque Catholicism could move the supplicant to appropriate Catholic sentiments and thus aid in enhancing appropriate forms of devotion.[7]

The ways in which the Coyaima believed and worshipped were crucial matters in terms of their identity as devoted and deserving vassals of the King, and these manners continued to be a preoccupation for various colonial officials. There are several complaints extant in the documentation regarding the Coyaima's religious faithfulness. At times these criticisms were launched by curates seeking to defend themselves and blaming failures on what they considered to be the indigenous populations' inherent weaknesses. In other cases complaints were made by the Coyaima against their priests, especially in reference to the management of their property tied up in the brotherhoods they had founded. Sometimes though, the documents detailing the practices of faith and belief by the Coyaima resulted from competition and intra-ethnic tensions as various factions within Coyaima lined up to accuse or defend the political figures in the community, usually the

---

[7]   Brian Larkin seeks to chart the shifts that were occurring in the seventeenth and eighteenth centuries regarding the ways in which worship should be approached. He argues that in New Spain, even though the church hierarchy sought to effect a transformation to a more inward piety, the general population continued to favor the traditional outward display and splendour of Baroque sensibilities and piety.

priest and the *corregidor*. The Coyaima availed themselves of the forms available through the Hispanic Baroque, including the Holy Office.

In 1645 a relation was made to the Inquisition tribunal regarding the case of don Juan Galindo, *corregidor* of the Coyaima.[8] He was accused by six Coyaima, but when Galindo was finally imprisoned and interviewed in 1649 it became evident that the real issue being contested was the complex nature of competition over *resguardo* land and the priest's involvement with non-indigenous competitors for that land. Galindo's actions upholding the Coyaima's rights led to the charges before the Inquisition made by six young indigenous men, all of whom were attached to the priest's household. They accused Galindo of having told the Indians that they should not venerate images of the saints, nor did they need to pay their *diezmo* (tithe). In his defense, Galindo argued that what he had really done was try to bring the Coyaima out of their idolatries. He claimed that they had not yet made the distinction between God and the saints and so he sought to teach them the first article of faith, that there was only one all-powerful God and that the images they venerated and treated as Gods were not in and of themselves divine. He taught them that the saints were exemplary human beings but that the Indians had to distinguish between the saints and the statues made from ordinary materials and to revere them only as representative of the saints (AHN, f. 188r). Contrary to teaching the Coyaima heresies, he claimed that his own unending attempts to indoctrinate the Coyaima had led to seven baptisms on different occasions as former pagans submitted to the faith (AHN, f. 189v).[9]

These early to mid-seventeenth century concerns regarding the nature of the Coyaima's Catholicism were revisited in other ways during the eighteenth century. Their exuberant celebration of fiestas notwithstanding, in 1749 their priest complained that he could not minister to the Coyaima because most of them lived too far outside the range of "son de campana", and even when they did gather for feast days, he was lucky if 40 of them appeared at mass.[10] He complained that those who did attend were usually drunk and loud and often there were fights in the church. The rest gathered outside to drink even though they heard the church bell perfectly well. His analysis of the problem led him to conclude that the Indians did not behave properly because they did not have the right cultural models. They lacked proper respect for the priest and

---

[8]   The details of the case can be found in the Archivo Historico Nacional de España, ff. 186r–190r, 246–247v.

[9]   When they were pressed the six indigenous accusers testified they had been pressured into denouncing Galindo by the priest, who was a great enemy of the *corregidor*. The case ended with Galindo's innocence being proclaimed publicly in the *audiencia* chamber and in the Cathedral (AHN, f. 247v).

[10]   This complaint was sent by the priest to Viceroy don Sebastian de Eslava. See AGN, Colecciones, ff. 136–137.

84   *The Transatlantic Hispanic Baroque*

the *corregidor* and they would not allow Ladinos into the town. They refused
to come to confession, even during Lent, nor were they capable of confessing
effectively because they were so ignorant of Christian doctrine and the mysteries
of the faith. Even many of the older ones did not know how to *persinar* (make
the sign of the cross). The Coyaima did fervently adhere to the forms of Baroque
Catholicism by conforming to the feast calendar and celebrating 29 fiestas, each
for a different saint. But, according to the priest, they honoured their patrons with
such disorder that on the eve of the saint's day they held dances in the church,
where they drank *chicha* and profaned the temple and committed numerous
other indecencies. The beleaguered priest whined that both he and *corregidor*
were like lambs among wolves in the town, especially since the Coyaima could
always count on the protection of the Crown. According to him, the Coyaima's
arrogance and independent behaviour undermined the authority of the local
officials and the problem was exacerbated by the refusal of the Coyaima to live
in a suitable urban setting like that demanded by civilized standards.[11]

The perspectives of the Coyaima themselves is revealed through the
documents generated in a later case. In the last decade of the eighteenth century
the Coyaima filed complaints of the cruel punishments inflicted on them by their
priest, don Luis de Torres and their *corregidor* don Fernando Benjumea (AGN
Colonia, Vol. 52, ff. 246–249, 993–1033; AGN Colonia, Vol. 60, ff. 813–906).
Their first claim was that they were loyal vassals of the crown and then they
proceeded to decry the abuses the priest was visiting upon them. These referred
to the 15 *cofradías* that had been founded in the town and the fact that the priest
was culling their herds for *fiestas* in the Villa de la Purificación. In this complaint,
the treasurers of the brotherhoods carefully located their Christian devotion
in a long history of conversion since they explained that the *cofradías* and the
means to sustain them had been established by their legitimate ancestors (AGN
Colonia, Vol. 52, ff. 998–999). The problem was that when they complained
to the *corregidor* about the priest they were punished. They again called upon
the legitimacy of their grandparents who founded the brotherhoods and begged
the Crown's charity and the favor which they had always been accorded. The
corregidor defended the priest, stating that the herds were mismanaged and that
the church required an infusion of capital so that the needs of the divine could
be met. He further argued that the Coyaima were so involved in their *fiestas* that
they would deplete the herds to pay for festivities and there were so many natives
with access to the *cofradía cajas* (strongboxes) that this was a real danger (AGN
Colonia, Vol. 52, ff. 1009–1010v).

The priest responded with harsh words, decrying the Indians as very bad
Christians and unworthy vassals (AGN Colonia, Vol. 52, ff. 1019–1021). He

---

[11]   To this end the priest quotes Cicero and the Second Council of Lima regarding the
reduction of indigenous populations (AGN, Colecciones, f. 137v).

Autonomy and Collective Identity in Coyaima 85

stated that because the natives completely controlled the property that belonged to each brotherhood they let the church slide into decay, and the property of the *cofradías* was being wasted and depleted through fraud. The Coyaima argued within the context of both the moral and physical damage being caused by the priest's excesses. The abuses committed by the two officials meant that the Indians were fleeing the town, and so were unable to comply with their spiritual duties or their fiscal responsibilities to the Crown.[12] The case in fact had been taken up by several of the town's captains. They laid out very clearly all of the feast day celebrations and the cost of those rituals. In their pleas for justice they drew out the intimate link between their expressions of Baroque Catholicism in the *cofradía* celebrations as a reflection of their Christian piety, and the well-being of the colonial economy guaranteed by their devoted vassalage.

In June 1774 Dr don Pedro Joseph de la Portela, then the vicar in Mariquita, wrote a letter of merit in which he compared the Natagaima against the Coyaima. He claimed that his zeal and conviction resulted in success with the Natagaima despite the fact that "those Indians were in their very being wild and haughty, and very similar to the Coyaimas who live nearby, who have in the last few years given ample evidence of their nature with the excesses they have committed against their *corregidor*." Because of the priest's service the Indians of Natagaima were reduced to domesticity and they "retained their civility and Christianity and have not given any problems to the superior authority like the Coyaimas have" (AGI, Santa Fe). This reputation of the Coyaima as inveterate troublemakers was based on an especially notorious conflict that developed over several years in the 1760s and came to a climax with the murder of the *hacendado* and *corregidor*, don Miguel Correcha in 1770.

Correcha had established himself as a renter of the Hato de la Iglesia of Coyaima in 1751 (Clavijo Ocampo 324).[13] Beyond this, in a uniquely ironic twist, he was also the *corregidor* of the Yanaconas of Purificación; their town, San Antonio, had been created in 1760 specifically to stand as a bulwark against possible aggressions from the Coyaima. The Yanaconas were a group of Indians that the Coyaima considered to be Ladinos or not really "true" Indians (Clavijo Ocampo 324; see AGI, Quito). By this time then, the Coyaima were feared as a dangerous collective who needed to be buffered by other more pliant Indians, Ladinos, who conformed more closely to Hispanic expectations.[14]

---

[12] See the case against the priest and corregidor in AGN Colonia, Vol. 60, ff. 813–906.

[13] The Correcha case ranges over different document collections, but is mostly concentrated in AGN Colonia, Vol. 41, ff. 77–136, ff. 519–31; Vol. 9, ff. 987–1000; Vol. 44, ff. 529–681; and Vol. 59, ff. 504–592. The case is also treated extensively in the epilogue to Triana Antorveza, *La colonización*. See also Soulodre-La France, *Región e Imperio*.

[14] It is noteworthy that the Yanacona became identified by their original lack of place in colonial society. The term Yanacona referred to indigenous people who left their traditional collectives and attached themselves to Spaniards as individuals.

86 *The Transatlantic Hispanic Baroque*

Throughout this land dispute the Coyaima sought legal resolutions but the situation gradually escalated into ever increasing violence. The struggle between the natives and Correcha continued for some ten years with varying degrees of violence against property perpetrated by both sides, until finally the Indians resorted to physical violence against the *hacendado* himself. They dragged him out of his house and beat in his brains after which they threw his body into the river, burned his *hacienda*, and imprisoned their own *corregidor*. Subsequently the tumult had to be put down by the military intervention of the provincial governor (Clavijo Ocampo 335). This traumatic series of events may have shaped the Coyaima's ever closer identification with their land in the eighteenth century, even while their control of that land came under increasing attacks as the colonial period waned.

Though the Coyaima expressed their identity in land conflicts, they also reflected shifting patterns of identity transformation through town leadership. In 1644 a group of Pijao were in the process of being reduced and aggregated into the Coyaima. The challenge of integrating the Pijao and their families made the choice of captain a crucial issue. The delicate question required a person who would be acceptable to the newcomers, one who would care for them and help them become a part of Coyaima while simultaneously being able to convince them to attend mass and embark upon the process of indoctrination and conversion. They chose for this purpose don Andres Alagua because he was of their nation, but he was also "ladino" and was quite capable. The others respected him because he was known as a community leader and his father had been a captain before they agreed to submit to Spanish rule. The Pijao needed a leader who was of their nation but who was also able to guide them into cultural consonance with the Coyaima, who were already Christianized. The *Protector de Naturales* argued that if someone from another nation were put in charge this would not be as effectively accomplished (AGN Colonia, Vol. 62, ff. 87–90).

The choice of leaders continued to be a crucial element in the politics of the royal town. In 1651 the *cacique* of Coyaima, don Melchior Cuque, named don Diego Biuche as his successor. Biuche was one of the *indios principales* in the town, a good Christian, capable and devoted to serving his community. The town leaders all agreed to his election because he was a good captain, plus, he knew how to read and write (AGN Colonia, Vol. 62, ff. 87–90). The integration of the Coyaima into the lettered culture of the Hispanic Baroque was well under way by the 1650s and was recognized as a powerful instrument by indigenous leaders, so Biuche's identification as a home-grown Ladino could serve a useful purpose as the indigenous population sought to adapt and use the Hispanic institutions they had been forced into.

There was, however, a perceptible shift in identity by the end of the eighteenth century in terms of acceptable characteristics for town leadership. In 1793 there was a tumultuous incident as the indigenous population sought to eject their *teniente*, Andres Parra. They stated that he had been foisted upon them by the priest and *corregidor*. The complaint was launched in January 1793 and the discourse deployed by both the Coyaima and their Hispanic handlers, the priest and the *corregidor*, employed images referring to categories of identity. The captains of Coyaima sought to deal with the problem of Andres Parra by calling a *cabildo* to elect another *teniente*. They wanted someone considered a "hijo del pueblo." They chose Agustín Tapiero as the likely candidate and asked the Crown to confirm his election. They also sought permission to expel all the Ladinos who lived in the town since their recent problems seemed to originate with them (AGN Colonia, Vol. 47, ff. 994–995v). The Coyaima used language of exclusion—"*esta dicha gente*"—when arguing their point. Parra's very identity as an Indian was challenged by the Coyaima, though according to the priest, his mother was an Indian Coyaima. However, Parra was born in Chaparral, and so his belonging to the *resguardo* could be challenged (see AGN Colonia, Vol. 43, ff. 564–566v). For town leaders his actions belied his identity as one of them. He was accused of having deprived the indigenous residents of their mines and given them over to Ladinos and of forcing local girls to perform personal service for the priest and *corregidor* (AGN Colonia, Vol. 46, ff. 994–995v). When they gathered to confront Parra and remove him, the Coyaima met fierce opposition from the Ladinos. The *corregidor* and the priest interpreted this series of events in the same vein as the earlier clash over land between the Coyaima and Correcha that had ended in frightening violence. That mark of violence was at the forefront of the image of the Coyaima presented by Fray Josef Thomas Lis in 1793 when he commented upon the struggle over Parra's office-holding. He argued that Ciprian Montiel, one of the men who launched the first complaint against Parra, belonged to a family heavily implicated in Correcha's murder (AGN Colonia, Vol. 43, ff. 562–563v). As he argued that these indigenous were bad vassals, Lis also presented them as bad Christians. He decried their ignorance, drunkenness and vices and attributed these to a single issue: the immensity of the land that they controlled. He added that they did not produce much on that land, and their ability to lose themselves far from the town itself, meant that they remained insubordinate and outside crown control (AGN Colonia, Vol. 43, f. 566v). In the circling round back to the Correcha case from the original objections to Parra in the 1790s we can discern the intimate connection between the Coyaima's identity and their belonging to their land. In the priest's formulation, that land was also the cause of their failure as Christians and vassals.

The tradition of seeking redress against local exactions by appealing to centralized authority continued into the early nineteenth century as the Indians of the town of Coyaima made a representation in Santa Fe asking to be exempted from public works because of the gold they contributed to the economy through their tribute. Thus in 1817 an order was issued that they not

88   *The Transatlantic Hispanic Baroque*

be forced to work on road building or in personal service or other public works (AGN Colonia, Vol. 32, ff. 60–61). In the Republican period there was a shift in discourse as indigenous people were no longer necessarily characterized as lazy, stupid and vice-ridden. However, their identity was shaped by the belief that communal landholding inhibited production and had a negative impact on them. It was argued that self-interest through individual property holding would solve the problems so starkly evident (Safford 9–15). The struggle to maintain their land continued to signal a defining feature of the Coyaima in the nineteenth century then as they objected to and resisted the application of various laws from the mid-century into the beginning of the twentieth century. Liberal attacks were particularly destructive, until finally in the 1890s the Governor of the state declared that there were no Indians in Tolima. They had been re-identified as "civilized" beings and their contrary Indianness and identity as Coyaima were simply dismissed as non-existent (Triana Antorveza, "Los resguardos" 100–105).[15]

The twentieth century brought added violence and pressures that effectively dispossessed indigenous people of their land in Tolima in 1945 (Consejo). Through all of these struggles the Coyaima survived and eventually began to reverse some of the patterns of identity integration that had been imposed upon them since early Spanish colonization. In recent times the typical direction of identity politics toward the Eurocentric ideal of whiteness has been challenged by people such as the Coyaima, who had been largely redefined as *mestizo* peasants by the middle period of the twentieth century. After the 1991 Constitution was signed and Article 70 guaranteed traditional rights to land held by indigenous and Afro-Colombian groups, the Coyaima once again took up the instrument of identity to secure their survival. The irony is that the old trajectory to success as one became whiter has been overturned and now survival can depend on being identified as Indian. This is a process that is not dependent on cultural diacritics, but on a sense of identity (Chaves and Zambrano 8). That identity as Pijao has come full circle and is expressed through claims to colonial *resguardo* land titles (Chaves and Zambrano 10). So though the Coyaima now speak Spanish and live like *mestizo* peasants they are nonetheless determined to reclaim their identity as Pijao. They are manifesting that re-Indianization by cultivating traditional medicinal practices, by continuing the collective struggle for survival in local and national contexts of extreme violence and as Pijao they are demanding their traditionally held lands (Espinosa Arango 67).

Peeling back the layers of identity manifested by the Coyaima at various moments in the last several hundred years we can infer some of the "cultural tremors" that inspired them to claim particular characteristics as essential to

---

[15]   This is the same type of 'definition out of existence' that was imposed upon the Mapuche by the Pinchet regime. See Lewis.

their collective survival. They were effective in adopting the cultural forms provided by the Hispanic Baroque and using them as tools to preserve the essential elements of their distinctiveness. While over time their unique markers became transformed by the cultural *milieu* they experienced with the conquest, colonizing and subsequent nation building projects, in the end the cultural system of the Hispanic Baroque provided them with mechanisms to firmly establish an indomitable connection between their sense of being and their land. Their identity was formed and reformed along the spectrum of ethnicity as Pijao, but the Hispanic Baroque was a malleable enough context that they were able to deploy various strategies within identity politics to preserve that crucial and unique characteristic. That history of interaction would help ease their way through twenty-first century political mazes as they remained focused upon what and where it means to be Coyaima.

Bibliography

Archivo General de Indias (AGI). Quito 284, No. 17. Expediente respondido del señor Fiscal a cerca del estado de las Provincias de Guayaquil, Santiago de las Atalayas, Neyba y Loxa. 1758.
———. AGI Audiencia de Santa Fe, leg. 752. Cartas de virreyes, Audiencia, cabildos seculars y eclesiasticos de Santa Fe informando sobre los méritos y servicios de personas seculares y eclesiásticas. 1770–1780.
Archivo General de la Nación (AGN). Colecciones, Fondo Enrique Ortega Ricaurte. Serie Virreyes. Box 206, folder 758. ff. 136–137.
———. AGN Colonia, Caciques y Indios, Vol. 9, ff. 987–1000.
———. AGN Colonia, Caciques y Indios, Vol. 32, ff. 60–61.
———. AGN Colonia, Caciques y Indios, Vol. 33, ff. 956–959.
———. AGN Colonia, Caciques y Indios, Vol. 41, ff. 77–136, 519–31.
———. AGN Colonia, Caciques y Indios, Vol. 43, ff. 562–563v.
———. AGN Colonia, Caciques y Indios, Vol. 44, ff. 529–681.
———. AGN Colonia, Caciques y Indios, Vol. 47, ff. 993–998.
———. AGN Colonia, Caciques y Indios, Vol. 52, ff. 246–249, 993–1033.
———. AGN Colonia, Caciques y Indios, Vol. 59, ff. 504–592.
———. AGN Colonia, Caciques y Indios, Vol. 60, ff. 813–906. 1793–1796.
———. AGN Colonia, Caciques y Indios, Vol. 62, ff. 87–90.
———. AGN Colonia, Fábricas Iglesias, Vol. 15, ff. 143–160. 1621–1623.
Archivo Historico Nacional de España (AHN). Inquisición de Cartagena, Libro 1021. Relaciones de Causas de Fe desde el año de 1638–1655, ff. 186r–190r, 246–247v.

Ceballos-Bedoya, Nicolás. "Usos indígenas del Derecho en el Nuevo Reino de Granada. Resistencia y pluralismo jurídico en el derecho colonial. 1750–1810." *Revista Estudios Socio-Juridicos* 13.2 (2011): 223–47.

Chaves, Margarita and Marta Zambrano. "From *blanqueamiento* to *reindigenización*: Paradoxes of *mestizaje* and Multiculturalism in Contemporary Colombia." *Revista Europea de Estudios Latinamericanos y del Caribe* 80 (April 2006): 5–23.

Clavijo Ocampo, Hernán. *Formación Historica de las Elites Locales en el Tolima.* Vol. 1. 1600–1813. Bogotá: Banco Popular, 1993.

Colmenares, Germán. "La sociedad Indigena y su evolución posterior a la Conquista." *La Nueva Historia de Colombia.* Ed. Dario Jaramillo Agudelo. Bogotá: Instituto Colombiano de Cultura, 1976. 67–172.

"Colombia: Indigenous Delegation Abducted." *Actualidad Etnica*, August 27, 2004. January 23, 2013. <http://www.tulane.edu/~libweb/RESTRICTED/WEEKLY/2004_0904.txt>.

Consejo Regional Indigena del Tolima. *Tercer Congreso Consejo Regional Indigena del Tolima. Ortega Tolima Colombia, dic. 1987.* Ortega, Tolima: Consejo Regional Indígena del Tolima, 1987.

Cutter, Charles. *The Legal Culture of Northern New Spain, 1700–1810.* Albuquerque: University of New Mexico Press, 1995.

Espinosa Arango, Mónica L. "Memoria cultural y el continuo del genocidio: lo indígena en Colombia." *Revista de Antropología y Arqueología* 5 (July–December 2007): 53–73.

Hernández de Alba, Gregorio. "The Highland Tribes of Southern Colombia, The Culture of the Pijao." *Handbook of South American Indians, Volume 2: The Andean Civilizations.* Ed. Julian H. Steward. New York: Cooper Square Publishers Inc., 1963. 956–60.

Herrera Ángel, Marta. "Ordenamiento especial de los Pueblos de Indios, dominación y resistencia en la sociedad colonial." *Fronteras* 2.2 (1998): 93–128.

Jouve Martín, José Ramón and Renée Soulodre-La France. "Introducción: *The Hispanic Baroque Project* y la constitución del barroco." *La constitución del Barroco hispánico: problemas y acercamientos.* Special issue of *Revista Canadiense de Estudios Hispánicos.* Ed. José Ramón Jouve Martín and Renée Soulodre-La France. 33.1 (Autumn 2008): 1–10.

Larkin, Brian. *The Very Nature of God. Baroque Catholicism and Religious Reform in Bourbon Mexico City.* Albuquerque: University of New Mexico Press, 2010.

Lewis, Stephen E. "Myth and the History of Chili's Araucanians." *Radical History Review* 58 (1994): 112–41.

Panich, Lee M. "Missionization and the Persistence of Native Identity on the Colonial Frontier of Baja California." *Ethnohistory* 47.2 (2010): 225–62.

Parkinson Zamora, Lois and Monika Kaup. "Introduction. Baroque, New World Baroque, Neobaroque: Categories and Concepts." *Baroque New Worlds: Representation, Transculturation, Counterconquest.* Ed. Lois Parkinson Zamora and Monika Kaup. Durham, NC: Duke University Press, 2010. 1–35.

Phelan, John Leddy. "Authority and Flexibility in the Spanish Imperial Bureaucracy." *Administrative Science Quarterly* 5.1 (1960): 47–65.

———. *The People and the King: The Comunero Revolution in Colombia, 1781.* Madison, WI: University of Wisconsin Press, 1978.

Pineda, Roberto, ed. *Tierra Profanada. Grandes proyectos en territorios indígenas de Colombia.* Bogotá: Disloque Editores Ltd, 1995.

Reichel-Dolmatoff, Gerardo. "The Agricultural Basis of the Sub-Andean Chiefdoms of Colombia." *Peoples and Cultures of Native South America.* Ed. Daniel R. Gross. Garden City, NY: Doubleday and Natural History Press, 1973. 28–36.

Restall, Matthew. *Seven Myths of the Spanish Conquest.* New York: Oxford University Press, 2003.

Robertson, Jamie M. "Evolutionary Identity Formation in an Indigenous Colonial Context: The Torres Strait Experience." *Nationalism and Ethnic Politics* 16 (2010): 465–82.

Rubio Orbe, Gonzalo. "Colombia Indigena." *América Indigena* 32.4 (1972): 1091–1108.

Safford, Frank. "Race, Integration, and Progress: Elite Attitudes and the Indians in Colombia, 1750–1870." *Hispanic American Historical Review* 71.1 (1991): 1–33.

Salinas Leal, Héctor Hernando. "Coyaima de la Real Corona. Entre la legalidad y la violencia. Conflicto agrario en un pueblo de indios durante la segunda mitad del siglo XVIII." *Memoria y Sociedad* 6.11 (April 2002): 85–100.

Soulodre-La France, Renée. *Región e Imperio: El Tolima Grande y las reformas borbónicas en el siglo XVIII.* Trans. Antonio Jara. Bogotá: Instituto Colombiano de Antropología e Historia, 2004.

———. *"Los esclavos de su majestad:* Slave Protests and Politics in Late Colonial New Granada." *Slaves, Subjects and Subversives: Blacks in Colonial Latin America.* Ed. Jane G. Landers and Barry M. Robinson. Albuquerque: University of New Mexico Press, 2006. 175–208.

Triana Antorveza, Adolfo. *La colonización española del Tolima. Siglos XVI y XVII.* Bogotá: FUNCOL and Cuadernos del Jaguar, 1992.

———. "Los resguardos indígenas del sur del Tolima." *Encrucijadas de Colombia Amerindia.* Ed. Luis Guillermo Vasco Uribe and François Correa Rubio. Bogotá: Instituto Colombiano de Antropología, 1993. 99–140.

PART II
Hispanic Baroque: Religion, Politics, Society

Chapter 5

Baroque Religion in Spain: Spanish or European?

Henry Kamen

Though the characteristics of Baroque culture have been well explored in nations such as Italy and Germany, Spain has suffered from a considerable neglect of how the basic elements of its religious tradition evolved during the seventeenth and eighteenth centuries. The bibliography on the subject offered in 1979 by the most outstanding Spanish expert, Antonio Mestre, said little about religion and was dominated by French scholarship that limited its attention to the later eighteenth century and to literary and political themes such as "Jansenism" (584–5). Since then, not much attention has been paid to the broad lines of the subject. Nearly 200 years of the practice and belief of the Catholic religion (as distinct from ecclesiastical matters) were left in great measure forgotten and undefined by peninsular historians. There has been no researched discussion in Spanish of what may seem a simple question: Was there a Spanish Counter Reformation? Nor has there been much discussion of the equally pertinent question: Was there a religious dimension to the Spanish Baroque?

These questions need some comment because, of course, religion was the fundamental vehicle of social expression in the pre-industrial age. Any attempt to study intellectual or literary trends while ignoring completely the socio-religious context, will arrive inevitably at incomplete conclusions. It has been habitual, for instance, to approach the advent of new ways of thinking in the peninsula through the texts of individuals rather than through their social impact.[1] The writings of Erasmus and of Feijoo, and later of Mayans, have often been focused on as though their words were both widely read and influential, when the truth is that very few people in Spain had any access to these authors. We should perhaps give less significance to the texts than to the people who helped to disseminate them: their friends and colleagues, members of the public, local bookstores, and contacts they may have had outside the limited radius of their residence.

---

[1]   See Deacon 129–40, for a review of four recent studies that concentrate on the literature and ideas of the Baroque period.

96 *The Transatlantic Hispanic Baroque*

In short, from where did Spaniards receive the ideas that shaped their lives? Were they cut off from the outside world? This chapter considers some aspects of that extremely complex theme of isolation. For many specialists in history and literature, Spain was cut off from and never passed through the phases of Reformation or Counter Reformation, but proceeded straight to the glories of Baroque. Why so? Simply, runs the argument, because the Inquisition shielded it from the Reformation, and because Spain was *already reformed*, so that the changes offered by a Counter Reformation were superfluous. A leading Spanish historian maintained that Spain at the dawn of the sixteenth century, long *before* any other nation did so, completely reformed its clergy, initiated a "religious awakening," and launched "a militant Catholicism which found its most typical expression in Spain," with a "Spanish" religious order (the Jesuits) that pioneered change, and a reforming Council of Trent in which the Spaniards, though a minority, "should be given first place" (Domínguez Ortiz 200–203). "The revival came long before the so-called Counter Reformation" (Domínguez Ortiz 124), he assured us. This presentation, for which there is absolutely no support in the historical evidence, was a faithful reflection of Menéndez Pelayo's ideas of nearly 100 years before, and is still held by many British and American experts. In 1982 American scholars concluded: "In Iberia the cause of Catholicism and of civilization became one. Not only was Hispanic Christianity immune to alternatives, but it became a central resource for the renewal of Catholicism. The soldiers and saints of Iberia made Hispanic Catholicism the wellspring of Counter Reformation piety" (Weinstein and Bell 191–2). In other words, Spain *exported* its religion, rather than importing any outside influences. The same line of thinking was followed by Otis Green when, after several pages defining the place of Counter Reformation and Baroque in Spanish literature, he concluded that Spain enjoyed "an age that gave new strength to Europe" (Green 4: 182). The meaning cannot be clearer: Spain gave *to* Europe rather than receiving *from* it.

The central thesis of these writers was the assumption that Spain already had a religious fertility that it produced from within itself. The possibility of interchange with external culture was not only rejected by them, it was pushed aside and forgotten. Spanish religion became a stage on which no change took place, because it flourished splendidly in isolation. As the ideal to which everyone looked, Spain could afford to reject anything that came from Europe, since it was *more* Catholic than Europe and even more Catholic than the pope.[2]

---

[2]   Needless to say, this argument is deeply rooted in traditional Spanish thinking. Ramón Menéndez Pidal argued that the city of Rome was destroyed by the troops of Charles V in 1527 because of "Spanish indignation at the conduct of the pope, who would not support the aspirations of Spain in favor of European Catholicism." In his *Defensa de la hispanidad*, Ramiro de Maeztu stated: "In the history of the world there is nothing comparable to what was achieved by Spain, because we incorporated into Western civilization all the peoples

Baroque Religion in Spain: Spanish or European?   97

This exclusion of Spain from the influential currents of thought in Europe was an act perpetrated by scholars who loved Spain and therefore insisted on its uniqueness. There may have been a brief moment (they conceded) when Spaniards appreciated Europe, but that only happened with Erasmus, and he was soon excluded. Through this simple conclusion, the concept of reform and Counter Reformation was rendered irrelevant for Spain.[3]

But there was more to come. Spain, the argument went, not only gave a new Catholicism to Europe, it also gave the Baroque, which would not have existed but for Spain. Those who attributed Spanish origins to the Baroque were confident of their conclusions. A French art historian stated in 1951 in the journal *Annales ESC*: "Baroque was born in Italy only as a consequence of the forceful entry of certain forms of religion that came from Spain" (quoted in Maravall 40 n.37). When Jose Antonio Maravall published his pioneering *La cultura del Barroco* in 1975, he apologized for his temerity in identifying Spain with the Baroque, but took as his defense the fact that many non-Spanish scholars had suggested (Maravall 41) that everything in the European Baroque originated from Spain, above all from Spanish religion. French, British and German scholars seemed to agree that Spain was the source for trends in religion and mysticism. One of them wrote: "It was Spain which experienced the Baroque most intensely. The Baroque is Spain's true form and fulfillment" (Friedrich 50).

Was Spain really the most Baroque nation in religion? If true, this would have been extremely strange, since not a single Spanish historian had ever published a learned study of the art and religion of Spain's Baroque. The one scholar to venture into mainly socio-political aspects of the field, José Antonio Maravall, began by fixing—as historians tend to do—its chronology: he stated that it "consists of the first three quarters of the seventeenth century" (Maravall 24). He also added that there was during the eighteenth century a subsequent "restoration" of Baroque. To my knowledge, no other scholar took any learned interest in the subject. Because historians abandoned the field, the analysis of traditional culture was necessarily taken up by literary experts, from Menéndez Pelayo to (in our own time) Aguilar Piñal and Mestre, who were obliged to use literary sources to describe social phenomena.[4] Since literature became the main evidence, Spanish scholars tended to discount any consciousness of the Baroque in terms of religion, and restricted the concept to a question of literary (Green 4: 216) or artistic extravagance.[5] Was there then no religious meaning to Baroque?

---

who were under our influence. During its two great centuries the whole of Spain was on a mission."

[3]   The French scholar Marcel Bataillon argued, however, that Erasmus effectively contributed to Spain's Counter Reformation (770).

[4]   "It is enough to read our own authors," notes Mestre at one point (4: 600).

[5]   Especially with the creative artists, from Carreño de Miranda to Churriguera, mentioned in Kamen (*Spain* 315–16).

98   *The Transatlantic Hispanic Baroque*

Though the word "baroque" appears everywhere in books about Spain, it is difficult to find what it might signify in religious terms. In *La cultura del Barroco* [*The Culture of the Baroque*], Maravall overcame the defect by suggesting that "Baroque" was a continent-wide phenomenon, a sort of Zeitgeist, that did not have its origins in any specific country but could be found equally in every nation. The emphasis in art on violence and blood, for example, he interpreted as "a common theme, particular to the historical moment of the Baroque in all of Europe" (Maravall 332). This ingenious argument of "a common theme," a Zeitgeist, immediately solves one of the major issues of Spanish historiography, namely the alleged isolation of Spain from Europe. Maravall was the only Spanish historian of his day to insist, in all his writings, on the cultural heritage that Spain shared with other Europeans. He therefore accepted that Spain had a Counter Reformation just as it had a Baroque, because both were expressions of the same Zeitgeist.

One suspects, however, that Maravall unconsciously came to see Baroque as a sort of *projection of Spain*. Since all countries shared the same Zeitgeist, then unusual and exotic manifestations such as bullfights could be seen as an expression of Baroque (Maravall 334). It followed that rejection of bullfights could be seen as anti-Baroque. Maravall cites an incident in Madrid when the Danish ambassador asked to attend at a bullfight, and fainted when he saw so much blood. "One might almost think," Maravall comments, "that it is understandable why there was no Danish Baroque" (335). The principal features of Spain's culture were presented by him as co-extensive with the European experience and quintessential examples of Baroque. The image we obtain from his book is of a Spain that was completely at the heart of Baroque in all respects, including art and literature. Spain, effectively, *was* Baroque.

Among its many virtues, the Zeitgeist model saves us from the problem of having to enquire into cultural transference, because it saves us from any of the bother of finding out where Counter Reformation and Baroque came from or where they went to. Maravall cites a religious procession in Madrid in 1623, when the monks paraded through the streets with acts and symbols of flagellation and blood, as a case of "the pedagogy of violence feelings in the Baroque" (334). This may well be true, but surely an enquiring historian would wish to ask whether the monks had done this always, or only in the last 20 years, or whether it was a practice imported from abroad and widely accepted in Spain. If it was universal practice across Europe to have flagellation, and could be specifically identified with the period, then a Zeitgeist would be a reasonable explanation.

The principal weakness of Zeitgeist, evidently, is that it imposes a model without any attempt to search for specific evidence relating a phenomenon to its context in time and space. For example, Maravall followed other famous experts, such as Mâle and Tenenti, in emphasizing the alleged obsession of Baroque with the theme of death (Maravall 336), notably through the depiction of death in paintings. Recent scholarship, in contrast, has attempted to be more specific, by analyzing attitudes to death according to period, region, class, and person, most notably through an analysis of testaments. The entire context of death in Spain, indeed, is so complex—as Eire's brilliant book reveals (40–45)—that particular rather than general perspectives are always the most illuminating. Modern research makes it impossible for us to rely any more on vague global concepts such as "obsession." A concern for death obviously existed equally in Spain and in other European countries, but its context varied widely from region to region.

At this point, it is relevant to link the points that have been touched on. I have suggested that there has been a failure to give a specific researched dimension to developments in Spanish religion. "In Spain, there is a lack of serious study in religious sociology of Spanish history, and it is my impression that we would be late to arrive at such study" (Mestre 4: 587). Twenty years after those words were written by Mestre, the picture seemed not to be so bleak, because research students were beginning to imitate some of the methods of French historians. Archives all over Spain were combed for statistics, above all statistics from testaments, and the results were presented as evidence of Spanish "attitudes to death." It looked like a swift and sure method of penetrating the secrets of what French scholars termed "les mentalités" [the mentalities]. However, this admirable activity took place (in Spain) without much corresponding research into the cultural context of religion, and a good deal of the data collected in that period can now be seen to be unhelpful.

Moreover, the research did not change the broad traditional lines of interpretation, which continued to state that Spain had no need for a Reformation or Counter Reformation, and was instead the creator of Baroque. "The Spanish Church was reformed *before* the Reformation," a historian insisted boldly as recently as 2001 (Ruiz 232), despite the complete absence of visible proof for such a claim. The same scholar logically omitted any consideration of "Counter Reformation" from his discussion. This inevitably creates problems for researchers who suspect that there may be evidence of European influence in early modern modes of religion, not to mention in art, music and literature. In the same way, if no convincing explanation is given for Baroque, we are left to puzzle how such a phenomenon is related to Spain's alleged isolation from the outside world. How can the country, at one and the same time, be isolated from Europe yet also be at the heart of Baroque?

When, in 1983, I first began studying the process of religious change in seventeenth-century Catalonia, I commenced with the accepted view that there was no Counter Reformation. By the time I finished my book on the subject ten years later, the picture had, for me, changed radically. Though I was careful to state that my conclusions were valid only for Catalonia, I came to see that interaction between all levels of the Christian community, at a European level, was a potent basis for asserting that a Counter Reformation not only happened

100   *The Transatlantic Hispanic Baroque*

within Spain, but also received a mighty stimulus from outside. In every respect, from parish reform to modification of rituals and processions, from adoption of art and customs and saints to copying the style of sermons and prayers, Europeans (notably Italians and, in particular, the Jesuits) made a solid contribution that probably extended throughout Spain but certainly had a marked impact on the Mediterranean provinces.

Subsequent studies of religious reform, undertaken by American scholars, supported the idea that a Counter Reformation took place in Spain.[6] These new perspectives emphasized that over the generations there were significant changes in the allegedly eternal, unchanging, religion of Spaniards. In short, none of the statements that follow, taken from a scholarly presentation made by a Spanish expert in 1979 (see Mestre 4: 586–602), can be accepted as valid if not placed within a specific context of period and place:

> The devotion with which Spaniards attend to the officiating priest seems clear, as much as it might be surprising to foreigners [...]. Attending Mass was not the only form of devotion in Spain. Saying the rosary was a well-established, popular practice. Saying the rosary was common in all parishes [...] Attending Sunday Mass was common [...] One must also recall the vast number of [religious] celebrations. A classical sermon was an important element of any celebration [...]. Along with sermons, processions were an essential part of all celebrations. Any student of the eighteenth century in Spain must be aware of the abundance of processions. In addition to those of Holy Week, the processions of Corpus Christi were of notable splendour.

The evidence suggests that these statements are not true for a good part of Spain during the early modern period (Kamen, *Phoenix* 82–9). Up to around the year 1600, there is no remarkable evidence of devotion to the priest, or of widespread assistance at mass, or of praying the rosary, or of an excess of fiestas, or of abundant sermons, or of regular processions, or of popular devotion to Corpus Christi. What happened is that at some time between the end of the sixteenth century and the early eighteenth century, significant changes occurred that left their mark on Spanish religion and culture. And since—as we shall see—those changes can be documented, we are faced by two fundamental questions. Why, in the first place, do scholars often cling to the fictitious image of a Spain that was unchangingly Catholic and impervious to change? Second, why do many continue to pass over the real religious practice of Spaniards, which was no better or worse than that of other Europeans, in favor of purely literary concepts,

---

[6]   Apart from Kamen, *The Phoenix*, the Counter Reformation in the peninsula is explored by Bilinkoff, Nalle, and Poska.

deemed moreover to be uniquely Spanish, such as "the mystical tradition of the Baroque age in Spain" (Green 4: 182)?

Was Spanish Catholicism not part of a worldwide Christian Church? It is true that in Spain, as in most countries, huge sections of the population had little contact with the outside world, and even less with the continent of Europe. In this respect, the little 1981 study by William Christian Jr, *Local Religion,* has rightly been seen as pioneering. His book centered on a sample of villages in sixteenth-century Castile that were subjects of a government survey. He argued that religious devotions were firmly rooted in the local community, and that though "there was a persistence of local religion from the mid-sixteenth to the late eighteenth century, the piety of the universal Church was adopted and domesticated for local use" (Kamen, *Phoenix* 434). I arrived at a similar conclusion in my study of Catalonia, which emphasized that even the local community was not closed off from European culture, and that religious change in the Baroque, far from being limited to urban centers, could also affect remote communities.

Baroque was, above all, an extension of the Counter Reformation, during which significant changes took place in Spain's religion.[7] Spanish religion of the early sixteenth century was still in all essentials late mediaeval: an easy-going combination of vague theology and irregular practice, with a heavy emphasis on local rituals and folk religion. Reform attempts in Spain were of long standing, but nothing significant was achieved by Cardinal Cisneros or by Ferdinand and Isabella. A generation after the death of Ferdinand, in 1540 the new reforming bishop of Pamplona was attempting to introduce basic changes such as the preaching of a sermon on Sundays, reservation of the sacrament on the altar, and the keeping of baptismal records. These piecemeal local efforts in various dioceses were reinforced in the 1560s by the authority of the Council of Trent and that of Philip II, who in 1567, for example, was urging forward on his bishops in Catalonia "the task of the reformation" (Kamen, *Phoenix* 69). By confirming previous trends, notably in the reform of religious orders, and by its own innovations, Trent revolutionized Spanish Catholicism.

Of the significant religious changes that occurred from the end of the sixteenth century, the first was the abolition of variations in liturgy and the imposition of the new Roman Missal and Breviary. Distinctive and curious local ways of saying mass in, for example, Mallorca and Asturias, were phased out. By 1571, the nuncio in Madrid reported to Rome, all the dioceses and orders (Toledo with its ancient Mozarabic rite was a permitted exception) had accepted the changes. This was certainly optimistic, for the "*nuevo rezado*" [new way of praying] was not accepted without murmurs, particularly since the new

---

[7]   All the information that follows is summarized from the documented details in several pages of my *Phoenix.*

missal involved the abolition of many local saints and feast-days in favor of saints recognized by the universal Church. In 1588 it was reported from Mallorca that less than a third of the clergy in the diocese were using the new Roman rite, over 15 years after its introduction.

The authority of bishops was strengthened, and material changes were made in education, so that the teaching of the faithful advanced significantly. In most parishes the priest was now enjoined to preach a sermon at Sunday mass, an innovation as startling for the congregation as it must have been onerous for the incumbent. At the same time religious instruction had to be given during mass, and Sunday schools for the children of the parish were made obligatory. Many of these reforms brought in by Trent were, as one might expect, never enacted. In the parish of San Vicente in San Sebastián, in the margin of the official record enforcing sermons on Sunday a seventeenth-century hand wrote: "This has never been done." Poor and ignorant clergy continued to be common, but gradually by the early seventeenth century the combined efforts of bishops, religious orders and the Inquisition managed to coax Spaniards into observing many of the practices of the new Catholicism. A striking feature of the new parish structure was the organization of confraternities, intended to encourage loyalty to the parish but also to heighten devotion, since confraternity rules stipulated regular confession and communion.

There were profound differences between the new Catholicism and the old. The changes brought from Europe into Spanish religion of the Baroque age introduced a revolutionary sense of the sacred that endured for generations. Where the church had been used for communal meetings and festivities, it was now totally separated from all secular use; all religious rites, and all baptisms were to be performed in the church and in no other place; clergy were ordered to wear distinctive robes to separate them from laity (in Mallorca in 1578 many still refused to wear clerical dress); priests were no longer to attend wedding parties and similar celebrations; carnivals, plays and dances were banned from church; processions with any hint of non-religious ritual were abolished; certain feast days (such as Corpus Christi) which had become laicized, were reclaimed for the Church. A worshipper in post-Tridentine Spain would experience, among other innovations: whitewashed walls in church, paintings purged of sensuality, a pulpit if there had not been one before, an eternal flame before the tabernacle, a sacristy to which no women were allowed access, strict separation of sexes among the worshippers, a wooden confessional to separate priest from penitent (introduced in Barcelona, for example, from 1566), sermons (an innovation outside the major cities), and a new liturgy, including the popularization of the Rosary (1571) and the introduction of the Forty-Hours devotion (brought from Italy to Barcelona by the Capuchins in 1580). New rules imposed on the parish priest included having to keep a record of all baptisms, marriages and burials.

Parishioners were obliged to attend mass every Sunday and take communion at Easter, all of this being recorded by the priest.

From faith and worship, the impact of these changes extended to all aspects of Christian life. The reforming outlook produced a generation of composers of sacred music, culminating in the magnificent motets (composed, it should be stressed, entirely in Italy) of Tomás Luis de Victoria (d. 1611). On literature and theatre, unfortunately, the impact was equivocal. It has often—and mistakenly—been thought that the Inquisition alone was responsible for pressure on creative writers. In practice the Inquisition was more concerned with the published word, whereas the one art form accessible to the mass of the illiterate general public—the theatre—was more normally subject to the local civic authorities and ultimately to the council of Castile. A clear effect of the new Catholic spirit was the evolution in the late sixteenth-century theatre of *autos sacramentales*, plays performed specially for the newly emphasized feast of Corpus Christi. For the dramatist and priest Lope de Vega the *auto* was "a confounding of heresy and a glory of our faith." On the other hand, many Counter-Reformation clergy, led by Jesuits like Mariana and Ribadeneira, thought the stage a source of immorality and mounted a campaign which led to the closing of all theatres from 1597 into the early years of the next century. The new moral spirit extended also into family life. The rules for what constituted marriage were clarified and enforced, and parish priests were encouraged to check on the sex lives of parishioners (an area that the Inquisition also attempted to control).

As the preceding summary has emphasized, many of the new cultural trends were imported into Spain, not exported by it. Popular devotions, even those with prior existence in the peninsula, such as the Rosary, owed their growth to foreign influence (Kamen, *Phoenix* 148–9). Virtually unknown a generation before, the Rosary flourished in the seventeenth century. In the same period we find the first significant use of the Christmas crib, imported, it appears, from Germany by the Jesuits and commonly found in the 1580s. The Angelus was similarly brought in from Italy and became popular. From the end of the sixteenth century, popular processions were enriched by a new form of piety, brought in by Jesuits from Italy: the "holy discipline," that is, flagellation, which became popular and was often deemed by visitors to the peninsula to be quintessentially Spanish. During a Lenten mission organized by the Jesuits in Vilafranca del Penedès in 1653, a member of the order reports, "the high point was a procession of penitence in which eighty penitents went whipping blood and were preceded by over a hundred barefoot young girls dressed in white, their faces covered with black veils" (Kamen, *Phoenix* 435).[8]

---

[8]   For many other types of public piety that the Jesuits brought into Spain, compare the Jesuit practices in the kingdom of Naples (a territory governed for much of the period by

The existence of changes cannot now be disputed. If we ignore the European dimension it becomes difficult to understand what really happened in Spanish religion. For example, scholarly treatment of the sermon as a cultural form often tends to look no farther than the frontiers of Castile. In discussing "The witty of the Holy Rhetoric," a scholar refers to the sixteenth century as one in which "the great preachers [...] lived in a thriving cultural era and reached the highest levels of perfection in rhetoric," which he contrasts with "The decadent Baroque at the end of the seventeenth century" (Mestre 4: 591). The problem with this opinion is that it is untrue. There was no "thriving cultural era," not even in Castile, and there was no "perfection" of any sort. "The decline," the same authority continues, "reached its lowest point in the first half of the eighteenth century." The conclusion is meant to encourage us to see the later eighteenth century—the period of Jansenist thought—as the epoch of real reform (see Saugnieux). More recent research disproves this assumption, concluding that "Preaching was, during this [seventeenth] century, not only the most useful means of conversion to Christianity, but also of acculturation" (Núñez Beltrán 34).

The historical context is that pre-Baroque Catholicism in Spain did not have sermons outside the king's court and the big cathedrals, and the gospel was not significantly communicated through the spoken word. Furió Ceriol in his *Bononia* (1555) pointed out that sermons were almost unknown in Spain (Kamen, *Phoenix* 357–62), a lack that the early Jesuits attempted to remedy, since they were aware that there had been no "flourishing cultural era." In their instructions to clergy, bishops attempted to explain what material should feature in sermons, but it was difficult to explain something that had seldom been practiced. The bishop of Tortosa at the end of the seventeenth century ended up recommending his clergy to preach "in the Italian way," and for many Spaniards the model adopted was Cardinal Borromeo of Milan. If there were bad sermons in Baroque Spain, it was because it was a discipline that many clergy had not yet begun to master; and it seems fair to say that there was no notable decadence. The use by priests of the spoken word, whether through the sermon or through the confessional, was a slow development. Borromeo, it is timely to recall, was immensely influential in Spain for several reasons, and his invention of the wooden confessional was perhaps his most notable contribution to peninsular Catholicism.

In brief, the idea of a "golden age" that was followed by "decadence" is a literary conceit that does not always coincide with historical evidence. The stylistic prose of sixteenth-century court sermons may appeal more to the modern professor of literature, but the effective achievement was that of sermons preached by ordinary clergy, who learned much from foreign methods, especially those

---

Spain), see Gentilcore.

brought in from Italy. As Pérez Magallón has emphasized, the influence of Italy, well into the reign of Philip V, continued to be significant (320).

At this point, we may venture a word on a theme that appears to arouse no doubts: the role of the Inquisition in the Baroque experience of Spain. It was with the Inquisition in mind that an American historian asserted that Spain "seems more truly akin to the spirit of the Baroque than perhaps any other nation in Europe" (Friedrich 226), and a British historian concluded that "the top-heavy Church of Baroque Spain had little to offer a passive population but an unending succession of sedatives and heavy ceremonial which ministered to its apparently insatiable passion for display" (Elliott 369). These antiquated judgments may have had in mind the impressive canvas, now in the Museo del Prado, of the Madrid *auto de fe* of 1680. Or they may be based, as in a famous study of Baroque by Victor-Lucien Tapié, on the view that blood and flagellation are typical of the Spanish character. Exotic interpretations of the Holy Office still abound, but the fact is that its activity in the late seventeenth and early eighteenth centuries was modest, and in matters of religious practice and belief it had a minimal role. As I have stressed elsewhere, with respect to Catalonia, "in over ninety per cent of the towns and villages, during more than three centuries of existence, the Holy Office never once intruded" (*Phoenix* 436).

Was the Inquisition in Baroque Spain an obstacle to contact with progressive thought? There were constant complaints—as there were also in Feijóo's correspondence—about the closed minds of the inquisitors (Kamen, *Spain* 300). But the fact is that the reverend fathers controlled little, and impeded little. Books flowed in across the Pyrenees with no hindrance from inquisitors (Kamen, *Phoenix* 422). Anyone who had the interest could import literature. In the late seventeenth century, Spaniards purchased books freely in Paris and brought them home, while traders from France and Italy brought books to sell together with their other goods. Members of the elite, until well into the eighteenth century, never had any problem about foreign books (Fayard 502–519), though many intellectuals had a major cultural problem, an inability to read any foreign languages. Only a very few were able to, like the soldier-diplomat Rebolledo, who lived for 12 years in Denmark and there built up a library (which he brought back to Spain in 1660) that included not only prohibited books but also the works of Théophile Viau and the French libertines.

With respect to Spain's alleged isolation from European currents of thought, it is important to eliminate from consideration the supposed ban on movement of students. It used to be believed that Philip II, in a decree of 1559, prohibited Spain's students from studying abroad. Two centuries after 1559, Gregorio Mayans claimed that "one of the causes of the great decline in the Arts and Sciences was the law created by Phillip the Second that prohibited study in foreign universities" (quoted in Gil Fernández 476). There was no such prohibition (see Kamen, *Spanish Inquisition* ch. 6), though it has not prevented

106 *The Transatlantic Hispanic Baroque*

allegations that the said decree contributed to "stifle the exchange in knowledge and ideas that nourishes Culture and Sciences" (Gil Fernández 475). Maybe one day a researcher will attempt to identify the names and details of the scores of Spanish students who allegedly abandoned their studies in Louvain, Oxford, Paris, Heidelberg and Rome, and returned home; or of the British, French, German and Italian students who flocked to Alcala de Henares and were driven out; but this is unlikely, for they never existed.

Of all west European countries, Spain stood out for its failure to send students to foreign universities, or to receive foreign students. Few testimonies are as damning as that of the Flemish humanist Bonaventura De Smit, in his comments on the state of Castile's universities during the supposed golden age.[9] The country also stood out for its complete lack of interest in experimental research. Spaniards in the early modern period had possibly the least dedication to science, measured by the university affiliation of scientists (Gascoigne 250), of any nation in western Europe. Those who took learning seriously went to Italy. Thanks to access to Italian and foreign scholarship, scientific enquiry did not collapse. Technology filtered into the country: foreign treatises were translated; engineers were imported by the state. Foreign technicians—all of them Catholic—came to the peninsula with their expertise. The Inquisition, for its part, did not normally interfere.

The Holy Office palpably had nothing to do with the failure of the Spanish intellectual world, and it is grotesque to claim that "fear of the Inquisition, restricting freedom of expression and thought, also suppressed the desire to think" (Gil Fernández 492). Though it has been very justifiably claimed that there was an "almost total rift from the book culture of Europe" (Pardo Tomás 87),[10] the Holy Office was hardly the culprit. If ordinary Spaniards did not read foreign authors it was for the very same reason that prevails today in the twenty-first century: the books were not available in Spanish, or did not appeal to their tastes. Nor, apart from specific outbreaks of persecution, when it carried out localized (and sometimes harsh) campaigns against persons of Portuguese (Kamen, *Spanish Inquisition* ch. 13), Muslim and Jewish origin,

---

[9]   "In Hispania omnibus maximum fit studiorum detrimentum. Inter aulicossumma con miseria degitur. Compluti nullus fere est profitendi locus cum utilitate conjunctus, na milli suas habent cathedras, quas vocant, neque iis nisi Hispanos praeficiunt. Praterea aestate summa hic per totos quinque menses solitudo est. Salamantiae vigent leges, sordet medicina, sordent literae" (in Vries de Heekelingen 28). De Smit (Latinized as Vulcanius) was private secretary to the cardinal of Spain, Cardinal Mendoza, and left Spain for Belgium in 1570 in the company of the duke of Medinaceli. He died in 1614, as professor of Greek in Leiden.

[10]   Pardo Tomás expresses this opinion because a report of the Inquisition in 1632 stated that "very few of the books written by heretics make their way to Spain." The phrase clearly refers only to heretical books; but foreigners also flooded the Iberian market with non-heretical books.

did the Inquisition play any significant part in repressing the religious life of Spaniards during the century preceding the famous case of Pablo de Olavide in the 1770s. In every field of interest, whether because of profession, commerce or the army, or for adventure and curiosity, Spaniards were free to move around Europe, America and Asia, and hundreds of thousands did so. They were also free to read the books they wished, and neither booksellers nor readers were punished in any way for using their capacity to think.

In conclusion, Spain remained a Catholic country, and retained its Inquisition, but it was not impervious to outside influences. There is no reason to consider innovation of thought in the late seventeenth and early eighteenth century as an exceptional development that took place in a previously isolated Spain. The individuals now termed by scholars "innovators" were unquestionably heirs to a significant period of cultural interchange, and shared with other Spaniards the possibility of a broad range of contact with other Europeans. Throughout the seventeenth century in Spain, there was continuous change and modification in the modes of everyday religion, and by extension in the associated modes of thought. In particular, there was active interchange between Italy, France and Spain, at all levels from movement of persons to exchange of printed literature and popular devotions. Spain always had open frontiers, and the Inquisition was never an effective barrier against outside influences. Already in the late sixteenth century, the book market in the peninsula was "colonized" (Pettegree ch. 14) by imports, and the situation had not changed a century later. From my own analysis of the lists of Spanish books drawn up by Nicolás Antonio at the time, it can be seen that "about a quarter of the religious works published by Spaniards during the Counter Reformation came from foreign presses" (*Phoenix* 413). Thousands of books, on a broad range of themes, were freely imported into Spain from all parts, mainly France and Italy. The marvelous catalog of Toda y Güell, which I have used for an analysis of the import of Italian books to Spain (*Phoenix* 404), demonstrates this conclusively. "If the interchange of ideas between intellectuals continued at an unduly low level it was for reasons unconnected with the accessibility of foreign literature" (*Phoenix* 401).

A far more serious barrier to change than the Inquisition, was (as I have noted above) the widespread ignorance of foreign languages (including Latin) among all sectors of the educated elite—clergy, university professors, and bureaucrats. By the early eighteenth century Castilian had become widely known in the western world, and the major works of the peninsula were translated into other European tongues. The negative face of this picture was that Spaniards did not translate works from other nations (with the outstanding exception of Italy), and tended to cut themselves off from other cultures (see Kamen, *Empire* 339). Attention should also be paid to the fact that Spain's upper classes, unlike those of other European states, had little interest until well after the Baroque period in improving their cultural perspectives by dedicating themselves to the Grand

Tour. A study of sections of the elite, along the lines of Janine Fayard's analysis of government officials of the Baroque period, might help to explain why this was so.

Changes in the Catholic religion of Spain during the epoch known as Counter Reformation and Baroque have usually gone unrecognized by scholars who, in default of available research, have tended to apply stereotyped labels instead of historical evidence. This failure to analyze has been most notable in the case of the visual arts—a discipline outside the limits of this chapter—where the enormous contribution of Italian and French styles and spirituality has often been ignored, and works of art located in Spain have been identified simply as Spanish. It is a pleasure, then, to observe that the two most notable paintings depicting Spain's role in religion come from the beginning and the end of the so-called Baroque period, and both were done by Italians, not by Spaniards. The first and best known is Titian's "Spain succouring Religion," finished in 1575 and now in the Prado. The other notable work, this time from the late Baroque in Spain, is the fresco decorating a ceiling in the Royal Palace in Madrid, titled "Religion protected by Spain." It is a fine title, and a fine painting, but it was painted in the 1750s by an Italian, Corrado Giaquinto, a pupil of Luca Giordano and for a while director of the Real Academia de San Fernando.

The contact with Europe was crucial to many changes. By the time of the Baroque, "universal" rather than "local" saints became the focus of popular devotion (Kamen, *Phoenix* 136), a feature of some importance for promoting the international religion of the Church. At every stage, new religious life was brought into Spain by foreign contacts, foreign missionary orders, foreign devotions and practices, foreign saints (Carlo Borromeo, Filippo Neri), and foreign literature (including the substantial number of books by peninsular authors published abroad, in the Netherlands, France and Italy) (Kamen, *Phoenix* 413). In brief, Spanish Catholicism, thanks in great measure to its links with the universal Church,[11] did not remain impervious. Baroque religion was not exclusively a product of Spanish mentality and culture, it was also in many respects European, and all its new characteristics were imported from Europe. Historians have now grown to recognize that there was a vigorous entity known as Baroque religion, and they have studied several aspects of it brilliantly (see Foster). Many of these Baroque influences penetrated the peninsula, but they seem to have created no conflict of identity, and in time became an integral part of Spanish religious practice.

That did not necessarily make Spain more Catholic. The common picture of a devout people thronging to mass must be looked at critically. "For very many,

---

[11]   Likewise, the universal Church aided Spanish Catholicism, as with the many foreign Jesuits who formed the backbone of the missionary effort in South America; see Kamen, *Empire* 280.

Baroque Religion in Spain: Spanish or European?

both before and after Trent, mass was primarily a communal gathering, of which the part over which the priest officiated was not necessarily the most important" (Kamen, *Phoenix* 119). Popular assistance at masses, theatres and *autos de fe* was never proof of piety, though it was always undoubted proof of sociability. People went to religious gatherings for motives that were not necessarily religious, and the clergy were well aware of it, which explains why they supported the periodic visits of missions, a common feature of the Baroque period. We need look only at the amazing missions preached throughout Spain between 1665 and 1676 by the Jesuits Tirso Gonzalez and Gabriel Guillen, with massive participation of the population everywhere (Astraín 6: 76).

By way of epilog, it was logical that the cultural interchange of the Baroque should include some *export* of influences, but the theme has been little examined by scholars from the peninsula. Perhaps the only substantial area studied is that on the diffusion of the *picaro* novel. In art, reference is made inevitably to the significance of Bernini's statue of St Teresa in Santa Maria della Vittoria, but the broader context of Spain's cultural impact on Italy has been neglected. In the same way, reference is often made to the crucial role that Teresa's Carmel—and indeed the saint's other writings as well—played in the "invasion mystique" patronized by Bérulle and others in France in the early seventeenth century (see Bremond). Perhaps the most famous Spaniard of the Baroque age in terms of spirituality was the priest Miguel de Molinos (1628–1696), whom the poet Antonio Machado once placed among "the four Miguels [Miguel Servet, Miguel de Cervantes, Miguel de Molinos y Miguel de Unamuno] who represent and sum up the essence of Spain" (214). In the whole of Spanish history few individuals have made such a mark on European religious thought. From 1662 his life and career centered on Italy. In 1675 he published two books that sent shockwaves through Catholic Europe. The first of these was the *Short Treatise on Frequent Communion*. The second book, also published the same year in Rome (first in Spanish then in Italian), was a more solid item with the title *Spiritual Guide*. The *Guide* was published in Italian, in Latin (in Germany), in French, English, Dutch and German, not to mention a very late version in Russian in 1784. A transatlantic version came out in Philadelphia in 1885. Molinos' doctrine, which was in essence a harmless application of mystical principles related to Quietism, continued to survive in religious confessions (such as the German Pietists) far removed from his own. The Church, especially in Spain, expunged him from its collective memory and banned all his works. Down to today, there are no substantive studies in Spanish of his life or ideas (see Tellechea).

Finally, we may venture to ask: How Catholic was Spain on the eve of the age of Enlightenment? The question is relevant because of the common supposition that Spain was solidly Catholic and that this represented a barrier to new ways of thought. The firmness with which Spain seemed to resist dissenting movements, from Protestantism to Quietism, confirmed its reputation as the most inflexibly

110 *The Transatlantic Hispanic Baroque*

Catholic country of Europe. According to this view, the people remained faithful to their beliefs until innovators in the eighteenth century created a conflict by attacking the Church. The interpretation pervades most studies of Spanish religion, which are inevitably written by clergy committed to a specific way of thought.[12]

My own minority and dissenting opinion is that Spaniards, rather than being solidly Catholic, seem always to have accepted little more than outward forms of the official religion. Unfortunately, there is no compelling evidence for one or the other point of view. Fragments of information exist about hostility to the Church, the Inquisition, and the clergy, but they cannot be used to construct a convincing picture, and even the evidence for anticlericalism—a notion that may have had a role in the expulsion of the Jesuits in 1767—is equivocal. The religious impulse of the Counter Reformation in Spain faded away in the course of the seventeenth century, and no significant changes in the religion of the people occurred over the next two centuries. People probably took part in the social activity of the Church—in festivities such as Winter Carnival, Holy Week, Corpus Christi and midsummer celebrations such as the feast of St John—in the way they do today, that is, without necessarily believing in any of it. And all the while, century after century, they might be harboring resentment against the small and privileged group of persons who dominated religious and social life, ran the schools, intruded into details of personal and family behavior, and dictated all sexual norms. Throughout peninsular history there was evidence of opposition to clergy. "The poor," stated a man in Granada in the 1620s, "pay tithes to the clergy so they can get fat and rich." Another stated that "there should be no more than four priests in the world, and even these should be hanged." Hostility to the clergy, both priests and nuns, took so many different forms that it is still impossible to reduce the matter to dimensions that are easy to understand.

Bibliography

Astraín, Antonio. *Historia de la Compañía de Jesús en la asistencia de España*. 7 vols. Madrid: Sucesores de Ribadeneyra, 1905–1925.

Bataillon, Marcel. *Erasmo y España. Estudios sobre la historia espiritual del siglo XVI*. 2nd edition. Trans. Antonio Alatorre. Mexico, DF: Fondo de Cultura Económica, 1966.

Bilinkoff, Jodi. *The Avila of Saint Teresa: Religious Reform in a Sixteenth-Century City*. Ithaca, NY: Cornell University Press, 1989.

---

[12] The authoritative *Historia de la Iglesia en España* in five volumes is notably clerical in inspiration and opinion.

Bremond, Henri. *Histoire littéraire du sentiment religieux en France. Vol. 2: L'invasion mystique, (1590–1620)*. Paris: Bloud et Gay, 1923.

Christian Jr, William. *Local Religion in Sixteenth-Century Spain*. Princeton: Princeton University Press, 1981.

Deacon, Philip. "Early Enlightenment and the Hispanic World." *Eighteenth-Century Studies* 37.1 (2003): 129–40.

Domínguez Ortiz, Antonio. *The Golden Age of Spain 1516–1659*. Trans. James Casey. London: Weidenfeld & Nicolson, 1971.

Eire, Carlos M. *From Madrid to Purgatory: The Art and Craft of Dying in Sixteenth-Century Spain*. Cambridge: Cambridge University Press, 1995.

Elliott, John H. *Imperial Spain 1496–1716*. Harmondsworth: Penguin, 1970.

Fayard, Janine. *Les membres du Conseil de Castille à l'époque moderne (1621–1746)*. Geneva: Librairie Droz, 1979.

Foster, Marc R. *Catholic Revival in the Age of the Baroque: Religious Identity in Southwest Germany, 1550–1750*. Cambridge: Cambridge University Press, 2001.

Friedrich, Carl J. *The Age of the Baroque: 1610–1660*. New York: Harper & Row, 1952.

Gascoigne, John. "A Reappraisal of the Role of the Universities in the Scientific Revolution." *Reappraisals of the Scientific Revolution*. Ed. David Lindberg and Robert Westman. Cambridge: Cambridge University Press, 1990. 207–260.

Gentilcore, David. "'Adapt Yourselves to the People's Capabilities': Missionary Strategies, Methods and Impact in the Kingdom of Naples, 1600–1800." *Journal of Ecclesiastical History* 45.2 (1994): 269–96.

Gil Fernández, Luis. *Panorama social del humanismo español (1500–1800)*. Madrid: Alhambra, 1981.

Green, Otis H. *Spain and the Western Tradition: The Castilian Mind in Literature from "El Cid" to Calderón*. 4 vols. Madison: University of Wisconsin, 1963–1966.

Kamen, Henry. *Spain in the Later Seventeenth Century, 1665–1700*. London: Longman, 1980.

———. *The Phoenix and the Flame: Catalonia and the Counter Reformation*. London and New Haven, CT: Yale University Press, 1993.

———. *The Spanish Inquisition: A Historical Revision*. London and New Haven, CT: Yale University Press 1998.

———. *Empire: How Spain Became a World Power 1492–1763*. New York, NY: HarperCollins, 2003.

Machado, Antonio. "Unamuno." *La Guerra. Escritos: 1936–1939*. Ed. Julio Rodríguez Puértolas and Gerardo Pérez Herrero. Madrid: Emiliano Escolar Editor, 1983. 213–15.

Maeztu, Ramiro de. *Defensa de la hispanidad*. Madrid: s.n., 1934.

Maravall, José Antonio. *La cultura del Barroco*. Barcelona: Ariel, 1983.

Menéndez Pidal, Ramón. *Idea imperial de Carlos V*. Madrid: Espasa, 1940.

Mestre, Antonio. "Religión y cultura en el siglo XVIII." *Historia de la Iglesia en España*. Dir. Ricardo García-Villoslada. 5 vols. Madrid: Biblioteca de Autores Cristianos, 1980. 4: 583–745.

Nalle, Sara T. *God in La Mancha: Religion, Reform and the People of Cuenca 1500–1650*. Baltimore, MD: Johns Hopkins University Press, 1992. The Library of Iberian Resources Online. 30 July 2012. <http://libro.uca.edu/nalle/gmc.htm>.

Núñez Beltrán, Miguel Ángel. *La oratoria sagrada de la época del Barroco. Doctrina, cultura y actitud ante la vida de los sermones sevillanos del siglo XVII*. Seville: Universidad de Sevilla, 1997.

Pardo Tomás, José. *Ciencia y censura. La Inquisición española y los libros científicos en los siglos XVI y XVII*. Madrid: Consejo Superior de Investigaciones Científicas, 1991.

Pérez Magallón, Jesús. *Construyendo la modernidad: la cultura española en el tiempo de los novatores (1675–1725)*. Madrid: Consejo Superior de Investigaciones Científicas, 2002.

Pettegree, Andrew. *The Book in the Renaissance*. London and New Haven: Yale University Press, 2010.

Poska, Allyson M. *Regulating the People: The Catholic Reformation in Seventeenth-Century Spain*. Leiden, Boston and Cologne: Brill, 1998.

Ruiz, Teófilo. *Spanish Society, 1400–1600*. London: Longman, 2001.

Saugnieux, Joël. *Les Jansénistes et la renouveau de la prédication dans l'Espagne de la seconde moitié du 18e siècle*. Lyon: Presses Universitaires de Lyon, 1976.

Tapié, Victor-Lucien. *The Age of Grandeur: Baroque Art and Architecture*. 2nd ed. Trans. A. Ross Williamson. New York, NY: Praeger, 1966.

Tellechea, José Ignacio. "Molinos y el quietismo español." *Historia de la Iglesia en España*. Dir. Ricardo García-Villoslada. 5 vols. Madrid: Biblioteca de Autores Cristianos, 1980. 4: 478–523.

Vries de Heekelingen, H. de. *Correspondance de Bonaventura Vulcanius pendant son séjour à Cologne, Genève et Bâle (1573–1577)*. The Hague: M. Nijhoff, 1923.

Weinstein, Donald, and Rudolph M. Bell. *Saints and Society: The Two Worlds of Christendom, 1000–1700*. Chicago: The University of Chicago Press, 1982.

Chapter 6

The Baroque and the Influence of the Spanish Monarchy in Europe (1580–1648)[1]

José Javier Ruiz Ibáñez

For Oscar Mazín

Introduction

Historiographically, it is a commonplace to consider that the final decades of the sixteenth century and at least the early decades of the seventeenth century marked the height of the expansion and dissemination of Spanish culture and religion. Nevertheless, there are not too many overviews on the effect that this influx had on the areas in proximity to the dominions of the King of Spain (Hillgarth, Part II; Ruiz Ibáñez, *Vecindades*). Based on this observation, it is necessary to reflect whether and to what extent this phenomenon caused, enabled, or restricted the political dominance of the King of Spain, in which ways, and within which timeframe.

During his visit to the court of Philip II to report on his diplomatic activities in Flanders and France, Antonio de Frías Salazar drafted an extensive report summarising the political means that, in his opinion, might be implemented by the Catholic King in order to establish his power both in the Low Countries, recently occupied by Farnese, and in France, where the Spanish ministers were seeking mechanisms to coordinate with the numerous powers of the League rebelling against Henry IV (Vázquez de Prada 418). Like so many others serving the Spanish sovereign (Vázquez 3: 96), Frías assessed the development of Catholicism in these territories with reference to the situation in Spain and

---

[1]   This work has been undertaken within the context of the research project "Hispanophilia, The Political Influence of the Spanish Monarchy (II): Policies of Prestige, Migration and Representation of Hegemony (1560–1650)," Ministry of Science and Innovation (Spain), HAR2011-29859-C02-01.

114 *The Transatlantic Hispanic Baroque*

with the forms of devotion existing in the Peninsula. On the Low Countries, he wrote:

> Something that I have seen in these countries of your Highness which has truly shocked me are the strange temples and modest clergymen who pass through the streets to the sick without any ceremony so that ordinarily the Blessed Sacrament is transported by the cleric only accompanied by a boy with a lantern, for there are no brotherhoods of the Blessed Sacrament in the parishes. (Archivo)

From his experience in Rouen (Benedict ch. 8), Frías knew that the Duke of Mayenne, *lieutenant général* of France through the agency of the Catholic League, had bestowed upon such brotherhoods goods that had been confiscated from the Protestants (Ruiz Ibáñez and Sabatini 676–80):

> something that could equally be done in Flanders to favour those who accompany so that along this path devotion and reverence might grow for the Blessed Sacrament, the lack of which in those parts I see as the main cause of all their painful endeavours. (Archivo)

This report clearly illustrates the difficulty in understanding the Catholic mobilisation north of the Pyrenees, if this was not carried out in accordance with Spanish ways. At the same time, Frías Salazar himself identified in Rouen the advent of Iberian devotional practices, due to the action of agents (Ruiz Ibáñez and Sabatini) who were certain to have had such an impact subsequently, as in the case of Jean de Brétigny de Quintanadueñas (Casado Alonso; Morgain, *Pierre* ch. 1). Indeed, figures such as he were to be at the centre of the Catholic renewal embarked upon with devotion after 1598, a reform that coincided with the Baroque and which adopted much from the Iberian practice of religion. The question is, to what extent was this reception during peacetime an expression of the political success of the Monarchy or palpable proof of its failure?

1570–1598: Catholic Rebellion and Spanish Religion

The second half of the sixteenth century saw the Crusade being revived as a very important military exercise given the series of conflicts with the Ottoman Empire which linked combat in the Mediterranean with the outbreak of the Long War between the Emperor and the Sultan in 1596 (Dupront). The renewal of the conflict with the Turks coincided and overlapped with the development of a new kind of belligerence in Western Europe – borne out of the rulers' desire to impose the principle of *cuius regio, eius religio* in their own territories, thus redefining the balance of power in their favour (Sacerdoti ch. 1 and 2) – which led to the emergence of political and religious rebelliousness that took the form of numerous civil wars. The mutual allegiance between subject and sovereign, fairly sound in the first half of the century, now seemed to have become extremely fragile. The legitimacy of the monarch was cast into doubt and even contested by both Protestants (in England, Scotland, the Low Countries and France) and Catholics (in France, Ireland and England) (Souriac and Souriac; Kaiser; Figeac; Le Roux, *Les Guerres*). Just as Mary, Queen of Scots, was deposed because of her practice of the "old religion," two French sovereigns (Henry III and Henry IV) were assassinated by religious fanatics who reproached their kings for their lack of Catholic zeal (Greengrass; Le Roux, *1er août*; Cottret).

This scenario of strife was central to the growth of religion, as may be seen in the predominantly Catholic territories where there was the perception of being a world under threat and attack in which co-religionists were pursued and tormented from Japan to England or the Low Countries (Dillon, El Kenz, Arblaster). Furthermore, the crisis of prestige of the monarchies seen to be promoters of or compliant with the Protestant Reformation meant that, with the Catholic insurgency, there were attempts to replace the kings themselves with a foreign monarch capable of sustaining the Faith. The support, actual or hoped for, of the King of Spain's forces for such rebellion caused him to be identified among parts of the Catholic world as the leader of a universal plan and the Catholicism developed in his territories as a sure way of re-establishing religious vitality.

This does not mean to say that there was a direct mimesis between Spanish Catholicism and the Catholicism that the Catholic rebels throughout the Continent were seeking to develop. The militant affirmation of a suffering church, which could immediately become a faith of expansion, was seen as a reaffirmation of the cult linked with a global understanding of its protection, promotion and safeguarding. Two areas of tension, which had been widely developed since the middle of the century, coincided at this point. On the one hand, a Catholic response, which might be considered as both *popular* (with all the reservations that come with this term) and Pre-Tridentine,[2] and on the other the Catholic Reformation which, promoted by the Reformist clergy, sought to define both the dogma and, with the same enthusiasm, the way in which it should be developed (Po-Chia Hsia, *The World* ch. 1–4). Of course, tensions occurred when it came to uniting these two elements, which could be contradictory and whose cultural roots did not always coincide. Nevertheless, the success of the dissemination of the new idea of Catholicism throughout this century was notable. The reasons for this may be found in the fact that both arguments,

---

[2]   There is a debate, which there is no room to develop here, concerning lay people and the significance of the Catholic insurgency in these decades. See Wanegffelen, Ramsey, Judith Pollmann, "Countering" 83–120, and "Catholics and Community."

116 *The Transatlantic Hispanic Baroque*

the Pre-Tridentine reaction and the project-mongering of the Council, took shape in the form of a common political action in defence of the traditional faith against attack both from political powers and from denominational rivals. After all, the theological subtleties of the Council did not have to be developed immediately and, truth be told, the means were not available to do so in any event. Moreover, we should not forget that the very existence of such an impetus was neither wholly accepted nor fully implemented in any Catholic territory in the following century (Fernández Terricabras, "Éxitos y fracasos"). Nonetheless, it did serve as a symbolic source of legitimacy for the Catholic reaction rather than as a tangible reality for immediate development, at least for the majority of the population involved. In his book of 1596, *La Bellone Belgica*, Hendrick de Wachtendonck, a leading figure from Mechelen, heavily involved in the restoration of Catholicism and in its defence in Flanders, stated that Catholics could rely on the saints and the Pope, whereas Protestantism had only brought to the Low Countries division, conflict, martyrs and war (Ruiz Ibáñez, "La Guerra Cristiana"). This was not a subtle theological speech, but it sufficed to define who was following the Old Faith and persevering with that of their fathers. Although his book contained strong Irenicist statements, the final point was a clear and united Catholic reaction and neo-Tacitism: the charisma of the king, of a Catholic king, was what would bring order to a confessional society.[3]

To the despair of papal diplomacy (Hortal Muñoz), the continental geopolitical balance bestowed on the Spanish Monarchy a new form of leadership and made of its actions exemplary politics by religion. The major role played by the King of Spain in protecting Catholics allowed his allies to argue the idea of the *truly* Christian monarch by connecting his foreign policy and his domestic religious reforms. Naturally, this argument was only fully accepted in its entirety by the most radical of those who supported a common international Catholic policy and who were prepared to subordinate local interests or traditional claims to a large policy whose indisputable leader seemed to be the son of Charles V (see Ruiz Ibáñez, "Inventar"; "Percepciones"). Many of these radicals, together with others of a more moderate stance, defeated in the various wars in which they were involved in their own countries in defence of the old faith, ended up taking refuge in the territories of Philip II, seeking to immerse themselves within the programme for the integration of religious exiles which grew to unprecedented levels until then from the 1580s (see Pérez Tostado and Ruiz Ibáñez). Although the dissemination of the image of Philip II as "Abraham, a father of many nations," was always limited and kept in check in the countries of origin, this was not so when his actions were considered the appropriate model for the effective implementation of the new Catholicism.

---

[3] A similar development was taking place in France, see Crouzet, *Les guerriers de Dieu* II ch. 20.

The existence of a Spanish reform (Fernández Terricabras, *Felipe II*), which should not be confused with Roman Catholicism in general, does not mean that its representation was directly based on what had happened in the Iberian Peninsula as one model among many (Tallon part II; see Dubet and Ruiz Ibáñez). Rather, for the emerging European Catholicism, the positive affirmation of the existence of an ideal environment was more important than the direct mimesis of reality on which such an affirmation was founded. Consequently, it is not difficult to detect the spreading of practices, religious expressions, institutional frameworks or forms of devotion and patronage of Iberian origin into European territories (France, the Low Countries, England, Central Europe and, to a lesser extent, Italy) (see Brunet) before the peaceful years of 1598–1604. To say that this was simply the transposition of the peninsular religion is not enough, since in each area such conceptions and practices conveyed or established local tendencies which were born of internal development into certain home-grown Catholicisms whose mobilisation still had much of the Late Middle Ages in their make-up.

The report by Antonio de Frías shows that, in the eyes of a Catholic brought up in the Iberian world, the religious practices of his potential allies were barbaric and archaic. However, the Spanish diplomat could not fail to acknowledge the commitment of his allies to the defence of the Faith and the enormous political potential. Put simply, all of these energies had to be directed in a specific direction and under the appropriate leadership – precisely what was about to happen with the effective implementation of the Counter-Reformation, except that this leadership was not going to be that of the King of Spain.

Post-1598: New Religious Expressions and Royal Power

The turn of the century brought about a major change in scenario. Relations between the Spanish Monarchy and the Papacy improved and the court of Madrid identified increasingly with the papal version of the Counter-Reformation (Martínez Millán, "La crisis"; "La transformación"). Meanwhile, the return to the international scene of France as a Catholic power enabled the Roman See to detach itself from the protection of Spain. We should not forget either that religion in Spain itself was also in the process of change from the end of the sixteenth century and on into the beginning of the next century. Also, in Europe, the strengthening of the power of the sovereigns that had led to the defeat of the Catholic insurgency brought about the redefinition of the very meaning of that power. Incapable of following through, some of the Catholic opposition movements attempted, with greater or lesser success, to adjust to the new situation and to act from within their own countries (the *appellants* in England, the *dévots* in France or the Catholics themselves in the United Provinces in spite

118   *The Transatlantic Hispanic Baroque*

of their political marginalisation).[4] This change in position constituted a radical transformation, which involved renouncing a more immanentist, belligerent religion (Descimon and Ruiz Ibáñez 21–36), and the forms of universalism, in favour of a royal Catholicism, which would incorporate religion into the state. "Hispanophilia" could no longer mean the acceptance of the political leadership of the Catholic King, but the adoption of those elements which had potential for activating the religious re-conquest of each particular territory, but under the leadership of the local sovereign (see *Table ronde*). The various different European Catholicisms were becoming increasingly politically autonomous and universalism was now becoming a dual relationship between these sovereigns and the Pope.

The affirmation of the Catholicism of the Counter-Reformation in the various European settings shows the influence of practices that were strengthening control and discipline over society itself (Po-Chia Hsia, 'Disciplina social'). This reaffirmation of social order, as a value in itself, coincided with the political consolidation of the various Monarchies, which ended up discarding the subversive nature of Catholicism. The processes of conversion to the old religion were no longer solely or predominantly focused on the reformed or Islamic population, but on the Catholic masses themselves, those who had remained more or less distanced from the theological content of Trent, but who had strengthened their conviction of loyalty to a Catholicism that they saw as being under attack. Both in the territories in which they were in the majority (France, Catholic Low Countries) and in those in which they were a persecuted denomination (England, Valtellina, parts of the Empire) or where religion went hand in hand with military conquest (Bohemia), the aim was to convert them into Catholics of the Counter-Reformation, thus setting in motion a discipline which would not necessarily be alien to the local customs and which would enjoy long-lasting success. The urgency to develop such a vast project made use of successful experiences, in Italy and the Iberian Peninsula, validated by the Council and soon endorsed by the canonisations of the seventeenth century. The influence of this *Spanish model* should certainly not be underestimated in terms of the justification, mobilisation and the raising of the prestige of the transition towards a new religious form which grew extremely quickly, due precisely to its adaptability to the multiple scenarios. Just as in America, each society took those elements they were interested in up to the point where they had made them their own and could declare, as would the France of Louis XIV, that it was precisely

---

[4]   There is an extensive bibliography on the forms of reconstruction, to a greater or lesser degree effective, of the dissident Catholic communities at the end of the Wars of Religion and their connection with international politics. This bibliography, however, cannot be reproduced here; for an introduction to this central theme, which should be read as a global movement, see Diefendorf; Tutino; Parker.

on their land that elements which on the Iberian Peninsula had merely been outlined were developed in a coherent way (Schaub; Sabatier and Torrione).

Faced with the disorder of the Reformation and the Catholic reaction itself at the end of the sixteenth century, the new religion placed a particular emphasis on demonstrating that what was needed was a society that was ordered precisely by religious deeds that justified the hierarchies, but which, at the same time, served to bind together and integrate its elements. In the Catholic Low Countries, the recovery, and redefinition, of the urban ritual (Thøfner part III) insisted on the municipal corporation as an organic whole dominated by a legitimate and paternal political power which could find justification only in its own faith and which had resulted in the previous purge of the populations suspected of heresy (Junot; Goosens, *Inquisitions* 1: ch. 5); and we should not forget that this was a tendency also present in the major French cities (Schneider; Amalou ch. 6–8). The feasts and processions of a religious nature (see Thomas), interrupted by the Reformation, now reappeared in greater splendour. This signified a clear, symbolic re-occupation of the urban space, which also extended to rural areas through the promotion of pilgrimages to sanctuaries dedicated to the Virgin Mary. The reception of new orders in turn allowed for a new form of devotion to flourish under the direct control of the Church. The return of the Jesuits and the selection of the population accompanying the Farnese re-conquest is paradigmatic (Soen), but so, too, was the attention paid to contemplative orders such as the Carthusians. The same may be said of the reception and undeniable success of the Discalced Carmelites and of the new forms of devotion (to St Joseph and, after 1624, to St Teresa of Jesus) involved here. It was not so much a case of a Catholic re-conquest, but rather the reconstruction and renovation of the Catholic world, in which the local elite were the major protagonists in close collaboration with the sovereign power (Junot 111–12; Lottin and Guignet ch. 7). At the same time there was probably much popular feeling concerning such a reconstruction based on the definition of the urban community, as can be seen from the involvement of the local bourgeoisie in the defence of the Monarchy in the following decade (Herrero Sánchez and Ruiz Ibáñez 286–96).

This was a case of a coherent policy of the Archduke's government (1598–1621) in the Low Countries (Pollmann, *Catholic Identity* ch. 6), but was not only limited to the action of a power that was seeking to capitalise on its legitimacy following the years of revolt. Urban history shows how the different native elites were being defined through the implementation of their firm support for the new forms of devotion, for the new orders, for the persecution of dissidence and/or for the projection of the new religion through the stimulus for religious celebrations or the training of boys and girls (see Lottin, *Lille Citadelle*; Être et croire). The success and relatively swift dissemination among the population of these confessional mutations seems to prove that the elements of popularisation of the same (repression, dissemination, participation, mimesis and multiplication) were perfectly suited to the religious needs of a large part of the population, who assimilated them with notable speed (re)identifying in them the sense of their old practices largely due to the militancy inherited from the military conflict with the "rebels," now seen, first and foremost, as "heretics."

It should not be forgotten that the Catholic Low Countries were a true testing ground, as they had an additional part of the population involved in religious reform in the form of the Catholic refugees from England, Ireland, Scotland, the United Provinces or even France itself, who sought to apply in their land of exile the confessional ideal that they had not been able to put into practice in their places of origin (Goosens, "Les Pays-Bas"; Janssen, "Quo Vadis?"; Pérez Tostado and Ruiz Ibáñez; Pollmann, *Catholic Identity* 150). In many cases, these agents only spent part of their career in their new land and, therefore, acted as instruments of cultural circulation playing a decisive role in the importing of worship, relics and practices. Certainly, they were not the only ones to participate by such mobility in the forming of a global Baroque cosmos. The Spanish and Italian ministers who held posts at that time in Flanders, the nuns who were setting up foundations (Brunet), the Jesuits, the members of the Nunciature, the very soldiers who formed the Flemish army, in addition to the persistence, albeit limited, of a Luso-Hispanic community in Antwerp and Bruges, triggered the favourable reception of the forms and content that we consider as Baroque (Casado Alonso). For the first decade of the seventeenth century, Flemish Baroque had become a true paradigm of cultural export: with the dissemination of Rubens prints and of the many books coming off the printing presses, the environment that had essentially been one of reception and recovery now became an exemplary place for the emission of religion.

The case of France bears significant similarities to that of Flanders, but there are also differences. The inheritance of the radical *ligueur* Catholicism and the outright condemnation of the most radical forms of *espagnolisation* seemed to indicate a marginalisation of the concept of an Iberian political leader at the expense of a royal Catholicism personified by Henry IV and the 'good French' (Descimon and Ruiz Ibáñez, Introduction). Nevertheless, the power of the French Catholic movement was much stronger than the easy victory of the King from 1594 onwards seemed to indicate. Hispanophilia now resulted in the acceptance, and the promotion, of the Iberian devotions, integrated, it is true, in the affirmation of loyalty to the devout Christian king as a religious arbitrator. The ties between the *ligueurs* families and the extremely strong French devout movement are clear, but this extends far beyond purely mechanical continuism (Cassan, "Laïcs, Ligue" 159–70; *Le temps des guerres*). This expansion of brotherhoods and the tendency to order society under the authority of the Church, at the same time reinforcing the authority of the bishops and the Jesuits, channelled the religious emotions that had presided over the kingdom at least since the 1570s (Crouzet, "Un imaginaire"). Faced with the disorder of the white processions that burst on to the political-religious scene of France decades earlier, or of the ritual celebrations of the League, the focus was now on reaffirming the authority of the devout Christian king. The Jesuits themselves, following their return to the parliament district of Paris from where they had been expelled in 1594, and their rapid integration into French academic and political life (Blet), insisted on affirming their allegiance to the local monarchy (Nelson ch. 3 and 5), even joining parliament in its condemnation in 1610 of the most compromising aspects of the work by Juan de Mariana by order of General Aquaviva on 6 July 1610, did not support the proposals condemned by the decree of the Parliament of Paris (see Gabriel) and insisted on the Catholic and French nature of their celebrations of the canonisation of Ignatius of Loyola and Francisco Javier (Cassan, "Les fêtes"). This was a general movement: the evolution of the Franciscans or the reform of the Capuchins had gone from the autonomy of the League to joining the construction of a royal state (Armstrong; Pierre ch. 8)—as long as the latter had a devout king, a figure that Louis XIII would personify to perfection (Morgain, "L'Église").

This process of appropriation of the forms of Iberian origin may also be identified in the reception and expansion of the Discalced Carmelites, thanks to, among others, Bèrulle (Morgain, *Pierre de Bérulle*, Part II), who allowed them to be naturalised and so shed their subversive image (Houdard ch. 2). Following an initial phase dominated by the Spanish nuns, the order was able to be clearly defined as an instrument of devotion of the French royal state. The Carmelites became part of a distinguished movement that would include the reception of the new forms of sanctity (Bergano, ch. 1; Suire ch. 3), the development of missions to the marginalised population and towards the rural communities, well-illustrated in the actions of Vincent de Paul or François de Sales, the establishment of large centres of pilgrimage, the development of conversion projects in New France, the expansion of the worship of the Blessed Sacrament[5] and of eremitism, the generalisation of Marian brotherhoods (Chatéllier), the confirmation of a Monarchy as an example of devotion (Diefendorf; Dillon, "Henri IV"), and the development of the very concept of the Crusade (Sauzet ch. 1–4). As in the case of Flanders, it was not just a question of the actions of an active minority concentrated in the court, but of a widespread movement in which the local elite were actively involved and which succeeded in conveying, within such far more coded devotion and rituality which was controlled by a clergy subjected to the Monarchy, the religious forces exerted by a very significant part of the population.

---

[5]   Something that would have undoubtedly pleased Antonio de Frías, although it involved debates on the opportunity for public exposure—debates that very clearly showed the tensions between the desire to disseminate and the desire to control the forms of dissemination; see Meunier.

The masses, who during the conflict with the Protestants and *politiques* had found a means of expressing their defence of the old faith and the urban ideal, were now finding this in the development of certain forms of religion that were highly ritualised, where collective participation was a means of showing world order and the way in which this was established. As in the Low Countries, in France the Catholic population was the main object of this process of conversion to a Tridentine religion. Once again, the goal was to convert Catholics into *true* Catholics and, to this end, all of the resources of discipline and propaganda, so dear to the Baroque, were made available (Deslandres part II). Generally speaking, the operation was a great success, turning a religion from the Late Middle Ages, and in some cases a humanist religion, into a faith, and a practice, that was openly Baroque, firmly rooted in the very people who would resist the attempts at political modernisation made in France during the next three centuries.

Conclusions

The height of Spanish political influence came prior to the expansion as such of the Baroque and was more a characteristic of the period of Catholic reaction against Protestant expansion (around 1570–1600). It is true that in this mobilisation, the mechanisms of Spanish Catholic affirmation were to be seen, and to be considered as exemplary. In the following decades, the examples of France and Flanders show how the presence of elements pertaining to the Iberian religion is easy to detect: reception of the worshipping of Iberian saints, expansion of the Spanish devotion to the Virgin Mary beyond the borders of Spain, dissemination of Spanish mysticism and a taste for Golden Age literature. However, identifying the Baroque as a means of expansion of Spanish hegemony was not easy at that time, however persistent the accusation this timely reception was merely being an instrument of Spanish design. Nevertheless, the growing significance of the role played by these elements was not in absolute symmetry with that existing in the sixteenth century. At that time, the perception of peninsular religion had been formed more through its idealised representation than through the adoption of a specific, consistent, and thoroughly Iberian programme; now the complete opposite was happening.

Thus, there was a clear paradox: when the influence of Spain on the internal politics of these countries was at its greatest, the reception of the religious forms from the Peninsula (which were claimed to justify this influence) was incomplete and contradictory; and when these forms *were* directly received, their effect was to bar the possibility of influencing these politics effectively. The Spanish elements of the Baroque did not contribute towards enhancing a renewed sense of hispanophilia, but instead constituted the affirmation of the hierarchies

The Baroque and the Influence of the Spanish Monarchy 123

pertaining to the societies to which they applied; hierarchies which, in general, had been reconstructed against Spanish hegemony at the end of the sixteenth century. With its insistence on order and dependence of this on the figure of the king, the Baroque was, in fact, obstructing the mechanisms of rebelliousness that had allowed Spanish hegemony to erode the political foundations of its rivals and to provide Philip II with supporters beyond his borders. The processes of religious discipline confirmed the ordering of the world, denying the people the ability to judge monarchs and establishing a religion in which the sovereign would increasingly occupy the position of intermediary between God and man. If this acted as a central factor in the reaffirmation of obedience under the Spanish Monarchy in Flanders, it did the same in France with royal Catholicism, which put an end in the medium term, and in spite of a series of specific episodes, to the image of leadership that the King of Spain may have enjoyed at different, more radical times.

In short, there is nothing contradictory in the statement that the more present the Iberian cultural influence, rooted on its own reality, the less feasible was the possibility of political intervention, since precisely the elements of Spanish Catholicism that had been identified and incorporated across the length and breadth of Europe had lost their Spanish political meaning. Their very naturalisation enabled such reception, at the time when the affirmation of contributing to an ordered society that they brought with them involved the denial of the political universalism on which Spanish hegemony had been founded.

Bibliography

Amalou, Thierry. *Le Lys et la Mitre. Loyalisme monarchique et pouvoir épiscopal pendant les Guerres de Religion*. París: Éditions du Comité des travaux historiques et scientifiques, 2007.

Arblaster, Paul. *Antwerp & the World. Richard Vestegan and the International Culture of Catholic Reformation*. Leuven: Leuven University Press, 2004.

Archivo General de Simancas, Valladolid. Ek (Estado-Francia) 1579, No. 80, [September?] 1591, Antonio de Frías Salazar a Felipe II.

Armstrong, Megan C. *The Politics of Piety: Franciscan Preachers during the Wars of Religion, 1560–1600*. Rochester, NY: University of Rochester Press, 2004.

Benedict, Philip. *Rouen during the Wars of Religion*. Cambridge, London and New York: Cambridge University Press, 1981.

Bergano, Mino. *La science des saints. Le discours mystique au XVIIe siècle en France*. Grenoble: Jérôme Milon, 1992.

Blet, Pierre. "Les jésuites et les libertés gallicanes." *Archivum Historicum Societatis Iesu* 24 (1995): 165–88.

Brunet, Serge. "¿Una religiosidad hispánica en Francia y en Europa en los siglos XVI y XVII?" *Las vecindades de las Monarquías Ibéricas.* Ed. José Javier Ruiz Ibáñez. Madrid: Fondo de Cultura Económica, 2013. 375–402.

Casado Alonso, Hilario. "El papel de las colonias mercantiles castellanas en el imperio hispánico (siglos XV y XVI)." *Las vecindades de las Monarquías Ibéricas.* Ed. José Javier Ruiz Ibáñez. Madrid: Fondo de Cultura Económica, 2013. 355–74.

Cassan, Michel. "Laïcs, Ligue et réforme catholique à Limoges." *Histoire, Économie & Société* 10.2 (1991): 159–75.

———. *Le temps des guerres de Religion. Le cas du Limousin (vers 1530–vers 1630).* Paris: Publisud, 1996.

———. "Les fêtes de la canonisation d'Ignace de Loyola et de François Xavier dans la province d'Aquitaine (1622)." *Les Cérémonies extraordinaires du catholicisme baroque.* Ed. Bernard Dompnier. Clermont-Ferrand: Presses Universitaires Blaise-Pascal, 2009. 459–76.

Chatéllier, Louis. *L'Europe des dévots.* Paris: Flammarion, 1987.

Cottret, Monique. *Tuer le tyran?: le tyrannicide dans l'Europe moderne.* Paris: Fayard, 2009.

Crouzet, Denis. *Les guerriers de Dieu: la violence au temps des troubles de Religion (vers 152–vers 1610).* 2 vols. Seyssel: Champ Vallon, [1990].

———. "Un imaginaire au travail. Le catholicisme militant pendant les guerres de Religion." *Religion et confession. Un bilan franco-allemand sur l'époque moderne (XVIe–XVIIIe siècles).* Ed. Philippe Büttgen and Christophe Duhamelle. Paris: Maison des Sciences de l'Homme, 2010. 541–58.

Descimon, Robert and José Javier Ruiz Ibáñez. *Les ligueurs de l'exil: Le refuge catholique français après 1594.* Seyssel: Champ Vallon, 2005.

Deslandres, Dominique. *Croire et faire croire. Les missions françaises au XVIIe siècle.* Paris: Fayard, 2003.

Diefendorf, Barbara. "Entre la Ligue et les dévots: les ultra-catholiques français face à la paix de Vervins." *Le traité de Vervins.* Ed. Jean François Labourdette, Jean-Pierre Poussou and Marie-Catherine Vignal. Paris: Presses de l'Université Paris-Sorbonne, 2000. 431–53.

Dillon, Anne. *The Construction of Martyrdom in the English Catholic Community, 1535–1603.* Aldershot: Ashgate, 2002.

———. "Henri IV, the *Dévots* and the Making of a French Catholic Reformation." *Politics and Religion in Early Bourbon France.* Ed. Alison Forrestal and Eric Nelson. New York: Palgrave Macmillan, 2009. 157–79.

Dompnier, Bernard, ed. *Les cérémonies extraordinaires du catholicisme baroque.* Clermont-Ferrand: Presses Universitaires Blaise-Pascal, 2009.

Dubet, Anne and José Javier Ruiz Ibáñez, eds. *Las monarquías española y francesa. ¿Dos modelos políticos?* Madrid: Casa de Velázquez, 2010.

Dupront, Alphonse. *Le mythe de croisade.* 4 vols. Paris: Gallimard, 1997.

El Kenz, David. "Les victimes catholiques au temps des guerres de Religion: la sacralisation du prêtre." *Les victimes des oubliées de l'histoire?* Ed. Benoît Garnot. Rennes: Presses Universitaires de Rennes, 2001. 191–9.

Fernández Terricabras, Ignasi. *Felipe II y el clero secular: la aplicación del concilio de Trento.* Madrid: Sociedad Estatal para la Conmemoración de los Centenarios de Felipe II y Carlos V, 2000.

———. "Exitos y fracasos de la Reforma católica. Francia y España (siglos XVI–XVII)." *Manuscrits. Revista d'història moderna* 25 (2007): 129–56.

Figeac, Michel, ed. *Les affrontements religieux en Europe. Du débout du XVIe siècle au milieu du XVIIe siècle.* Paris: Sedes, 2008.

Gabriel, Frédéric. "An Tyrannum opprimere fas sit? Construction d'un lieu commun: la réception française du *De Rege et regis institutione* de Juan de Mariana (Tolède, 1599)." *Les Antijésuites: discours, figures et lieux de l'antijésuitisme* à l'époque moderne. Ed. Pierre-Antoine Fabre and Catherine Maire. Rennes: Presses Universitaires de Rennes and Société d'Histoire et d'Archéologie de Bretagne, 2010. 241–64.

Goosens, Aline. *Les Inquisitions modernes dans les Pays-Bas méridionaux, 1520–1633.* 2 vols. Brussels: Université de Bruxelles, 1997.

———. "Les Pays-Bas méridionaux, refuge politique et religieux à l'époque du traité de Vervins (1590–1598)." *Le traité de Vervins.* Ed. Jean François Labourdette, Jean-Pierre Poussou and Marie-Catherine Vignal. Paris: Presses de l'Université Paris-Sorbonne, 2000. 203–233.

Greengrass, Marc. "Regicide, Martyrs and Monarchical Authority in France in the Wars of Religion." *Murder and Monarchy. Regicide in European History, 1300–1800.* Ed. Robert von Friedeburg. New York: Palgrave Macmillan, 2004. 176–92.

Herrero Sánchez, Manuel and José Javier Ruiz Ibáñez. "Defender la patria y defender la religión: las milicias urbanas en los Países Bajos Españoles, 1580–1700." *Las milicias del rey de España. Política, sociedad e identidad en las monarquías ibéricas.* Ed. José Javier Ruiz Ibáñez. Madrid: Fondo de Cultura Económica, 2009. 268–96.

Hillgarth, Jocelyn N. *The Mirror of Spain, 1500–1700: The Formation of a Myth.* Ann Arbor: University of Michigan Press, 2000.

Hortal Muñoz, José Eloy. "La lucha contra la *Monarchia Universalis* de Felipe II: la modificación de la política de la santa sede en Flandes y Francia respecto a la Monarquía Hispana a finales del siglo XVI." *Hispania* 71.237 (2011): 65–86.

Houdard, Sophie. *Les invasions mystiques. Spiritualités, hétérodoxies et censures au début de l'époque moderne.* Paris: Les Belles lettres, 2008.

Janssen, Geert H. "Quo Vadis? Catholic Perceptions of Flight and the Revolt of the Low Countries, 1566–1609." *Renaissance Quarterly* 64.2 (2011): 472–99.

Junot, Yves. *Les bourgeois de Valenciennes. Autonomie d'une élite dans la ville (1500–1630).* Villeneuve d'Ascq: Presses Universitaires du Septentrion, 2009.

Kaiser, Wolgang, ed. *L'Europe en conflits. Les affrontements religieux et la genèse de l'Europe moderne, vers 1500–vers 1650*. Rennes: Presses Universitaires de Rennes, 2008.

Le Roux, Nicolas. *1er août 1589. Un régicide au nom de Dieu. L'assassinat d'Henri III*. Paris: Gallimard, 2006.

———. *Les Guerres de religion, 1559–1629*. Paris: Belin 2009.

Lottin, Alain. *Lille Citadelle de la Contre-Réforme (1598–1668)*. Dunkirk: Les éditions des Beffrois, 1984.

———. *Être et croire à Lille et en Flandre XVIe–XVIIIe siècle*. Arras: Artois Presses Université, 2000.

———, and Philippe Guignet. *Histoire des provinces françaises du Nord de Charles Quint à la Révolution française*. Arras: Artois Presses Université, 2006.

Martínez Millán, José. "La crisis del 'partido castellano' y la transformación de la Monarquía Hispana en el cambio de reinado de Felipe II a Felipe III." *Cuadernos de Historia Moderna. Anejos* 2 (2003): 11–38.

———. "La transformación del paradigma 'católico hispano' en el 'católico romano' durante la época del Quijote." *La orden de San Juan en tiempos del Quijote*. Ed. Francisco Ruiz Gómez and Jesús Molero García. Toledo: Universidad de Castilla la Mancha, 2010. 85–126.

Meunier, Alexis. "Nécessités publiques 'dévotion des peuples': les polémiques autour de l'exposition fréquente du Saint-Sacrament." *Les Cérémonies extraordinaires du catholicisme baroque*. Ed. Bernard Dompnier. Clermont-Ferrand: Presses Universitaires Blaise-Pascal, 2009. 63–78.

Morgain, Stéphane-Marie. *Pierre de Bérulle et les Carmélites de France*. Paris: Cerf, 1995.

———. "L'Église est-elle dans l'État ou L'État est-il dans L'Église? La révolution des années 1615." *Pierre d'angle* 5 (1999): 73–86.

Nelson, Eric. *The Jesuits and the Monarchy: Catholic Reform and Political Authority in France (1590–1615)*. Aldershot, Burlington and Rome: Ashgate and Institutum Historicum Societatis Iesu, 2005.

Parker, Charles H. *Faith On The Margins: Catholics and Catholicism in the Dutch Golden Age*. Cambridge: Harvard University Press, 2008.

Pérez Tostado, Igor and José Javier Ruiz Ibáñez, eds. *Los exiliados del rey de España*. Madrid: Fondo de Cultura Económica, 2013.

Pierre, Benoist. *La bure et le sceptre: la congrégation des Feuillants dans l'affirmation des États et des pouvoirs princiers (vers 1560–vers 1660)*. Paris: Publications de la Sorbonne, 2006.

Po-Chia Hsia, Ronald. *The World of Catholic Renewal, 1540–1770*. Cambridge: Cambridge University Press, 2005.

———. "Disciplina social y catolicismo en la Europa de los siglos XVI y XVII." *Manuscrits: Revista d'història moderna* 25 (2007): 29–43.

Pollmann, Judith. "Countering the Reformation in France and the Netherlands: Clerical leadership and Catholic Violence, 1560–1585." *Past and Present* 190 (2006): 83–120, 188–95.

———. "Catholics and Community in the Revolt of the Netherlands." *Living with Religious Diversity in Early-Modern Europe*. Ed. C. Scott Dixon, Dagmar Freist and Mark Greengrass. Farnham and Burlington: Ashgate, 2009. 183–202.

———. *Catholic Identity and the Revolt of the Netherlands, 1520–1635*. Oxford: Oxford University Press, 2011.

Ramsey, Ann W. *Liturgy, Politics, and Salvation. The Catholic League in Paris and the Nature of Catholic Reform 1540–1630*. Rochester, NY: University of Rochester Press, 1999.

Ruiz Ibáñez, José Javier. "La Guerra Cristiana. Los medios y agentes de la creación de opinión en los Países Bajos Españoles ante la intervención en Francia (1593–1598)." *España y las 17 provincias de los Países Bajos. Una revisión historiográfica*. Ed. Ana Crespo Solana and Manuel Herrero Sánchez. Córdoba: Universidad de Córdoba, 2002. 291–324.

———. "Inventar una monarquía doblemente católica. Los partidarios de Felipe II en Europa y su visión de la hegemonía española." *Estudis. Revista de Historia Moderna* 34 (2008): 87–109.

———. "La percepciones de la Monarquía hispánica como un proyecto universal." *António Vieira, Roma e o universalismo das monarquías portuguesa e española*. Ed. Pedro Cardim and Gaetano Sabatini. Lisbon: Centro de História de Além-Mar; Universidade Nova de Lisboa; Universidade dos Açores, 2011. 29–52.

———, ed. *Las vecindades de las Monarquías Ibéricas*. Madrid: Fondo de Cultura Económica, 2013.

———, and Gaetano Sabatini. "Entre Aguirre y el gran rey. Los discursos de la elección de Felipe II al trono de Francia en 1591." *Hacer historia desde Simancas: Homenaje de José Luis Rodríguez de Diego*. Ed. Alberto Marcos Martín. Valladolid: Junta de Castilla y León, 2011. 661–84.

Sabatier, Gérard and Margarita Torrione, ed. ¿Louis XIV espagnol?. *Madrid et Versailles, images et modèles*. Paris: Centre de Recherche du Châtateau de Versailles and Maison des Sciences de l'Homme, 2009.

Sacerdoti, Gilberto. *Sacrificio e sovranità. Teologia e política nell'Europa di Shakespeare e Bruno*. Turin: Einaudi, 2002.

Sauzet, Robert. *Au Grand Siècle des âmes. Guerre sainte et paix chréstienne en France au XVII siècle*. Paris: Perrin, 2007.

Schaub, Jean-Frédéric. *La France espagnole. Les racines hispaniques de l'absolutisme français*. Paris: Seuil, 2003.

Schneider, Robert A. *Public Life in Toulouse, 1463–1789: From Municipal Republic to Cosmopolitan City.* London and Ithaca, NY: Cornell University Press, 1989.

Soen, Violet. "Reconquista and Reconciliation in the Dutch Revolt: The Campaign of Governor-General Alexander Farnese (1578–1592)." *Journal of Early Modern History* 16.1 (2012): 1–22.

Souriac, Pierre-Jean and René Souriac. *Les affrontements religieux en Europe. Du début du XVIe siècle au milieu du XVIIe siècle: Historiographie, Bibliographie, Enjeux.* Paris: Belin, 2008.

Suire, Éric. *La sainteté française de la Réforme catholique (XVIe–XVIIIe siècles) d'après les textes hagiographiques et les procès de canonisation.* Bordeaux: Presses Universitaires de Bordeaux, 2001.

Table ronde internationale: Mutations de l'hispanophilie entre guerres et réformes religieuses de la Ligue aux dévots (1580–1635). Montpellier: Université Paul Valéry Montpellier III, forthcoming.

Tallon, Alain. *Conscience nationale et sentiment religieux en France au XVIe siècle.* Paris: Presses Universitaires de France, 2002.

Thøfner, Margit. *A Common art: Urban Ceremonial in Antwerp and Brussels During and After the Dutch Revolt.* Zwolle: Waanders Publishers, 2007.

Thomas, Werner. "La fiesta como estrategia de pacificación en los Países Bajos Meridionales, 1598–1621." *El legado de Borgoña. Fiesta y Ceremonial cortesano en la Europa de los Austrias, 1454–1648.* Ed. Krista De Jonge, Bernardo García García and Alicia Esteban Estringana. Madrid: Fundación Carlos de Amberes and Marcial Pons, 2010. 267–304.

Tutino, Stefania. "Thomas Preston and English Catholic Loyalism: Elements of an International Affair." *The Sixteenth Century Journal* 41.1 (2010): 91–111.

Vázquez, Alonso de. *Los sucesos de Flandes y Francia del tiempo de Alejandro Farnese.* 3 vols (LXXII–LXXIV). Madrid: Imprenta de Miguel Ginesta, 1879–1880.

Vázquez de Prada, Valentín. *Felipe II y Francia (1559–1598). Política, religión y razón de Estado.* Pamplona: Eunsa, 2004.

Wanegffelen, Thierry. *Une difficile fidélité, catholiques malgré le concile en France, XVIe–XVIIe siècle.* Paris: Presses Universitaires de France, 1999.

Chapter 7

Rethinking Identity: Crisis of Rule and Reconstruction of Identity in the Monarchy of Spain[1]

Pablo Fernández Albaladejo

'In what way does Spain resemble itself? In no way' (1669)

Whilst recognising that the pamphlet literature of the *ancien regime* largely deserves to be called printed poison, it must at least be accepted that the statement above – the epigraph to the document quoted here (Maura y Gamazo 2: 497-8) – addressed one of the key issues concerning the monarchy from the final third of the seventeenth century and for quite some time afterwards. After criticising those who in one way or another had been involved in the monarchy's government, the pamphlet, in its final conclusion, warned of a crucial change which, initiated earlier, by then was becoming perfectly apparent. The essence of what was being stated was not without significance: *Spain* had simply ceased to be what it had once been. At the beginning of the reign of Charles II, *Spain* was experiencing an identity crisis, an upheaval so profound that the party concerned seemed not to recognise its own reflection.[2]

Within their appropriate context, the aims of such lampooning were perhaps somewhat more limited and the change in identity was invoked in a more instrumental rather than truly analytical, sense. The text was a direct consequence of the plot which between October 1668 and March 1669 had in fact succeeded in stripping the Jesuit Everardo Nithard of his status as *valido* (favourite) of the Regent Mariana of Austria, a dismissal that would immediately

---

[1]   Research project HAR-2011 27562-HIST.

[2]   The document to which we refer, entitled "*Papel de los símiles, hecho para el verdadero conocimiento de los sujetos y divertimiento de los cortesanos en preguntas y respuestas*," was used recently by Pilo ("*Casi todos los hombres*" 257–75); the date of the original manuscript is 12 May 1669. The generic characterisation of the pamphlet as *printed poison* has been taken from Sawyer; it is the usual characterisation seen in the Spanish pamphlet literature of the period.

130   *The Transatlantic Hispanic Baroque*

be followed by his expulsion from the kingdoms of Spain.[3] The noise of the conspiracy scarcely obscured the acknowledgement that something deeper was happening. The crisis formed the backdrop and the stage for a decisive internal political conflict which, ultimately, merely served to ratify the true gravity of the situation. Hence, although the subversive text contained to a sequence of censures predominantly directed against those who had been occupying positions of power in the monarchy, there was, nevertheless, scarcely any criticism of the figures who had pulled the strings of the 1668–1669 conspiracy. In this respect, the authors of the text did not necessarily identify with the members of the conspiracy movement. Far from taking refuge in a partisan position, the writers of the pamphlet were making a criticism *in totum* of the very period in which they were living. They highlighted a state of collective demoralisation and, more specifically, a pessimistic conviction in relation to the pointlessness of the recent changes at the heart of the Spanish monarchy. There is nothing more tempting for the historian than to turn the pamphlet into one more item of proof of the crisis, a possibility that must nevertheless be handled with a certain amount of care. Accustomed to seeing the reign of Charles II as definitive confirmation of a prolonged decadence, we often forget the reactive changes that came about at that very time, reorientations and responses that did not necessarily bear any relation to the constantly-cited economic recovery or to the reception of the culture of a foreign pre-enlightenment. There was also a clear desire to redefine Spain's own identity, to fabricate some assumptions of identity with which to place oneself within a European setting which, rejecting any claim of imperial hegemony, proceeded to be organised according to the grammar of 'balance'. The following pages aim to reconstruct the context in which that attempt to redefine Spain's identity came to light, and to highlight those features which initially articulated that process of a new construction of meaning (see Martucelli, Ch. 4; on the European context, see *Ideology*).

Crisis of Empire

1669 is, to all intents and purposes, a good reference point. That year would bring to a close a decade that had seen crucial changes in the development of the monarchy, including the Peace of the Pyrenees (1659), the death of Philip IV (1665), the political uncertainty brought about by the fragile health of his last son and the establishment of a regency, the rumours that were beginning to circulate surrounding a possible partition of the monarchy, and, finally, the

---

[3] Pilo's work (*"Casi todos los hombres"*) carefully reconstructs the connections and provenance of the key figures involved in the plot, research that has been completed with his recent contribution in collaboration with Juana Salado.

recent independence gained by Portugal (1668). Reading about these events left little room for doubt: the aim of acting as a dynastic imperialist power, to which Philip IV had been committed, attempting to uphold the great "Monarchy of Spain" designed by his grandfather, was now ultimately proving impossible. From abroad, the messages were no less conclusive. The consequences of military defeat could now be seen in the significant field of representation, where a diminished image of the monarchy was beginning to be projected. The Royal House of France emerged as the main instigator of these changes, even though its action seemed to respond to an imperial logic rather than to the assumptions of the balance of powers. Thus Louis XIV expressed in 1662 a not undisguised satisfaction at the way in which the diplomatic incident that had occurred in London in October of the previous year had finally been resolved. Baron de Watteville, the Spanish ambassador, had been reluctant to give right of way to the carriage of the French ambassador on the occasion of welcoming the Swedish ambassador, a decision that immediately led to a dispute between the two parties. The symbolic aspect of the incident was no less significant, as Louis XIV himself would endeavour to point out immediately. The revocation of the ambassador imposed on Philip IV was accompanied in March 1662 by a solemn declaration in the "grand cabinet" of the Louvre, where the *Roy Très Chrétien* announced that "le roi Catholique, avait donné ordre a ses embassadeurs de ceder la préséance aux miens en toutes sortes d'occassions." At the hand of Le Brun, Versailles would include in its décor strategic references to this new situation, in a repeated theme whose inspiration was no other than to artistically display the "Prééminence de la France reconnue par l'Espagne." In his *Mémoires*, Louis XIV would refer to the significance of an event which could be considered as "le plus glorieux" of the monarchy, a tribute, in short, to the monarchy of France which in this way would become "la première de toute la chrétienté" (quoted in Sabatier 309–310; see Álvarez López 131–4, 327–9; Ochoa Brun).

The long debate surrounding this pre-eminence, which had been continuing since the second half of the sixteenth century—and reaching its climax during the 1635–1659 war—thus concluded by proclaiming unilaterally a new hierarchy between the two royal houses.[4] Whilst important, the newly-proclaimed superiority over the Spanish monarchy did not eliminate the imperial *effect* which would still continue to be projected by the Kingdom of Spain north of the Pyrenees. Not without reason, some authors have mentioned the existence of a "Charles V complex" which seemed to govern the offensive movements of

---

[4]   As Ochoa Brun notes, the proclamation intentionally emphasised a loss of pre-eminence decided unilaterally by the French monarch, something which the solution provided for the event itself and the subsequent diplomatic relations do not confirm. For the debate surrounding the pre-eminence, see Haran ch. V and VI; Jover *1635*; Fernández Albaladejo, *La crisis de la Monarquía* 131–46.

Louis XIV during the early stages of his reign, accompanied by a militant anti-Habsburg iconography which would continue up until the death of Charles II (see Zeller 523; Ziegler). All within a political practice which, contradicting the responsibilities corresponding to a so-called imperial power, did not hesitate to subject itself completely to the criteria of the *raison d'État*, as demonstrated by the resounding absence of the French monarch in coming to the defence of Vienna when it was besieged by the Turks (1683).[5] It was the Emperor himself who, after this victorious defence, would end up capitalising on the event by reaffirming the imperial dignity and, consequently, his own House. Minimising the effects of the constitutional limitations imposed in Westphalia by the members of the Empire, Leopold I came to be seen as a true *Carolus redivivus*. In the 1687 almanac celebrating the re-conquest of Buda of the previous year, the hand of Leopold I appeared resting on the globe, thus highlighting his imperial status (Haran 338; Monod 234–42; Ziegler 80).

Underlining this sense of exaltation of imperial power, the Dutch engraver Romeyn de Hooghe composed around that time an imaginary triumphant entry of Leopold I into Brussels with the wish to celebrate the defeat of the Turks in Buda, an engraving in which the Emperor's triumphant air contrasted in this case with the deferential and supplicant attitude of his nephew Charles II. Independently of a symbolic request for refuge against the offensives being launched by Louis XIV against those territories since the War of Devolution, Hooghe illustrated to what extent the pre-eminence between the two branches of the House had ceased to reside in the Spanish complex, passing into the hands of the cadet branch.[6] This new relationship between the two branches emerged within a context in which large cracks were starting to appear in the inter-dynastic solidarity, and were already showing during the Thirty Years' War. In 1646, the Count of Peñaranda, ambassador plenipotentiary at the Münster congress, had written to the governor of the Spanish Low Countries, the Marquis of Castel-Rodrigo, making him see that the monarch had to become accustomed to "living by himself," given that "there is no Empire in Germany, or kinship, or blood, or friendship, or honour, or respect" (quoted in López Cordón; see Fernández Albaladejo, *La crisis de la Monarquía* 336–9). Soon afterwards, Philip IV himself was the one who was complaining bitterly to Sor María de Ágreda that the signing of the Peace of Westphalia by the Emperor had been undertaken "leaving me out and with all the enemies in" (146). Making a virtue of necessity,

---

[5] Very different from the previous interventions against the Turks (Saint Gotthard, 1664). In relation to the complexity of Louis XIV's eastern policy, interpreted pragmatically, rather than out of concern for an imperial dream, see Bérenger, "La politique ottomane" 87–107.

[6] On this subject, warning of the status of the engraver as an unconditional servant of the House of Orange—and consequently of the presence of a Dutch interest in this request for refuge—see Álvarez-Osorio.

Rethinking Identity 133

the Spanish monarch wanted to believe that this decision had been imposed by "the rulers of the Empire and their ministers" (146), against the very will of the Emperor. An active tradition of *Austro-Hispanism* was pressurising this form of solidarity,[7] but the erosion of the amicable relationships between the members of the House was clear. The marriage of one of the daughters of Philip IV to the French monarch and of another to the Emperor reflected the uncertainty surrounding the direction to be followed by the monarchy, aggravated by the concerns – in relation to succession – raised by the birth of Charles II in 1661.

Whilst clouded by uncertainty, the period stretching between the Peace of the Pyrenees and the death of Philip IV was not short of a route map.[8] The death of the *valido* Luis de Haro in 1661 led to a series of key developments. On the one hand, it resulted in the monarch announcing his decision to assume the responsibilities assigned to him by his position, in line with the actions of Louis XIV (1661) and, subsequently, of Leopold I (1665) (see Hermosa Espeso, "Ministros"; Valladares, "Haro sin Mazarino" 349, 374; on the European dynamics of the time, Bérenger, "La supresión"). As an immediate result of this measure, the figure of the *valido* lost its visibility and the key role which—in spite of the fall of Olivares—it had been enjoying up until then, in a process that went hand in hand with the restoration of the role of Council of State and of its ministers. But the status of the royal favourite would not disappear. As seen by the actions of the Duke of Medina de las Torres, the post became one of a ministerial nature.[9] Acting from that position, Medina steered the international policy of the monarchy in a different direction from the previous *valido*. As opposed to Haro's aim of maintaining the hegemony of the House of Austria at all costs and to fight France, the Portuguese rebellion became Medina's priority as part of a general approach which included the territorial withdrawal from the European scene. The "dynastic pre-eminence" of Haro's policy had to be replaced by a pre-eminence of peninsular issues (Valladares, "Méndez de Haro"), a call that ultimately aimed at repositioning the strategic importance of the Spanish territories within the monarchy as a whole and at emphasising the importance of the substratum of Hispanic identity.

Everyone's eyes were therefore on Portugal, seen from a perspective which, whilst not identical to that of 1580, nevertheless fell within a logic of incorporation. It was not an unreal option. In certain respects, the events of the past twenty years were endorsing it (Valladares, *La rebelión*; Barreto and

---

[7]   Visible in the works of Claudio Clemente, *El machiavelismo degollado por la christiana sabiduría de España y Austria*, 1637; José Pellicer, *Fama Austríaca*, 1641; Jean Chiflet, *Vindiciae hispanicae*, 1645; Saavedra Fajardo, *Corona gótica, castellana y austríaca*, 1646. On *Austro-Hispanism*, see Didier, *Vida y pensamiento* 91–110, and also Martín Polín.

[8]   On the stances being debated at that time, Stradling, and Hermosa Espeso, *Una mirada*.

[9]   Reaffirming this dual status, Hermosa Espeso, "Ministros" 67; "En torno."

134   *The Transatlantic Hispanic Baroque*

Cardim). From the outset, the rebellion in Portugal had been far from bringing together a compact block of national interests directly opposed to Castilian domination. Aside from and on top of a widespread national feeling, there was a solid network of cross-cutting interests, personalised in the alliances existing between noble families either side of the border between the kingdoms, and also in the political posts held by members of this same aristocracy or prominent bureaucrats. Neither was the existence of a feeling of loyalty towards the dynasty established in 1580 insignificant, perceptible in the presence of pockets of loyal subjects to the Habsburgs within the kingdom who intermittently drew attention to themselves (Schaub, *Le Portugal*; "Le sentiment"; Bouza Álvarez, *Portugal* ch. 8 and 10; Soares da Cunha; Terrasa Lozano; De Bernardo Ares).

It can therefore be understood that by 1641 – and from within Portugal – proposals had been formulated that aimed at restructuring the cluster that was the Catholic monarchy, including Flanders and the Italian territories among the members of the House and, meanwhile, allowing the three Crowns of Aragon, Castile and Portugal to continue "governing themselves [...] by their laws with equality" (Valladares, *La rebelión* 297), even considering the presence of the monarchs in Lisbon for a period of time. Going one step further, the possibility of quashing the Portuguese rebellion by means of peninsular reunification was an option considered by those involved in the conspiracy of the Duke of Hijar (1648), which revealed a glimpse of the existence of a plot to kidnap the daughter of Philip IV in order to wed her to the son of John IV of Portugal, the newly proclaimed king and member of the House of Braganza. One year later, the same idea of forming a "marriage between Portugal and Castile" (Valladares, *La rebelión* 297) would instigate a complex plan led by the Jesuit Antonio Viera, which would take him to Rome, although the Iberian *restauraçao* being pursued would in this case be led by Portugal, with a view to the advent of a "fifth empire" that would put an end once and for all to the destructive power of the House of Austria and the very memory of the German Empire (Valladares, *La rebelión* 104–109; Didier, "Lusitaniae"; Cardim). A strictly Iberian horizon would therefore control the movements of a reconstructed *Spanish* monarchy. In different formats, the idea of a reunion would continue. A few months before the Peace of the Pyrenees, Pedro de Valenzuela was committed to "a united and separate Portugal," a work in which the political reality of the peninsula was presented as a community of "Provincial nations" based on a common identity (Fernández Albaladejo, *La crisis de la Monarquía* 258–9). New proposals would continue to fuel the debate during the final years of Philip IV, within an unfolding of arguments in which the unionist approaches went hand in hand with a strict political reasoning, and without ruling out matrimonial union as an effective solution (Jover, "Tres actitudes"; Fernández Albaladejo, "Entre la razón católica").

Whilst ignored, the mere presence of these proposals was bound to constitute a call to redirect, from a peninsular perspective, the global policy of the monarchy. This possibility, however, was proving increasingly difficult in view of the sensitive situation that had arisen following the death of Philip IV in September of 1665. The timing was particularly complex. Designed to avoid any possible royal favour, the creation of the *Junta de Regencia* (Regency Council) represented in itself a major factor of instability, given the aversion it created among those who, in addition to seeing the possibility of gaining royal favour being removed, also saw themselves excluded from the new body. Furthermore, the rumours surrounding the fragile health of the heir brought to the fore the question of the partition of the monarchy, an issue which was already being observed with concern in Europe, where France made no attempt to hide its intention to cut off the path to the cadet branch of the House of Austria. Despite what was at stake, relations between the members of the House did not improve. Leopold I was not prepared to overlook the deliberate delays, caused by the court of Madrid, with regard to the betrothal to Margarita María of Austria, daughter of Philip IV and Mariana of Austria, and the decisive *argument* with regard to a possible succession. The marriage, which finally took place by proxy in April 1666, would not improve these relations. The Emperor tried to establish an imperial strategy from Vienna rather than from Madrid. In any event, he did not hide his fascination with the political model of Louis XIV or his relative willingness to form agreements with the latter with regard to a possible partition of the monarchy, something about which there had already been rumours not long before the death of Philip IV (Oliván Santaliestra 282–328; Pilo and Salado 73–8).

The court of Vienna was thus becoming the backdrop for a complicated game of factions where the Emperor was attempting to reach an understanding with the French monarch, in that his key minister (the Count of Auersperg) was leading the pro-Spanish faction of the court itself, in turn closely connected with the pro-imperial faction of Madrid. In the latter seat, the situation was no less complicated. In a text from April 1666, it was acknowledged that the court was divided between a faction of "imperialists" and another of "Spaniards," and where at the same time the regent was refusing to adhere unconditionally to the guidelines set by her brother, the Emperor. Faithful to the ties of family loyalty but at the same time determined to protect her son and to ensure the continuity of Nithard, Mariana of Austria presided over a Regency Council whose composition and actions reflected those same divisions. In an attempt to procure his own space, Nithard's actions accentuated these tensions even further. In Vienna, his role was deemed highly disloyal to the interests of the Emperor, as was reiterated in the reports compiled by the imperial ambassador, the Count of Pötting, who in fact liaised openly with the sectors opposed to the Jesuit.

With his wife claiming her hereditary rights over a part of Flanders, Louis XIV started a war of "devolution" in the middle of 1667, which, ultimately, constituted a considered strategic challenge to the power of the House of Austria:

136 *The Transatlantic Hispanic Baroque*

whilst they were the inheritance and property of the Spanish branch, the Low Countries at the same time formed part of the imperial circle of Burgundy. The interests of both parties were therefore affected, but the possibility of an effective and coordinated action seemed highly remote. There was also pressure from the unresolved conflict with Portugal, as demanding in resources as it was scarce in possibilities of a military solution and an acceptable agreement. In May 1667, the imperial ambassador in Madrid, Count of Pötting, had recorded in his diary "the remarkable daring of the French monarch" (300) in the recent invasion, but this observation was not followed by the subsequent declaration of war—on the part of the Emperor—that was expected at the court of Madrid. The news of the signing of a treaty of partition of the monarchy of Spain, carried out in January 1668 between the Emperor and the French monarch, highlighted these internal tensions even more (Bérenger, "An attempted"; Valladares, *La rebelión* 207–221). Although in the end the treaty dissolved into an ephemeral attempt at *rapprochement* between its signatories, the mere fact that the Emperor had come round to signing it amounted to—as Louis XIV himself would note in his *Memoirs*—"a wonderful confirmation of the rights of the queen and an express confession of the nullity of the renunciation, all the more important given that it was undertaken by the same party that had intended to maintain it" (quoted in Gómez-Centurión Jiménez 826). The treaty rendered meaningless any possible allusion to "the bonds of blood and unity" or to the "common cause" between the two branches of the House of Austria. In a significant turnaround in its politics, the diplomacy of the monarchy—from the platform of the Burgundy circle—gave value to its status as a member of the Empire, acting as a German power and consequently requesting the help of the other members in order to defend the German liberties against the dominant demands of Louis XIV (Oliván Santaliestra ch. 4; Bérenger, *Finances* 93–5).[10]

Whilst the partition of the monarchy of Spain agreed between Leopold I and Louis XIV had questioned the internal solidarity of the House, the signing of the Treaty of Lisbon in February 1668—one month after the signing of the treaty of partition and just a few months before the Treaty of Aix-la-Chapelle, which would bring an end to the War of Devolution—in turn raised some equally pressing questions, resulting in this case from the difficult assimilation of peace itself. A concise text of 13 chapters resolved a conflict that had been dragging on for 28 years and in whose first section, "the Catholic King and King of Portugal," in their name "and in that of their kingdoms," signed up to this peace. The possibility of an agreement in "from king to king" terms had been rejected in the latter years of the reign of Philip IV, opting instead for a solution under the terms of the truce signed with the Dutch rebels in 1609. The last military defeats on the Portuguese front and the success of the occupation

---

[10]   On the new direction of the monarchy in the context of the Empire, see Störrs.

of Louis XIV finally forced independence to be recognised, within a process of negotiation that made even more visible the climate of internal confrontation in which the regency government was developing. Ultimately, the conclusion of peace could be seen as a weakness considering the wider interests of the House, and as giving priority to the Low Countries. Aware of the situation, the regent kept her distance in relation to what could be interpreted as pure adaptation to the interests of Vienna. Flaunting a consultative approach, she even attempted an announcement from the Courts of Castile to lend more legitimacy to the signing of the peace with Portugal.

It is therefore understood that Medina de las Torres, defender of a peace agreement strictly in order to *preserve* the monarchy, had informed the regent—in his vote on the negotiation with Portugal expressed in the State Council on 11 August 1666—that her status as guardian would always leave the door open to future claims, since "the rights of the kingdoms cannot be relinquished without the Courts." In this respect, the signing of peace could be seen as an act which—legally—did not relinquish the right of "*restitutio in integrum*" once Charles II came of age (in Cánovas del Castillo 759).[11] The political events taking place in Portugal at the same time as the negotiations, meanwhile, provided further grounds, from the other side of the border, for the treaty to be viewed with this connotation of reversibility. The fall on 3 September 1667 of Castel Melhor, the strong *valido* of Alfonso VI of Portugal, was followed two months later by the "replacement" of the monarch by his brother Peter, leading to a period of confrontation between parties in relation to the direction to be taken by the Braganza revolution. The fact that Peter himself would accept no title other than Prince Regent added to the uncertainty. Hence the hope maintained for reintegration that he continued to support in the segregated kingdom and which, over a period of time, would nurture a climate of permanent Spanish conspiracies (Barreto and Cardim 183–220; Martín Marcos, "1668"; "Visiones").

Aside from the impact on the image of the monarchy itself, Portugal's independence was seen as a distancing of identity. The Duke of Alba brought this to the attention of the regent in April 1666, explaining in his capacity as State advisor that he was obliged to prevent "such an essential and key part as a kingdom within Spain from crumbling away from the Crown." When all is said and done, the particular difference that may exist between the nouns "Lusitanians" and "Castilians" should not obscure the fact that "they are both brought together under the general term of Spanish"; Spain should remain "united as when ruled by the Romans" (in Cánovas del Castillo 495). There were also constitutional reasons. In the memorandum by the jurist García

---

[11] Mariana's status as a guardian and the fact that 'the rights of the Kingdoms cannot be relinquished without the Courts' supported this possibility of restitution.

Alexandre published at the end of 1667 it was insisted upon that, prior to the signing of any peace agreement, there was no avoiding a constitutional debate between the corporate political subjects inhabiting the "Continent of the Spains."[12] Clearly, the visible nostalgia for Spain was not far removed from the factional confrontation existing at court, where Mariana's actions and Nithard's influence seemed to be directly responsible for the loss of Portugal and the far-from-honourable Treaty of Aix-la-Chapelle. The consequences of this situation were: as of May 1667 Cardinal Moncada informed the Marquis of Grana, "the Regency has been reduced to tyranny; the monarch is Everardo Nithard," a situation whereby, inevitably, "nobility is insulted and determined not to tolerate it." The fact that "the lord Emperor" had "dismissed the servants he had in Spain," as well as compromising the prestige of the House itself, to some extent legitimised the reaction of the key figures in Spain to put an end to this situation (Pilo and Salado 79).[13]

In *Causas no causas*, the exculpatory manuscript written by Nithard after his fall, the Jesuit continued to note the anti-imperialist climate existing among "the Spanish." This consisted of a series of "very serious grievances" which had been accumulating since Philip the Fair and the Emperor Charles V, continuing up until the Emperor Leopold I, whose understanding with the French king was deemed completely unacceptable. As a consequence of all of this, "Spain" was "highly offended and opposed to that Austrian line" and, no less serious a matter, the Spanish were not prepared to accept the Emperor as a possible successor in the "terrible event" of the death of Charles II. Whilst the rejection of the candidature of Louis XIV was a result of "the natural antipathy" between the two neighbouring nations, in the case of Leopold I it was more a personal disaffection. So much so, that the Spanish had begun to set "[their] sights on the figure of Don John of Austria" (in Pilo and Salado 247–9). The latter's sudden appearance at the forefront of the political scene was nothing new in itself. But the circumstances in which this was occurring were certainly new. He had been removed from his political duties by testamentary decision of his father and had also tried—unsuccessfully—to gain the support of Nithard. Above all, it was the health of his stepbrother and the recent Portuguese regency established by Peter that would give him a decisive added value. In fact, the possibility—following Nithard's dismissal—that the bastard son of Philip IV would end up declaring himself "king or governor" was given serious consideration among government circles in Lisbon, appeared in the *décimas* circulating around Madrid and was

---

[12]   Having to take into account in this respect "the view of all the towns and cities concerned and even if without a vote in the Courts, or being called, and not just taking those of Castile, but of all the first cities of the other Kingdoms and dominions of the Continent of the Spains" (cit. by Bouza, *Papeles* 141–2)

[13]   See the nuances of this process in Carrasco Martínez.

Rethinking Identity 139

recognised by the French ambassador in 1670 (Valladares, *La rebelión* 263).[14] The search for a high-level matrimonial tie—unsuccessfully attempted on two occasions—did nothing to belie these aspirations.[15]

Redefining Identity

Although imposed by this context, the alliance between the most conspicuous members of the Castilian aristocracy and the natural son of Philip IV was something more than *déjà vu*, starting in particular with Don John himself. Between the conspiracy against Nithard at the end of 1669 and his appointment as first minister at the beginning of 1677 (preceded shortly before by the fall of Valenzuela), Don John's activities made it clear that the political game was being played by new rules. His successful war against Mariana's two favourites was more one of words than of arms, owing more to the shifting of public opinion than to the game of court intrigues; his own support, meanwhile, was to be found less in the area of Madrid than outside the Crown of Castile. The very justification of his movements can neither be presented as a "conspiracy," nor simply likened to a *coup d'état*. As cleverly pointed out by Héloïse Hermant, Don John introduced a new way of negotiating by influencing the decisions of the monarchic power through advice (issued in pamphlets) and, ultimately, by gaining power through open letters to the Regent. Rather than reflecting "public opinion," his writings attempted to "persuade" by means of a logical polemic. His aim was to "resist without disobeying," by distributing manifestos which, performatively, hastened the outcome (see Hermant, "La publicité"; *Guerres*).

As he himself had demonstrated to the regent in the manifesto of Torrejón, it was a question of restoring Spain's "lost reputation," which inevitably gave his proposals a *nacionista*, and at the same time redeeming, tone.[16] He was acting in

---

[14]   In one of the *décimas* of the time, it was stated "that Don John has no intention/ other than to ascend the throne" (in Egido 187); the printing was ratified in 1670 by the French ambassador (Álvarez López 119).

[15]   Specifically, with the sister of the Duke of Enghien (1665), a possible successor to the Polish throne, and with the Archduchess Claudia Felicitas (1666), which would open the door to the government of Tyrol (Oliván Santaliestra 91–9). In the aforementioned manuscript by Nithard *Causas no causas*, it is written that 'Don John in times past received predictions from various judicial astrologists that Our Lord and King [...] would die at a tender age of very few years and that Don John would ascend the throne [...] and hoped to be pronounced King of the Spains or at least of some other foreign kingdom, such as that of Poland' (127).

[16]   On the subject of the manifesto, Ruiz Rodríguez (327). As is known, the term *nacionista* was coined by Feijoo, who used it in an ironic sense to describe those who only admired new developments abroad; it can, however, be understood as a form of "national

the name of all Spaniards. The characterisations of Don John as "our restorer," as the "Phoenix of Spain," corresponded with those of "*caudillo*" (leader), or "Messiah," with those of someone who, also imagining himself as "Hercules" or "Atlas Politicus", seemed to be the only one capable of supporting the weight of the Spanish monarchy/world.[17] In comparison with the "foreigner" Nithard, Don John exemplified the "son of the family," although the *nacionismo* with which his figure was adorned was more in response to an orientation imposed by the circumstances of the time than to an attitude originating from earlier times. In any event, the bastard could read and lend political influence to the climate of reaffirmation of identity that was beginning to emerge on the peninsula. It was no coincidence that Nithard's camp criticised the constant readiness of Don John to offer himself as "the nation's saviour" or that the signatories of the manifesto against Valenzuela in December 1676 considered the followers of the new *valido* to be "sworn enemies of the king and the nation" (Ruiz Rodríguez 414). The allusions to the nation were far from coincidental. Even the treaties on the prince's education that were being printed at that time were already full of it. The *Nudrición real* (1671) with which González de Salcedo aimed to feed the political imagination of Charles II stressed the need for monarchs to be brought up "by teaching them to love their Land or Nation" (González de Salcedo 58–9):[18] a recommendation that was reiterated in the *Reynados de menor edad y de grandes Reyes*, by Ramos del Manzano (1672), thus elaborating on the need to resort to the *exempla* of history itself. The *nutriment* in question had to be obtained by attending to "the native aspect of the natural land, the virtue and nature of Spain," far from any imitation of "foreign and strange documents" (quoted in Fernández Albaladejo, *La crisis de la Monarquía* 418–20).

Clearly, the historiography was not far removed from this growing patriotic indigenism either. Dedicated to the "Tutrix of Charles the Desired," the *Corona Real de España por España* (1668), by the Benedictine friar Gregorio de Argaiz, strived to leave a record of the signs pertaining to identity, to make the regent see the importance of the three Spanish crowns (one made from the gold of Castile and Asturias, another from the silver of the Pyrenees and Andalusia, and a third from the iron of Cantabria) of which she was the custodian and which by no means would compare unfavourably with those which had been adorning the holder of the Empire (Argaiz 90–91; on the imperial coronation, see Cavina). It was worth highlighting above all the last of these crowns of Spain, given that the one flaunted by the Romans and Carthaginians "did not pertain

---

passion," of a love for oneself, completely different from the sacrificial demands and the driving role of history that nineteenth-century nationalism assigned to the nation.

[17] Such as that incorporated by the engraver Pedro de Valenzuela in the second edition of *De lege política*, by Pedro González de Salcedo (1678).

[18] On the importance of this turnaround, see Fernández Albaladejo, "Lecciones de Roma."

Rethinking Identity 141

to natural Monarchs," as was also the case with the Goths. The crown whose history was of interest at this point could only be "that of our leading Spaniards, that of the Cantabrians, that of our old Castilians" (n.p.). The passing of the leading role of the Goths into the hands of the *montañeses* ("mountain people," the Castilian inhabitants of the Santander region) sanctioned a new alliance of forces in the ever-tricky territory of the founding times of the monarchy (Fernández Albaladejo, "Entre godos"). However illustrious their presence may have been in the past, the Goths were losing the leading role that the Gothic, Castilian and Austrian Crown of Saavedra Fajardo had recognised in them in 1646. Significantly, Alonso Núñez de Castro, the author of a "second part" of this work that appeared in 1671, underlined the importance of the history subsequent to the "loss" of Spain, a period whose glorious deeds had been led by "*montañeses* and Asturians." In the third part, appearing six years later, Núñez de Castro offered the monarchy, "by the hand of His Serene Highness Don John," a list of political dogmas derived from the actions of "Ferdinand the Saint, Alfonso the Wise, Sancho the Brave and Ferdinand the Summoned"; to these—declared the author—"Your Majesty owes the Crown," and their lessons of wisdom were what mattered. In practice—and to make the task easier—it sufficed to look at Ferdinand III, elevated to sanctity in the same year in which the book appeared, whose life alone, as written in the dedication, "is enough as a library" (Núñez de Castro, ¶4).

Reflecting this dynamic of Hispanicisation of identity and of an underground anti-Austrianism, Antonio Calderón and Jerónimo Pardo had already eulogised in 1658 the *Excelencias y primacías del apóstol Santiago el Mayor*, a work that rejected the ideas of the Austro-Hispanist Nieremberg expressed in *De la devoción y patrocinio de San Miguel, antiguo tutelar de los godos y protector de España* (1643), and where the "warrior archangel" was placed above the "Moor-slayer apostle." Calderón and Pardo harboured no doubts about the role played by the apostle in leading "the Spanish from the Mountains," the "primitive Spanish" throughout the reconquering process (Calderón and Pardo 252; Didier, *Vida* 91–107; Fernández Albaladejo, *La crisis de la Monarquía* 510–11). Even if we go back to that primitive time, there were still equally fundamentalist references to be found, albeit supported by other examples. In this case they were provided by the life of *El ayo y maestro de príncipes Séneca* (1674), the biography of "a vassal of this Crown" who, having become an icon of the doctrinaire moralists of seventeenth-century Spain, was used by Juan Baños de Velasco to continue arguing in favour of the expectations created by neo-Stoic epistemology.[19] Such an "arduous and difficult" matter as politics

---

[19] From the same "argument" in the book: "understanding metaphysics of state is not demonstrative, but conjectural. A design of what it was must be created, for what it will be or can be" (n.p.); see Blüher and the excellent work by Robbins (ch. 2).

142   *The Transatlantic Hispanic Baroque*

could be considered in a different way and, in this respect, Seneca's work could be considered as a monument to an early "National politics" (Baños de Velasco n.p.). The vicissitudes of the philosopher were highly illustrative when it came to putting together a description of Spain which exalted its "Standing, Religion, Fertility and Nobility," along a path marked by the tracks and deeds of "the invincible Cantabrians" (8). Cantabria ratified its status as a true *depôt* of Hispanic essences, as endorsed by its inhabitants being direct descendants of Tubal, the coming of St James and the maintaining of the true religion from the outset; and no less, the presence of its own dress (completely removed from "the Roman, Goth or Arab") and of a language which, like Basque, demonstrated strict loyalty to those origins. As descendants who were from those "legitimate Spanish," Pelayo and Garci Ximénez could only have descended from those Cantabrians, far removed from any Gothic origin. Seneca finally established himself as a founding reference when it came to shedding light on the new patriotic memory on which he was obliged to reflect: "May the Spaniard see what sons his Nation had, and may other Kingdoms admire what Nation this is, the origin of such illustrious Spaniards" (1–2).

Both aristocratic and patriotic, Baños de Velasco's description of Spain did not however add much new in relation to the question of origins, a debate that was being held in the European Republic of Letters due to the appearance of the *Geographia Sacra* by Samuel Bochart (1646) and which at that time was becoming rather complex. It was the entity of "ancient history," the very possibility of addressing that time, that was in question. Between the demands of *criticism* and the abyss that was opening up with *Pyrrhonism*, some members of the *Republic* were trying to lend intelligibility to a period in which, furthermore, a bitter debate was brewing in relation to the origins of each of the *nationes* (see, for example, Borghero ch. 1–3; Grell 983–1003; Pouloin 253–67; Kidd 9–34). The appearance of the *Población y lengua primitiva de España* (1672), by Joseph de Pellicer, is a much overlooked Hispanic contribution to this debate, which also served to air some internal issues.[20] His work proceeded to look into the "primitive history" of Spain, beyond "the brief and simple news left by our forefathers," going back to a time well before that left by Jiménez de Rada or Lucas de Tuy. The result of their investigations suggested "another Spain, most unlike the one that had been recorded until now," and from which there was also emerging "a different Empire" inhabited by "different (if not uncertain) inhabitants" (Pellicer, *Prefación* 3). As opposed to the leading role that had been

---

[20]   *Poblacion y lengua primitiva de España recopilada del Aparato a su Monarchia Antigua en los tres tiempos, el Adelon, el Mithico y el Historico*; the *Aparato* had been completed in 1671, but would not see the light of day until 1673; also of interest, *Beroso de Babilonia en Caldea, distinguido de Beroso de Viterbo en Italia, con la cronología de los reyes antiquísimos de Asiria y Babilonia* (1673). On this subject, see Botella Ordinas, "Los novatores."

played by Tubal as the first inhabitant of Spain, Pellicer decidedly advocated in favour of Tarsis—the grandson of Jafet—whom he claimed to be the first king of Spain and to whom he attributed the origin of its monarchy. Pellicer's operation thus cleansed part of history itself of the disrepute back into which it had been made to fall by the false chronicles. Tarsis gave Spain's first inhabitant an exotic, oriental provenance which, at the same time, enabled him to get round the ever-delicate problem of establishing where the "nest" of the monarchy, the seat of the first inhabitants, lay (Pellicer, *Población* 17–25).

Pellicer's proposal attempted to disregard the debate surrounding "which part of Spain started to become inhabited first" (Moret 78) which had been initiated shortly before by the Jesuit Moret in his *Investigaciones históricas*, but inevitably the debate continued beyond this initial moment. There was pressure from certain regional political communities which, ignored by the imperial argument, were seeking to secure a space of their own within this process of re-establishment. In this respect, to prove the presence of the first inhabitant in their region was also to open up the possibility of their own legislation and monarchs, of a community of *montañeses* who could claim the status of *original Spaniards*, of inhabitants of the region in which Spain *began*. The debate surrounding the first king of Spain after its *loss* thus went hand in hand with the argument surrounding the essence of the first legislation, of what the nature of the founding charters of the community in question could be. In some way, Pellicer warned that Spain's crisis of imperial identity had opened the way for a dynamic of redefining identity which, in the face of the emergence of histories of the peninsular *nationes*, ran the risk of blurring the visibility and virtual unitary entity of *Spain* to propose a conglomerate of concurrent histories of the nation's inhabitants, another idea of Spain. Hence, previously, his antiquarian investigation had resorted to recreating a history and to proposing a memory in accordance with its original status of "different empire," an empire of its own which "with more or less sovereignty" had been maintained in spite of the "invasions" by the Romans, Carthaginians and Goths. And where, furthermore, the Spanish had never lacked "a natural king," even if he was "stationed in this or that corner of its provinces" (Pellicer, *Población* 3–5).

The presence and importance of the Goths was indisputable but, in accordance with the origins being considered, it was of interest to blur the Gothic-Scandic connection and to explain their arrival in Hispania in another way. The split from the *Gothic crown* of Saavedra was crystal clear. Far from originating from "the outer-most parts of the North," the Goths originated from the Orient, identifying with the *Getae*, a branch of the Scythians. Arriving finally in Spain, "as far as their colonies remain today," their identification with the Hispanic land was formed from the very first moment (Pellicer, *Prefación* 136).[21] The diversity shown by its members did not prevent a unit from being established to twin them. The detail was not insignificant. The actions of the *Getae* offered a unifying pan-Hispanism that Pellicer used to explain and define the process of constructing Spain's identity.[22] The presentation of Pelayo as the "only King of Spain," the natural successor to the "Ancient Right of its Spanish Monarchs" formed part of this logic. His *Annales de la Monarchia de España después de su pérdida* recreated and carefully recalled the moment in which "the Christians of Asturias, and of the Pyrenees" proceeded to elect the "King and Leader to govern them." Not without warning that, previously, the "commissars" elected for this purpose took care of establishing "sixteen laws" drafted "for election of a King of Spain; not of Aragón, of Navarra, or of Sobrarbe, but universal to all Christians of the League of the Pyrenees, who represented, as free subjects, the Ancient Gothic, and Spanish, Monarchy." The laws in question were no more than "those known today as *Fueros de Sobrarbe*," the true "Fundamental law of the Monarchy of the Spains." A single king and common legislation supported the new imperial memory. There could be other monarchs and other legislation, but they were understood to be subsequent, like branches torn away from a single trunk, ultimately limbs of a single monarchic "body" whose head was no other than Pelayo (Pellicer, *Annales* 31–3, 104–106, 157–8; see Botella Ordinas, "La constitución").

Pellicer died in mid-December 1679, scarcely three months after the death of Don John of Austria. The end of that year offered at the same time the first balance in the complex attempt to redefine identity that had been initiated ten years earlier. Whilst impossible to execute officially, the split from the Austrian origins and the Gothic-Scandic races appeared to be firmly established. But there was no such agreement when it came to assuming in shared terms a past which, from its alleged origins, was nevertheless perceived to be its own. In reality, the dispute surrounding the interpretation of the history of Spain was not so much a debate on the actual reality of Spain as one on which—which community within it—could assume the *label* of Spanish primogeniture. It is a question that would therefore mark the years leading up to 1700. Unlike the royalist dynamic that had been imposed in France, in Spain the debate was more around the enlargement and affirmation of each of the *nationes Hispaniae* than around

---

[21] Specifically, and in relation to the rejection of the traditional provenance of the Goths, Pellicer writes: "May it be the proposed deceit of the *Gothic crown*, which brings the Goths, from the outer-most parts of the North to Spain, and of greater deceit the *Historic Investigations*." On this relocation of European scope, see Johnson.

[22] The projection over the present moment was clear: if "whenever one speaks in the actions of the Castilians they are Spain; and those of Aragonese are Spain; and in this consequence those of the Navarrans, Andalusians, Valencians and Vizcayans, all are of Spanish; and also those to whom the Getae were referring" (Pellicer, *Prefación* 135).

the expectations of *grandeur* that the head of the monarchy might be able to offer. It is an approach that largely explains the dynastic options faced and that would manifest themselves from 1700 onwards, and the leading role that the construction of a Spanish national identity would finally assume throughout the eighteenth century (Fernández Albaladejo, "Dinastía"). The unresolved contradictions of this process would, as is known, mark the history of subsequent times and even that of our present day. As if—refuting the statement in the 1669 pamphlet—*Spain* still remained committed to continuing to resemble itself.

Bibliography

Álvarez López, Ana. *La fabricación de un imaginario. Los embajadores de Luis XIV y España*. Madrid: Cátedra, 2008.

Álvarez-Osorio Alvariño, Antonio. "Virtud coronada: Carlos II y la piedad de la Casa de Austria." *Política, religión e inquisición en la España moderna*. Ed. P. Fernández Albaladejo, J. Martínez Millán and V. Pinto Crespo. Madrid: Universidad Autónoma de Madrid, 1996. 29–57.

Argaiz, Gregorio de. *Corona Real de España por España, fundada en el crédito de los muertos*. Madrid: Melchor y Alegre, 1668.

Baños de Velasco y Acebedo, Juan. *El ayo y maestro de príncipes Séneca en su vida*. Madrid: Imprenta del Reyno, 1674.

Barreto, Angela and Pedro Cardim, eds. *D. Afonso VI*. Lisbon: Círculo de leitores, 2006.

Bérenger, Jean. *Finances et absolutisme autrichien dans la seconde moitié du XVII siécle*. Paris: Imprimerie Nationale, 1975.

———. "An attempted *Rapprochement* between France and the Emperor: the Secret Treaty for the Partition of the Spanish Succession on 19 January 1668." *Louis XIV and Europe*. Ed. R. Hatton. London: Macmillan, 1976. 133–52.

———. "La politique ottomane de la France dans les années 1680." *Frankreich im Europäischen Staatensystem der Frühen Neuzeit*. Ed. Rainer Babel. Sigmaringen: Thorbecke, 1995. 87–107.

———. "La supresión del ministro-favorito, o el crepúsculo de un modelo político: el caso austríaco." *El mundo de los validos*. Ed. John H. Elliott and L. Brockliss. Madrid: Taurus, 1999. 365–79.

Blüher, Karl A. *Séneca en España desde el siglo XIII al siglo XVIII*. Madrid: Gredos, 1983.

Borghero, Carlo. *La certezza e la storia. Cartesianismo, pirronismo e conoscenza storica*. Milan: Angeli, 1983.

Botella Ordinas, Eva. "Los novatores y el origen de España. El vocabulario hispano de probabilidad y la renovación del método histórico en tiempos de Carlos II." *Obradoiro de Historia Moderna* 14 (2005): 39–64.

146   *The Transatlantic Hispanic Baroque*

———. "La constitución de los territorios y la invención de España: 1665–1700." *Estudis* 31 (2005): 223–52.

Bouza Álvarez, Fernando. *Portugal no tempo dos Filipes. Politica, cultura, representaçoes (1580–1688)*. Lisbon: Cosmos, 2000.

———. *Papeles y opinión. Políticas de publicación en el Siglo de Oro*. Madrid: Consejo Superior de Investigaciones Científicas, 2008.

Calderón, Antonio and Gerónimo Pardo. *Excelencias y primacías del apóstol Santiago el Mayor*. Madrid: Imp. Gerónimo Rodríguez, 1658.

Cánovas del Castillo, Antonio. *Estudios del reinado de Felipe IV. Obras completas*. Vol. 2. Madrid: Fundación "Cánovas del Castillo," 1987.

Cardim, Pedro. "António Vieira e o universalismo dos séculos XVI e XVII." *António Vieira, Roma e o universalismo das monarquías portuguesa e española*. Coord. P. Cardim and G. Sabatini. Lisbon: CHAM, 2011. 13–27.

Carrasco Martínez, Adolfo. "Los Grandes, el poder y la cultura política de la nobleza en el reinado de Carlos II." *Studia Historica. Historia Moderna* 20 (1999): 77–136.

Cavina, Marco. *Imperator Romanorum triplice corona coronatur*. Milan: Giuffrè, 1991.

De Bernardo Ares, José Manuel. "El iberismo como alternativa político-dinástica al francesismo y al austracismo." *Anais de Historia de Alem-Mar* 8 (2007): 11–36.

Didier, Hugues. *Vida y pensamiento de Juan E. Nieremberg*. Madrid: Fundación Universitaria Española, 1976.

———. "'Lusitaniae est imperare orbi universo.' El padre António Vieira (1608–1697) y los autores 'austrohispanistas' de Castilla." *Literatura portuguesa y española. Cuadernos de Filología*. 31 (1999): 143–53.

Egido, Teófanes. *Sátiras políticas de la España Moderna*. Madrid: Alianza, 1973.

Fernández Albaladejo, Pablo. "Dinastía y comunidad política: el momento de la patria." *Los Borbones. Dinastía y memoria de nación en la España del siglo XVIII*. Madrid: Marcial Pons, 2001. 485–532.

———. "Entre godos y montañeses: reflexiones sobre una primera identidad española." *Materia de España*. Madrid: Marcial Pons, 2007. 287–321.

———. *La crisis de la Monarquía*. Madrid: Crítica and Marcial Pons, 2009.

———. "Entre la razón católica y la razón de Estado: senderos de la *raison politique* en la monarquía de España." *Transitions: Journal of Franco-Iberian Studies* 5 (2009): 97–116.

———. "Lecciones de Roma. Monarquía y patria común en el reinado de Felipe III." *Homenaje a Antonio Manuel Hespanha*. Lisbon, forthcoming.

Gómez-Centurión Jiménez, Carlos María. "La sucesión a la Monarquía de España y los conflictos internacionales." *Calderón y la España del Barroco*. Ed. José Alcalá-Zamora and Ernest Belenguer. Madrid: CEPC, 2001. 805–835.

González de Salcedo, Pedro. *Nudrición Real*. Madrid: Imprenta Bernardo de Villadiego, 1671.

Grell, Chantal. *Le Dix-huitième siécle et l'antiquité en France*. Oxford: Voltaire Foundation, 1995.

Haran, Alexandre Y. *Le lys et le globe. Messianisme dynastique et rêve impérial en France aux XVIe et XVIIe siècles*. Paris: Champ Vallon, 2000.

Hermant, Héloïse. "La publicité au service de la dissimulation: don Juan José de Austria en Machiavel?" *Mélanges de la Casa de Velázquez* 38 (2008): 219–40.

———. *Guerres de plumes. Publicité et cultures politiques dans l'Espagne du XVII siècle*. Madrid: Casa de Velázquez, 2012.

Hermosa Espeso, Cristina. "Ministros y ministerio de Felipe IV (1661–1665)." *Investigaciones Históricas* 27 (2007): 47–76.

———. "En torno a la Secretaría de Estado de Felipe IV (1661–1665)." *Cuadernos de Investigación Histórica* 26 (2009): 159–91.

———. *Una mirada a la Monarquía española a finales del reinado de Felipe IV. José Arnolfini de Illescas*. Valladolid: Universidad de Valladolid, 2010.

Johnson, James W. "The Scythian: His Rise and Fall." *Journal of the History of Ideas* 20.2 (1959): 250–57.

Jover, José María. *1635. Historia de una polémica y semblanza de una generación*. Madrid: Consejo Superior de Investigaciones Científicas, 1949.

———. "Tres actitudes ante el Portugal restaurado." *Hispania* 10 (1950): 105–170.

Kidd, Colin. *British Identities before Nationalism: Ethnicity and Nationhood in the Atlantic World, 1600–1800*. Cambridge: Cambridge University Press, 1999.

López Cordón, María Victoria. "La paz oculta: propaganda, información y política en torno a Westfalia." *Pedralbes* 19 (1999): 71–93.

María de Jesús de Ágreda. *Correspondencia con Felipe IV. Religión y Razón de Estado*. Ed. Consolación Baranda. Madrid: Castalia, 1991.

Martín Marcos, David. "1668: una paz 'inacabada' entre España y Portugal." Congreso *As relaçoes entre Portugal e Hespanha de 1668 a 1758*. Lisbon: Comunicación fotocopiada, 2011.

———. "Visiones españolas de algunos anhelos prohibidos en el Portugal de los Braganza (1668–1700): en torno a una nueva unión ibérica." *Ler História* 61 (2011): 67–84.

Martín Polín, Raquel. "Pellicer de Ossau: una visión de la monarquía católica en torno a 1640." *Espacio, Tiempo y Forma* series IV 13 (2000): 133–63.

Martucelli, Danilo. *Grammaires de l'individu*. Paris: Gallimard, 2002.

Maura y Gamazo, Gabriel. *Carlos II y su Corte. Ensayo de reconstrucción biográfica*. 2 vols. Madrid: Revista de Archivos, Bibliotecas y Museos, 1911 and 1915.

Monod, Paul Kléber. *The Power of Kings: Monarchy and Religion in Europe, 1589–1715*. New Haven: Yale University Press, 1999.

148   *The Transatlantic Hispanic Baroque*

Moret, José de. *Investigaciones históricas de las antigüedades del Reyno de Navarra*. Pamplona: Imp. Gaspar Martínez, 1665.

Núñez de Castro, Alonso. *Corona gótica, castellana y austriaca*. Vol. 3. Madrid: García de la Iglesia, 1677.

Ochoa Brun, Miguel Ángel. "El incidente diplomático hispano-francés de 1661." *Boletín de la Real Academia de la Historia* 201 (2004): 97–159.

Oliván Santaliestra, Laura. "Mariana de Austria en la encrucijada política del siglo XVII." Ph.D. thesis. Universidad Complutense, 2006.

Onnekink, David and Gijs Rommelse, eds. *Ideology and Foreign Policy in Early Modern Europe (1650–1750)*. Farnham: Ashgate, 2011.

Pellicer, Joseph de. *Prefación de la Monarchía de los Godos. Bibliotheca formada de los libros y obras públicas de don Joseph Pellicer de Ossau y Tovar*. Valencia: Gerónimo Villagrasa, 1671.

———. *Población y lengua primitiva de España recopilada del Aparato a su Monarchia Antigua en los tres tiempos, el Adelon, el Mithico y el Historico*. Valencia: Benito Macè, 1672.

———. *Beroso de Babilonia en Caldea, distinguido de Beroso de Viterbo en Italia, con la cronología de los reyes antiquísimos de Asiria y Babilonia*. Valencia: Gerónimo Villagrasa, 1673.

———. *Annales de la Monarquía de España*. Madrid: Francisco Sanz, 1681.

Pilo, Rafaella. "Casi todos los hombres del cardenal Moncada. La conjura de otoño. Octubre de 1668–marzo de 1669." *La sucesión de la monarquía hispánica 1665–1725*. Ed. J.M. de Bernardo Ares. Córdoba: Universidad de Córdoba, 2006. 257–75.

———, and Juana Salado. *Juan Everardo Nithard y sus "Causas no causas." Razones y pretextos para el fin de un valimiento*. Madrid: Silex, 2010.

Pötting, Francisco Eusebio de. *Diario del Conde de Pötting, Embajador del Sacro Imperio en Madrid (1664–1674)*. Ed. M. Nieto Nuño. Madrid: Escuela Diplomática, 1990.

Pouloin, Claudine. *Le temps des origines*. Paris: Honoré Champion, 1998.

Robbins, Jeremy. *Arts of Perception: The Epistemological Mentality of the Spanish Baroque (1580–1720)*. Glasgow: University of Glasgow Press, 2007.

Ruiz Rodríguez, Ignacio. *Don Juan José de Austria en la Monarquía Hispánica*. Madrid: Dikynson, 2007.

Sabatier, Gérard. *Versailles ou la figure du roi*. Paris: Albin Michel, 1999.

Sawyer, Jeffrey K. *Printed Poison: Pamphlet Propaganda, Faction Politics, and the Public Sphere in Early Seventeenth-Century France*. Berkeley: University of California Press, 1990.

Schaub, Jean-Frédéric. *Le Portugal au temps du Comte-Duc d'Olivares*. Madrid: Casa de Velázquez, 2001.

———. "Le sentiment national est-il une catégorie pertinente pour comprendre les adhesions et les conflits sous l'Ancien régime?" *Le sentimente national* dans l'Europe meridionale aux XVIe et XVIIe siècles. Coord. A. Tallon. Madrid: Casa de Velázquez, 2007. 155–68.

Soares da Cunha, Mafalda. "Títulos portugueses y matrimonios mixtos en la Monarquía católica." *Las redes del imperio: élites sociales en la articulación de la Monarquía hispánica, 1492–1714*. Coord. Bartolomé Yun Casalilla. Madrid: Marcial Pons and Universidad Pablo de Olavide, 2009. 205–232.

Störrs, Christopher D. "Germany's Indies? The Spanish Monarchy and Germany in the Reign of the Last Spanish Habsburg, Charles II, 1665–1700." *The Lion and the Eagle*. Ed. Conrad Kent, Thomas Wolber and Cameron M.K. Hewitt. New York: Berghahn Books, 2000. 107–129.

Stradling, Robert A. "A Spanish Statesman of Appeasement: Medina de las Torres and Spanish Policy 1639–70." *Spain's Struggle for Europe 1598–1668*. London: Hambledon Press, 1994. 147–76.

Terrasa Lozano, Antonio. "De la raya de Portugal a la frontera de la guerra: los Mascarenhas y las prácticas nobiliarias de supervivencia política durante la guerra de la *Restauraçao*." *Las redes del imperio: élites sociales en la articulación de la Monarquía hispánica, 1492–1714*. Coord. Bartolomé Yun Casalilla. Madrid: Marcial Pons and Universidad Pablo de Olavide, 2009. 233–60.

Valenzuela, Pedro de. *Portugal unido y separado*. Madrid, 1651.

Valladares, Rafael. *La rebelión de Portugal 1640–1680*. Valladolid: Junta de Castilla y León, 1998.

———. "Haro sin Mazarino. España y el fin del orden de los Pirineos." *Pedralbes* 29 (2009) 339–92.

———. "Méndez de Haro y Guzmán, Luis." *Diccionario de Historia de España*. Madrid: Real Academia de la Historia, 2011.

Zeller, Gaston. "Les rois de France candidats a l'Empire. Essai sur l'ideologie imperiale en France." *Revue Historique* 173 (1934): 497–534.

Ziegler, Hendrik. "Le lion et le globe: La statue de Louis XIV par Domenico Guidi ou l'Espagne humiliée." *¿Louis XIV espagnol? Madrid et Versailles, images et modèles*. Ed. Gérard Sabatier and Margarita Torrione. Paris: Centre de Recherche du Château de Versailles and Maison des Sciences de l'Homme, 2009. 75–94.

Chapter 8

The Preacher Feeds and the Sermon Soothes: Body and Metaphor in Jesuit Preaching

Carlos-Urani Montiel and Shiddarta Vásquez Córdoba

Sed quoniam inter se habent non-nullam similitudinem vescentes atque discentes, propter fastidia plurimorum etiam ipsa sine quibus vivi non potest *alimenta condienda* sunt. [But as there is a certain analogy between learning and eating, the very food without which it is impossible to live *must be flavored* to meet the tastes of the majority].

Sancti Augustini, De doctrina christiana (IV, xi, 26).[1]

The subject of this chapter is the transmission of meanings through the *conceptual metaphor*, which serves not only as a figure of speech but as a tool of thought that enables us to gain access to an experience without having lived it. If this type of metaphor emphasises images or vital functions of the human body, such as that mentioned by Saint Augustine with respect to teaching and nutrition, then its lexical content transcends its meaning and stretches into other semantic fields. The corporeality reiterated in the Viceregal homily leads the preacher and his congregation to share and understand the concepts of THE PREACHER FEEDS and THE SERMON SOOTHES,[2] far beyond its metaphorical meaning. This cognitive process structures the composition and delivery of the discourse, turning it into a means of communication capable of preserving the identity of an audience.

Our aim is to study this process in two different sermons from Quito: one a funeral sermon, delivered by Alonso de Rojas in 1645, and the other a sermon of circumstances, preached from the pulpit of another Jesuit Father, Isidro

---

[1] Alonso Núñez de Haro, Archbishop of Mexico, paraphrases this passage in his "Pastoral letter I": "as St. Augustine teaches, spiritual food and corporeal food bear a certain similarity; and the dislike or fastidiousness of many makes it necessary to season even those very foods without which life cannot be preserved" (64–5).

[2] We follow the convention of writing conceptual metaphors in upper case.

152 *The Transatlantic Hispanic Baroque*

Gallego, on the occasion of the earthquakes that shook Lima in 1687. To this end, we are dividing the work into three sections: theory, tradition and analysis. Firstly, cognitive linguistics provides the theoretical support for the study of the organisation, storage and transmission of meaning present in units of language. The second section deals with the sacred oratory produced by the same Order to which the selected pieces belong, as the training of Jesuits articulates it within their own tradition. The final section analyses the "Sermon in honour of Mariana de Jesús" and the "Sermon of San Jerónimo, patron saint of tremors," where the metaphors reveal a semantic mapping moving from the corporeality of the congregation to their actual cohesion as a Catholic community.[3] In this way we attempt to link the precepts of the ministry of the word with the theoretical apparatus, and thus, to study particular cases delivered from the Viceregal pulpit, "[an] important vehicle of dissemination, [which] aims to resolve the most frequent cases in order to move the collective conscience and preserve public order" (Río Parra 17).

Cognitive Linguistics and Embodiment

The object of cognitive linguistics is meaning and how it is conveyed. The description in official terms, either of syntactical structures or of combinatorial rules and restrictions, are not the priority in a discipline which, rather than a theory of language, constitutes a flexible theoretical framework. Cognitive linguistics suggests that communication defines man as a social being; that the experience of the individual forms the basis of language; and, thus, its description is pragmatic and reconciles the mental plane with the cultural environment.[4] Consequently, the distinction between a more profound type of language, which we refer to as thought, and another superficial type, which would be language production, places the sensorimotor experience on a protagonic plane

---

[3]   For Fernando R. de la Flor, "to concern oneself with the sermon and orality is to ask oneself also about the body." Furthermore, "the awareness of that corporeality is fully recorded—and since ancient times—in the codes—that is to say, in the rhetorics—that regulate the function of the word in preaching" (124). For her part, Lina Rodríguez traces recurrences relating to healing and physical pain in Renaissance prose. The whole structure of the body as a focus for comparisons in sermons and symposia opened up "an extremely broad field of study yet to be explored" (257).

[4]   Already in 1936 Benjamin Lee Whorf noted that "We are inclined to think of language simply as a technique of expression, and not to realize that language first of all is a classification and arrangement of the stream of sensory experience which results in a certain world-order, a certain segment of the world that is easily expressible by the type of symbolic means that language employs" (130–31).

The Preacher Feeds and the Sermon Soothes 153

and considers language as a tool for organising, processing and transmitting information about that experience.

Conceptual metaphor is the distinctive theme of cognitive linguistics.[5] The essential idea is that many concepts, abstract concepts in particular, are structured and represented mentally by means of metaphors that determine their understanding and usage in language, not only in the language of poetry or literature, but also in conventional language. The identification of this metaphor is due to the generalisation of different linguistic expressions from which a recognisable pattern is abstracted, summarising the general meaning of them all. A metaphor is conceptual when it has a decisive role in the mental representation of abstract concepts or concepts that are not clearly outlined in our experience, such as intangible ideas (TIME IS MONEY), emotional states (AFFECTION IS WARM) or states of alteration/change (ARGUMENT IS WAR).[6]

George Lakoff and Mark Johnson, pioneers in the subject, state that "Our ordinary conceptual system, in terms of which we both think and act, is fundamentally metaphorical in nature" (39). They locate the patterns that govern metaphorical expressions, not in language, but in thought and conclude that for their description, there is a mental mapping that projects a source or start domain towards a target or end domain. This mapping occurs on an individual level: the external stimuli are represented through internal images and the processing of these images generates linguistic expressions. Thus, for every metaphor, the mental operation runs through the long-term memory, retrieves or generates an image and, finally, activates the concept concerned. However, this process reduces efficiency and disregards any inference. Cognitive networks, on the other hand, extend beyond the individual and store units of information externally.[7] This idea assumes that culture itself supports interaction between conceptual domains, where patterns of behaviour reduce the mental operation of the user, and places the latter in a physical, three-dimensional space, in which the body is the prime filter. The conceptual metaphor enables meanings to be distributed in the cultural environment and thus, the community increases its speed and potential for problem solving, decision making and language use.

Around 1725, Giambattista Vico recognised that the meaning of a metaphor was the product of abstract thought and that "it is worthy of observation that in all languages most expressions for inanimate objects are formed on the basis of

---

[5]   For an overview of the complete programme of the discipline, see the introduction by Dirk Geeraerts to the monograph on the subject (1–28), or the book by María Josep Cuenca and Joseph Hilferty.

[6]   In "Las dos grandes metáforas" (The two great metaphors), of 1924, José Ortega y Gasset defined these as "an essential mental instrument" that consists of "an intellectual procedure whereby we manage to learn what lies beyond our conceptual potential [...] it is a supplement to our intellectual arm" (387, 391).

[7]   The stance defended by Edwin Hutchins, Raymond Gibbs, *inter alia*.

transpositions of the human body, and of its parts, as well as human senses and emotions" (197–8). Centuries later, Lakoff and Johnson would confirm that "our experiences with physical objects (especially our own bodies) provide the basis for an extraordinarily wide variety of [...] ways of viewing events, activities, emotions, ideas, etc., as entities and substances" (64). This embodiment assumes that nerve endings are key to the processing of external stimuli and to the definition of thought processes. From this perspective, the opposition of substantialist dualism remains excluded, as the body/soul coexist as one, make use of reason and learn from the cultural ecosystem.

A corporeal metaphor is based on a correlation of experience between a particular sensorimotor domain and another target domain pertaining to abstract thought (judgement, reflection, learning, creativity). This activation offers the conditions for the mapping of entities, structures and relationships of the source domain towards the target domain. Mark Johnson establishes that the main means of reasoning depends, almost entirely, on the functioning of corporeal metaphors, as they allow for the appropriation of the semantics of the sensorimotor domain to understand and integrate a structure of knowledge of an abstract domain. The recurrence of the interaction of the body with its means begins to create patterns of inference that facilitate the processing of sensations and emotions. Metaphorical reasoning responds to a corporeal logic suitable for deducing a mapping already produced previously and for making the corresponding move towards the target domain. However, inference is not the only channel for conceptualising old or new experiences, as teaching, imitation and consensus enable metaphors to be shared among a specific community.

The everyday experience of correlation (sensorimotor/reasoning) within a wide network of users seems to be automatic and unconscious. The variety of models of feeling/thinking in transatlantic culture at the beginning of the modern era enables us to consider the body as a privileged place of composition for the distribution of messages. The corporeal domain as a focus of observation, a literary theme, a semantic and iconographic channel, was affected by a standard for each of its activities. It is no surprise that the *Spiritual Exercises*, the founding text of the Jesuits, imposes a regime that distances the reader from mundane pleasure and trains it for a metaphysical experience by controlling the corruptible body. Ignatius of Loyola writes an explanatory note on how to punish the body: "What appears most suitable and most secure with regard to penance is that the pain should be sensible in the flesh and not enter within the bones, so that it give pain and not illness" (56).

Preaching in the Company of Jesus

The sacred oratory is intended as a practice of social communication. Its association with cognition becomes apparent when comparing the three evidential perspectives of the homily: that of the preacher (and the realms of orality),[8] that of the argument (of the sermon itself regulated by the precepts), and that of the faithful.[9] Consequently, speeches are formed on the basis of instructions on the capacity of composition and execution of the speaker (*inventio, memoria, pronuntiatio*), the social coherence of the discourse (*dispositio, elocutio*), and the handling of the response from the audience. Whilst it is true that rhetoric dwells on non-verbal discursive proposals that the human figure of the priest must adopt,[10] the ultimate goal of the sermon is the disturbance of the body and soul of his congregation by means of the correct assemblage of the aforementioned five classic operations of the rhetorical device.

The inventory formed by Fernando Rodríguez de la Flor on the role of the preacher's body, as the deliverer of the word, gives precedence to his action and movement, as in the case of the mnemonic hand and the cry in full execution.[11] Nevertheless, the same researcher indicates that there is another body involved, one that is "subject to mimetic movements" and "placed in specific demand of the sacred annotation." A certain vocabulary, set of instructions governing body movement, is aimed at the spectator who "in countless metaphors is always in the end *penetrated* by the oratorical word" (146). And so, on the level of reception, from the analysis of the discourse and identification of the metaphors, it is possible to reflect upon the perception, the processing of information, the collective experience, the knowledge acquired or reactivated and the response produced.

---

[8]   On orality and rhetoric, see the article by María Dolores Abascal.

[9]   These focuses coincide with the emission, the object and the reception (Cerdan 61); and they also agree with Aristotle's concepts of *ethos, logos* and *pathos*.

[10]   For example, the homily of the Jesuit-trained preacher Caramuel does not only show "the whole traditional apparatus of movement: it rationalises it, legitimises it and makes it an indispensable condition of the effectiveness of the discourse, of its persuasive ability" (Robledo Estaire 147).

[11]   José de Ormaza, SJ, notes in 1648 that the audience celebrates the preacher: "Some, because he talked of many places, say: A great man!; he has the Scripture in his hands" (51). Another member of the Company, Juan Bautista Escardó, wrote a chapter "In which they give signs that facilitate the motion of emotion; especially tears." In addition to taking to the pulpit devout images, crucifixes or skulls, the condition is that "in order to move others the preacher has to be moved," that "the orator should think and pass through his imagination the images that represent what he is addressing." Motion as a craft requires that "the orator should not look at the cause as alien, but as his own" (333r–336r).

156 *The Transatlantic Hispanic Baroque*

Preaching in the Company of Jesus is part of a large-scale common project of evangelisation.[12] The 1550 version of the *Formula of the Institute* is clear on how to spread the faith: "by means of *public preaching*, lectures and any other ministration whatsoever of the Word of God, and further by means of retreats, the education of children and unlettered persons in Christianity" (Corella 30). The Jesuits codified the ministry of the word in their colleges and through their rhetorical precepts, and so they could be said to have a tradition of their own, which began around 1555 with the *Brief Treaty of How to Preach the Holy Gospel*, by Francisco de Borja, written at the request of Ignatius himself (438–59).[13] The Castilian version appears as an appendix to the author's biography, written by Father Rivadeneyra in 1592. The eight chapters of the *Treaty* contain practical and concise notes for before, during and after the exercise. The advice is intended for the physical and mental preparation of the orator. Tables 8.1 and 8.2 show the recurrence of expressions which construct the underlying conceptual metaphors in the text: THE PREACHER FEEDS and THE SERMON SOOTHES.

Table 8.1   Mapping between different conceptual domains (THE PREACHER FEEDS)

Mapping between different conceptual domains	
Source Domain	Target Domain
Feeding	*elocutio*/teaching
– abstract	+ abstract
Underlying conceptual metaphor: THE PREACHER FEEDS Expressions: 'Having read the interpreters, *ruminate* and *digest* the entire substance with careful consideration'. 'The little *bread* of doctrine that he [preacher], as an ignorant man, takes to the pulpit, is multiplied by his divine hands and distributed to the congregation'. The preacher, then, sustains the people with spiritual *delicacy* which he tastes and *swallows* so that it passes through his chest, converted into sustenance provided to the *stomach* of the people'. The preacher confesses and asks for fire for the sacrifice to be consumed, 'without this fire the delicacy will be *raw* and taste so unpleasant that the guests cannot digest it'.	

The target domain is the instruction of the audience, obtained with the correct elocution (style and composition) of the sermon. Father Álvaro Cienfuegos copies a passage where the third General of the Company relates that "we would

---

[12] The most comprehensive study of Spanish sacred oratory is the one by Félix Herrero Salgado. His third volume is exclusively on *Preaching in the Company of Jesus*.

[13] 'The most often reprinted and translated of Borja's writings, it presents preaching as a religious act, effective only insofar as God operates through it' (O'Malley 99).

provide equally for the villages, as for the most refined towns," as "if truths, he said, are not digested with understanding, they rarely nurture the audience with their beautiful light" (217). Francisco de Borja reuses the metaphor of food in his *Treaty*, so apparent in the biblical episodes of the forbidden fruit and the last supper. Communion itself and the mystery of transubstantiation reveal an organic mechanism; "it is that brilliant metaphor—the one whereby bread becomes the body of Christ—which opens up the description of the body as a laboratory and office of pity" (Rodríguez de la Flor 129).

The projection of the following metaphor is as below:

Table 8.2   Mapping   between   different   conceptual   domains   (THE SERMON SOOTHES)

Mapping between different conceptual domains	
Source Domain	Target Domain
corporeal health	*spiritual wellbeing*
– abstract	+ abstract
Underlying conceptual metaphor: THE SERMON SOOTHES	
Expressions: The preacher seeks that 'like a true doctor of ill souls, he distributes to his listeners the syrups and medicines of his gospel'. 'If it is sometimes deemed necessary, for the health and preservation of he who is to be cured, to open the wound with the rough cautery of correction, do not delay or forget the application of the oil of tenderness'. 'A wise doctor sweetens the pill, so that the lean stomach may receive it gently, and it will not cease to be effective because it is sweetened'.	

Here the semantic field of the source domain starts to become populated with all kinds of references to illnesses to which the body is exposed and which find relief on a spiritual plane, thanks to the homily. In the *Spiritual Exercises* there is an annotation from Mateo (10:1) which justifies the spreading of the Gospel: "Christ calls his beloved disciples and gives them the power to rid human bodies of demons and to *cure* all *illnesses*" (125).

The *Ratio studiorum* is the syllabus followed by every college in the Company. The final version of 1599 summarises the intellectual work of over 50 years of operations and describes the ministry of education in a hierarchical form. Its formulary document helps to identify objectives; the main one being to teach through disciplines that are in line with the Institute so that in so doing "they move towards the knowledge and love of our Creator and Redeemer" (67). Among these, rhetoric forms the basis of the curriculum and pursues "perfect eloquence" (209). The method for its study regulates creation, i.e. *inventio*. The interpretation of sources is controlled and the techniques of the art of oration are taught. On the one hand, the *Ratio* specifies: "only ancient classics are explained,

158   *The Transatlantic Hispanic Baroque*

under no circumstances more modern authors" (197) and it lists the authorities: Aristotle, Cicero, Quintilian; but it later clarifies: "so that they are expurged" (219). In fact, the *Arte Retórica* by Father Cipriano Suárez (1568) is the resource that filters examples and sets exercises of imitation, memory and recital, similar to being on stage. With this well understood, the syllabus continues, the student is ready to "take from rhetorical and topical places an abundance of arguments in favour of any thesis" (213) and to allocate "grammatical figures and metaphors to the chosen arguments" (290).

In the middle of the seventeenth century, two other precepts predominated.[14] We have that of Juan Bautista Escardó, "the ultimate work on sacred rhetoric, the most comprehensive, extensive and well-written in existence in our language" (Herrero García xv). The aim of the *Rhetorica christiana*, as the full title indicates, is the *fruit of the souls* and the *benefit of the listeners*. The Jesuit Father understands that one must preach with spirit, in other words, "any movement of the soul, any impetus, impulse or instinct." Escardó quotes another member of his Order, Cornelio A. Lapide, who says that "*spiritus*" applies to any habit, action and vital act through metaphor and almost always implies a deed governed and aspired in another place. Thus, the emphasis is not in the cries or in corporal actions, but in recognising that "words that are soft and modest, but full of great spirit and effect, move the listeners greatly, and overcome them, and persuade them: so that beneath the golden layer of a *pill*, is the hand of a *Rebarbaro* [purgative], that stirs the humours of the *sick*, and gives them *health*" (6v–7r). The effectiveness of the sermon lies in the structure of the discourse, but the mechanism of arguments uses the same projection between domains stretching from corporeal references to the spiritual world.

One century after the appearance of Borja's *Treaty*, the Atlantic expansion still required manuals for preaching the Gospel in contexts where the Jesuit missionaries and teachers held a monopoly. The *Christian Orator*, by Father Antonio Jarque, condemns the stylistic abuses of preaching and offers weapons for administering the doctrine overseas. We know that both the work and the author had an American presence (Rey Fajardo and González 262). The invectives of the *Orator*, of 1660, reworked the metaphor THE SERMON SOOTHES, based on particular cases: "The Lord behaved in this like a celestial *doctor*, who seeing, that in this general *Hospital* of the world are without further comparison the *sufferers*..." (3); "If I stop manifesting my *sores* to the *doctor* of my soul, I become *ill* and mortal..." (268); and:

---

[14]   The debate between the *Censura de la elocuencia* by José de Ormaza (1648) and its counterpart, the manuscript *Trece por docena*, by Valentín de Céspedes (1669), strays from our subject matter. On this controversy between ancient and modern or between high and popular discourse, see the article by Luis López Santos and the introduction to the book by Céspedes (Cerdan and Laplana).

The Preacher Feeds and the Sermon Soothes 159

> The Christian orator must *ingest* the memory of Hell, that the listeners being *ill*, imprudent would be the *doctor*, who in not tormenting them, ceased *prescribing* this *purge*, which although bitter, brings with it *health*, and the expulsion of the bad *humours* that lead to eternal death. (402)

The images of the fire that cooks the delicacy for the stomach of the people, like that of the doctor who gives treatment, highlight the value of the body in preaching. Borja instructed the preacher of his Order so that from every sermon he would take "a morsel and beneficial point" from the soul of his listenings/listeners (451).

Of *finis* and Tremors

We finally come to the Jesuit Province of the New Kingdom of Granada and Quito, established between 1611 and 1619 following the decrees of the Generals Aquaviva and Vitelleschi. "The Jesuit work established a communication network between the vast dominions of the European monarchies, acting as a point of contact, not only between the colleges and churches of the Company, but between their own congregations" (Montiel 79). The educational sites were the connecting points in the network of knowledge which enabled the circulation of manuscripts and printed matter.[15] In 1622, the year in which St Xavier and St Ignatius were canonised, the College of Quito acquired the title of *Real y Pontificia Universidad de San Gregorio Magno*, granted by Philip III. During the middle of the century, the rector Juan Severino obtained the document that gave professors the authority to grant all degrees, including doctorates. A member of this University was the Andalusian Alonso de Rojas (1588, Bujalance–1653, Quito) who studied philosophy and theology in Cartagena and, once ordained, obtained the prefecture at the San Gregorio Magno University.[16] Also there,

---

[15] 'In Quito there were large libraries in the San Luis Seminary, at San Gregorio and the Máximo College, the latter boasting 14,892 volumes (O'Neill and Domínguez 2: 1189).

[16] Rojas participated in the transcription of several Amazon expeditions (Díaz). Augustin de Backer states that he was Procurator General of the New Spain (252–53 and Addendum II). Rey Fajardo agrees with Backer on several points (places and dates of birth and death, acceptance into the Company, a period at the College of Panama, the role of preacher), but does not mention his brief stay in New Spain (*Biblioteca* 583–5). Perhaps the editor Sommervogel mistook our preacher for a Procurator of Mexico with the same name (Rey Fajardo, *Biblioteca* 65), although the coincidences would suggest to the contrary, and we add one more. The Procurator Alonso de Rojas was involved, along with the aforementioned Antonio Jarque, in a lawsuit concerning licences to preach and confess in Puebla de los Ángeles, from where they write a letter, published in Madrid in 1650, *To the king our lord, on*

160   *The Transatlantic Hispanic Baroque*

Isidro Gallego taught dogmatic and moral theology.[17] They were both renowned as excellent orators due to their narrative production and, above all, to their command of the congregation from the pulpit.

The selection of the sermons is justified not by their recent publication, but because they refer to experiences that have taken place, or have direct consequences, in parts far from where they were delivered. In these we shall see how the conceptual metaphors, THE PREACHER FEEDS and THE SERMON SOOTHES, are implied. Both the funeral sermon for a well-known figure in Quito, printed in Ciudad de los Reyes, and the earthquake that shook the same city of Lima and alarmed the inhabitants of Quito, reflect the communicative link between the Viceroyalties. Its modern editor, Hernán Rodríguez Castelo, states that this society, "founded on radicalised and exacerbated oppositions—body and soul, matter (or flesh) and spirit, sin and virtue," needed heroes to overcome these contradictions; "and these incarnations were the saints" (xxxi).

In 1645, Mariana de Jesús Paredes y Flores died, and Alonso de Rojas, her mentor and spiritual leader, delivered the funeral oration, which, writes the historian Pablo Herrera, "made such a great impression on the congregation, that they immediately sent it to print in the Capital of the Viceroyalty" (37).[18] *La Azucena de Quito* (The Lily of Quito) was beatified on the return of the Company to Ecuador in 1850 and canonised a century later. The "Funeral oration in honour of Mariana de Jesús" develops three coded matters of Ecclesiasticus (36:10): the hastening of time (*festina tempus*), the memory of death (*et memento finis*) and the dissemination of wonders (*ut enarrent mirabilia tua*); or as it appears in the *Biblia vulgata latina*: "Hasten the time and remember the end, that they may declare thy wonderful works" (Scio 321). The congregation was enthralled by the homily once their attention was caught: "my faithful." The occasion is these exequies and the intention is not to designate miracles "that is the role of our Mother, the Church," but to be aware of "a life without the *ailments* of blame" (38). On this path, a single argument structures the rest, as Mariana was predestined from her first steps: "she did not want to accept the gift that was presented to her by the breasts on which she *was raised*" (38) and Rojas insists: "*food* almost non-existent; her *abstinence* unprecedented" (48). At the age of ten, her vows of chastity, poverty and obedience came as no surprise. A life without sin guaranteed her "all the goods *she could wish for (a*

---

behalf of the province of the Company of Jesus of the New Spain: for the benefit of a book by the visitor bishop Iuan de Palafox.

[17] We have less information on Gallego. Manuel Sánchez Astudillo talks of a "distinguished teacher Father Isidoro Gallego who certainly taught in Quito" and quotes without reference a catalogue from that Province: "born in Puebla de España in the year 1647" (28).

[18] The quotations from the sermon come from this edition, which reproduces it in its entirety (Rojas 37–49).

pedir de boca" (41). Refusal of her mother's milk and fasting as she travelled the world were due to the transubstantiation that turned the little she ate into her entire sustenance: "she would move so quietly, in silence and unearthly quietude, which would often cause her to move as if outside of herself, and like a small bee she would feed on the chest of Christ, sucking his blood" (48).

The "daily exercises": fasting, not sleeping, examining her conscience, "discipline of one hundred lashes," "beans on her feet" and "a wire cilice, wound four times around the waist" (43), renew the virtue of this "seraph in human flesh." But how can someone so young display such fervour? The preacher replies: "The elderly girls are those who anxiously run after the smell of the *ointment* of Christ" (40); girls in terms of age, but elderly women in terms of virtue. Youth and old age are comparable because "whilst far apart in physical terms, they are alike in spiritual terms" (42). The misalignment of time reveals the objective of the discourse; that the value of actions prolongs the time of their duration. The best example of this is her death itself:

> Listening to a sermon (16 March 1645) by Father Rojas on the danger of an earthquake and epidemic in Quito, as had just occurred in Riobamaba, she offered herself to God for the good of her fellow citizens. On returning home, she was already ill and died soon afterwards. Her funeral was a popular outburst of devotion. (O'Neill and Domínguez 3: 3043)

The passing of Mariana takes us back to the source: "bring an end as soon as possible to the ills and hardships that we suffer and remember the oath you took" (Ecclesiasticus 36:10). The sacrifice, "in the final illness, meant to be in her desires with affectionate signs." The *memento mori* led her to have "become a mass death, of an entire nature (peregrine invention!), which she called her portrait" and instructed her towards the "contempt of all honours." Rojas states: "I have always wished to know what *antidote* she used against the *poison* of sin," and senses that "it was the memory of death" (46). The hagiographies of Teresa of Ávila and of Rose of Lima are the model for the saint from Quito, written by Jacinto Morán, SJ in 1696, who "reevaluated the historically hegemonic relationship between Lima, the Viceregal capital and archdiocesan see, and his own city and region" (Morgan 276). The sermon makes the body of Mariana the religious text and the place of spiritual and exemplary authority. Her actions contain the relief and antidote conveyed by the homily for the good of the community.

When Father Isidro Gallego delivered his sermon at the end of 1687, he did so in the midst of a political storm within the Company. In the 1630s the Mainas missions were established, the colleges of Cuenca and Popayán opened and the Jesuits decreed in the Court of Quito the foundation of its own Province, denied by Vitelleschi. Halfway through the century the academic prestige of

162   *The Transatlantic Hispanic Baroque*

the Gregorian University and the tensions with Santa Fe continued to increase, whilst the people and the Jesuits had adopted the image of *La Azucena* (The Lily) as their banner. By 1685 the Provincial Congregation insisted on the separation of provinces. Two years later, Tirso González, a former theologian and preacher, was appointed as General of the Company and at the beginning of 1688 he sent the Representative Francisco Altamirano to the lands of Quito; a visit that would last for eight years, but which came to an end, finally, with the establishment of the Province of Quito in 1696.[19]

The "Sermon of San Jerónimo, patron saint of tremors," was delivered on the occasion of the earthquake and tsunami that shook Lima, particularly in the area of Callao, on 20 October 1687, much to the anguish of the inhabitants of Quito.[20] Rodríguez Castelo, editor of the manuscript, tells us that the city entrusted Gallego with the homily of San Jerónimo, "who had been chosen as a protector against these type of threats," although his feast day was 30 September. "The oration was given in the cathedral, before a mixed and tense congregation" (liii). The choice was not by chance, as at the end of the sixteenth century,

> as the city of Quito was gravely afflicted by continuous plagues and tremors, the City Council decided to choose a saint as the patron and special protector of the city against tremors. As the names of many saints were documented, one was chosen, at random, and this was San Jerónimo, whom they took a vow to celebrate his solemn feast with a procession. (González Suárez 399–400)

The nature of the cause meant that the exordium began with an outburst towards the congregation: "Catholics." The preacher used and abused the word that shook everyone at the time and rebuked the Saint with it: "Tremble, Jerónimo; tremble, doctor maximus of the people [...] tremble, lord, and honour of the desolate [...] tremble example of ruins and falls." The authority on earth movements is Seneca but his use is not exact. Gallego quotes: "*Cum aliquid peccatum peccatur*, said Seneca, *tunc velut aegritudo corporis motus est*" (167); however, the alliteration and derivation do not come from the source, *Natulares quaestiones*: "cum aliquid peccatur, tunc velut aegri corporis motus est" (Seneca 168). Whilst an impersonal disorder stirs an infirm body, Gallego says that "when someone commits a sin, it is as if the body is cleansed of the *illness*." Thus, the direct relationship is established between "Jerónimo, distinguished patron saint of Quito," who trembles "ridding you of penitence and pain with strong

---

[19] See the historiographies by Torres Saldamando (274); José Jouanen; Ángel Santos (96–120) and Teófanes Egido (201–203).

[20] An account of the event was recorded in 1725 by Juan Barrenechea in his *Reloj astronómico de temblores* (Odriozola 23–36).

blows," and the building of the "City so stable that it would seem to have been erected on the high mount of perfection."

The Jesuit, still towards the same interlocutor, glosses the words with which Christ addressed his disciples (Mateo 5:13): "you are the *salt* of the earth, effective for *healing it* from tremors to which it is subjected by the accidents of our sins like a malign *fever*" (167). The paradox between firmness and movement activates the conceptual metaphors, the subject of our study, to convey the content of the sermon. One element becomes a key point: "the remedy for this ailment lies in *salt*" and in its properties: it seasons food, preserves from decay and promotes purity. Thus, "that trembling of the wrath of God, as is the *medicine* that Jerónimo *administers to us* in the effectiveness of his *salt*, is the firmness that establishes it, the stability that perpetuates it and the calm that in his movement stills and assures it" (168). San Jerónimo himself teaches in his *Epistles*: "there is nothing in this life that gives men more strength, or is healthier for them, than after committing sin, not delaying the *medicine* of confession and penitence" (227). Along these lines, Gallego incites "to tremble in order not to fall, to die in order to stand." The sacrament of the communion with which the discourse ends "goes public today" because "this divine *delicacy* must be *seasoned*, in order to be of *benefit* to the soul, with the *salt* of Jerónimo, which is the reckoning of accounts demanded by the fear of judgement" (169).[21]

In conclusion, the way in which Jesuit preaching questions people, seeks to discipline them and give them certain abilities to act and respond, is in a process of semantic construction that starts with rhetorical precepts, which instruct the preacher to activate the thoughts of the congregation based on their sensorimotor experience. In his *Oráculo manual*, Gracián recommends "to procure human means, as if there were no divine means, and the divine means, as if there were no human means" (429). This is achieved through a symbolic/ Catholic universe that is superimposed on daily life and adds a spiritual content to any secular activity, such as eating, health or teaching.

Here is where the conceptual metaphor comes in, consisting in the projection of a source domain—with its entities and relationships—on to another target or end domain. The transmission of experiences particular to those who have not been direct witnesses and in itself, the transfer of meanings through metaphors is more effective when the discourse reiterates elements on corporeal mechanisms personified by the spectator. The conceptual metaphors THE PREACHER FEEDS and THE SERMON SOOTHES resort to physiological functions and make the homily a spectacle that cures and nurtures. Its functioning also determines the cognitive process; to think something is to form a mental image; understanding

---

[21] Baltasar Gracián had already formed this food metaphor relating to Holy Communion, an occasion "To take communion, as in an open banquet" (*Comulgatorio* 474–6).

164 *The Transatlantic Hispanic Baroque*

the thought means comprehending that image. The greatest concern of Jesuit evangelisation focused on mediating and regulating the forming of these images and concepts among the faithful, bearers of one identity. The sermons delivered by professors of the Gregorian University of Quito reflect upon the proximity of death, they strengthen their argument with biblical examples and promote the leading of an exemplary life. The insistence on body functions—feeding and curing—enables the transformation of pain/fear in the face of death, into hope and spiritual relief. The orator makes the handling of abstract images into an instrument of accessible and immediate emotions.

The aim is to move the congregation to transmit global standards and consensus. The effect on the receiver implies an idea of permanence that reduces variables of behaviour, regulates passion or affection and gives the spectator a major role in the continuation of their community. The rhetorical formulas and figures on the one hand, and a collection of Catholic norms on the other, are subject to the clear and explicit objective of "shaking the public," as we are reminded by Dámaso Alonso (96). In the act of the homily, the correlation of the sensorimotor experience with the cognitive experience occurs on a collective level, where it would be impossible not to acquire these metaphors and make use of some form of conceptual reasoning, *a distinguishing feature* of the communities belonging to the Hispanic dominions at the dawn of the modern era.

Bibliography

Alonso, Dámaso. "Predicadores ensonetados. La oratoria sagrada, hecho social apasionante del siglo XVII." *Del siglo de oro a este siglo de siglas*. Madrid: Gredos, 1962. 95–104.

Backer, Augustin de. *Bibliothèque de la Compagnie de Jésus*. Vol. 7. Ed. Carlos Sommervogel. Brussels: Schepens, 1896.

Borja, Francisco de. *Tratado breve del modo de predicar el santo evangelio. Tratados espirituales*. Ed. Cándido de Dalmases. Barcelona: Juan Flors, 1964. 438–59.

Cerdan, Francis. "El sermón barroco: un caso de literatura oral." *Edad de Oro* 7 (1988): 59–68.

———, and José Laplana. "Introducción." *Trece por docena*. By Valentín de Céspedes. Toulouse: Université du Mirail, 1998. 10–74.

Cienfuegos, Álvaro. *La heroica vida, virtudes y milagros del grande S. Francisco de Borja*. Madrid: Viuda de Juan García, 1717.

Corella, Jesús, ed. "Fórmula del Instituto. Texto paralelo de las tres redacciones." *Constituciones de la Compañía de Jesús*. Ed. Santiago Arzubialde, Jesús Corella and Juan Manuel García-Lomas. Bilbao: Mensajero, 1993. 30–40.

Cuenca, María Josep and Joseph Hilferty. *Introducción a la lingüística cognitiva*. Barcelona: Ariel, 1999.

Díaz, Rafael. "Introducción." *La aventura del Amazonas*. Madrid: Historia 16, 1986. 7–36.

Dolores Abascal, María. "Oralidad y retórica en el Barroco." *Barroco*. Ed. Pedro Aullón de Haro. Madrid: Verbum, 2004. 349–75.

Egido, Teófanes, ed. *Los jesuitas en España y en el mundo hispánico*. Madrid: Marcial Pons, 2004.

Escardó, Juan Bautista. *Rhetorica christiana*. Mallorca: Herederos de Gabriel Gualp, 1647.

Gallego, Isidro. "Sermón de San Jerónimo, patrón de temblores." *Letras de la Audiencia de Quito, período jesuítico*. Ed. Hernán Rodríguez Castelo. Caracas: Biblioteca Ayacucho, 1984. 167–9.

Geeraerts, Dirk. "Introduction: A Rough Guide to Cognitive Linguistics." *Cognitive Linguistics: Basic Readings*. Berlin: Mouton de Gruyter, 2006. 1–28.

Gibbs, Raymond. "Taking Metaphor Out of Our Heads and Putting it into the Cultural World." *Metaphor in Cognitive Linguistics: Selected Papers from the Fifth International Cognitive Linguistics Conference, Amsterdam, July 1997*. Ed. Raymond Gibbs and Gerard Steen. Amsterdam: Benjamins, 1999. 145–66.

González Suárez, Federico. *Historia eclesiástica del Ecuador: 1520–1600*. Quito: Imprenta del Clero, 1881.

Gracián, Baltasar. *Agudeza y arte de ingenio; Oráculo manual; El comulgatorio*. Antwerp: Geronymo y Iuanbaut, 1669.

Herrera, Pablo, ed. *Antología de prosistas ecuatorianos I*. Quito: Imprenta del Gobierno, 1895.

Herrero García, Miguel. *Sermonario clásico, con un ensayo sobre la oratoria sagrada*. Madrid and Buenos Aires: Escelicer, 1942.

Herrero Salgado, Félix. *La oratoria sagrada española de los siglos XVI y XVII*. 5 vols. Madrid: Fundación Universitaria Española, 1996–2006.

Hutchins, Edwin. *Cognition in the Wild*. Cambridge: MIT Press, 1995.

Ignacio de Loyola. *Ejercicios espirituales*. Ed. Jordi Groh. Barcelona: Abraxas, 1999.

Jarque, Antonio. *Tomo cuarto de la primera parte del Orador Cristiano, sobre el Salmo del Miserere*. Zaragoza: Miguel de Luna, 1660.

Jerónimo. *Epistolas del glorioso doctor de la Yglesia, San Geronimo*. Ed. Francisco López Cuesta. Madrid: Luis Sánchez, 1613.

Johnson, Mark. *The Meaning of the Body: Aesthetics of Human Understanding*. Chicago: University of Chicago Press, 2007.

Jouanen, José. *Historia de la Compañía de Jesús en la antigua provincia de Quito: 1570–1774*. Quito: Ecuatoriana, 1941.

Lakoff, George and Mark Johnson. *Metáforas de la vida cotidiana*. Madrid: Cátedra, 1986.

López Santos, Luis. "La oratoria sagrada en el seiscientos. Un libro inédito del P. Valentín de Céspedes." *Revista de Filología Española* 30 (1946) 353–68.

Montiel, Carlos-Urani. "Labor jesuita en Nueva Francia y hagiografía en Nueva España: un ensayo de replicación cultural." *Transitions* 5 (2009): 79–96.

Morgan, Ronald. "'Just like Rosa': History and Metaphor in the Life of a Seventeenth-Century Peruvian Saint." *Biography* 21.3 (1998): 275–310.

Núñez de Haro, Alonso. *Sermones escogidos, pláticas espirituales privadas, y dos pastorales.* Madrid: Imprenta Hija de Ibarra, 1807.

O'Malley, John. *The First Jesuits.* Cambridge: Harvard University Press, 1993.

O'Neill, Charles and Joaquín Domínguez. *Diccionario histórico de la Compañía de Jesús (DHCJ).* 4 vols. Rome: Institutum Historicum, 2001.

Odriozola, Manuel de, ed. *Terremotos: colección de las relaciones de los más notables que ha sufrido esta capital y que la han arruinado.* Lima: Aurelio Alfaro, 1863.

Ormaza, José de. *Censura de la elocuencia.* Ed. Giuseppina Ledda and Vittoria Stagno. Madrid: El Crotalón, 1985.

Ortega y Gasset, José. "Las dos grandes metáforas." *Obras completas. Vol. 2: El Espectador.* Madrid: Alianza, 1983. 387–400.

"Ratio studiorum." El sistema educativo de la Compañía de Jesús. Ed. Eusebio Gil and Carmen Labrador. Madrid: Universidad Pontificia Comillas, 1992. 61–295.

Rey Fajardo, José del. *Biblioteca de escritores jesuitas neogranadinos.* Bogotá: Pontificia Universidad Javeriana, 2006.

———. *Los jesuitas en Venezuela, Vol. 5: Las misiones germen de la nacionalidad.* Caracas: Universidad Católica Andrés Bello, 2007.

———, and Felipe González. *Los jesuitas en Antioquia, 1727–1767: aportes a la historia de la cultura y el arte.* Bogotá: Pontificia Universidad Javeriana, 2008.

Río Parra, Elena del. *Cartografías de la conciencia española en la Edad de Oro.* Mexico, DF: Fondo de Cultura Económica, 2008.

Robledo Estaire, Luis. "El cuerpo como discurso: retórica, predicación y comunicación no verbal en Caramuel." *Criticón* 84–5 (2002): 145–64.

Rodríguez, Lina. "Los símiles corporales entre el sermón y el coloquio misceláneo: las *Comparaciones* de Pérez de Moya." *Le corps comme métaphore dans l'Espagne des XVIe et XVIIe siècles.* Ed. Augustin Redondo. Paris: Université de la Sorbonne Nouvelle III, 1992. 245–57.

Rodríguez Castelo, Hernán. "Sociedad y literatura en la Audiencia de Quito." *Letras de la Audiencia de Quito, período jesuítico.* Caracas: Biblioteca Ayacucho, 1984. xi–lxxxi.

Rodríguez de la Flor, Fernando. "La oratoria sagrada del Siglo de Oro y el dominio corporal." *Culturas en la Edad de Oro.* Ed. José María Díez Borque. Madrid: Universidad Complutense, 1995. 123–48.

Rojas, Alonso de. "Oración fúnebre en honra de Mariana de Jesús." Ed. Pablo Herrera. *Antología de prosistas ecuatorianos I*. Quito: Imprenta del Gobierno, 1895. 37–49.

Sánchez Astudillo, Manuel. *Textos de catedráticos jesuitas en Quito colonial*. Quito: Casa de la Cultura Ecuatoriana, 1959.

Santos, Ángel. *Los jesuitas en América*. Madrid: Mapfre, 1992.

Scio, Phelipe. *La Biblia vulgata latina, Vol. 11*. Madrid: Benito Cano, 1796.

Seneca, Lucius Annaeus. *Naturales quaestiones II*. Ed. Thomas Corcoran. Cambridge: Harvard University Press, 1972.

Torres Saldamando, Enrique. *Los antiguos jesuitas del Perú*. Lima: Imprenta Liberal, 1882.

Vico, Giambattista. *Ciencia nueva*. Ed. Rocío de la Villa. Madrid: Tecnos, 1995.

Whorf, Benjamin Lee. "The Punctual and Segmentative Aspects of Verbs in Hopi." *Language* 12.2 (1936): 127–31.

PART III
The Urban World and the Hispanic Baroque

Chapter 9

The Creole Metropolis

Manuel Lucena Giraldo

In 1684, the young Alonso Ramírez, born in San Juan in Puerto Rico, boarded the Manila galleon and set sail for the Philippines, in search of his fortune. This was an act of desperation, as he had come to the Viceroyalty of New Spain in the hope of carving out a future for himself, but this had not turned out as planned. But the worst was yet to come. Held captive by English pirates, he was taken on a dreadful journey of pillage, destruction, rape and cannibalism, stretching from Vietnam to China and from the Indian Ocean to the Atlantic. When he finally arrived in Yucatán, having travelled around the world, the news of his ordeal reached the ears of the Viceroy, the Count of Galve, who ordered the eminent Viceroyalty-born Carlos Sigüenza y Góngora to spread the news of his ordeal, for the edification and to the amazement of all. The result of this was, in fact, a fundamental text entitled *Infortunios de Alonso Ramírez* (Misfortunes of Alonso Ramirez), published in Mexico in 1690 by Sigüenza, "cosmographer and Professor of Mathematics of the King Our Lord in the Mexican Academy" (13).

The universal nature of Ramírez's experience was as engaging as the presence of the cities in his life, as in these lay his hope, whilst in the frontier spaces surrounding them, and the dark seas in particular, his misadventure unfolded. A collective mentality can be seen in this particular reasoning, typical of the Spanish rule, with its Mediterranean and Greco-Roman traditions. In fact, since the reign of Philip III, cities had become spaces with their own identities, a process often characterised by conflict but also always dynamic and creative. More than a century after the discovery of the New World, the largest of these cities aspired to become metropolis, and all of them, sooner or later, began to acquire their own idiosyncrasies.[1] The metropolitan intentions of the cities under the rule of the Spanish monarchy—the first global empire in history, the expression of a polycentric character visible across four continents—fitted well with the model of distant government Habsburg monarchs exercised over the

---

[1]   Metropolis, for the Greeks, was the mother city and, for the Romans, the capital of a province. In 1611 it was defined as the "main city from which many neighbouring towns depending on it have emerged" (Covarrubias 548). In the first edition of the *Diccionario* of the RAE, it is defined as the "main city that has control or rules over the others." It is also the main church or See, thus metropolitan, of an archiepiscopal city, according to Terreros Pando (580).

opulent kingdoms of the Indies and its dependencies, so far from the hardship and wars of seventeenth century Europe (Gruzinski, *Las cuatro* 45). Thus, the metropolitan projects of Mexico and Lima, the head cities of the Viceroyalties of New Spain and Peru, were not only compatible with loyalty to the monarch and his viceroys, but reinforced it and expressed it to the full. They also had an emulating effect on smaller governments and entities (Bravo Lira 398). In terms of symbolic construction, the determining factor was the overseas presence of the viceroys, who were seen as an extension of the monarchy—"the king in the flesh," as the Marquis of Cañete remarked (cited in Aldana Rivera 195)—demonstrating the power of his righteousness and goodness to the inhabitants of the Spanish American city. The cities celebrated their newly-acquired universal body as well as their right to proclaim themselves as the celestial city of Jerusalem and city of providence, the ubiquitous place indicated by God for the punishment and redemption of man (Rodríguez Moya 94).

Festivals and Baroque Politics

The elements of this self-referential urban construction, which made these cities unique places to which their inhabitants became attached through an incipient local patriotism, were projected by means of mass indoctrination, making the Baroque spectacle, so facilitated by the accumulation of political power, wealth and sanctity, an end in itself. The festivals "were" the Baroque metropolis; they established it, recreated it and preserved it. As stated in *Ecclesiastes*, they turned simulation into reality, through the promulgation of an ephemeral theatricality of martyrdom. In both spectacular and specular calendar cycles, the sphere of the sacred and the profane, the Creoles, aspiring to an important public role and frustrated at not achieving it, were able to emphasise the ceremonial and the formalities. They conformed to the appearance of things to the detriment of their substance. Meanwhile, the peninsular Spaniards sublimated the enormous effort involved in building a global monarchy and found an illusion of absolute control, a substitute representation which provided them with an escape from a reality that was impossible to endure. It was during that time that the political and moral economy typical of the Baroque period was created (Marzahl 638; Romero 73; Rodríguez de la Flor 37).

We often do not know for how long festivals lasted in the Spanish American cities of the seventeenth century, but we do know that their true vocation was to take possession of daily life, almost making it disappear altogether. Far from obeying a supposed counter-reformist obscurantism, this circumstance underlines the nature of Baroque politics, committed to the absolute, to the control over time and space. In the kingdom of Chile at that time there were 94 religious events, which, together with the 52 Sundays in the year, amounted to

146 special days (Cruz de Amenábar 122). They were of varying importance and duration. The *Limpia Concepción de María* was celebrated in Lima between 14 October 1656 and 10 March of the following year and included—in addition to the strict religious celebration of the dedication to the Virgin Mary—fireworks and street processions with floats displaying seven-headed serpents, mountain scenes with savages, flower carts, Paradise with Adam and Eve, sailing boats firing artillery and images of the Catholic monarch Philip IV. A masquerade funded by the University of San Marcos, particularly generous and high-handed on that occasion, was accompanied by six carts carrying 1,000 illustrious figures and 500 "fools" (masquerading). There was also a staging of a battle involving four galleys attacking a castle, provided by the city's blacksmiths and tailors, and there was a procession of black people, who provided a musical accompaniment to the event, both engaging and suspicious-sounding. They funded a bullfight, as it was common belief that this was of particular comfort to the dark-skinned *morenos* who worshipped it (Bernand 68). But most remarkable of all were the canonisations and beatifications, particularly in the case of Creoles, as they reaffirmed the providential content of the Spanish American metropolis.

Whilst Mexico experienced the growing devotion to the Virgin of Guadalupe, patron saint of the Viceroyalty of New Spain since 1747, Lima celebrated the canonisation of its former archbishop, Saint Toribio de Mogrovejo, the missionary and traveller Saint Francisco Solano, the *mulatto* and 'miraculous nurse' Saint Martín de Porres and the humble Creole Saint Rose of Lima (Vila 43). The latter was honoured in 1671 with *bando de luminarias*, a procession of the members of all monasteries and convents (only the Jesuits had the privilege of not attending), or honours of the troops and merchants—who paved their streets with silver bars and adorned it with damasks—bulls and greasy poles.[2] Eight years later, for the celebration of Saint Toribio, a procession was organised, including floats with young female instrumentalists dressed as nuns and statues portraying heroic deeds from his life, such as the baptism of Rose, also a future saint. In Mexico there was much celebration in 1621 for the sanctity of Ignatius of Loyola. Alongside the creation of wonderful altars, fireworks and processions, the most striking element was the procession that included a life-sized image of the saint—with a very devout face, a figure of Jesus on the cross in its right hand—and the line of five triumphant floats representing stages in his immortal life: youth, science, the triumph of faith over heresy, the conversion of peoples and the reformation of states (Bayle 735).

---

[2]   The ultimate "conventual city" of the Americas was Quito, which in 1650, with approximately 25,000 inhabitants, had a cathedral, five parish churches (and three more in outlying areas), four convents, five monasteries and two *recolecciones* (retirement convents). Lima had a large population of monks and nuns and a high number of "large" convents (Martín 174).

174   *The Transatlantic Hispanic Baroque*

Corpus Christi was soon adopted by the *cabildos*, or municipal governments, as their official festival, and therefore in cities such as Caracas and Guayaquil this led to disputes over pre-eminence. There may have been cases in which insolent people failed to respect the seats reserved for officials and the king's servants, conquistadors and honourable figures. It was usually celebrated with dances, processions and the staging of comedies and religious plays were performed in Lima in 1635: *La Margarita del cielo: Santa Margarita de Crotona*, a work featuring a Portuguese adventurer who had repented of his sins and become a clergyman, and *Las dos columnas de Hércules*. The following years saw the staging of *No está el cielo seguro de ladrones* (Lohmann Villena, "Las comedias" 866). In Caracas, for greater entertainment, the black population also organised parades with a monster, giants and little devils (Duarte 675). In Potosí, where the Feast of *Corpus* lasted six days, this was used to display its inhabitants' equestrian skills and inventiveness, thus dispelling the ill will towards them and their bad reputation, as their only sin was to have been blessed with good fortune (Mújica Pinilla 310). Bulls were a feature of both religious and secular festivals. Lima celebrated the days of the Epiphany, San Juan, Santiago and the Assumption, but bulls were also run to welcome viceroys, as in 1629. Or they were organised by the guilds of silversmiths, blacksmiths, confectioners or soldiers in celebration of their patron saints. Blacks, *mulattos* and Indians participated increasingly in bullfights and became peons or horsemen, thus diluting the aristocratic element of the festival (Iwasaki Cauti 318).

Secular festivals also provided ample opportunity for celebration. The *paseo del pendón* (procession of the standard) with the royal arms and those of the city was the most important and was held on the anniversary of the city's foundation. The ceremony, in accordance with the laws of the Indies, had to be similar, but with the customary casuistry, there were local variants. In Guatemala, the descendants of the allied indigenous peoples, who had participated along with the Spanish in the conquest, proudly formed processions. The locals dressed in their finest and the houses and streets were adorned with tapestries and drapes. The *alférez real*, the standard bearer responsible for covering the costs of the banquets, bulls and fireworks, was accompanied by a squadron of horsemen and the authorities according to their hierarchy, along with guards, footmen, macebearers and servants, in accordance with a complicated ceremonial reflecting each one's particular place. Royal deaths also played a key role, as they allowed for a display of loyalty and the advent of the succession to the throne (Ossorio 460–61). Funeral pyres or magnificent burial mounds were built in the churches, statues and linens placed thereon; judges and aldermen wore their mourning dress made with specific fabrics and royal officials competed in their displays of mourning. There was music, with discordant drums, and gun salutes. The death of Queen Anne of Austria in 1581 led Philip II to impose on cities under Spanish rule a public penance and general mourning, as he believed her

The Creole Metropolis 175

death to be linked to "the great sins of Christianity" (MacCormack, "El gobierno" 217). Proclamations, births and oaths of monarchs closed the cycle of pain and atonement, and not only involved the public procession of the standard but the procession of all hierarchies in the city, the erection of lights, the reading of royal letters, obedience (no oath) "on the heads of each and every one" and, finally, the customary cries of: "Guatemala, Guatemala for the King Philip II our lord, King of Castile and León and of the Indies," in the case of this monarch (Bayle 684).

The 1666 proclamation of Charles II in Lima became famous. In the main square, a temporary altarpiece/shrine was erected, where the monarch was depicted as an artistic figure accompanied by angels and the cardinal virtues, all crowned by the figure of Fame. On one side, an Inca offered him a golden crown, and on the other, a *coya*, or "Inca queen," offered one of flowers (Ramos Sosa 279). The ceremonies could be followed by dancing, discussions, bullfighting and comedies. Although everyone was obliged to attend, under penalty of a fine, a feeling of loyalty to the king that should be renewed and displayed in public was the norm. In Panama, the guilds of shoemakers, storekeepers, tailors, carpenters or silversmiths readily committed their funds in order to participate in demonstrations of loyalty. One extraordinary case was that of a black slave who bequeathed his entire meagre fortune to his beloved King of Spain (Castillero Calvo 270). The reception of the royal seal, arrivals of the viceroys and on a smaller scale those of the governors, could be extremely ostentatious, as they would last for months and include, in addition to their personal welcome, the presentation of gifts, travelling through triumphal arches, masquerades, fireworks, comedies, religious plays and dancing. Philip II tried to stem the costs of this squandering, both theatrical and political, which saw no bounds and would leave the *cabildo* in financial ruin, as in the case of Lima in 1606. The festivities for Carnival and Candlemas in Cartagena were also on a large scale. There were dances held in ballrooms for whites, *mulattos* and blacks in turn; the whites could attend the dances of the other two and the *mulattos* those of the blacks, but not vice versa (Rípodas Ardanaz 16). Finally, there were one-off festivals, ranging from those which may have been organised for the arrival of investigating judges—as in Mexico following the Martín Cortés rebellion—to those for consecrating cathedrals and churches, the inauguration of fountains and aqueducts, defeats of pirates or the victory over the Turks in Algiers or over the heretics in Flanders.

Creolism and Loyalty

Although the Spanish American metropolises were governed from an itinerant court, such as that of the Habsburgs, and on the basis of constant consensus and negotiation, during the seventeenth century a civilising process was created

176   *The Transatlantic Hispanic Baroque*

to make them "true cultural centres, recognisable by the individuality and inimitability of certain costly, complex and exemplary products" (Kubler 30). It could not be otherwise, as the bureaucratic *cursus honorum* was moving within a Spanish solar system whose cities in Asia, the Americas and Europe were like its constituent planets. This was an empire of cities. A member of the Council of the Indies, Eugenio de Salazar, expressed it fittingly when he mischievously recounted his own life:

> I was born and married in Madrid. I was brought up studying at the schools of Alcalá de Henares and Salamanca, I graduated from the University of Sigüenza, and gained a doctorate in Mexico. I was judge at the Royal Saltworks, customs on the border with nearby Portugal. As investigating judge I went to La Cortina, and governed in the Canary Islands. I was a judge in Hispaniola. I was public prosecutor in Guatemala, and then I went to Mexico as public prosecutor, and then judge. From there I went to the highest court of the Indies, to which God promoted me. There I embraced his divine fire. (Barrientos Grandón 633)

The inhabitants of the Spanish American metropolises could thus build up an urban identity by proclaiming themselves the centre rather than the periphery; they placed themselves in the first globalisation as emporia of a culture built from bits and pieces from home and abroad. This attitude in some way had been visible since the times of the conquest in the chronicles and accounts—in admiration of the utopian paradise gained, and in despair of the lack of reward and the unfairness of an unjust monarch towards the worthy conquistadors and their descendants. But from the latter decades of the sixteenth century, as well as from 1620 in particular, when the reforms of the government of the Indies forming part of the plans for restoring the monarchy to its former power, supported by the Count-Duke of Olivares, were seen by far-from-negligible sectors of the Creole aristocracy as an onerous and tyrannical way of ruling them, there emerged a series of imaginary representations of specific urban spaces, nurtured by classic traditions, biblical images and counter-reformist liturgies (Elliott 161). In the face of the Renaissance and empirical model implicit in chronicles of the Indies and geographical accounts, the Creole urban myths projected a new loyalty, based on a Baroque topology, with an exuberant reading of the symbols and rhythms of its own nature, also hagiographic due to its aim of exemplifying and disciplining those inhabiting it.

The word "Creole," from the Portuguese "crioulo," was used in the middle of the sixteenth century to refer to slaves born in the Indies. But by 1563, it was appearing as a way of describing the white Spaniard born in the Indies, used by the Bishop of Guatemala, for instance. The term soon became widespread in Peru and the Jesuits used it from then on in their correspondence with Rome and in edifying literature. The novelty of the term was expressed by the

The Creole Metropolis 177

Governor of Peru, García de Castro, when he remarked in 1567 to the President of the Council of the Indies that the Americas had become full of Creoles. The mistrust felt by the high officials towards the Spanish born in the Americas, a long-established sentiment, was accentuated during the reign of Philip II. The geographer López de Velasco had declared that they had darker skin than the Europeans and would eventually become *Indianised*, and in turn increasingly barbaric and stupid (Álvarez xcv). The lack of regard shown to the secular clergy born in New Spain, particularly of *mestizo* or mixed-race origin, in the allocation of Indian parishes was also related to their supposed disloyal, lazy and incompetent nature. In the final decades of the sixteenth century, faced with what they saw as an outrageous lack of confidence in their loyalty to the monarch and an unfair attack on just rights—suspiciously at the same time as the fervour in the peninsular cities for the purity of blood—the Spanish Americans began to express their Creolism assuredly and convincingly in order to flaunt their loyalty and to demand justice.

Yet it is not easy to determine when urban praise became one of their preferred cultural and political vehicles. Since the sixteenth century, local accounts, of humanist inspiration and Italian origin, had helped to disseminate an image of the city as a centre for the organisation and dissemination of faith in an extensive environment. In accordance with the canonical model of the heavenly Jerusalem, its values exhibited the city as a central, natural and providential site, organising the surrounding territory (Quesada 93). The mouthpieces of the incipient Creolism were masters at adapting local accounts to their circumstances, at using the existing utopian traditions to proclaim virginity, and even at reinterpreting, if required, the past of the indigenous peoples to make it part of their noble genealogy. The Creole capacity for producing opposing stereotypes to those imposed on them was remarkable. Whilst there were peninsular Spaniards who, for example, criticised the excessive freedom of women in the Americas—they were particularly scandalised by the fact that important ladies were allowed to play cards and dice in the company of other women and of men—the Creoles had no qualms about mocking the pathetic absurdity of the European greenhorn or *gachupín*, the peninsular Spaniard who was so ignorant of the New World that he was unaware of the greatness of its geography and confused Peru with Guatemala (Gerbi 226).

The tracing of a fabulous and fanciful genealogy of the Spanish American urban creation, manipulative of the records of its etymology and its toponymy, served the purpose of turning the Renaissance city of the conquistadors into a Creole metropolis. The natives were no longer corralled into a separate community—that "republic of the Indies" of the sixteenth century never existed—but became neighbours like everyone else, whilst blacks and castes "appeared" everywhere. There was no longer just a vision of the possible city, but an authentic, real place that offered a particular civilisation and existence

178   *The Transatlantic Hispanic Baroque*

(Szuchman 24). The Spanish American cities, since their foundation, had borne a name that indissolubly linked them to the patron saints and tastes of the founder, celestial guardian figures and often a coat of arms. There had been a need, however, to interweave the political and the cultural into a new genealogy that would exceed the narratives of the conquest to construct an urban account of the loyalty and exceptional nature of the Creoles worthy of justice, an epic of the Spanish city in the Indies. The two Viceregal capitals produced, not by chance, the most interesting and complex of these new genealogies.

Sublime Lima and Mexico

As the capital of the Viceroyalty of Peru was about to celebrate its centenary, the Creole from Chuquisaca, fray Antonio de la Calancha, the author of the influential *Crónica moralizada del orden de San Agustín en el Perú* (1638), recounted the edifying Augustine history of Peru. In his project of applying Genesis to the New World, he praised its climate, explained the stellar influences from which it benefited, presented the rivers, streams and springs, and evoked the fruits picked, the plants and trees, the birds and wild animals, to end in a vibrant tribute to mankind and the character of its natives (MacCormack, "Antonio" 67–8).

Almost one century earlier, the humanist Francisco Cervantes de Salazar had dared to overlook in his *Crónica de la Nueva España* (1564) the references to the Aztec city of Tenochtitlan, to describe instead the contemporary greatness of the metropolis, the majesty of the main square, the size of the viceroy's palace and the number of monasteries, churches, hospitals and charitable colleges, as well as the construction of the cathedral.[3] Around 1604, Baltasar Dorantes de Carranza echoed the growing disagreements brewing there between peninsular Spaniards and Creoles, and in the sonnet "El gachupín" he demythologised the viceregal reality, exposed the urban corruption with Arcadian enthusiasm and criticised the continuing injustice towards the conquistadors and founders of the kingdom and their suffering descendants (Lorente Medina 77).

---

[3]   There were two cathedrals in Mexico. The older, a church with three naves and a wooden roof, was built between 1524 and 1532 by the architect Juan de Sepúlveda. It was rebuilt in 1585 and demolished in 1626. The first stone of the current church, which was thought to be even larger than the enormous cathedral of Seville, although the more reasonable new cathedral in Salamanca was later chosen as the model, was laid in 1573. Claudio de Arciniega and Juan Miguel de Agüero were the authors of the project, which was completed in 1667, also the year of its consecration. The façade, which José Damián Ortiz began to execute after winning a tender in 1786, was completed by Manuel Tolsá. The work was concluded in 1813 (Toussaint 2–3).

The Creole Metropolis   179

That same year, the Creolised Bernardo de Balbuena from La Mancha published his famous tribute in tercets to the viceregal capital, *Grandeza mexicana*, which helped turned this city into a fundamental element of the identity of the Creoles of New Spain. As Alfonso Reyes indicated, it was a true poem of the polis: "It is Mexico in the worlds of the West / an imperial city of great district, / space, attendance and population" (cited in Gruzinski, *La ciudad* 200). Balbuena's aim of placing the centre of the continent in Mexico was shared by the Extremaduran Arias de Villalobos, for whom only Madrid was finer though the apologists for Lima were not dragging their heels. The peninsular Spaniard and convert Antonio de León Pinelo, affected by what he saw as the disdain and ignorance shown by the Europeans towards the Americas, took his argument to the extreme. In a planned *Historia de Lima* in four parts, which would in fact cover the entire viceroyalty, he wanted to dedicate his second book to the city, yet in his complex, encyclopaedic *Paraíso en el Nuevo Mundo* (1656), his messianic Creolism drove him to break the boundaries of urban providentialism and made him place Eden in the Amazon Basin (Lohmann Villena, "La 'Historia de Lima'" 766).

The comparisons, whilst odious, were unavoidable. The Seville-born Juan de la Cueva singled out Mexico in the late sixteenth century as a city with six excellent things of beauty, all beginning with the letter "c" (in Spanish): "*casas, calles, caballos, carnes, cabellos* y *criaturas*" (houses, streets, horses, meat, hair and creatures). Some later writers, such as the aforementioned Balbuena, Arias de Villalobos and the renounced Dominican Thomas Gage, did introduce some variety, although the theme reflecting public opinion most closely was that of the magnificent buildings of Mexico. Lima, on the other hand, boasted, according to its panegyrics, four prodigious "p's" in which it exceeded Mexico—recorded by Concolorcorvo at a later date in *El lazarillo de ciegos caminantes* (1776), and culminating in the beauty of the famous "covered" women and the pleasures of the table.

The cities were even given a physical appearance. Personified in statues bearing gifts that were characteristic of them, the nine major cities of New Spain attended in 1713, on an allegorical float, the festivities held in the capital in celebration of the birth of Prince Philip. Similarly, in 1725, the eight largest cities in Peru were present in the mausoleum erected in the metropolitan cathedral for the funeral rites of Louis I. The mining town of Potosí, stricken by fever but of sound mind, in 1800 managed to make its own will, in which, on entrusting to God its soul of pure silver, it asked not to be embalmed as it had already been "disembowelled alive." It instructed that its funeral should be attended by, among others, its father, Cuzco; by its son, "the child Buenos Aires, to whom I gave the Viceroyalty" and by Chuquisaca, "the foundling daughter and suckled at my breast" (Rípodas Ardanaz 19–20).

Creole Nature and Providential Debates

The power and wealth of the Spanish American cities had much to do with the extension and success of these innovative narratives with Creole roots. The progressive control of the Spanish Americans over the *cabildos*, sectors of the clergy and even the courts, the spreading of the universities, the relative loss of power on the part of the founding families descending from the conquistadors and *encomenderos*, or the emergence of powerful men of letters, merchants, military figures, landowners and traders born in the Americas, did nothing but give them political justification, readers and patrons. Without doubt, the sale of posts—which facilitated the control of new institutional spaces by the Creoles, particularly from 1687 onwards, when the Crown also began to alienate the posts of *oidor de audiencia* (court judge), thus allowing to talk of a true Creole state – facilitated the establishment of a plutocracy. And access to Castilian titles of nobility or the acquisition of habits of military orders played a key role in the expansion of prestige.

It is difficult to imagine the intensity of the debate surrounding the suitability of peninsular Spaniards and Creoles for holding different posts in the service of the Crown and the city, or the arguments relating to the limitations of their nature and, thus, the justice or lack of it in their appointment. Whilst there were those who believed that in the Indies there were no people of sufficient refinement, quality or wealth to hold a post or to be of any great benefit, there were those who defended the Creoles and maintained that they were only reacting, in search of justice, to the disregard and humiliating treatment to which they were subjected. The Viceroyalty-born Juan de Zapata maintained in *De iustitia distributiva* (1609) that those elected for the bishoprics of the Indies needed to know the indigenous languages; otherwise those electing them would be committing a mortal sin and the appointment would not be valid. The geographer Vázquez de Espinosa, author of the fundamental *Compendio y descripción de las Indias occidentales* (1630), pointed out that the students in Spanish American universities were performing highly, which contradicted the supposed negative influence of the climate on their intellectual development. As far as he could see, the only real reason for the difficulties they encountered on finishing their studies was the distance from the Court and their opportunities for patronage. Shortly afterwards, the great treatise writer Juan de Solórzano Pereira maintained in *Política indiana* (1647) that Spanish Americans should be considered identical to peninsular Spaniards and enjoy the same opportunities and privileges, as "there can be no doubt that they are true Spaniards" (Solórzano Pereira 219).

The controversial and courageous Juan de Palafox, one of the protégés of the Count-Duke of Olivares, great Bishop of Puebla, and briefly Viceroy of New Spain in 1642, was convinced that the conquest of the Americas had put the

Spanish monarchy in a terrible state. Yet he also demanded that every confidence should be placed in the Mexican Creoles, who were as worthy of such as were members of the Aragonese or Castilian elite. In his view, the legitimacy of the viceroy's power lay in his ability to impart justice, not to hand out posts. His determined struggle to ensure adherence to ecclesiastical rotation, organised in order to guarantee the granting of posts alternately to Creoles and peninsular Spaniards, earned him popularity along with a saintly reputation among the former and the exacerbated hatred of the latter (Álvarez de Toledo 82–3).

The regional variants, always with a blessed capital at the leader, did not take long to appear. Resorting to the climate, which played a key role in attributing inferiority to the New World, channelled the debate towards the issue of the quality and the site of the cities, which had become an element of observation and comparison, or a providential reflection of the divine will sowed by the New World of Creole metropolises. In 1618, the eminent Madrid-born doctor Diego Cisneros published *Sitio, naturaleza y propiedades de la ciudad de México*, one of the founding works of the Baroque of New Spain, dedicated to the study of the medical implications of the climate and the environment in the viceregal capital, geographical location, astronomic position, winds, waters, temperatures, properties of the soil and produce from the land, in order to deduce the temperament of its inhabitants and to prevent their illnesses. As he stated therein, Creoles, the sons and grandsons of Spaniards, could only be like their ancestors. In other words, of a spirited nature, bold, sharp and strong. The indigenous people, on the other hand, were melancholic or sanguine and, therefore, skilful and resourceful. As the Creoles of New Spain, concluded Cisneros, followed a diet similar to that of Castile, the differences between peninsular Spaniards and Creoles were in fact so slight that there was no reason as far as their nature was concerned to support any discrimination whatsoever (Cisneros 111).

The comparative arguments were highly imaginative. Lázaro de Arregui, for example, when referring to the Creoles of Nueva Galicia, claimed that they spoke a Spanish language as correct as that of Toledo, and Bernabé Cobo remarked that the inhabitants of Lima were 'Spanishified'. The Creole Dominican Alonso Franco argued that the mutual hostility between peninsular Spaniards and Creoles would have made some sense if it had been a matter of people who were different in some way, but as in reality they shared the same blood, language and traditions, there was no justification whatsoever. Esteban García, an Augustine chronicler and also a Creole, was more interested in demonstrating how the Mexican climate inspired obedience and respect for the Spanish institutions than in proving its suitability for intellectual development. Although the Creole authors could not accept that those native to the Americas were lethargic and apathetic in comparison with European Spaniards, they had no objection to acknowledging that they were idle. They attributed this fault to the long distance separating them from Europe and from the Court, as this circumstance led to

182 *The Transatlantic Hispanic Baroque*

a lack of stimulus, given that they encountered great difficulties and became disheartened when they hoped to gain employment in the service of the king or of the church. A derivative of idleness, indolence, had been characterising the condition of the urban Creole since the seventeenth century and later became part of the literary genre of *costumbrismo* in the nineteenth century, reaching the present day as an element of magic realism. The Viceroy Velasco had criticised the Mexican Creoles for refusing to perform manual work or crafts and for coming to the capital just to eat and to spend. Meanwhile, the ever-combative Palafox found the antidote to Creole idleness in trust and captured the attention of his successor, the Count of Salvatierra, with regard to the true victims of the situation, the indigenous people. As had occurred in the city of the conquistadors, reported to be the ideal place, the Creole metropolises suffered from a vicious identity, a violent constitution and a disregard for law by the powerful.

In the Creole mythology, the defence of the Baroque metropolis was associated with the imaginary and literary recreation of a city of God, a heavenly Jerusalem of an entirely free nature, with moderate and virtuous inhabitants, patriarchal family fathers who would one day inhabit the kingdom of heaven. The functionality of this structure, its brutal utilitarianism, can be seen when it is revealed that prominent Creole authors scarcely travelled beyond the spatial framework of the city and, on the contrary, were of the indigenous gentiles, so helpful when it came to inventing an alternative genealogy to that of the peninsular Spaniards. Thus, the Franciscan friar from Lima, fray Buenaventura de Salinas y Córdoba, in his *Memorial de las Historias del Nuevo Mundo: Perú* (1630) entered into the mysteries of the four pre-Incan ages. Though undoubtedly inspired by the memorable *Nueva crónica y buen gobierno* (1615) by Felipe Guamán Poma de Ayala, he went no further than to cover in his work the space contained within Lima and its surroundings, and referred to the rest of the Viceroyalty in a distant and allusive manner. Guamán Poma had not hesitated to present Lima as a royal court, the leading city in the kingdom of the Indies, the residence of the Viceroy and the Archbishopric of the Church.[4] Just as its chroniclers maintained that the calm environment of the Mexican capital made its inhabitants virtuous and healthy, he indicated that Lima boasted an agreeable temperature and clear air. Furthermore, it was neither shaken by thunder nor split by lightning, the hillsides were dotted with running deer and bucks, partridge hopping and coots flying, and birds rising at dawn, accompanied by roses, fragrant flowers, birds of heaven and songbirds. The people, as befitted his view, were gentle and kind, intelligent and noble.

---

[4] Luis E. Valcárcel and Warren L. Cook suggested that Guamán Poma was the source used by Salinas y Córdoba given the textual similarities at various points (Adorno).

The *Memorial* was an example of literature in true exaltation of the Creole which in the Baroque age, as opposed to what would tend to happen later, could recall the indigenous past, but would sometimes opt to ignore it. The Jesuit Bernabé Cobo in his *Historia de la fundación de Lima* (1639) recorded the barbarity of the Indian gentiles in contrast with those who had converted to Christianity, "our sacred religion of savage men who are more or less as fierce and incompetent as rough logs [...] powerful in making men human, living with reason and virtue" (in Esteve Barba 559). In this regard, it is symptomatic that the author of such a fundamental work in the Peruvian urban tradition as *Lima fundada o conquista del Perú* (1732), Pedro Peralta y Barnuevo, the famous "*Doctor océano*" who could write of astronomy, blood circulation or earthquakes, should opt in his colossal poem of 1,159 Sicilian octaves to claim positions and honours for the Creole nobility, but should limit the treatment of the pre-colonial era to a small fragment and should choose the arrival of Francisco Pizarro in Peru as the true moment of the initiation of the city and the Viceroyalty (Esteve Barba 566–7).

Such accounts of the past and present of Mexico and Lima as providential Creole metropolis were widely applicable and were reproduced in one way or another in many cities of Spanish America during the seventeenth and eighteenth centuries. The reasons are clear: it was this model I have described that inspired, supported, and directed the intention to reorganise the urban space and provided guidance for the needs and future ambitions of the emerging sectors of the urban elite. The walls and fortifications also contributed to this, defending the cities from pirates and corsairs, but also expelling undesirable sectors of the population to the surrounding areas. At the same time, as their public and private spaces were being Americanised and inhabited by all races (neutralising the peninsular Spaniards), the cities projected their aspirations of becoming a capital in their own right into the surrounding areas. That city, the lively, too lively Creole metropolis, has long been undervalued due to Enlightenment and modernist ignorance of the last two centuries, and their characteristic criticism of supposed Baroque "dark ages." But it is now high time that this came to an end. Latin American cities were and still are Baroque cities. That means cities which proclaimed from the very beginning to be at the centre of the world, not at the periphery.

Bibliography

Adorno, Rolena. *Guaman Poma and His Illustrated Chronicle from Colonial Peru: From a Century of Scholarship to a New Era of Reading*. Copenhagen, 2001. 31 August 2014. http://www.kb.dk/permalink/2006/poma/info/es/docs/index.htm

184 *The Transatlantic Hispanic Baroque*

Aldana Rivera, Susana. "Cañete del Perú, ¿para la defensa del reino? Un caso de burocracia y negociación política, Siglo XVII." *Andes* 19 (January–December 2008): 183–210.

Álvarez, Raquel. "El cuestionario de 1577. La 'Instrucción y memoria de las relaciones que se han de hacer para la descripción de las Indias de 1577.'" *Cuestionarios para la formación de las Relaciones Geográficas de Indias, Siglos XVI–XIX*. Ed. Francisco de Solano. Madrid: CSIC, 1988. xciii–cvi.

Álvarez de Toledo, Cayetana. *Politics and Reform in Spain and Viceregal Mexico: The Life and Thought of Juan de Palafox, 1600–1659*. Oxford: Oxford University Press, 2004.

Barrientos Grandón, Javier. "El *Cursus* de la jurisdicción letrada en las Indias (s. XVI–XVII)." *El gobierno de un mundo. Virreinatos y audiencias en la América Hispánica*. Coord. Feliciano Barrios. Cuenca: Universidad de Castilla-La Mancha, 2004. 633–710.

Bayle, Constantino. *Los cabildos seculares en la América española*. Madrid: Sapientia, 1952.

Bernand, Carmen. *Negros esclavos y libres en las ciudades hispanoamericanas*. Madrid: Fundación Mapfre, 2001.

Bravo Lira, Bernardino. "Régimen virreinal. Constantes y variantes de la constitución política en Iberoamérica (Siglos XVI al XXI)." *El gobierno de un mundo. Virreinatos y audiencias en la América Hispánica*. Coord. Feliciano Barrios. Cuenca: Universidad de Castilla-La Mancha, 2004. 375–430.

Castillero Calvo, Alfredo. *Arquitectura, urbanismo y sociedad. La vivienda colonial en Panamá*. Panama: Fondo Schell, 1994.

Cisneros, Diego. *Sitio, naturaleza y propiedades de la ciudad de México*. Preliminary study by José Luis Peset. Madrid: Fundación Ciencias de la Salud, 1992.

Covarrubias, Sebastián de. *Tesoro de la lengua castellana o española*. Madrid: Castalia, 1995.

Cruz de Amenábar, Isabel. "Una periferia de nieves y soles invertidos: notas sobre Santiago, fiesta y paisaje." *Tiempos de América* 5–6 (2000): 121–31.

Diccionario de Real Academia Española. Vol. 4. Madrid: Imprenta de Francisco del Hierro, 1734. 1 October 2012. <www.rae.es>.

Duarte, Carlos F. "Las fiestas de *Corpus Christi* en la Caracas hispánica (Tarasca, Gigantes y Diablitos)." *Boletín de la Academia Nacional de la Historia* 70.279 (1987): 675–92.

Elliott, John H. *El conde-duque de Olivares. El político en una época de decadencia*. Barcelona: Crítica, 1991.

Esteve Barba, Francisco. *Historiografía indiana*. Madrid: Gredos, 1992.

Gerbi, Antonello. *La naturaleza de las Indias Nuevas: de Cristóbal Colón a Gonzalo Fernández de Oviedo*. Mexico, DF: FCE, 1978.

The Creole Metropolis 185

Iwasaki Cauti, Fernando. "Toros y sociedad en Lima colonial." *Anuario de Estudios Americanos* 49 (1992): 311–33.

Kubler, George. "El urbanismo colonial iberoamericano, 1600–1820." *Historia y futuro de la ciudad iberoamericana.* Ed. Francisco de Solano. Madrid: CSIC, 1986. 27–45.

Lohmann Villena, Guillermo. "Las comedias del *Corpus Christi* en Lima en 1635 y 1636." *Revista de Indias* 10.42 (1950): 865–8.

———. "La 'Historia de Lima' de Antonio de Léon Pinelo." *Revista de Indias* 12.50 (1952): 761–81.

Lorente Medina, Antonio. "México: 'Primavera inmortal' y 'emporio' de toda la América." *De Arcadia a Babel. Naturaleza y ciudad en la literatura hispanoamericana.* Ed. Javier de Navascués. Madrid: Iberoamericana, 2002. 71–94.

MacCormack, Sabine. "Antonio de la Calancha: un agustino del siglo XVII en el Nuevo Mundo." *Bulletin Hispanique* 84 (1982): 60–94.

———. "El gobierno de la república cristiana." *El barroco peruano.* Ed. Ramón Mújica Pinilla. Vol. 2. Lima: Banco del Crédito, 2003. 217–49.

Martín, Luis. *Daughters of the Conquistadores: Women of the Viceroyalty of Peru.* Albuquerque, NM: University of New Mexico Press, 1983.

Marzahl, Peter. "Creoles and Government: The Cabildo of Popayán." *Hispanic American Historical Review* 54.4 (1974): 636–56.

Mújica Pinilla, Ramón. "Identidades alegóricas: lecturas iconográficas el barroco al neoclásico." *El barroco peruano.* Ed. Ramón Mújica Pinilla. Vol. 2. Lima: Banco del Crédito, 2003. 258–335.

Ossorio, Alejandra. "The King in Lima: Simulacra, Ritual and Rule in Seventeenth-Century Peru." *Hispanic American Historical Review* 84.3 (2004): 447–74.

Quesada, Santiago. *La idea de ciudad en la cultura hispana de la edad moderna.* Barcelona: Universidad de Barcelona, 1992.

Ramos Sosa, Rafael. "La fiesta barroca en ciudad de México y Lima." *Historia* 30 (1997): 263–86.

Rípodas Ardanaz, Daisy. *Las ciudades indianas.* Buenos Aires: Municipalidad de Buenos Aires, 1982.

Rodríguez de la Flor, Fernando. *Barroco. Representación e ideología en el mundo hispánico (1580–1680).* Madrid: Cátedra, 2002.

Rodríguez Moya, Inmaculada. *La mirada del virrey. Iconografía del poder en la Nueva España.* Castelló de la Plana: Publicacions de Universidad Jaume I, 2003.

Sigüenza y Góngora, Carlos de. *Infortunios de Alonso Ramírez.* Ed. José F. Buscaglia. Madrid: CSIC, 2011.

Solórzano Pereira, Juan. *Política indiana.* Madrid: Imprenta Real de la Gaceta, 1776.

Szuchman, Mark D. "The City as Vision: The Development of Urban Culture in Latin America." *I Saw a City Invincible: Urban Portraits of Latin America.* Ed. Joseph M. Gilbert and Mark D. Szuchman. Wilmington, DE: S.R. Press, 1996. 1–32.

Terreros Pando, Esteban de. *Diccionario castellano con las voces de ciencias y artes.* Vol. 2. Madrid: Imprenta de la Viuda de Ibarra, 1787.

Vila, Enriqueta. *Santos de América.* Bilbao: Ediciones Moretón, 1968.

Chapter 10

Foreign Communities in the Cities of the Catholic Monarchy: A Comparative Perspective between the Overseas Dominions and the Crown of Castile

Manuel Herrero Sánchez

A Polycentric and Multinational Monarchy: The Complex Definition of "Foreigner" in the Spanish Monarchy

Some years ago, Daniel Roche alerted us to the problems existing during the Ancien Régime in relation to ascertaining the correct definition of the term étranger (foreigner) and thus he concluded emphatically: "Comprendre l'étrangeté des étrangers n'est pas chose facile" (Roche 477). A difficulty that would have been seen to increase as a result of the lack of interest on the part of the different national historiographies in including in their respective historical accounts the role of certain communities which, in many cases, had acted as the necessary counterpoint to stress the exceptional and distinctive nature of each of these nation-states (Recio Morales 34–5). The low effectiveness of nationalist prejudices for a correct analysis of the polyhedral political and social nature of the state structures during the early modern period can be seen in the inability shown in the late sixteenth century by one of the key theorists of the concept of absolute sovereignty, Jean Bodin, to draw a clear distinction between the subjects and the foreigners in Book I, Chapter 6: "que si nous suyvions la varietè des privileges pour juger la définition du citoyen, il se trouveroit cinquante mil définitions de citoyen, pour la diversité infinie de prerogatives que les citoyens ont les uns sur les autres, et sur les estrangers. Et mesmes il se trouveroit que l'estranger en plusieurs lieux seroit plus vrai citoyen que le suject naturel" (141).

The plurality of situations for defining the citizen and distinguishing him from the foreigner was becoming even more complex in such a strongly disintegrated model as that of the Spanish Monarchy. A power structure characterised by the gradual process of incorporating a wide range of territories under the jurisdiction of the same sovereign who acted as the guarantor of privileges, liberties and immunities in each of the bodies, kingdoms or cities over which he exercised his rule (see Álvarez-Ossorio and García). Respect for legislative, cultural, linguistic, ethnic, social and political diversity was paradoxically becoming one of the key factors in the cohesion of the whole and strengthened the loyalty towards the king on the part of certain fragmented dominions, distant from one another and in their location on the globe. However, the mechanisms for negotiating between the sovereign and the local elite were not implemented only in one direction between the centre and the periphery. In line with the multinational and dispersed nature of the whole, it was more a case of a polycentric power structure within which each of the hubs forming it interacted not only with the sovereign and his representatives but also among themselves (Cardim et al. 3–4). The Spanish Monarchy was arranged around a powerful network of cities and courts which always retained extensive areas of autonomy and which, as opposed to what was happening in the French or British monarchy models, were not displaced by the leading role of certain capitals which like Paris and London gave greater cohesion to their respective government systems and allowed them to advance, through different channels, in the process of administrative centralisation at the expense of local privileges. In the Spanish Monarchy, there were other mechanisms designed for lending cohesion to such disparate dominions. Respect for jurisdictional diversity, the profession of the Catholic religion as the main identifying factor and obedience to one sovereign undoubtedly constituted the key elements for lending stability to the system. But they were not the only ones. The Crown also knew how to implement measures aimed at facilitating the mobility of the elite between such dispersed territories, leading to the establishment of a complex transnational framework of aristocratic, bureaucratic, commercial and religious networks concerned with maintaining the imperial structure (see Yun Casalilla; Crespo Solana, *Comunidades*; Pardo Molero and Lomas Cortés).

This took the form of an imposing space within which people, ideas, products, institutions and codes of conduct under a marked cosmopolitan stamp could circulate, encouraging communities from outside of the monarchy itself to join in. Foreign nations attracted by the possibilities for social promotion,[1] by the considerable business to be gained from such widespread and profitable markets or by the protection offered by the Crown to all the Catholics who were being persecuted for religious reasons in their own countries. Far from the monolithic and impenetrable image with which certain historiography strove to portray the Catholic Monarchy, this was a complex power structure

---

[1]   It should be stressed that we use the concept of "nation" in the same way as the contemporaries would have used it, i.e. as an area for the articulation of certain communities originating from the same geographical area in the form of consulates, exclusive brotherhoods, or other types of body. Thus, in the ports of Castile, both the king's subjects (of Neapolitan, Flemish, Catalonian nationality, etc.) and foreigners (of Dutch, French, English, Scottish, Irish, Genoese, Ragusan, Venetian, German nationality, etc.) were operating.

in which the coexistence within it of various different national communities would act as an additional factor in facilitating the arrival of a growing number of foreigners who, like the king's subjects, found themselves obliged to adapt to the mechanisms for inclusion pertaining to each of the local communities and cities in which they were seeking to settle. When all was said and done, in the Castilian cities, anyone from Catalonia, Naples, Flanders or Milan had to meet the same requirements as a Frenchman, a Genoese or an Englishman in order to take up residence or to become naturalised. There is no doubt that being a subject of the same king brought certain advantages or that being a Catholic was an essential requirement but, ultimately, neither vassalage nor religion would suffice in order for foreigners to become naturalised (Herzog, *Defining* 139).

Foreigners and subjects from the different nations belonging to the Monarchy were not only difficult to distinguish but moved around with relative ease between its different territories, even in those in which, as in the case of the Indies, their entry was prohibited without a permit granted expressly by the Crown. The difficulties that the Monarchy was forced to address in order to communicate with its dispersed dominions and to mobilise resources, soldiers or capital effectively obliged it to depend increasingly on the services that overseas businessmen were able to offer it. We have had the opportunity to analyse in detail the mechanisms for dependence and collaboration set up between the Catholic Monarchy and two of the main commercial republics of the time, Genoa and the United Provinces, whose naval and financial services were fundamental to maintaining the Spanish imperial structure. Their powerful commercial networks also enabled the agricultural produce from the Iberian, Italian or Spanish American elite to be channelled under the best conditions and this aristocracy to be supplied with a whole host of sumptuary products essential for maintaining their social status (see Herrero Sánchez et al., *Génova*; Israel; Herrero, "Republican"). It is true that the various foreign communities deployed different strategies for connecting with the local people or for accessing the system of royal patronage but, regardless of the depth of their roots, their networks led to an increase in communication within the Monarchy. Their businessmen were the best equipped to move freely within the hotchpotch of legal and monetary systems coexisting at its heart, facilitating the integration of certain marginalised territories into the international markets, as well as playing a key role in the Iberian process of Atlantic expansion (Crespo Solana, "Elementos" 58–60).

The Crown did not hesitate to make use of the interest roused by its markets as an effective tool for diplomatic negotiation through the granting of privileges or as a forceful weapon by means of the strict implementation of trade embargos which, in spite of their limitations, allowed for certain foreign nations to be favoured over others (Alloza Aparicio; Herrero Sánchez, "La monarchie"). The subjects of the Crown and its allies had a comparative advantage for operating within the dominions of the Monarchy as they were exempt from the policy of reprisals that affected the normal running of activities by those from enemy nations. Nevertheless, and in line with the complex definition of "foreigner" noted by Bodin, very often outsiders from allied nations enjoyed prerogatives which more than surpassed those of the king's actual subjects. This is demonstrated by the numerous accusations of the abuses carried out by the Genoese in Castile or in Naples, or the complaints of the states of Flanders concerning the advantages granted to the former Dutch enemies following the signing of the Peace of Westphalia. The growing dependence of the Crown on the services that foreigners were able to offer it, along with military defeat, forced the king to multiply the privileges and immunities in the subsequent trade treaties and peace agreements reached with the Hanseatic cities (1607, 1647), the United Provinces (1609, 1648, 1650), England (1604, 1630, 1667, 1670) and France (1659).

The mass presence of foreigners at the height of these concessions and the inability to compete with the products crafted overseas gave rise to significant xenophobic reactions in practically all of the dominions under the jurisdiction of the Catholic monarch and instigated the implementation of half-hearted protective measures, which were to fail miserably. As indicated by Domínguez Ortiz, in the majority of cities, the legislation designed to restrict the trading activities of foreign communities was not observed, as the local authorities considered these colonies as one of the main sources of prosperity (40). The high levels of tax revenue reaped by the Crown from trade also served to tone down the projects proposed by the *Cortes* of Castile or by certain individuals with a view to stopping the imports of products manufactured overseas. Furthermore, the very multi-territorial nature of the Spanish Monarchy made it unfeasible to introduce trade programmes similar to those implemented from the middle of the seventeenth century by England and France—and not just because the Dutch, French and English had in their respective treaties with the Crown managed to impose by force the clause of most favoured nation, but because any protective measure in defence of any of the dominions under the jurisdiction of the sovereign resulted in resentment at the inequality in relation to the interests of the other territories.

In a similar context, it is not surprising that in the latter decades of the seventeenth century the xenophobic attitudes eventually turned into open admiration for the political and economic models originating from northern Europe which were described as the panacea for restoring the former splendour of the Monarchy, but for whose implementation a complete transformation of the institutional and territorial structure of the Spanish imperial system seemed necessary—a transformation that limited the predominance of the local over the kingdom as a whole and which prioritised vassalage over residence.

Mechanisms for Taking Up Residence and for Naturalisation in the Spanish Monarchy

The high level of autonomy in each of the territories forming a polycentric structure such as that of the Spanish Monarchy, and the zealous defence of local privileges, meant that the Catholic King had to deal with different ways of gaining citizenship in each of his dominions. In Castile, as demonstrated through the sharp analyses of Tamar Herzog, the monarchy was incapable of turning the kingdom into a community of vassalage in the same way as in France and England, where the native tended to identify with the subject (Herzog, *Defining* 198–200).

Rather than as subjects, the Castilians liked to describe themselves above all as residents and as members of a local community integrated into the kingdom, whilst zealous defenders of its autonomy and privileges. In this respect, it does not seem too bold to observe concomitant circumstances under which such attitudes were held in other urban republics with which the Crown maintained close relationships of cooperation and which, it was no wonder, had formed part of the same political structure until the end of the sixteenth century. In Castile, as in the Catholic Low Countries or in the United Provinces (see Prak), the difference between foreigners and residents, i.e. those citizens who could access communal property, flaunt posts and positions, be members of the local civil militia or take part in particular ceremonies or bodies, was a question that depended on the consensus of each of the local authorities without having to resort to a legal recognition that would affect the kingdom as a whole. Residence had more to do with the deep-rootedness of the individual within the local environment, with the years of residence and with his willingness to integrate, than with the existence of defined legislation. It was a question of a process of adapting to the host community which could be two-way and which was equally applicable for inclusion within a larger community, the community of the kingdom.

In this way, the natives of Castile included anyone who took up residence in any of the municipalities of the kingdom, as well as a mid-range of individuals who complied with a series of common guidelines, such as use of the Castilian language or the Catholic religion, and who, as was the case with residents, expressed their wish to remain in the host community or brought benefits to the republic (Herzog, "Naturales" 26–7). Ultimately, it was a question of an implicit recognition that only required one legal document, naturalisation papers, in those cases in which there were conflicting situations. Foreigners could not become naturalised merely at the king's discretion, as this would go against a series of privileges reserved exclusively for natives of Castile, such as the monopoly of posts or the ability to trade with the Indies. From this perspective, it is no surprise that there were so many accusations lodged by the *Cortes*, which did not hesitate when it came to questioning the sovereign's capacity to graciously grant naturalisation papers to his subjects from other dominions under his jurisdiction or to bankers or royal servants who were not integrated into the kingdom according to the above guidelines, and if they did not meet the requirements for gaining naturalisation through the courts (Herzog, *Defining* 11, 76–8).

In spite of everything, the king continued to resort to these types of proceedings to obtain from the *Cortes* or from the Consulate of merchants of Seville new tax concessions in exchange for waiving his right to naturalise unilaterally particular foreigners. On other occasions, it was the sovereign himself who was inclined to apply severely the trade embargos against certain foreigners who had taken up residence and were deeply rooted in the community. Thus, in 1673, following the outbreak of war with France, the Crown immediately proceeded to confiscate the assets of Antonio Balmier, a French merchant who had been a resident of Madrid for over 22 years, had a Spanish wife and who, in principle, met all the requirements for naturalisation through integration, although not through royal papers. In the contraband trial held two years later, we have available a large part of the legislation relating to naturalisation processes which covered in detail all the criteria required for obtaining naturalisation papers (AGS, Contaduría). Some years earlier, in response to the protests of the Consulate of Seville in relation to the granting of naturalisation papers to the Genoese Consul in Cadiz, Antonio María Tasara, the Council of the Indies ratified the licence in the interest of justice as it complied with requirements, i.e. "that in order to be deemed naturalised, and to trade in the Indies and Western Islands, they should have lived in them, or these kingdoms, continuously for 20 years, having a home and good roots for ten and be married to a native or a daughter of foreigners born in these kingdoms" (AGI).

However, flexibility in the application of this legislation seemed to be the norm, as there was always the possibility of granting an exemption in the case of failure to comply with any of the criteria in return for a sum of money, providing that the candidate could show his intention to settle in the kingdom and prove that he formed part of the host community.[2] In spite of these situations of uncertainty, naturalisations were in no way the normal process for settling in Castile and represented an exceptional channel for the foreign communities established in the kingdom. According to the account given by Domínguez Ortiz of naturalisation papers for trading with the Indies issued throughout

---

[2]   The exemptions tended to range between 400 and 2,000 pieces of eight, as can be seen from an account prepared by the Council of the Indies on the 14 naturalisations processed between 1645 and 1671 (AGI 781). At the request of the Consulate of Seville, a Royal Decree was issued on 22 April 1645 revoking all "discretionary" naturalisations, i.e. those which were not acquired through the courts in accordance with the 1608 document. For the previous period, see Díaz Blanco.

the seventeenth century, most were granted to non-Castilian subjects of the king, particularly Flemish (98), who were afraid of being mistaken for Dutch and being accused of heresy, closely followed by Portuguese subjects (91), who were always being suspected of being Judaisers (Domínguez Ortiz 137–64). On the other hand, there were only 42 naturalisation papers issued to Genoese applicants, even though they were the foreign community with the deepest roots in Castile, could consider themselves to be faultless Catholics, had known how to integrate easily into the local society or relied on the protection of their respective consulates (Herrero Sánchez, "Génova"). The low number of papers obtained by the French (23), English (5) and Dutch (1) was not so much due to the state of war as to the fact that their respective governments had managed to secure many privileges from the Crown from the second half of the seventeenth century, thanks to which they were able to operate with even greater ease than the king's subjects themselves, thus removing the need for their naturalisation. It is true that the French had to suffer the consequences of a constant conflict with the Spanish Monarchy, but let us not forget that, unlike what was happening in Castile, the naturalised community in the kingdom of France had built themselves into a vassal community, and so whilst not residing within the kingdom, it was assumed that they maintained the links with their place of origin and, consequently, they found it more difficult to change their status and to become part of another nation (Herzog, *Defining* 194; Shalins).[3]

The Presence of Foreigners in the Indies, a Territory Restricted to the 'Natives of the Kingdoms of Spain'

In the Indies, although settlement and *vecindad* (residence) constituted, as in Castile, the fundamental mechanism for naturalisation and the consensus of the local communities was a determining factor, there were some significant differences resulting from the fact that, at least on paper, the presence of foreigners was prohibited, and there was therefore no room for conflict due to naturalisation such as those which arose between the king and the *Cortes* in Castile (Konetzke). Unsurprisingly, it was precisely in the Americas that for the first time, in a royal decree issued by Philip II in 1596, the concept of "natives of the kingdoms of Spain" was formed. This included those native to Castile, Aragon, Catalonia, Valencia, Mallorca, Menorca, Navarra and the three Basque provinces to which was reserved the right to trade with and emigrate to the Indies (Herzog, *Defining* 65).[4] The Crown managed to establish a community of vassals originating from its dominions on the Iberian Peninsula—excluding

---

[3]   For the guidelines for nationalisation in France see Shalins.

[4]   See *Recopilación de leyes de Indias*, law 28, title 27, book 9.

194 *The Transatlantic Hispanic Baroque*

Portugal—which were associated more with their otherness with respect to foreigners, than with their local belonging. A process of "nationalisation" of residence which, interestingly, adopted the opposite path to that of England, where the monarchy was implementing increasingly restrictive measures with respect to the naturalisation of foreigners in the metropolis, whilst applying a much laxer policy in the colonies (Herzog, *Defining* 198). In the Spanish Indies, there would even be failure for the subsequent proposals which, like the one put forward by Francisco Retama to the king in 1618, were aimed at encouraging the emigration of the king's Neapolitan and Flemish subjects as the best way of preventing non-Catholic foreigners or enemies from entering these lands (AGS, Estado leg. 634).

In spite of the abundant and reiterated punitive legislation designed to halt the influx of foreigners into the Indies, migration control was far from effective. The Iberian area of the Atlantic offered certain possibilities for promotion that were unknown in Europe. This, together with the process of economic expansion, the demographic crisis experienced by the indigenous communities and the growing need for a specialised workforce, turned the desire to reserve this space for the king's "Spanish" subjects into a pipe dream. Artisans, engineers, miners, servants, clergymen, sailors and businessmen, both from other dominions under the king's jurisdiction and from allied nations or even enemy nations, were soon inhabiting such vast dominions, thanks to the high level of flexibility shown by the local authorities and to the limitations of the Crown in effectively implementing such rigorous legislation. As occurred with the successive royal decrees to combat smuggling, a permanent space was established for negotiation between the king and the Creole elite to enable certain foreign communities to be favoured over others and to open up the way for the timely instigation of criminal proceedings or implementation of mechanisms for legalisation from which profitable benefits could be reaped (Herrero Sánchez and Pérez Tostado). It was no wonder that the increasing control over commercial dealings with the Indies held by foreign merchants led to protests from the Consulate of Seville and from its counterparts in Mexico and Lima, demanding the implementation of increasingly strict measures of control, culminating in 1608 with a tightening of the legal channels through which foreigners could access trade with the Indies (Herrero Sánchez and Poggio 267). Earlier, and pressurised by the needs of the Treasury, the Crown introduced a series of taxes aimed at gaining increasing revenue from its dominions in the Indies at the expense of the foreigners who had settled there. In 1591, the first of the *composiciones*, or "inventories" of foreigners was published, demanding the detention and subsequent expulsion of all those who, without being native to the kingdoms of Spain, had moved to the Americas without a permit from the Crown. As Eleonora Poggio highlighted recently, the *composiciones* neither fulfilled a regulatory function nor were designed to facilitate the integration of the foreigners who had met the requirements in

Castile for taking up residence.[5] It was more a mechanism whereby the King would grant his grace and pardon to all foreigners who had infringed the ban on going to the Indies without his permission, in return for a sum of money set by the local authorities, which were the bodies responsible for implementing the measure. A penalty that could only be collected on the assets that the foreigners had acquired in the Indies and whose payment enabled the monarch to grant them a favour, allowing them to remain in the Americas (Poggio).

The transnational networks that gave such dispersed territories homogeneity continued to operate through semi-official contraband, encouraged by the local authorities and thanks to the difficulties encountered by the sovereign in controlling dominions that were too far away and that enjoyed a significant degree of autonomy. Military defeat also forced the Spanish Monarchy to recognise the settlements that the other European powers had succeeded in occupying in the Americas. The acceptance of the enclaves of the Dutch in 1648, the English in 1667 and the French in 1697 increased the porosity of the inter-imperial borders overseas, which, together with the concessions made to foreign merchants through such important channels for eroding the trade monopoly as the *asiento de negros*, encouraged the presence of foreigners of all kinds in the dominions of the Catholic King. However, the Crown managed to establish in the Indies a community of natives in which foreigners became obliged to insert themselves into the existing gaps of sociability and to integrate with the "Spanish" if they wished to continue with their activities—behaviour that was far from voluntary and which we do not believe should be related to the classic Weber approach, according to which the merchants involved in worldwide transactions would become increasingly reluctant to join any kind of family, ethnic, residential or religious district.[6] It was more likely to have been motivated by the Crown's strong opposition to accepting in the Indies similar conditions to those enjoyed by foreigners in its European dominions, where they benefited from their own corporate structures (consulates, brotherhoods, hospitals, chapels, centres of worship and burial) from where they could operate mechanisms for solidarity, maintain their collective identity and even enjoy an exclusive justice system. In fact, we only need to look at how these same foreign nations designed their strategies in Madrid, the sovereign's place of residence, or in Cadiz, the bridgehead between the Indies and the Crown's European dominions, to understand how the mechanisms for corporate protection represented a major comparative advantage and continued to be fundamental

---

[5]   An approach supported by studies such as those by Rodríguez Vicente or Mörner.

[6]   "The market is fundamentally alien to any type of fraternal relationship" (Weber 2: 637); see Trivellato.

196 *The Transatlantic Hispanic Baroque*

as a key mechanism for structuring the different foreign communities that were operating in the heart of the Monarchy.[7]

Foreign Nations in the Court of Madrid

As the seat of the main administrative and financial bodies, the Court of Madrid appeared to be the best platform for social promotion and the most appropriate place for accessing the generous system of royal patronage. The capital of a multi-ethnic and multinational monarchy, Madrid became an eminently cosmopolitan city in which, as indicated by Eugenio de Salazar, it was normal to hear all kinds of languages in the streets (Herrero García 77). Consequently, it was not easy to distinguish those from the territories under the rule of the Catholic monarch from the rest of the colourful and diverse number of foreigners inhabiting the streets and whose main characteristic lay in their social and professional heterogeneity: renowned diplomats, retired soldiers, clergymen, aristocrats, artists, beggars or simple visitors joined the all-powerful merchants and financiers who were settling in the capital to conduct their business. The foreigners were also spread all over the city and were not concentrated in restricted neighbourhoods or areas. This, combined with the large contingent of floating population, makes it very difficult to provide statistics on their total percentage within the Madrid population (Montemayor). In contrast with what was happening in the other cities with large merchant communities of foreign origin, and as was happening in the Indies, the Crown would never accept procedures to establish in Madrid consulates responsible for protecting the interests of businessmen from the main foreign nations settled there.[8] With a view to compensating for the absence of an institutional framework capable of giving them their own identity, the different communities organised unofficial mechanisms for socialising, such as brotherhoods and hospitals, responsible for meeting their spiritual needs or for offering help to their members. The foreigners could also rely on the support of their respective diplomatic legations. Ambassadors often acted as intermediaries, took care of bribing influential members of the Court and strove to establish factions aimed at protecting the interests of the members of their nation. Embassies also became actual warehouses from which banned goods were brought in and all kinds of products were distributed, taking advantage of the privilege of holding stocks that were free from the payment of taxes

---

[7] For the cases of Madrid and Cadiz I offer on these pages an abbreviated version of my work, Herrero Sánchez, "La Monarquía Hispánica."

[8] The only serious attempt was the one launched by a royal decree on 9 February 1632 establishing the creation of a consulate in which the members of the four nations that formed part of the Monarchy were represented: the Aragonese, the Italians, the Portuguese and the Flemish. Nevertheless, the legislation was never implemented (Domínguez Ortiz 46).

Of the foreign businessmen residing in the Court, those who gained the highest social recognition were, without doubt, those working in high finance. Of the suppliers to the Crown, the Genoese, from the main families of the Ligurian nobility, were known for their aristocratic lifestyle and for their high level of inbreeding, except when they managed to marry into important families of the Castilian nobility.[9] Their magnificent residences, which also housed their stores and offices of business, were situated, like those of their Portuguese counterparts, on the spacious avenues near the Prado de San Jerónimo and the Retiro (Sanz Ayán 61–82). The key difference between both communities lay in the fact that the Portuguese, apart from the rejection they suffered at the hands of the population due to their suspected Jewish origins, were not merely involved in lending, but acted as tax farmers and had important links with the world of commerce.

Commercial activities formed the environment that interested a large number of foreigners and they were essentially concentrated in the most central areas, specifically in the area around the Plaza Mayor, the Puerta de Guadalajara, the Plaza de la Provincia and the Puerta del Sol. Places where the Judges of the Royal House and Court, responsible for the regulation of commerce and craftsmanship in the city, ordered the proclamations in which prohibitions were dictated, prices were fixed or auctions were held for confiscated goods. The foreign merchants formed the majority in the trading of what were referred to as *especierías*, a term covering a wide range of luxury products, from pepper and other kinds of spices to fabrics such as silk and velvet, as well as tapestries, carpets, precious stones and even combs, paper, drugs and musical instruments—objects that mainly came from outside of the kingdom and were seriously affected by the subsequent prohibitions against manufactured goods from enemy nations, and which required close commercial links to be maintained with overseas nations (Herrero Sánchez, "La política"). The smooth running of their businesses depended on the forging of solid kinships and close alliances with the other members of their community (Larquié; Alvar Ezquerra, "Mercaderes"). Finally, it is worth highlighting the important role played by the retailers and travelling merchants who allowed for a diversification and expansion of demand and facilitated small sums of credit. Viñas Mey provides us with some written testimonies relating to the contempt shown by the general public towards these street vendors who, like most of those dedicated to humble trades, such as locksmiths, water sellers, puppeteers, labourers and even beggars, came from France (28–30). The high level of xenophobia shown towards the French could only be compared with the

---

[9] On this subject, see the cases of the Serras analysed by Ben Yessef, the Spinolas, studied by Álvarez-Ossorio and Herrero Sánchez, or the Grillos by García Montón.

198   *The Transatlantic Hispanic Baroque*

hatred of the Portuguese converts, and explains the multitude of satires and also the creation of burlesque youth companies dedicated to attacking or ridiculing them in the street. The continued altercations resulting from these activities led the authorities to issue, in 1685, certain provisions against all those who came together to "shout at and follow foreigners in this Court and dressed as such, and they should not throw stones or harass them in any way" (Domínguez Ortiz 69–70).

The political element behind the development and urban identity of Madrid explains the major repercussions of the crisis of the Monarchy at the end of the seventeenth century and, in particular, from the arrival of the Bourbon dynasty in 1700. The loss of European possessions, the nationalisation of public finances and the decreased possibilities for social promotion led to a significant reduction in the influx of foreigners into the Court. At that point, Madrid had ceased to be the capital of the Spanish Monarchy and had simply become the capital of Spain.

Cadiz: "The World's Leading Marketplace" and the Main Hub for the Foreign Population in the Spanish Monarchy

The situation in Cadiz was very different. An eminently commercial city, it was to experience throughout the seventeenth century, particularly from the middle of the century onwards, spectacular demographic growth as a result of the gradual process of the Castilian economy moving out to the peripheries, the multiplication of the concessions granted to foreign commercial communities and the inability of the government to exert direct control over transactions with the Indies. Its strategic geographical location also helped to make Cadiz one of the main ports for transit and storage, an obligatory service stop for all transactions being carried out between the Atlantic world and the Mediterranean. Along with Amsterdam, it represented, in the words of Juan Cano "the world's leading marketplace" (Cano ch. 23), although this was only due to the control exerted over the consignments of precious metals coming in from the Americas and without which the European businessmen were incapable of maintaining trade with Asia or with the Levant of the Ottoman empire. It was therefore no coincidence that the main naval convoys formed by the Dutch, Flemish, English, Genoese or Hanseatic League had a naval base of the first order in Cadiz, or that the most important European commercial firms had commission agents based in the city, responsible for overseeing the efficient administration of their business. One, if not the main, reason for the displacement of Seville in favour of Cadiz as the governing city of the Spanish American monopoly lay in the greater opportunities available in the latter for the development of contraband and fraud (Girard; García Fuentes 55–66). Although trade with the Indies was, in principle, reserved for citizens, over 90 per cent of the consignments of precious metals coming from the Americas through the legally established system of fleets and galleons was delivered to foreign firms. Resorting to front men added to the activities of those known as "*metedores*," or smugglers, who were bringing in merchandise directly on the numerous ships anchored just off the coast and which in effect acted as warehouses for contraband goods (García-Baquero). Attempts to discourage this abuse by means of a policy of reducing taxes failed due to the impunity with which foreign businessmen operated, thanks to the successive privileges extracted from the Crown from 1648 onwards (see Pulido Bueno).

The main commercial nations had a consul responsible for ensuring that treaties were complied with, solving any internal problems within the community and acting as their representative before the authorities (AGS, Estado leg. 2867).[10] Furthermore, they were guaranteed swift justice thanks to the action of the *jueces conservadores*, judges responsible for processing all the cases in which they became involved and for putting a stop to any excesses on the part of the contraband inspectors.[11] Along with a significantly high floating population, whose presence in Cadiz was determined by the arrival of fleets or preparations for a military operation, as it was the seat of the Atlantic fleet, the *Armada del Mar Océano*, there was a large and influential foreign community firmly settled in the city. The risk involved in a cyclical trade determined by the arrival and departure of the fleets and galleons, the need to insure the cargo, the payment of high commissions and the systematic use of credit to alleviate the shortage of capital endured by the city for most of the year, made the presence of a permanent delegate an absolute requirement (see Carrasco González, *Los instrumentos*). As shown in the memoires of Raimundo de Lantery, one of the most valuable documents available to us on the world of commerce in Cadiz during the second half of the seventeenth century, mutual trust and personal ties were the key to the smooth running of businesses (Bustos Rodríguez, *Un comerciante*). Consequently, it was normal for most companies to be formed by members from the same nation and for family strategies to favour marriages within the national community (Carrasco González, *Comerciantes* 121–9). Each

---

[10]   The documents stored at AGS, Estado leg. 4191 and 4192 show that, by the end of the century, the list had increased enormously and that even the Poles asked for a consulate to be established, which they were denied (15-VI-1694).

[11]   The figure of the *juez conservador*, appointed by the king from the most highly-distinguished counsel, was one more conquest achieved by Hansa in 1647 and by the United Provinces in 1648 to speed up legal proceedings and to prevent the multiple jurisdictions existing within the kingdom from delaying rulings. His decisions could only ultimately be appealed before a court-martial. The foreign businessmen who enjoyed this privilege could request his appointment in those cities in which they deemed it pertinent. In 1680, the French ambassador would succeed in extending the duties of the *juez conservador* to both civil and criminal cases (AGS, Estado leg. 4192).

200 *The Transatlantic Hispanic Baroque*

community acted in a strongly corporate way and, in addition to the consulate, tended to avail of other areas of identification and support such as brotherhoods, charity, guilds and hospitals (Crespo Solana, *Entre Cádiz*; Bustos Rodríguez, *Cádiz*). In this respect, businessmen from Catholic nations found more suitable mechanisms for integrating into the city's social life, even if only because their faith enabled them to form ties through marriage with local families and thus to enjoy more options for obtaining naturalisation papers. Even so, Protestants enjoyed a wide margin of tolerance as long as they worshipped in private.

Cadiz was the most cosmopolitan city in the Monarchy and one of the European cities with the highest foreign population. From the middle of the seventeenth century and even more so throughout the next century, it became the leader in trading with the Americas and the main meeting point between Castile and the two major centres of commercial capital, Genoa and Amsterdam; the central enclave of a network of contacts not only on a European scale, but worldwide. This continuous flow of merchandise and of capital was accompanied by an equally active exchange of ideas and information and a palpable respect for diversity and for everything that came from overseas. It was in this highly open and permeable setting that, completely under siege by French troops, the first Spanish constitution was signed in 1812—a constitution which, as indicated by Tamar Herzog, adopted a definition of the Spanish nation based on the Castilian criteria of residence and naturalisation and which, far from defining the nation in cultural, linguistic and ethnic terms, described the Spanish as the people who resided permanently in Spanish territories both in the Old and the New World (Herzog, *Vecinos* 145).

Bibliography

Alloza Aparicio, Ángel. *Europa en el mercado español. Mercaderes, represalias y contrabando en el siglo XVII*. Valladolid: Junta de Castilla y León, 2006.

Alvar Ezquerra, Alfredo. *Algunos aspectos de las despensas de los embajadores extranjeros en Madrid en la primera mitad del siglo XVII*. Madrid: Ayuntamiento de Madrid, 1992.

———. "Mercaderes en Madrid (1540–1640). Primeras notas." *La burguesía española en la Edad Moderna*. Vol. 3. Ed. Luis Miguel Enciso Recio. Valladolid: Universidad de Valladolid, 1996. 1439–59.

Álvarez-Ossorio, Antonio and Bernardo García, eds. *La Monarquía de las naciones. Patria, nación y naturaleza en la Monarquía de España*. Madrid: Fundación Carlos de Amberes, 2004.

———, and Manuel Herrero Sánchez. "La aristocracia genovesa al servicio de la Monarquía Católica: el caso del III marqués de Los Balbases (1630–1699)." *Génova y la Monarquía Hispánica (1528–1713)*. 2 vols. Ed. Manuel Herrero

Sánchez, Carlo Bitossi, Dino Puncuh and Rocío Ben Yessef. Genoa: Atti de la Società Ligure di Storia Patria, 2011. 331–65.

Archivo General de Indias (AGI). Indiferente, leg. 781. Consulta del Consejo de Indias. Madrid, 12-11-1669.

Archivo General de Simancas (AGS). Contaduría del Sueldo, 2nd series, leg. 156. Juicio por contrabando contra Antonio Balmier. Madrid, 26-X-1675.

———. Estado leg. 634. Informe de Francisco Retama para evitar la expansión del comercio holandés en las Indias analizado en el Consejo de Estado. Madrid, 13-4-1618.

———. Estado leg. 2867, Lista de cónsules extranjeros en Cádiz enviada por el duque de Medina Sidonia. Sanlúcar, 4-II-1624.

———. Estado leg. 4192. Real Cédula sobre el nombramiento de juez conservador para la nación francesa en la Corte. 30-X-1680.

Bartolomei, Arnaud. "La naturalización de los mercaderes franceses de Cádiz a finales del siglo XVIII y principios del XIX." *Cuadernos de Historia Moderna* 10 (2011): 123–44.

Ben Yessef, Rocío. "Entre el servicio a la Corona y el interés familiar. Los Serra en el desempeño del Oficio del Correo Mayor de Milán (1604–1692)." *Génova y la Monarquía Hispánica (1528–1713)*. 2 vols. Ed. Manuel Herrero Sánchez, Carlo Bitossi, Dino Puncuh and Rocío Ben Yessef. Genoa: Atti de la Società Ligure di Storia Patria, 2011. 303–330.

Bodin, Jean. *Les six livres de la république*. Ed. Christiane Frémont, Marie-Dominique Couzinet and Henri Rochas. Paris: Fayard, 1986.

Bustos Rodríguez, Manuel. *Un comerciante saboyano en el Cádiz de Carlos II (Las memorias de Raimundo de Lantery, 1673–1700)*. Cádiz: Caja de Ahorro de Cádiz, 1983.

———. *Cádiz en el sistema atlántico: la ciudad, sus comerciantes y la actividad mercantil (1650–1830)*. Madrid: Silex, 2005.

Cano, Juan. *Reforma moral, política y cristiana del comercio que restaura 30 millones de a ocho de renta a la Monarquía española*. Madrid: s.n., 1675.

Cardim, Pedro, Tamar Herzog, José Javier Ruiz and Gaetano Sabatini. "Introduction." *Polycentric Monarchies: How did Early Modern Spain and Portugal Achieve and Maintain a Global Hegemony?* Ed. Pedro Cardim, Tamar Herzog, José Javier Ruiz and Gaetano Sabatini. Eastbourne: Sussex Academic Press, 2012. 3–8.

Carrasco González, María Guadalupe. *Los instrumentos del comercio colonial en el Cádiz del siglo XVII (1650–1700)*. Madrid: Banco de España, 1996.

———. *Comerciantes y casas de negocios en Cádiz (1650–1700)*. Cádiz: Universidad de Cádiz, 1997.

Crespo Solana, Ana. *Entre Cádiz y los Países Bajos. Una comunidad mercantil en la ciudad de la ilustración*. Cádiz: Fundación Municipal de Cultura; Cátedra Adolfo de Castro, 2001.

————, ed. *Comunidades transnacionales. Colonias de mercaderes extranjeros en el mundo Atlántico, 1500–1830*. Madrid: Doce Calles, 2010.

————. "Elementos de transnacionalidad en el comercio flamenco-holandés en Europa y la Monarquía hispánica." *Cuadernos de Historia Moderna* 10 (2011): 55–76.

Díaz Blanco, José Manuel. "*El conflicto entre los naturalizados de justicia y los naturalizados venales en la carrera de Indias (1629–1643)*." *Pueblos indígenas y extranjeros en la monarquía hispánica: la imagen del otro en tiempos de guerra (siglos XVI–XIX)*. Ed. *David González Cruz*. Madrid: Silex, 2011. 220–45.

Domínguez Ortiz, Antonio. *Los extranjeros en la vida española durante el siglo XVII y otros artículos*. Seville: Diputación de Sevilla, 1996.

García-Baquero, Antonio. "Los extranjeros en el tráfico con Indias: entre el rechazo legal y la tolerancia funcional." *Los extranjeros en la España Moderna*. Ed. María Begoña Villar García and Pilar Pezzi Cristóbal. Málaga: Ministerio de Ciencia y Tecnología, 2003. 73–99.

García Fuentes, Lutgardo. *El comercio español con América (1650–1700)*. Seville: Diputación de Sevilla, 1980.

García Montón, Alejandro. "Trayectorias individuales durante la quiebra del sistema hispano-genovés: Domingo Grillo (1617–1687)." *Génova y la Monarquía Hispánica (1528–1713)*. 2 vols. Ed. Manuel Herrero Sánchez, Carlo Bitossi, Dino Puncuh and Rocío Ben Yessef. Genoa: Atti de la Società Ligure di Storia Patria, 2011. 367–84.

Girard, Albert. *La rivalité commerciale et maritime entre Séville et Cadix jusqu'au XVIIIe siècle*. Paris: De Boccard, 1932.

Herrero García, Miguel. *Ideas de los españoles del siglo XVII*. Madrid: Gredos, 1966.

Herrero Sánchez, Manuel. "La política de embargos y el contrabando de productos de lujo en Madrid (1635–1673). Sociedad cortesana y dependencia de los mercados internacionales." *Hispania* 201 (1999): 171–91.

————. *El acercamiento hispano-neerlandés, 1648–1678*. Madrid: Consejo Superior de Investigaciones Científicas, 2000.

————. "La Monarquía Hispánica y las comunidades extranjeras. El espacio del comercio y del intercambio en Madrid y Cádiz durante el siglo XVII." *Torre de los Lujanes* 46 (2002): 97–116.

————. "Génova y el sistema imperial hispánico." *La Monarquía de las naciones. Patria, nación y naturaleza en la Monarquía de España*. Ed. Antonio Álvarez-Ossorio and Bernardo García. Madrid: Fundación Carlos de Amberes, 2004. 528–62.

————. "La monarchie espagnole et le capital marchand. Les limites de la guerre économique et la lutte pour la suprématie dans l'espace atlantique." *Guerre et économie dans l'espace atlantique du XVIe au XXe siècles*. Ed. Silvia Marzagalli and Brunot Marnot. Bordeaux: Presses Universitaires de Bordeaux, 2006. 195–209.

———. "Republican Monarchies, Patrimonial Republics: The Catholic Monarchy and the Mercantile Republics of Genoa and the United Provinces." *Polycentric Monarchies: How did Early Modern Spain and Portugal Achieve and Maintain a Global Hegemony?* Ed. Pedro Cardim, Tamar Herzog, José Javier Ruiz and Gaetano Sabatini. Eastbourne: Sussex Academic Press, 2012. 181–96.

———, Carlo Bitossi, Dino Puncuh and Rocío Ben Yessef, eds. *Génova y la Monarquía Hispánica (1528–1713)*. 2 vols. Genoa: Atti de la Società Ligure di Storia Patria, 2011.

———, and Eleonora Poggio. "El impacto de la Tregua en las comunidades extranjeras. Una visión comparada entre Castilla y Nueva España." *El arte de la prudencia. La Tregua de los Doce Años en la Europa de los pacificadores*. Ed. Bernardo García, Manuel Herrero Sánchez and Alain Hugon. Madrid: Doce Calles, 2012. 249–73.

———, and Igor Pérez Tostado. "Conectores del mundo atlántico: los irlandeses en la red comercial internacional de los Grillo y Lomelín." *Ireland and the Iberian Atlantic: Mobility, Involvement and Cross-Cultural Exchange (1580–1823)*. Ed. Enrique García Hernán and Igor Pérez Tostado. Valencia: Albatros, 2010. 307–322.

Herzog, Tamar. *Defining Nations: Immigrants and Citizens in Early Modern Spain and Spanish America*. New Haven: Yale University Press, 2003.

———. *Vecinos y extranjeros. Hacerse español en la edad moderna*. Madrid: Alianza, 2006.

———. "Naturales y extranjeros: sobre la construcción de categorías en el mundo hispánico." *Cuadernos de Historia Moderna* 10 (2011): 21–31.

Israel, Jonathan. *Dutch Primacy in World Trade, 1585–1740*. Oxford: Oxford University Press, 1989.

Konetzke, Richard. "Legislación sobre inmigración de extranjeros en América durante la época colonial." *Revista Internacional de Sociología* 3.11–12 (1945): 269–99.

Larquié, Claude. "Les Français à Madrid dans la deuxième moitié du XVIIème siècle." *Les Français en Espagne à l'époque moderne (XVI–XVIII)*. Paris: Centre Nationale de la Recherche Scientifique, 1990. 85–109.

Montemayor, Julián. "Les étrangers à Madrid et à Tolède. XVIe–XVIIe siécle." *Les* étrangers *dans la ville. Minorités et space urbain du bas Moyen* Âge *à l'époque Moderne*. Ed. Jacques Bottin and Donatella Calabi. Paris: Maison des Sciences de l'Homme, 1999. 53–63.

Mörner, Magnus. *Aventureros y proletarios. Los emigrantes en Hispanoamérica*. Madrid: Editorial Mapfre, 1992.

Pardo Molero, Juan Francisco and Manuel Lomas Cortés, eds. *Oficiales reales. Los ministros de la Monarquía Católica (s. XVI–XVII)*. Valencia: Universidad de Valencia, 2012.

Poggio Ghilarducci, Eleonora. "Las composiciones de extranjeros en la Nueva España, 1595–1700." *Cuadernos de Historia Moderna* 10 (2011): 177–93.

Prak, Maarten. "*State Formation and Citizenship: The Dutch Republic between Medieval Communes and Modern Nation States*." *The Long Road to the Industrial Revolution: The European Economy in a Global Perspective. Ed. Jan Luiten van Zandem. Leiden: Brill, 2009. 205–32.

Pulido Bueno, Idelfonso. *Almojarifazgos y comercio exterior en Andalucía durante la época mercantilista, 1526–1740*. Huelva: Artes Gráficas Andaluzas, 1993.

Recio Morales, Óscar. "Los extranjeros y la historiografía modernista." *Cuadernos de Historia Moderna* 10 (2011): 33–51.

Roche, Daniel. "Postface." *Les* étrangers *dans la ville. Minorités et space urbain du bas Moyen* Âge *à l'époque Moderne*. Ed. Jacques Bottin and Donatella Calabi. Paris: Maison des Sciences de l'Homme, 1999. 477–80.

Rodríguez Vicente, María Encarnación. "Los extranjeros en el reino del Perú a finales del siglo XVI." *Homenaje a Jaime Vicens Vives*. Ed. Juan Maluquer de Montes. Vol. 2. Barcelona: Universidad de Barcelona, 1967. 533–46.

Sanz Ayán, Carmen. "Bajo el signo de Júpiter: negocios y hombres de negocios en el Madrid del seiscientos." *El Madrid de Velázquez y Calderón. Villa y Corte en el siglo XVII. I. Estudios históricos*. Ed. Miguel Morán and Bernardo García. Madrid: Ayuntamiento de Madrid, 2001. 61–82.

Shalins, Peter. "La nationalité avant la lettre Les pratiques de naturalisation en France sous l'Ancien Régime." *Annales. Histoire, Sciences Sociales* 55.5 (2000): 1081–1108.

Trivellato, Francesca. "A Republic of Merchants?" *Finding Europe: Discourses on Margins, Communities, Images*. Ed. Anthony Molho and Diogo Ramada Curto. New York: Berghahn, 2007. 133–58.

Viñas Mey, Carmelo. *Forasteros y extranjeros en el Madrid de los Austrias*. Madrid: Librería Siete Soles, 1963.

Weber, Max. *Economy and Society: An Outline of Interpretative Sociology*. 2 vols. Ed. Guenther Roth and Claus Wittich. New York: Bedminster Press Inc., 1968.

Yun Casalilla, Bartolomé, ed. *Las redes del imperio. Élites sociales en la articulación de la monarquía hispánica, 1492–1714*. Madrid: Marcial Pons, 2009.

Chapter 11

Writing Madrid, Writing Identity: A Spatial Dialogue between the Seventeenth and Eighteenth Centuries

Jesús Pérez-Magallón

Perched at the top of the Empire State Building in New York, Michel de Certeau writes: "It [the city] turns into a text that we have before us, right in front of our eyes [...] It allows us to read it, to be a solar Eye, a glance from god" (140). He continues: "The 420-metre tower that serves as a prow for Manhattan continues to construct the fiction that creates readers, makes the complexity of the city readable, and immobilizes its opaque mobility in a transparent text" (141). Without needing to climb a city's tallest building, it can be clearly read from above, but also from below, since the individual's walking and strolling, this *flâner*—wandering and roaming through the streets—implies more than simply a journey; it suggests absorbed contemplation, emotional empathy, and speculative suggestion. But this is not a gaze from the solar eye or God, but rather from man. As De Certeau rightly says, it is this reading that turns what, in reality, is nothing more than opaque mobility into a transparent text. However, Burton Pike seems to qualify De Certeau's opinion by affirming that the stroller "basically experiences the city as a labyrinth, although one with which he may be familiar. He cannot see the whole of a labyrinth at once, except from above, when it becomes a map" (245). Once again, height becomes an inevitable physical position to interpret urban space that changes from a labyrinth into a mapping of reality, a map or a text. Burton Pike takes up and interprets Walter Benjamin's concepts of the city and body as a metaphor, describing the city as fragments rather than as a whole: "Therefore his impressions of it at street level at any given moment will be fragmentary and limited: rooms, buildings, streets" (245).

This is probably true for the strolling individual, but not for the critic who observes past realities from the study of his home. The city *in itself* is not a whole, but rather an imaginary construction of the person walking through it. At the same time, can we speak of a fictitious—imagined—whole that represents a national identity? If we consider the previously mentioned fragmentary nature of urban reality that the individual experiences while wandering, then the answer is no. However, if we contemplate the imaginary construction and invention of

206 *The Transatlantic Hispanic Baroque*

the city as a whole, then yes indeed. In *Le pli*, Gilles Deleuze quotes Leibniz's *Monadology*: "a city, looked at from various sides, appears quite different and becomes numerous in aspects" (monad 57). Leibniz and Deleuze allude to the city's various sides, aspects and depictions. This also means its various appearances, either stable and permanent or temporary and ephemeral. The city's fragments are embodiments in the retina of partial ghosts that refuse to present *the* single comprehensive view of the city. However, by reflecting on Cavafy's poem "The City," one can imagine that there may be only one city, that the city encompasses the entire world, and that a city's fragments remind us of all cities—a simplistic metaphor for a more tortured reality, but a symbolic image of the futility of all movement. Hafiz Amirrol writes that "The city is conceived as a spatial system composed of many different parts, and this spatial system is attached to nature and evolution of the city, and constitutes the city's image" (19). If we consider the role of the city as a text and memory space together, then the city becomes the written embodiment and incarnation of history. And history is inseparable from the diachronic construction of identities. It is indeed a map, labyrinth and text, but they write and inscribe the vicissitudes of identity(ies). Or, as Maurice Halbwachs said many years ago: "there is a close connection between a group's customs, spirit, and the appearance of the places where it lives" (45).

Any architectural and/or urban work is an ecological aggression—setting aside a city's foundation, in which such aggression takes on unprecedented dimensions—whose effects no one seemed to care about in seventeenth-century Madrid. However, it also imposes new texts or changes to the old ones on the previously written memory, which constitute the affirmation of the present on a perhaps inerasable past—yet erased to a certain extent. Pedro Montoliu summed it up thusly: "Hunting was banished, oak forests, holm oak, chestnut, walnut, pine, hazelnut and strawberry trees were cut down to build houses and to use as firewood. One hundred years after the court occupation of the village, very little of its natural wealth remained. Many rivers dried up, wheat and wine crops were lost, the Great Plains were scorched and cattle had to be relocated. As a result, the climate became harsh" (89). The city symbolically reveals the human race's condition as a devastator of ecosystems but also as a creator of new ones. This inevitable destruction and creation process continues to our present day.

According to Roger Chartier, the printing press led to an "uncontrollable textual proliferation" and, consequently, it was necessary to develop strategies to erase what had previously been written, a practice "as essential for [the act of] remembering as [that of] forgetting" (quoted in Safier 11). Metaphorically applying this view to the urban experience, it can be said that, in reality, the city is a palimpsest that not only traces the levels of depth since it was founded, in addition to layers that provide evidence of historical moments in its evolution—as beautifully exemplified in the Museum of London—but also tells the story of its own development and, with the material scars, it traces the identity marks of those who founded it. Commenting on Carl Sauer's pioneering work, Don Mitchell points out that he and his group "show how cultural development and transformation [...] constantly created and recreated the places and landscapes in which people lived" (28). In other words, this urban palimpsest is part of a successive and diachronic series of major or minor operations carried out on the landscape by communities and cultures in tension, which, in an increasingly distant time, was natural. And not so much due to the uncontrolled excess of urban or architectural "writing," but rather the limited space in which to write (i.e. land speculation problem). One can also interpret it as the spiritual and material forms of existence of the community that inhabits it, and therefore the traits that marked the identities of the people who embraced it. The city thus constitutes a cultural landscape *par excellence*, in which decisive gestures—foundation, destruction and reconstruction—accompany actions of lesser significance but which left their mark of the time: collective tribulations, the uprooting and anxieties that accompany humans' journey, as well as their hopes and beliefs, successes and fulfilled dreams.

In *La cultura del barroco*, José Antonio Maravall recalls that Carlo Argan had aptly described baroque Europe in the first half of the seventeenth century as *Europa de las capitales* (253); he also mentions that Braudel had indicated that the Baroque was "a product of imperial mass civilizations" (quoted in Maravall226), and then adds: "although in the Baroque, the initiative and direction of culture changed from the city to the state, this does not mean that the city, with its own specific characteristics, was not the setting for baroque culture" (227). David R. Ringrose establishes the same relationship between imperial capitals:

> Madrid was the model for the political city. From its rise at the end of the sixteenth century until the Napoleonic Wars, Madrid remained an imperial center much in the tradition of imperial Rome. Both cities have been described as economic parasites, consuming the wealth of their empires without directly contributing to the creation of that wealth. Like imperial Rome, Madrid organized and ran a worldwide political and administrative structure and used that political structure as a framework for controlling, taxing, and shaping a widespread system of commercial activity. Madrid was unique, however, since its location kept it from becoming the commercial as well as the political center of its empire. (4)

In fact, from the moment when Philip II decided in 1561 to turn Madrid into the location for his court (see Alvar Ezquerra, *Felipe II* 29–37; *Nacimiento*)—abandoning the temporary transfer to Valladolid (Alvar Ezquerra, *Cartapacio*) at the beginning of the seventeenth century—as Jesús Escobar explains, "The town underwent one of the most dramatic urban transformations in early modern Europe" (4). The most remarkable feature of the city of Madrid is that, for the first time in history, a city of secondary importance (about 3,000

208 *The Transatlantic Hispanic Baroque*

inhabitants in 1513) in the country's economic or strategic life—as opposed to Constantinople, Paris or London—was chosen to become the political centre of a vast empire, the capital of both worlds, the Palatine capital (Mínguez and Rodríguez 77), whose management involved unforeseeable complexities. The subsequent foundation of Washington or Ottawa or the construction of Brasilia would not surprise anyone, but in the sixteenth century, the choice of Madrid was a radically innovative bet that was clearly connected with certain utopian aspirations of the Renaissance King, or perhaps more pragmatically, as Kamen points out, because of "its location in relation to the royal residences" (189).

The conversion of Madrid into the political centre and seat of the court—María José el Río Barredo aptly described it as *urbs regia*, the ceremonial capital of the Spanish monarchy—led to a large-scale social metamorphosis and, as a result, a radical urban metamorphosis as well. The establishment of the court automatically included the entire central bureaucratic court, but also the aristocratic court, part of the nobility, and other privileged layers. This gave rise to an unusual and sudden demographic development to meet various needs of idle sectors *par excellence*, stimulating the settlement and growth of other productive groups. As a small village that became a city (Alvar Ezquerra, *Nacimiento* 15–104)—according to Louville, there were about 160,000 inhabitants in Madrid under Charles II, compared with 500,000 in Paris (Díaz-Plaja 108)—it is clear that Madrid kept areas with narrow, winding streets—as did all cities with a relatively old central area. At the beginning of the seventeenth century, streets were opened and some were expanded and aligned, squares and public fountains were built, marking the city's old settlement with new signs.

From Dodds' perspective, Madrid in its own way clearly reflected the political power of the monarchy and its privileged classes. Escobar points out that there was an absence of Roman imperial ideology in sixteenth-century Madrid culture, but also that "alternative representations of the empire existed in Madrid" (8). One might wonder why Roman ideology had to be adopted, as imperial ideology was clearly present (as can be seen in Pagden, for example). Escobar says that "The use of brick, granite, and iron characterized Madrid buildings and served as a further marker of the town's identity" (26). And if we imagine the spire-crowned towers and the use of black slate, then we can see that the city's architectural identity appears closely linked to El Escorial's construction, which "represents an apex in the international classicism of the sixteenth century" (Escobar 23), with its hybrid architecture derived from local traditions, the Italian Renaissance, and certain aspects of Dutch architecture. This is the architectural language of the Hispanic, transatlantic empire that expanded and asserted itself in various directions. Clearly reflecting the dynamics inherent in the arts, the new emerging powers first tried to imitate this style; then they opposed/refused this language and articulated their own, separate and distinctive language which, as seems to recur in the sporadic movements of humanity, was the opposite of it. However, it is a serious mistake not to interpret imperial architectural language as anything but what it really is.

In my book *Construyendo la modernidad*, I devoted a chapter to the relationship between the cultural plans of the *novatores* and questioning what could be called a "conservative" concept of national identity, i.e., "being Spanish." Since all of the traditional arguments aim to establish an indissoluble link between Galenism and Aristotelianism, and the scholastic and being Spanish, the *novatores* proposed a different equation, in which experimental medicine, free philosophy, sciences, and the concept and value of art were linked with *another way* of being Spanish. This *new and different* approach incorporated the *novatores'* work in various branches of knowledge and technical or artistic disciplines. This period was characterized by a movement away from antiquity in certain areas and a movement toward it in others. There was a break with excess and a desire for clarity of lines in some areas; in others, decorative elements of creative individuality were developed and enhanced. Without a doubt, figures such as José Benito Churriguera, Teodoro Ardemans and Pedro de Ribera belonged to the *novator* circle, individuals who carved lines and enduring curves into the urban palimpsest of Madrid. The city reflects the identity of the community that inhabits it. However, since identity is not unique or exclusive, it also shows the diversity of identity that inhabits it. For this reason, when I refer to the works by Ribera, Ardemans and Churriguera as part of the *novatores'* reform and renewal plan, I am referring to the range of concerns and attitudes in a variety of fields and disciplines held by those who belonged to the intellectual, professional and artistic circles that we have called *novator*. But I am also referring to the conflicting lines of neoclassicism.

What are the characteristics of the Spanish architectural and urban development plan in the era of Charles II, and how does this plan reflect on itself up until the third decade of the next century? In other words, what languages endured or clashed at a time when new agents attempted to write the city and the city's history? While it is true that the tremendous work of Juan Gómez de Mora during the first part of the seventeenth century was, as Virginia Tovar Martín put it, "pure architectural prose" (*Enciclopedia* 59), this metaphor could be extended by arguing that Churriguera, Ardemans and Ribera turned architectural and urban development language into highly poeticized prose. The goal is to mark their work with highly evocative and suggestive decorative elements; i.e., not creating spaces and buildings that appear to be erected or open *naturally*. Quite the opposite is true: they placed emphasis on signs that highlighted its artificiality, its artistic objects or spaces. Focusing on Madrid, Virginia Tovar Martín says that "the contributions of this last period are specific references to the typology created by Juan Gómez de Mora, which opened the way for innovation in early baroque architecture in Spain" (*Enciclopedia* 60). Furthermore, in *El siglo XVIII español*, this author writes that, upon the arrival of Philip V, "Spanish cities formed a unified spatial image through the use of building types whose co-existence had reached great typicity during the seventeenth century. They sought essential identity from the form and concept, and architectural dignity through the appropriation of methods, systems and clear principles, whose figurativeness is associated with the Habsburg Monarchy" (17), although not all historians share this view. According to Bottineau, "Spanish baroque architecture presented itself as original art, the result of experiments that began with enhancing facade lines and decorating arches with motifs similar to basketwork. This continued for several generations. It thus remained faithful to consistent patterns in nation-building: a combination of multiple spaces in the plans, facades and elevations using discontinuous, rather than straight, lines; composition of masses using geometric shapes whose structure is reminiscent of prisms; ornaments graciously arranged with rectangular paintings attached to the construction" (207). Attempting to highlight the originality of the Spanish architecture of this period, Kubler minimizes the relationships between Spanish and Italian architects, claiming that "although the name of the great Borromini was a favourite term of abuse among Spanish critics of eighteenth-century architecture, it is now clear that his forms were almost entirely ignored in Spain until about 1700" (28). However, Bottineau disputed this view, highlighting not only this relationship through the dissemination of treatises and illustrations that accompanied them, but also drawing attention to the profound Italian influence on the architects of the time.

Although the last quarter of the seventeenth century cannot be considered an era of overwhelming architectural euphoria, it was not a period of total inactivity, however modest the results may have been. Improvement, reform and beautification work was carried out in the urban planning, municipal architecture, courtly and religious fields. Furthermore, Charles II considered abandoning classical Herrerian architectural criteria in order to create more typically baroque forms. However, Herrerian style did not disappear. The opposite is indeed true, as evident in the works by José Benito Churriguera or Ardemans. Thus, on the one hand, the apex of the Baroque is exemplified in works by Pedro de Ribera, which amalgamated various Spanish and European influences; the survival of classical concepts—obviously, not without evolving—in works by Ardemans and Churriguera; and the influence of Italian baroque architecture in works by Contadini and Fontana, which provided continuity in the work of other Italians under Philip V. Moreover, in the first quarter of the eighteenth century, certain forms emerged that could be likened to Rococo style. In other words, if we ascribe—with good reason—certain aesthetic forms to certain ways of conceiving national identity, although this concept of course had not yet been developed (i.e. we are talking about identity before the term existed), about 50 years later we see clear signs of conflicting understandings of this identity in the city.

Virginia Tovar Martín emphasized an aspect of early-eighteenth-century architecture that seems to be absolutely essential: there is continuity in the idiomatic foundations of planning and building, although there is also a dialogue with the Renaissance Herrerian style. Furthermore, the historian points out that "there is no conflict or division between the national plan at the institutional or private level and plans with purely classroom-based guidelines that are usually put in the hands of foreigners. It is basically *a national activity* that is considered with the same stimuli of demand and renewal" (*El siglo XVIII* 20). The architecture that developed during this period thus maintains some signs of identity, but, as this author points out, it is not "a *castizo* or populist plan, with varying quality or creativity and French or Italian-style influences" (*El siglo XVIII* 20). On the contrary, it is a process of manipulating exterior and interior spaces that could be described as an imaginative amalgamation within the general European movement of baroque architecture, since, as Virginia Tovar Martín says, "eighteenth-century Spanish art should be and deserves to be considered within Western art, with the value that it has, and the peninsula should be included within this nation. It is part of the powerful expansion of its baroque alternatives or those that are inspired by ancient art imitations" (*El siglo XVIII* 20). Without a doubt, these words also apply to what was produced in the last quarter of the seventeenth century.

Upon the change in dynasty in 1700, town planning and municipal architecture in Madrid closely depended on Teodoro Ardemans and Pedro de Ribera, under the direction of Marqués de Vadillo, Mayor of Madrid (1715–1729). Despite his modest output of architectural work, José Benito Churriguera enjoyed private patronage provided by Juan de Goyeneche (see Bonet Correa). The bourgeois patrician designed the plan for Nuevo Baztán (1709–1713, built 1715–1721). Nuevo Baztán's design is a kind of utopia—in a certain sense similar to the utopia presented in *Sinapia*—in which private life, work and social relations should be combined, but also a sign of control and desire for public utility. The other assignment that Goyeneche gave to him—and whose significance in Madrid town planning was transcendent—was the building of a palatial home on Calle de Alcalá, whose facade had a plinth made from stone blocks in the form of a breakwater on which was first erected a padded body followed by pilasters, culminating in a balustrade crowned by statues; the door was framed by estipites and bead moulding. But this facade—execrated by the neoclassicists, like everything by Churriguera—was restored in 1773 according to completely different criteria in order to clearly convey another way of understanding identity and its marks on the city. As Bonet Correa said, "Villanueva, who purified, or rather 'shaved,' the facade to give it a neoclassic look that the institution required, imbued it with new aesthetic ideas, drastically eliminated the plinth or natural base of rocky ashlars, the rustic padding on the first floor, the pilasters straddling the two upper floors,

212 *The Transatlantic Hispanic Baroque*

and the balustrade which, crowned with sculptural busts, crowned the whole" ("Juan de Goyeneche" 112). As a matter of fact, Diego de Villanueva's work was limited to eliminating the more eye-catching ornaments and plinth to give the building a distinct appearance, since, as Juan José Martín González says and Bonet Correa reiterates, "the key elements remained intact" (113). However, as Bonet Correa correctly points out, "From the historical perspective, this stately mansion marked an extremely important starting point [...] The new appearance and splendour of the palaces built by 18th-century nobles and important figures gave the Spanish capital a fresh new look" (113).

The work by Ardemans and Ribera was of much greater significance for the capital's urban planning and architecture—both civil and religious. Ardemans settled in Madrid in 1688. In 1691, Cardinal Portocarrero appointed him Master Builder of Catedral de Toledo. A senior palace and villa official, he clearly dominated Madrid's architecture until his death on February 15, 1726. He oversaw the main design of the capital, and in 1722, he delivered the plans for Iglesia de San Millán. He also published two works: *Declaración y extensión sobre las Ordenanzas de Madrid, que escribió Juan de Torija, y de las que se practicaban en Toledo y Sevilla, con algunas advertencias a los alarifes* (1719) and *Fluencias de la tierra y curso subterráneo de las aguas* (1724). His collaborator in municipal activities was Pedro de Ribera, and their work seems to become amalgamated. Around 1690, he presented Ardemans with his design of the Town Hall courtyard and participated in the completion of the towers and facade. In 1700, along with Felipe Sánchez—architect of the Dukes of the Infantado—he designed the plan for a house on Calle de Toledo; and in 1704, he presented a project for the Puerta de Segovia; at the beginning of the century, he also remodelled the Casa de corredor del duque del Infantado. A designer of burial mounds, without a doubt, the most significant and evident part of his work as *tracista* is found in La Granja and Balsaín.

Although Francisco Sabatini, under Charles III, carried out the construction of the Madrid sewer system, on November 5, 1717, Ardemans presented the plan for a network of sewers that completed the already operational underground passages (*Fluencias* 243–78). In Chapter 10 of *Declaración y extensión*, he proposed measures to enlarge the stone pavement of the sidewalks (implemented in specific places in the capital). However, in addition to all of his achievements as Madrid master builder, royal work master builder and designer, Madrid master plumber, and Philip V's court painter and royal architect, his concern for and reflection on the city's urban development and architecture is best revealed in his *Ordinances* (1719). Placed within the municipal bureaucracy, he had to do a great deal of reflection in order to overcome the obstacles involved in such dynamics. "We should therefore not be surprised about his "dictatorial" attitude, which is a prevalent feature of his life, his constant complaints about the bitter reality of the time, as well as his search for solutions: sometimes through the defense of *modern* ideas developed by the architects of his previous generation, and other times through his belief in the Bourbon renewal and full acceptance of his reformist approach" (Blasco Esquivias xxiii). This aptly summarizes the duality that characterized so many individuals in this era, as well as their work as painters, urban planners and architects. But they also reflect the professional commitment to the urban renewal of Madrid, which in many ways is a continuation of others from the previous century and a preview of what would take place during the rest of the century. There were clear signs of a modernization perspective.

Although Pedro de Ribera was supported to a certain extent by the king, who subsidized the statue of the saint above the Hospicio de San Fernando entrance in Madrid and permitted, at the very least, his urban development work—or did not directly oppose it—he was not named master builder of royal works to replace Ardemans, but he did replace him in his duties at the Madrid City Hall. It seems that his career was essentially devoted to the protection of Marqués de Vadillo from 1712 until his death in 1729, although in fact his career lasted much longer. He was thus not a court architect, but rather an urban development architect. The capital was the scene where Pedro de Ribera carried out "a magnificent urban development effort, which foreshadowed that of Charles III, but which was different in spirit" (Bottineau 370). He was largely responsible for a significant change in Madrid's image and its urban landscape. The urban planning work of Ribera, which set a clear precedent for what would take place under Charles III, consisted of "beautification activities, creation of various works capable of establishing monumental, vertically accented visual focal points within the horizontal extension of the city [...] through the adoption of a formal language which amalgamated the two most important 17th and 18th-century European styles, French classicism and Italian Baroque, characteristics of our intrinsic form of expression" (Verdú Ruiz 44–5). On the initiative of Marqués de Vadillo, Ribera undertook the design of the Virgen del Puerto hermitage and the urbanization of the surrounding area, to the west of Alcázar and along the banks of Manzanares, "one of the most important urban transformations that would be carried out in the court before the time of Charles III" (Verdú Ruiz 31), and which is the earliest in Spain. It was Ribera's innovative, indelible mark on Madrid's skin. Since Marqués de Montealto was a magistrate, in 1733, Ribera presented the designs and plans for the Real Convento de Nuestra Señora de Atocha, a key space in the city. As Madrid's Lieutenant Master of Works and Fountains, he was in charge of everything to do with "the design, management and supervision of the works that would make it possible to expand Viaje Bajo de Abroñigal by incorporating water from Tres Caños de la Venta del Espíritu Santo, increasing the flow of Viaje Alto de Abroñigal [...] and expanding Viaje de la Castellana through aggregation of water discovered in Valle de San Antón" (Verdu Ruiz 44). He probably designed the new public fountains of Antón

214 *The Transatlantic Hispanic Baroque*

Martín, Red de San Luis and Plaza de San Juan; and he remodeled the fountains of Puerta del Sol, Matalobos, Cura, San Antonio de los Portugueses, and Calle Valverde (see Martínez Alfaro).

As an architect, Ribera developed a language of comprehensive and ambitious experiments, "from his early work, to meet the vehement art of his time, he helped develop a unified art reconciling contemporary ideas, which he successfully combined" (Tovar Martín, *El siglo XVIII* 22). In 1717, he completed the design of Cuartel de Guardias de Corps (Cuartel del Conde-Duque)—that depicts a new location of the military at the heart of the city—and the following year, he designed the Puente de Toledo; in 1725, the Puente de la Casa de Campo; the Puente Verde in 1728, and the following year the Puente sobre el Arroyo de Abroñigal. In 1721, Ribera designed and completed the reconstruction work of Portillo de Jilimón de la Mota, in Plazuela de Armas. One year later, he began to rebuild Hospicio Municipal del Ave María y San Fernando, with the great portal's opulent facade, "an overwhelming theatrical scene, a stunning, ostentatious whirlwind of sculptures placed like a screen between the citizens and dispossessed members of society, hidden behind their walls" (Verdú Ruiz 42), but also—or better yet—as an eye-catching sign to force passers-by to stop and contemplate the facade, and to reflect on the fate of those who lived inside. If, according to Lefebvre, it can be said that where you live and where others live with respect to you determines your identity, then we are not only talking about the identity of the city and country, but also of the individuals who live there. The facades that Ribera designed vary according to the buildings' function and their own stylistic evolution: as Kubler points out, they highlight the military severity in Cuarteles del Conde-Duque (1720) and textile motifs in Hospicio de San Fernando (1722), his most famous and most despised work, which this author considers to be Ribera's study of French architecture (Kubler 38, 39). In the private homes that can be attributed to him, "he remained true to the modest schemes imposed by Juan Gómez de Mora at the beginning of the previous century, with the addition of matched modillions under the eaves from the second half of that century" (Tovar Martín, *El siglo XVIII* 42), but not forgetting to mark each of the works with superb decorative details on the balconies and facades. As for the interior, the rooms face courtyards, with spacious but not formal staircases, so that nobles' or bourgeois' staircases only seemed to differ from the rest by the size of the lots. Commenting on this domestic architecture, Verdú Ruiz recalled that the desired Ribera-style frame "was rooted in late 17th-century Madrid architecture" (68–9). According to Bottineau, "in the capital, he is credited with many palace doors typical of large Madrid residences, which are much different than Parisian hotels of the same period" (371), in particular, the palaces of Miraflores, Ugena, Perales, Torrecilla and Santoña. However, Verdú Ruiz clarified that "no documentary data confirms this" (43), since it was only the main door frame that led to this credit, as was the case with the chapel facade of Monte de Piedad, which is still preserved. However, the main door frame is an essential way to locate the fragment built within the urban context while signing its authorship. In reality, the facade is the semiotic sign that draws the attention of passers-by to the splendour of the building and the wealth and prestige of its inhabitants. It is a closed threshold, a notice to passers-by to not "forget" the mansion that they are walking past, a gesture aimed at highlighting the visibility of the home and its owners. This is particularly significant, considering some comments from travelers who mentioned that the great Spanish nobles' mansions were not at all ostentatious. On the other hand, like other designers, painters and writers, Ribera participated in ephemeral art of the period, and on November 24, 1719, he was appointed to oversee the "security and splendour of the theatres and stage machinery" (Verdú Ruiz 31).

Paradoxically, but understandably so, Pedro de Ribera was one of the most criticized architects by the neoclassicists. Referring to Churrigueresque style—interestingly, the most denigrating adjective is not *riberesco*, but *churrigueresco*—Ceán Bermúdez said that "If we had to award the title of the inventor of this ridiculous caste in Spain, no one is more deserving than Pedro de Ribera" (in Bottineau 371 n. 33). On the contrary, in Pedro de Ribera's library, alongside Italian translations of treatises by Palladio, Serlio, Vitruvius and Tolomeo, Bottineau finds Ribera to be highly significant and with a much more complex dialogue than the reductionist presumed by Ceán: "the exceptional nature of his genius was always the combination of architectural purity and decorative passion within the refinement of a strong and subtle sensitivity" (371). Verdú Ruiz concluded that he was "an expert on the great 16th-century classical treatise writers, mathematics and geometry treatises, Herrera's works, the teachings of masters such as Felipe Sánchez and Teodoro Ardemans, who conveyed 17th-century Madrid's innovative architectural experiences, and some 17th and 18th-century European achievements" (35). This scholar offered an innovative interpretation of Ribera by saying that "on Madrid soil, he takes all of the valid theoretical or practical experience and attempts to adapt their achievements to European experiences" (34). She later said that Ribera tried to mark the city by "participating in the severe, compelling, magnificent, sumptuous, ornamental and exuberant characteristics which, within a formal baroque grammar, were the prevalent features of the two dominant European styles respectively, but not forgetting to do so using a formal language with Spanish roots" (35). I do not think it is necessary to emphasize the "Spanish" character of Ribera, as it is absurd to question it, and there is no point in arguing the issue with those who have a different understanding of the architectural experience—or cultural experience in a broad sense—that took place in Europe. What I find remarkable is the approach and depth of the scars that Ribera left on the city's skin, his incisive writing on the capital's text. Above all, we have attempted to show how, through the clear marks left by Gómez de Mora in the first half of the seventeenth century, during the passage from one century to the next, new languages were introduced, which led urban and architectural agents to write and inscribe the city with the marks of identity of the most advanced intellectual circle of the time.

Bibliography

Alvar Ezquerra, Alfredo. *Felipe II, la corte y Madrid en 1651.* Madrid: CSIC, 1985.

———. *El nacimiento de una capital europea: Madrid entre 1561 y 1606.* Madrid: Turner, Ayuntamiento de Madrid, 1999.

———, ed. *El cartapacio del cortesano errante.* Facsimile edition. Madrid: Imprenta artesanal de Madrid, 2006.

Amirrol, Hafiz. *Regeneration of Decaying Urban Place Through Adaptive Design Infill.* 2011. May 3, 2012. <http://www.scribd.com/doc/51605698/13/III-2-3-Theory-of-Permanence-and-Monuments>.

Ardemans, Teodoro. *Declaración y extensión sobre las Ordenanzas que escribió Juan de Torija.* Madrid: Francisco de Hierro, 1719.

———. *Fluencias de la tierra y curso subterráneo de las aguas.* Madrid: Francisco del Hierro, 1724.

Blasco Esquivias, Beatriz. *Arquitectura y urbanismo en las "Ordenanzas" de Teodoro Ardemans para Madrid.* Prologue by A. Bonet Correa. Madrid: Ayuntamiento de Madrid. Gerencia Municipal de Urbanismo, 1992.

Bluche, François. *La vie quotidienne au temps de Louis XIV.* Paris: Hachette, 1984.

Bonet Correa, Antonio. "Los retablos de la iglesia de las Calatravas de Madrid." *Archivo Español de Arte* 35 (1962): 21–49.

———. "Juan de Goyeneche, su palacio y la academia." *Juan de Goyeneche y el triunfo de los navarros en la monarquía hispánica del siglo XVIII.* Exhibition catalogue, Royal Academy of San Fernando. Madrid, October–November 2005. Madrid: Fundación Caja Navarra, 2005. 105–113.

Bottineau, Yves. *L'Art de cour dans l'Espagne de Philippe V. 1700–1746.* Bordeaux: Féret & Fils, 1960.

Bustamante García, Agustín. *El siglo XVII. Clasicismo y Barroco.* Madrid: Sílex, 1993.

Chueca Goitia, Fernando. *El semblante de Madrid.* Madrid: Revista de Occidente, 1951.

Curtius, Ernst R. *Literatura europea y Edad Media latina.* Trans. Margit Frenk Alatorre and Antonio Alatorre. 2 vols. Mexico, DF: Fondo de Cultura Económica, 1955.

De Certeau, Michel. *L'invention du quotidien. Vol. 1: Arts de faire.* Ed. Luce Giard. Paris: Gallimard, 1990.

Deleuze, Gilles. *Le pli. Leibniz et le Baroque*. Paris: Les Éditions de Minuit, 1988.

Díaz-Plaja, Fernando. *La vida española en el siglo XVIII*. Barcelona: Alberto Martín, 1946.

Dodds, Jerrilynn D. *Architecture and Ideology in Early Medieval Spain*. University Park, PA: Pennsylvania State University Press, 1990.

Escobar, Jesús. *The Plaza Mayor and the Shaping of Baroque Madrid*. Cambridge: Cambridge University Press, 2003.

Fernández Álvarez, Manuel. *El establecimiento de la capitalidad de España en Madrid*. Madrid: Instituto de Estudios Madrileños, 1960.

Gaya Nuño, Juan Antonio. *Historia del arte español*. 4th edition. Madrid: Plus-Ultra, 1968.

Gramsci, Antonio. *Letteratura e vita nazionale*. Rome: Editori riuniti, 1996.

Halbwachs, Maurice. *La mémoire collective*. 1950. January 15, 2013. <http://classiques.uqac.ca/classiques/Halbwachs_maurice/memoire_collective/memoire_collective.html>.

Kamen, Henry. *Felipe de España*. Madrid: Siglo XXI, 1997.

Kubler, George and Martin Soria. *Art and Architecture in Spain and Portugal and their American Dominions, 1500 to 1800*. London: Penguin, 1959.

LeGates, Richard T. and Frederic Stout, eds. *The City Reader*. London and New York, NY: Routledge, 1996.

López Izquierdo, Francisco. "Plazas de toros de madera de la Puerta de Alcalá (1741–1748)." *Anales del Instituto de Estudios Madrileños* 14 (1977): 241–59.

———. *Plazas de toros de Madrid (y otros lugares donde se corrieron)*. Madrid: El Avapiés, 1985.

Lyotard, François. Économie libidinale. Paris: Minuit, 1975.

Maravall, José Antonio. *La cultura del barroco*. Barcelona: Ariel, 1980.

Marcos Marín, Alberto. "Percepciones materiales e imaginario urbano en la España moderna." *Imágenes de la diversidad. El mundo urbano en la corona de Castilla (s. XVI–XVIII)*. Ed. José Ignacio Fortea Pérez. Santander: Universidad de Cantabria, 1997. 15–50.

Martínez Alfaro, Pedro E. "Historia del abastecimiento de aguas públicas a Madrid. El papel de las aguas subterráneas." *Anales del Instituto de Estudios Madrileños* 14 (1977): 29–53.

Maura Gamazo, Gabriel. *Vida y reinado de Carlos II*. Madrid: Aguilar, 1990.

Mínguez, Víctor and Inmaculada Rodríguez. *Las ciudades del absolutismo. Arte, urbanismo y magnificencia en Europa y América durante los siglos XV–XVIII*. Castelló de la Plana: Publicacions de la Universitat Jaume I, 2006.

Mitchell, Don. *Cultural Geograpy: A Critical Introduction*. Malden, MA: Blackwell, 2000.

Montoliu, Pedro. *Madrid, villa y corte. Historia de una ciudad*. Madrid: Sílex, 1996.

Mumford, Lewis. "What Is a City?" *The City Reader*. Ed. Richard T. LeGates and Frederic Stout. London and New York, NY: Routledge, 1996. 183–8.

Orozco Díaz, Emilio. *El teatro y la teatralidad del barroco (Ensayo de introducción al tema)*. Barcelona: Planeta, 1989.

Pagden, Anthony. *Spanish Imperialism and the Political Imagination*. New Haven, CT: Yale University Press, 1990.

Pike, Burton. "The City as Image." *The City Reader*. Ed. Richard T. LeGates and Frederic Stout. London and New York, NY: Routledge, 1996. 243–9.

Quiroz-Martínez, Olga. *La introducción de la filosofía moderna en España. El eclecticismo español de los siglos XVII y XVIII*. Mexico, DF: El Colegio de México, 1949.

Ribot García, Luis Antonio. "La España de Carlos II." *Historia de España Menéndez Pidal. Vol. 28: La transición del siglo XVII al XVIII. Entre la decadencia y la reconstrucción*. Coord. P. Molas Ribalta. Madrid: Espasa-Calpe, 1993. Madrid: Espasa-Calpe, 1993. 61–203.

Ringrose, David R. *Madrid and the Spanish Economy, 1560–1850*. Berkeley, CA: University of California Press, 1983.

Río Barredo, María José del. *Madrid Urbs Regia. La capital ceremonial de la Monarquía Católica*. Prologue by Peter Burke. Madrid: Marcial Pons, 2000.

Rodríguez G. de Ceballos, Alfonso. *Los Churriguera*. Madrid: CSIC, 1971.

Safier, Neil. *Measuring the New World: Enlightenment Science and South America*. Chicago, IL: The University of Chicago Press, 2008.

Shergold, Norman D. and John E. Varey. "Tres dibujos inéditos de los antiguos corrales de comedias de Madrid." *Revista de la Biblioteca, Archivo y Museo* (1951): 391–445.

Tovar Martín, Virginia. *Enciclopedia de Madrid. II. Arquitectura civil*. Madrid: Giner, 1988.

———. *El siglo XVIII español*. Madrid: Historia Viva, 2000.

———. "Arquitectura barroca occidental." *Barroco*. Ed. Pedro Aullón de Haro. Madrid: Verbum, 2004. 251–62.

Valdivieso, Enrique. "Arquitectura." *Historia del arte hispánico. IV. El Barroco y el Rococó*. Ed. E. Valdivieso, R. Otero and J. Urrea. Madrid: Alhambra, 1980. 1–92.

Valencia Idiáquez, Juan A. de. *Diario de noticias de 1677 a 1678, en Colección de documentos inéditos de la historia de España. Vol. 67. Por el marqués de la Fuensanta del Valle y José Sancho Rayón*. Madrid: Imprenta Miguel Ginesta, 1877. 69–133.

Verdú Ruiz, Matilde. *La obra municipal de Pedro de Ribera*. Madrid: Ayuntamiento de Madrid, Área de Urbanismo e Infraestructuras, 1988.

Wirth, Louis. "Urbanism as a Way of Life." *The City Reader*. Ed. Richard T. LeGates and Frederic Stout. London and New York, NY: Routledge, 1996. 189–97.

Chapter 12

The City and the Phoenix: Earthquakes, Royal Obsequies, and Urban Rivalries in Mid-Eighteenth-Century Peru[1]

José R. Jouve Martín

Philip V died in Madrid on July 9, 1746 at the age of 62. He had ascended to the throne of Spain on November 1, 1700, after Charles II, the last of the Habsburg kings to rule the country, died without an heir and named him his successor. Philip's long reign had been marked by the War of the Spanish Succession, the Treaty of Utrecht, and the Nueva Planta decrees. Remarkably, he became King of Spain not just once, but twice. To the surprise of many in Spain and other European courts, he abdicated the throne in favor of his son, Louis I, on January 15, 1724, purportedly to retire from public life and devote the rest of his life to the service of God.[2] Unfortunately, Louis fell ill a few months later and passed away on August 31 of that year. Philip returned to the throne just six days later. This circumstance reinforced Philip's association with the image of the Phoenix, a metaphor that had played an important role in the Spanish political imagination since the late sixteenth century. As Mestre and Fernández Albadalejo have shown, the iconography of the Phoenix had been relevant during the last years of Philip II's reign when it embodied the desire for the renewal of a monarchy in crisis (Mestre and Fernández Albadalejo 10). Other Spanish kings, such as Philip IV, had also been associated with the mythological bird both in poetry and public ceremonies (Azanza López 42; Carreira 71–2). In fact, it was an image that was appropriated not just by kings, but also by many other relevant figures of the time, as the case of Lope de Vega—commonly referred as

---

[1]   This research was made possible by the generous support of the Canadian Social Sciences and Humanities Research Council (SSHRC) and the Spanish National Research Council (CSIC).

[2]   There has been considerable controversy on the reasons that led Philip V to abdicate the throne in favor of his son Louis Philip. While the King had clearly manifested a few years earlier his intention to withdraw from public life and devote the rest of his time to prayer and meditation a few years earlier, some scholars have suggested that his true ambition was to be able to exercise his dynastic rights to become King of France. For a discussion of Philip V's abdication see Kamen (139–68).

220 *The Transatlantic Hispanic Baroque*

the Phoenix of Spain—illustrates (Sánchez Jiménez 81–3; Cull 131–2). Given its wide symbolic and political currency at the time, it is not surprising that it was adopted by those who supported the Bourbon king. Gabriel Álvarez de Toledo had already described Philip in the early years of his reign as the new Phoenix that had emerged from that other "living Phoenix" ("ce Fenix vivant") that was the French king Louis XIV, Philip's grandfather (Álvarez de Toledo 15; Mestre and Fernández Albadalejo 11).[3] The association of Philip V with the mythological animal reappeared in the account that described the obsequies that the city of Granada organized on the occasion of the death of Louis I in 1725. Philip V, who had just reassumed his duties as king, is described in this text as the "Crowned Phoenix of Spain" (San Lorenzo n.p. [preamble dedicated to King Philip V]). Despite the best intentions of his apologists, the Phoenix was nevertheless a double-edged sword as a metaphor with which to describe both the monarch and—by extension—the Empire. Although the mythological bird carried the promise of its future resurrection, it also implied in its own nature the certainty of its irremediable decay and destruction.

Shortly after his death, the body of Philip V lay in state for three days in the Palacio del Buen Retiro to give his vassals the opportunity to pay their last respects (Kamen 216). Escorted by the royal Garde du Corps, the coffin was then taken to the church of San Jerónimo el Real for a *responso* or funeral prayer prior to its departure to the royal palace of La Granja de San Ildefonso, in Segovia, in whose church the monarch had requested to be buried (Kamen 214–18). By then, Philip's heir, Ferdinand VI, had already dispatched a royal decree informing his officers throughout the empire of his father's passing and prescribing the protocol to be observed during the obsequies. According to his instructions, the funeral had to follow the same set of principles and rules established by his progenitor on the occasion of the death of Louis I (Sainz de Valdivieso Torrejón 11), which in turn Philip V had based on the regulations known as *pragmática de los lutos* issued by Charles II in 1692 and first implemented in the obsequies for Queen Mariana of Austria in 1696 (Torrejón 22r). As Bertelli has pointed out, the passing of a reigning king created a momentary power vacuum that was particularly noticeable at the symbolic level. Royal funeral ceremonies were designed to fill that void (Bertelli 214–31). By adopting the funerary dispositions of the Habsburgs, Ferdinand VI aimed not just to keep the body politic together in the public imagination, but to reaffirm the temporal

---

[3]   Gabriel Patricio Álvarez de Toledo y Pellicer de Tobar (1662–1714) was a descendant of the House of Alba, a founding member of the Real Academia de la Lengua in 1714, King Philip V's librarian, and one of the most distinguished Spanish humanists at the turn of the eighteenth century. For more information about his life and works see Hill (95–146).

continuity of the Spanish monarchy despite the change of dynasty, just as his father had done before him during the obsequies for his brother.[4]

The degree to which the Spanish monarchy successfully imposed a standardized ritual for the funerals of their kings has led researchers to assert that royal obsequies in the Spanish empire were basically empty simulacra of each other that had no other purpose but to reassert the power of the monarch. Rodríguez de la Flor has argued that royal funeral ceremonies and the lengthy accounts written to commemorate them were for the most part "mechanisms" for doctrinal unification and integration, whose objective was to restore and homogenize "the fractured and dispersed imagination of an Empire structured by a providential worldview" (169). Similarly, Alejandra Osorio has suggested that these ceremonies helped establish the presence of royal authority in the king's dominions through a theatrical and ritual re-enactment of the king's persona through paintings, poems, and architectural structures (Osorio 84). For his part, Valenzuela Márquez has pointed out that royal obsequies were primarily designed as a way to convey the sacredness of the Catholic monarchy and the place of the king as intermediary between the celestial and terrestrial worlds (192–3). Thus, these views coincide in reducing the various performative and social aspects of royal obsequies to mere products of the ideological apparatus of the monarchy that the metropolis was able to impose throughout the Hispanic world.

While the Spanish monarchy obviously sought to instrumentalize its funerary rituals to its own advantage, I argue in this article that these rituals need to be interpreted in the context of local politics and imaginaries. The concrete meaning of these elaborate displays was, by its own nature, not fixed, but fluid, plural, and ephemeral. In order to avoid competing—and potentially troublesome—interpretations of the myriad of texts and hieroglyphs, and the actions that took place during these ceremonies, cities appointed *relatores de exequias* or chroniclers of obsequies with the double task of creating an univocal description of the events and fixing its intended meaning. Despite their obvious similarities in style, the accounts of these *relatores* became means through which the main cities of the Empire competed among themselves to assert, define, and establish their identity and privileges. Their books seized the opportunity offered by the king's passing not only to assert a city's allegiance to the monarchy, but to reflect on its past, present, and future and, by extension, on that of the

---

[4] While the Bourbons adopted the funerary ceremonies of the Austrias, this does not mean that they did not change other aspects of the Spanish royal protocol. On the contrary, as Castro has pointed out, Philip V tried "to put an end to the protocol of the House of Austria that had placed the king out of public view and made visible only to the grandees of Spain. It was necessary to make him visible to the nobility and the people in general and that the Court adopted the political role of exalting its Sovereign, as it was the case in Versailles" (43). See also Gómez-Centurión Jiménez (880).

imperial body politic. In this regard, the funeral obsequies for King Philip V organized by the cities of Lima and Cuzco and their subsequent celebration of the crowning of Ferdinand VI constitute a case in point. As I show in the following pages, the ceremonies held by both cities and the books written to commemorate them cannot be dissociated from their competition for political and cultural hegemony in the context of the Viceroyalty of Peru.

Surprisingly, researchers have paid little attention to the role that the funerals for Philip V played in the Spanish colonial world. Studies of royal obsequies have tended to concentrate on the formal and historical continuities observed in the conception and staging of these ceremonies as a whole rather than on the local and supra-local significance of specific cases (Varela; Allo Manero 2003; Rodríguez de la Flor). When they do so, they concentrate overwhelmingly on the obsequies organized by Spanish or Italian cities such as Madrid, Salamanca or Rome as the main models on which the other cities of the empire based their own rituals. This has introduced a certain Eurocentric bias in the analysis of the royal obsequies that took place in colonial Spanish America. Scholars either approach them to underline their similarities with the metropolitan ones, to the detriment of their own specificity, or they dismiss them altogether as mere repetitions of their European counterparts. This is particularly evident in the case of the few studies to focus specifically on the funerary ceremonies for Philip V. Azanza Lopez has analyzed the connections between the obsequies for Philip IV in Madrid and those that the city of Pamplone organized for the Bourbon king. For his part, Alberto Fernández González has studied the ceremonies that took place in Santiago de Compostela while Mónica Riaza de los Mozos and Emanuela Garofalo have concentrated on the funerals that took place in Rome and Palermo, respectively. The funerary structure erected in Lima in memory of Philip V is mentioned in passing by Lorene Pouncey in her survey of Peruvian catafalques as well as by Allo Manero in her study on the Sevillian influence on Limean and Mexican funerary structures (1989). Significantly, one of the studies to pay more attention to the funeral ceremonies held in Lima for the first Bourbon king does not focus primarily on the history of these rituals at all, but rather on the 1746 earthquake and its aftermath (Walker 167–72).

In order to understand the role that the obsequies for Philip V played in the power struggles between the former capital of the Inca empire and the city founded by Francisco Pizarro in January 1535, this chapter starts precisely with a discussion of how the huge earthquake that desolated the city of Lima and the port of El Callao in1746 shaped the interpretation of Philip V's death; and, vice versa, how the king's passing gave new meaning to the events suffered months earlier. The second part of this chapter then changes its focus to Cuzco, to analyze the way in which Lima's destruction, Philip V's death, and Ferdinand VI's coronation gave the city an unexpected opportunity to reclaim its old political centrality, and helped foster its ambitions to become once again the capital of Peru. In the last section of this chapter, I turn again to Lima to address how, in light of these events and to avoid challenges to its hegemonic position, the identity of the city was re-codified during the celebrations for Ferdinand VI's ascension to the throne. In my concluding remarks, I address the way in which the accounts that describe these ceremonies became vehicles for a reflection on the future of an empire that, while hoping it could once again rise from its ashes, was increasingly being seen as marked by its ephemerality.

The Phoenix and the Earthquake

News of Philip V's death arrived in Lima on February 21, 1747, nearly four months after one of the most devastating earthquakes ever to hit the capital of the Viceroyalty of Peru. The tremor had occurred on October 28 of the previous year at about half past ten in the evening. At precisely that moment, the Earth began to move so violently "that it seemed as if the bowels of Earth rose up as enemies of the city; the combination of water, fire, and wind violently destroyed everything that the intensity of the earthquake had not. Unable to withstand such powerful forces, small and large buildings alike fell down burying alive many of the city residents" (Llano and Zapata 1). The magnificent temples and rich palaces that "had taken 211 years to build" collapsed within just three minutes. The city suffered such a tremendous loss that it was doubted "that another two centuries would give us enough time to rebuild it or that 200 million would be enough to cover the losses" (Llano and Zapata 1).[5] The city's cathedral was among the buildings most affected by the quake. According to a contemporary account, "its impressive structure was the cause of its demise" as the high towers that flanked it collapsed over its vaults and chapels "destroying everything that the earthquake had left standing", making "incredibly expensive just to clear away the rubble" and turning "the task of rebuilding it almost impossible" (Lozano 4). The buildings that housed the main political institutions of the city did not fare any better: the palace of the Viceroy, the offices of the Real Audiencia, the Tribunal de Cuentas, the Tribunal de la Inquisición, the university, as well as many other proud edifices were all but reduced to "a terrifying shadow of what they once were" (Lozano 5).

---

[5]   There are several sources that describe the earthquake of 1746, among them the anonymous *Noticia analítica y estado del puerto del Callao* (1747), the poem by Juan Antonio Tristán del Pozo *Relación fúnebre* (1746), *Narración circunstanciada de la deplorable catástrofe sufrida en la ciudad de Lima* (published in 1863) by José Eusebio de Llano and Zapata, and the description by Pedro Lozano *Individual y verdadera relación de la extrema ruina que padeció la ciudad de los Reyes* (1747), the latter being one of the most widely translated contemporary accounts. For a discussion of these and other sources, see the studies of Walker and Ribas.

224 *The Transatlantic Hispanic Baroque*

Many in Lima attributed the tremor to the lack of piety of its inhabitants for it was thought that "the sudden impact of earthquakes is the most terrible way through which Nature manifests that the supreme force of its powerful hand serves the Almighty to exact revenge for the many outrages committed against his Divine Justice" (Lozano 1). However, the fact that a large number of its residents miraculously survived amid the rubble also proved God's mercy and that "He does not wish the sinner to die, but to repent" (Pozo 18). Alongside this religious view of the events emerged another, more philosophical interpretation connected with the baroque idea of the *vanitas*. At the beginning of the seventeenth century, the growth of Lima had led writers such as the Franciscan friar Buenaventura de Salinas y Córdova to praise the city's design and magnificence, the proportion of its squares and streets, the splendour of its temples, and the beauty of its striking balconies and windows (Salinas y Córdova 108; also see Oña 18–19). The topic was taken up in the eighteenth century by writers such as Peralta Barnuevo, who dedicated the eighth book of his *Lima fundada* to singing the praises of a city where "squares, streets, temples and buildings, / everything evokes a firm sense of artistic accomplishment" (Peralta Barnuevo 306).[6] By 1746, it was suggested that Lima had arrived "to the point of uppermost perfection a city was capable of in the new world" (Lozano 3), finding itself "at the highest peak and most elevated sphere that any royal Court could ever hope to achieve" (Pozo 7). The earthquake transformed this dazzling colonial metropolis into a "ruined Babylon" in just a few minutes (Pozo 7). Some in Lima considered it not simply an accident of Nature, but the ultimate proof of "the intimate, ephemeral nature of its being" and of all human designs in general (Lozano 3). The arrival of the royal decree informing of Philip V's death further accentuated this general perception of fugacity and mortality. As Sainz de Valdivieso Torrejón, who was the chronicler charged with the task of describing the royal funeral, put in his book: "If Time can bring new occasions with which to take grief to its supreme extreme, it could not have found better means to do so [than the announcement of the death of the King], for the havoc that the fatal earthquake created on October 28, 1746 had already transformed this city into the land of dismay and the country of laments" (Sainz de Valdivieso Torrejón 11v–12v).

With the cathedral turned into a pile of rubble, the Viceroy ordered the construction of a wooden structure in the main square of Lima. Its purpose was not just to accommodate the city's notables during the funeral, but also to

---

[6]   One of the most important Limean intellectuals of the early eighteenth century, Pedro de Peralta Barnuevo (1664–1743) was a poet, historian, and professor of mathematics and astronomy at the University of San Marcos. His book *Lima fundada o conquista del Perú* (1732) was a heroic poem about the conquest of Peru and the founding of the City of the Kings. For more information about his life and work see Hill (147–90).

house the royal catafalque, which was designed in the baroque style of those erected in Lima on previous occasions (Pouncey; Sainz de Valdivieso Torrejón 18r–34r). As the preparation for the obsequies progressed, Sainz de Valdivieso Torrejón highlighted something that must have been obvious to many of his contemporaries: the connection between the fate of the city, the fate of the king, and, by extension, the fate of the empire. Prior to the earthquake, Lima viewed itself not simply as another colonial city but as "the center of the Spanish empire in South America" (Walker 56). It was a city whose political relevance went hand in hand with its religious importance, as evidenced by the many canonization processes sponsored by the city during the seventeenth and eighteenth centuries (Jouve Martín; Mills). For 200 years, its main mission had been to control and "civilize" a vast hinterland populated by indigenous peoples and where European presence was often barely noticeable. The earthquake had not only called into question Lima's "civilizing" role; it even threatened its own survival as a unified and functioning *civitas*. Their homes demolished, Sainz de Valdivieso Torrejón points out how the inhabitants of Lima "stopped being residents of a city to become fugitives, and society itself became dispersed. Science disappeared, reason became useless, and the arts degenerated into idleness" (Sainz de Valdivieso Torrejón 12v). Thus, the blissful Lima extolled by Pedro de Oña and Peralta Barnuevo became dismembered, and the many piles of debris and the disappearance of entire city blocks gave birth to "another Lima divided into many settlements" (Sainz de Valdivieso Torrejón 12v).

Some of the emblems used in the obsequies for Philip V visually emphasized the connections between the king's death and the situation of the capital of the Viceroyalty. One of them depicted a city in ruins and a heart lying on the ground followed by four verses that stated, "My heart fell down like a building in my breast announcing, as an oracle, Philip's death" (Sainz de Valdivieso Torrejón 67r). Another emblem remembered the destruction of the statue of Philip V that, until the fateful day of the earthquake, had crowned the bridge over the Rímac River. It lamented that both the statue and his model existed no longer: "Her lovely original now lifeless! The foundations of Lima, the beautiful, turned now to dust! / O flood of sadness! / So many blows all at once? What a torment!" (Sainz de Valdivieso Torrejón 74r). As a third writer pointed out, it was as if the city itself, reduced to ashes, aimed at occupying the place and function played by the catafalque erected by the Viceroy and aspired to become at the same time the king's "mourner and his grave" (Sainz de Valdivieso Torrejón 118v). As Alejandra Osorio has noted, Lima was built during the seventeenth and eighteenth centuries as a synecdoche for Peru (60–61), and the silver of Potosí helped turn Peru into a synecdoche of the empire. As a result, the death of Philip V and the destruction of Lima came to be seen as two terms of the same equation: both embodied the monarchy. Underlining this connection, Sainz de Valdivieso Torrejón concluded his account of the funerals for Philip V

226 *The Transatlantic Hispanic Baroque*

by describing how the firing of the canons from the ruins of the once proud fort of El Callao with which the funeral ceremonies ended appeared to many as "a last-ditch effort after which the entire empire perished" (46r).

Head and Court of Peru

Meanwhile, in the Andes, the decree announcing Philip V's passing was received in a radically different way. The destruction of Lima and the upcoming coronation of Ferdinand VI were seen in Cuzco as an opportunity to reclaim the political and symbolic status lost in the sixteenth century in favor of the City of the Kings. To mark the momentous event, the town council ordered an account be published that, with the title *La lealtad satisfecha,* promulgated "the exalted joy and fond recognition of the loyalty with which the Muy Noble y Gran Ciudad of Cuzco expressed its feelings in the obsequies for the magnificent S.D. Philip V (may God have him in His holy glory) and festively applauded the glorious exaltation of the august and serene name of His Sacred Catholic Royal Majesty Ferdinand VI" (Santander, cover page). Given Lima's dilapidated state in the aftermath of the earthquake of 1748, the book—one of the few of its kind ever to be published by the city of Cuzco—must have taken on a special significance. While all cities in the Spanish empire organized obsequies in honor of the king and informed royal authorities of their acts, only a few of them considered necessary to publish a book describing their ceremonies on a regular basis. The production of such books was an expensive and difficult literary endeavor. Furthermore, while they presented an opportunity to advance their status in the empire, they also posed some risks to their reputation. In order to avoid them, cities were forced to spend lavishly in these ceremonies as to guarantee that their description merited the attention of the king and the admiration of other cities. They also needed to make sure that there were, among their residents, at least some who were talented enough to write the account of the obsequies and the multitude of other texts that accompanied them in the hermetic style characteristic of the genre. Not surprisingly, many cities decided that the effort was not worth the costs. Such was the case of Cuzco prior to 1748.[7] The publication of *La lealtad satisfecha* was therefore a momentous occasion intended to send a very clear message to other cities of the empire and particularly to the capital of Peru.

---

[7]   While it seems that no accounts of obsequies sponsored by the city of Cuzco appeared in print prior to 1748, there is at least one published funerary sermon in memory of Queen Isabel de Borbón published in 1646 with the title *Oracion funebre en las honras que la ciudad del Cuzco celebro a la memoria de la Serenissima Reyna ... Doña Ysabel de Borbón,* pronounced by Vasco Valverde y Contreras.

The expression "Muy Noble y Gran Ciudad del Cuzco" [Very Noble and Great City of Cuzco] that appeared in the cover page of *La lealtad satisfecha* acknowledged not just the customary and honorary title that Francisco Pizarro had conferred upon it almost 200 years earlier – it was also an indirect reminder of the fact that the Spanish conquistador had awarded the city jurisdiction over most of the lands once governed by the Incas, making it for a short period of time "at once the center (at least in terms of its jurisdiction) and most powerful municipality in the new province of Peru" (Osorio 38). Cuzco's political aspirations were also clearly reflected in the authorization for publication issued by the Jesuit Joseph de Paredes. Paredes claimed that, in organizing such rich and elaborate ceremonies for the Spanish monarchs, the city had really proved to be the "Head of the Peruvian Empire and truly the Court of its former Kings" (Santander 1). His reference to Cuzco as "Court" and "Head" of the Peruvian empire was anything but innocent. Both denominations had been at the center of a bitter legal dispute between Lima and Cuzco at the beginning of the seventeenth century regarding their respective rights as the political center of the Viceroyalty of Peru. As Osorio has noted, "Cuzco's claim to head status was based on its greater Indian population, its illustrious Inca past as 'Head of their Empire,' and its having been discovered and founded by Francisco Pizarro before Lima" (39). Lima, however, was able to successfully retain its hegemonic position thanks "to its greater number of vecinos or notable Spaniards residing in the city to its being the seat of the viceregal court and the archbishop—the *in situ* sources of all imperial powers mundane and spiritual" (Osorio 39). However, by the time *La lealtad satisfecha* was published in 1748, the material foundations of those powers lay in ruins.

Contrary to the dominant perception in Lima, Philip V's death and the beginning of Ferdinand VI's reign were seen in Cuzco not so much as a parable of the ephemeral nature of all worldly aspirations, but rather as a symbol of the resurrection of the monarchy and the renewed political aspirations of the city itself. The image chosen for this purpose was not the Phoenix, but the Sun. It was a convenient metaphor. Even though it had not been employed often during Philip V's reign due to its association with the French king Louis XIV and the fear of the interference of France in Spanish affairs, the sun had been used as a metaphor for the Spanish monarchy for well over two centuries (Bridikhina 196). As we shall see, the celebrations held in Cuzco re-contextualized this metaphor by connecting symbolically the Spanish monarch not with the French dynasty—to which Philip V was in fact linked by blood—but with the royal lineage of the Incas. The metaphor of the sun also allowed Joseph de Paredes to highlight Cuzco's role as the beacon of the empire. In this regard, he wrote how, after learning of the passing of its king, "a dark night covered this city as it had already covered the rest of the empire, but Cuzco, as the city of the Sun, to which it was consecrated in former times, made possible the dawn of a new day

228 *The Transatlantic Hispanic Baroque*

in which, leaving behind the dusk, the monarchy was reborn" (Santander 2). The image of Cuzco as the new light of the empire could not offer a starker contrast with Lima's real and symbolic decline. One of the poems written in Cuzco for this occasion graphically illustrated the change of fortune experienced by the capital of the Viceroyalty when stated that "breathless after such a bitter blow Lima had bent its head and surrendered its three crowns" (Santander 82).

Cuzco's decision to publish in the same volume the account of the obsequies for Philip V and the celebrations for Ferdinand VI's ascension to the throne clearly played well with the idea of the city's rebirth and renewal. Referring to Lima's central role in maintaining the colonial order, the erudite Limean savant Peralta Barnuevo had proudly declared in his book *Lima inexpugnable*: "Remove Lima from Peru and there will be no empire" (Peralta Barnuevo, *Lima inexpugnable* xxxiv). José Antonio Santander, the writer charged by Cuzco with the task of narrating the events, showed in his text just how wrong Peralta Barnuevo had been in his appreciation and defended Cuzco's ability to fill the void Lima had left. According to Santander, the funerals for Philip V in the Andean city were conducted with all of the splendour one would expect of a former imperial capital to the point that "it was difficult to believe that such abundance of lights and adornments and so many beautiful objects could exist if it were not for the fact that Cuzco was known around the world for its greatness as a producer of gold and silver" (Santander 3). As for the catafalque erected for the occasion, Santander claimed that it competed in greatness with the "ostentatious machine" of the cathedral itself. But it was the mausoleum, and not the cathedral, which caused the most admiration in the eyes of the beholders "for the multiple candles that illuminated it with their sad lights to reflect misfortune; for its extraordinary height that symbolized pain; and for its expensive adornments and careful construction that conveyed amazement; it [the catafalque] was an eloquent expression of everything Art has to offer when moved by the chisel of loyalty" (Santander 26–7).

The celebrations for the coronation of Ferdinand VI that followed the funerals for Philip V served to reaffirm even more clearly the ability of Cuzco to act as a true imperial capital. As Santander explains:

> If it were not for the fact that the magnificence of this Noble and Great City of Cuzco is already well-known around the world thanks to its opulence, I would have kept for myself many of the details of my narration as not to be accused of pretending to pass as true my own fictional, fabulous, and chimeric inventions. But the demonstrations of joy were such and the splendor and expenses so great on the day of the acclamation of our August and Most Serene Lord King Ferdinand VI (may he live long and happily) that, even if I wanted to exaggerate them, my words would never be able to fill the echo that their pomp left in our admiration. (90–91)

As customary, representatives of the main political, ecclesiastical, and economic institutions and social groups marched through the city streets to show their allegiance to their new sovereign. Among them, Santander singled out the parade organized by the indigenous communities that lived in the outskirts of the city. According to the chronicler, the procession was headed by a group of Indians who "imitated fierce, strange animals" accompanied by the sound of "countless *pututos*, instruments made with conch shells, whose melancholic accent mimics that of the natives of this nation" (Santander 171). They were followed by 64 Indians disguised as "noble squires of the former rulers of this empire, dressed with their traditional garments, and wearing on their breast an insignia of the Sun that hanged from two thick chains" (Santander 171). For Santander, the solar insignia displayed by the Indians was at the same time a reference to the ancient Sun (the god of the Incas) and to the modern Sun (Ferdinand VI), being that "ancient Sun," but an "imperfect simulacrum of his [the King's] persona" (Santander 95–6). The procession concluded with "twenty-nine Incas, whose solemn costumes and brilliant jewelry grabbed everyone's attention." The last of them embodied the continuity between the Incas and Bourbons by representing "our Lord and King Ferdinand with the Royal Banner in his hands and was followed, as his greatness demanded, by a magnificent, graceful and striking Triumphal Chariot" (Santander 171–3). While the use of Inca costumes allowed the Indians to not only keep alive the memory of their empire, but also negotiate their identity vis-à-vis the colonial authorities (Dean; Macera; Bradley and Cahill 87–151), Cuzco's creole elite saw in the participation of the Indian population a way to foster their political aspirations by grounding them on the indigenous past. In this regard, the message that the authorities of Cuzco wanted to transmit to anyone who cared to read Santander's account of the festivities could not be more eloquent: With Lima's power waning as a result of the earthquake, Cuzco was in position once again to become Head of Peru and the true "American Court of the unrivaled King Ferdinand" (Santander 95–6).

Death and Rebirth

Meanwhile, many in Lima understood quite well that if the city was to retain its privileged position after the earthquake, it was necessary not only to rebuild it as soon as possible, but to reaffirm its place as capital and viceregal court both politically and symbolically. As in Cuzco, the city's elite thought that celebrations for the ascension of Ferdinand VI to the throne of Spain offered such an opportunity. To this end, the Viceroy Count of Superunda had an account of the festivities published with the title *El día de Lima* that left no doubt about the place of the City of the Kings within the empire. While its Andean rival had presented itself as "the Head of the Peruvian empire," Lima

230 *The Transatlantic Hispanic Baroque*

went even further, calling itself "la muy noble y leal Ciudad de los Reyes, cabeza de la América Austral" [The very noble and most loyal City of the Kings, Head of Austral America] (Ribera, cover). As the Jesuit priest Juan Antonio Ribera, the chronicler who wrote the book, proudly suggested, "Lima is to the empire what the Earth is to the Universe: its center" (Ribera 123). As Santander did in *La lealtad satisfecha*, Ribera also used the metaphor of the Sun to represent the relationship between the city and its new sovereign in the book *El día de Lima*. But, while in Cuzco this metaphor associated the Spanish monarchy with the former Inca dynasty, the sun was primarily interpreted in Ribera's book as a symbol of the king himself (Ribera 5) and an embodiment of "the new dawn that illuminated Lima in the night of its misfortunes" (Ribera 35). Those misfortunes were obviously linked to the effects of the recent earthquake. However, despite its destructive power, the earthquake itself had not been the worst calamity. The loss of houses, palaces, and churches had fundamentally shattered "the dominance that this city enjoyed for many years, for kingdoms are sustained by their opulence," and having lost the basis of that opulence "it can be said that this city died of an even more furious death" (Ribera 57).

As in Cuzco, the celebrations for the coronation of Ferdinand VI began in Lima on September 23, 1747, coinciding with the birthday of the new monarch (Santander 99; Ribera 110). They were designed to demonstrate the ability of the City of the Kings to rise from its ashes only 11 months after the earthquake that had devastated it. In this regard, the Viceroy wrote to the monarch that "the aspect of this city appeared completely changed on the day of the royal proclamation. Its residents took off the sad clothes they had been wearing and put on their best robes. The streets were free of the horrors that had filled them, the grief had disappeared, and the city, filled with light and joy for the repairs and adornments of its many buildings, gave the impression of a pleasing and peaceful theatre" (Manso de Velasco 1v). According to the Count of Superunda, the coronation of Ferdinand VI had given Lima the impulse needed not only to raise "from the dust in which it had been buried," but also to rebuild it "in a new a better way" (Manso de Velasco 1v). As part of his plans to use the widespread destruction produced by the earthquake to the advantage of the capital of the Viceroyalty, the Viceroy had proposed "widening the streets, tearing down the top floor of two-storey buildings, and limiting the number of facades and bell towers" (Walker 13). In so doing, he was hoping that a more enlightened city could emerge from the ashes of the old one.

The celebrations that Lima held in honor of Ferdinand VI did not just reinterpret the solar metaphor that had also been used in Cuzco in order to symbolize this new beginning. Lima also appropriated as its own the historical narrative of the Incas. As in Cuzco, the processions that marched through the streets of Lima included one organized by the *indios naturales*. Some of those Indians paraded in the traditional costumes of the ancient *caciques* of the region, while others dressed as the Inca kings to whom those caciques were subjected. Among the historical figures they represented was the entourage of the Great Chimo, "the monarch who ruled the valleys around Lima" (Ribera 243), followed by the Inca Emperor Huascar accompanied by his knights and the Gran Coya, his wife, "carried on their vassals' shoulders on top of a sublime throne made of gold" (Ribera 250). Behind them came the rest of the Inca kings who had ruled Peru, beginning with Manco Capac and excepting only the "illegitimate" Atahualpa. All of them swore allegiance to their new sovereign, Ferdinand VI, thereby ritually "consenting" in the name of those of their social group to the colonial order imposed by the Monarch and the Spanish authorities.

Having Inca kings marching through its streets enabled Lima to appropriate as its own a historical narrative closely associated with Cuzco and to deny its competitor of its monopoly over it as a source of political legitimacy. It was certainly not the first time the Incas had paraded through the streets of the City of the Kings. Although the first occurrence of Indian participation as a separate group in Limean dynastic festivities took place in 1659 during the celebrations for the birth of Prince Philippe-Prosper, it was in the second decade of the eighteenth century that it had become customary (Périssat 252). Dressing as Incas during these occasions was important not just for the Indians of the city as a means through which to forge their identity, as Calvo correctly suggests (73; 81–8). Driven by their own ambitions, the political elites of both Lima and Cuzco considered their association with the Inca past an important element in their struggle to define who truly was the political and symbolic "Head of the Peruvian Empire."

In the end, in spite of the attempts to present the death of Philip V and the proclamation of Ferdinand VI under the best possible light, both events underlined the growing internal tensions between the coast and the Andean world. In the case of Lima, the Count of Superunda and his successors devoted a great deal of time and effort to rebuilding the city according to a more rational plan that called for a more effective use of its resources and a greater control over its residents (Walker 12–13; see also Moreno Cebrián and Sala i Vila). However, despite their herculean efforts to get the city back on its feet, the celebrations in honor of Ferdinand VI could not hide the devastation that this baroque city had suffered, nor the calamitous state of the buildings that embodied its political power. Furthermore, some of the Indians who had actively participated in the ceremonies for the king and who embodied in part the city's desire for its return to greatness were later discovered to have played a leading role in the Lima and Huarochirí rebellions and were found guilty of conspiring to overthrow the same colonial order that they had sworn their allegiance to (Dueñas 65–78). In the case of Cuzco, the ceremonies for Philip V and Ferdinand VI's coronation did constitute a turning point in the perception of the city's identity and an important step on the road to its symbolic recognition as the capital of the

232 *The Transatlantic Hispanic Baroque*

"Peruvian Empire." This road culminated with its designation as Real Audiencia in 1787. This fact, along with the establishment of the Viceroyalty of the Río de la Plata ten years earlier, contributed to further undermining Lima's aspirations of becoming the "Head of Austral America." Paradoxically, the rebirth of Cuzco as a political and administrative center was also to be threatened by the descendants of those Inca kings who had walked through its streets during Ferdinand VI's proclamation, as the rebellion of Túpac Amaru II in 1780 illustrates. Thus, the funerals for Philip V served in the end to highlight the ephemeral nature of the colonial order. As that crowned Phoenix had done after the death of Louis I, Lima and the monarchy rose once again, but not for long. As the many devastated buildings left behind by the earthquake of 1748 ominously seemed to foretell, Lima and the monarchy were just beginning a cycle that would culminate with the destruction of the empire and with the capital of the Viceroyalty of Peru forever renouncing its name of true City of the Kings.

Bibliography

Allo Manero, María Adelaida. "Aportación al estudio de las exequias reales en Hispanoamérica. La influencia sevillana en algunos túmulos limeños y mexicanos." *Anuario del Departamento de Historia y Teoría del Arte de la Universidad Autónoma de Madrid* 1 (1989): 121–37.

———. *Exequias de la Casa de Austria en España, Italia e Hispanoamérica*. Zaragoza: Universidad de Zaragoza, 2003.

Álvarez de Toledo, Gabriel. *Obras posthumas poéticas, con la Burrumaquia*. Madrid: En la Imprenta del Convento de la Merced, 1744.

Azanza López, José Javier. "Los jeroglíficos de Felipe IV en la Encarnación de Madrid como fuente de inspiración en las exequias pamplonesas de Felipe V." *Emblemata aurea: la emblemática en el arte y la literatura del Siglo de Oro*. Ed. Rafael Zafra and José Javier Azanza López. Madrid: Ediciones AKAL, 2000. 33–56.

Bertelli, Sergio. *The King's Body: Sacred Rituals of Power in Medieval and Early Modern Europe*. University Park, PA: Pennsylvania State University Press, 2001.

Bradley, Peter T. and David Patrick Cahill. *Habsburg Peru: Images, Imagination and Memory*. Liverpool: Liverpool University Press, 2000.

Bridikhina, Eugenia. *Theatrum mundi: entramados del poder en Charcas colonial*. La Paz: Plural Editores, 2007.

Calvo, Thomas. "Proclamations royales et Indiens au XVIIIe siècle: enjeux politiques et sociaux." *Anuario de Estudios Americanos* 68.1 (2011): 73–103.

Carreira, Antonio. "Góngora y su aversión por la reescritura." *Criticón* 74 (1998): 65–79.

The City and the Phoenix 233

Castro, Concepción de. *A la sombra de Felipe V: José de Grimaldo, ministro responsable (1703–1726)*. Madrid: Marcial Pons, 2004.

Coello de la Rosa, Alexandre. "El Fénix en las Marianas (1747)." *Revista de Indias* 70.250 (2010): 779–808.

Cull, John. "El teatro emblemático de Mira de Amescua." *Emblemata aurea: la emblemática en el arte y la literatura del Siglo de Oro*. Ed. Rafael Zafra and José Javier Azanza López. Madrid: Ediciones AKAL, 2000. 127–42.

Dean, Carolyn. *Inka Bodies and the Body of Christ: Corpus Christi in Colonial Cuzco, Peru*. Durham, NC: Duke University Press, 1999.

Dueñas, Alcira. *Indians and Mestizos in the "Lettered City": Reshaping Justice, Social Hierarchy, and Political Culture in Colonial Peru*. Boulder, CO: University Press of Colorado, 2010.

Fernández González, Alberto. "Las exequias de Felipe V en Compostela." *Compostellanum: revista de la Archidiócesis de Santiago de Compostela* 46.3–4 (2001): 715–36.

Gadow, Marion Reder. "Exequias y pompas barrocas en tiempos de Felipe V." *Baética: Estudios de arte, geografía e historia* 6 (1983): 289–94.

Garofalo, Emanuela. "I Solenni Funerali di Filippo V nella Cattedrale di Palermo." *Espacio, tiempo y forma: serie VII, historia del arte* 13 (2000): 221–44.

Gómez-Centurión Jiménez, Carlos. "La corte de Felipe V: el ceremonial y las casas reales durante el reinado del primer Borbón." *Felipe V y su tiempo: congreso internacional*. Ed. Eliseo Serrano Martín. Vol. 2. Zaragoza: Institución Fernando el Católico, 2004. 879–914.

Hill, Ruth. *Sceptres and Sciences in the Spains: Four Humanists and the New Philosophy (ca. 1680–1740)*. Liverpool: Liverpool University Press, 2000.

Jouve Martín, José Ramón. "En olor de santidad: Cultos locales y política de canonizaciones en el Virreinato del Perú." *Colonial Latin American Review* 13.2 (2004): 181–98.

Kamen, Henry. *Philip V of Spain: The King Who Reigned Twice*. New Haven, CT: Yale University Press, 2001.

Llano y Zapata, José Eusebio de. *Narración circunstanciada de la deplorable catastrofe sufrida en la ciudad de Lima e inundación del puerto del Callao*. Lima: Imprenta de la Libertad, 1863.

Lozano, Pedro. *Individual y verdadera relacion de la extrema ruina que padecio⊠ la Ciudad de los Reyes*. Lima: Por la viuda de J.B. de Hogal, 1747.

Macera, Pablo. *El Inca colonial*. Lima: Universidad Nacional Mayor de San Marcos, Fondo Editorial, 2006.

Manso de Velasco, José Antonio, Virrey Conde de Superunda. "Carta del Conde de Superunda al Rey." Archivo General de Indias 417. Lima, 29 October 1749.

Maravall, José Antonio. *La cultura del barroco*. Madrid: Ariel, 1975.

Mestre, Antonio and Pablo Fernández Albaladejo. *Fénix de España: modernidad y cultura propia en la España del Siglo XVIII (1737–1766)*. Madrid: Marcial Pons Historia, 2006.

Mills, Kenneth. "Diego de Ocaña's Hagiography of New and Renewed Devotion in Colonial Peru." *Colonial Saints: Discovering the Holy in the Americas, 1500–1800*. Ed. Allan Greer and Jodi Bilinkoff. New York, NY: Routledge, 2003. 51–76.

Moreno Cebrián, Alfredo and Núria Sala i Vila. *El "premio" de ser virrey: los intereses públicos y privados del gobierno virreinal en el Perú de Felipe V*. Madrid: Consejo Superior de Investigaciones Científicas, Instituto de Historia, 2004.

Noticia analítica y estado del puerto del Callao. Lima: Imprenta de los Niños Expósitos, 1747.

Oña, Pedro de. *Arauco domado*. Valparaíso: Imprenta Europea, 1849.

Osorio, Alejandra B. *Inventing Lima: Baroque Modernity in Peru's South Sea Metropolis*. New York, NY: Palgrave Macmillan, 2008.

Peralta Barnuevo, Pedro de. *Lima fundada o conquista del Perú*. Lima: Imprenta de F. Sobrino y Bados, 1732.

———. *Lima inexpugnable*. Ed. Luis Antonio Eguiguren. Lima: Liurimsa, 1966.

Périssat, Karine. *Lima fête ses rois (XVIe–XVIIIe siècles): hispanité et américanité dans les cérémonies royales*. Paris: Harmattan, 2002.

Pouncey, Lorene. "Tumulos of Colonial Peru." *The Art Bulletin* 47.1 (1985): 18–32.

Pozo, Juan Antonio Tristán del. *Relacion funebre, poema tragico, que del funesto terremoto acaecido en la corte del Perú; y deplorable inundacion del presidio y puerto del Callao, año de 1746*. Lima: s.n., 1746.

Riaza de los Mozos, Mónica. "'Solenne pompa celebrate in Roma': Ferdinando Fuga y las exequias de Felipe V en la iglesia de Santiago de los Españoles." *Congreso Internacional Imagen Apariencia*. November 19, 2008–November 21, 2008. Murcia: Servicio de Publicaciones de la Universidad de Murcia, 2009. May 29, 2012. <http://congresos.um.es/imagenyapariencia/imagenyapariencia2008/paper/viewFile/2731/2671>.

Ribas, Nicolás de. "Le tremblement de terre de Lima de 1746: témoignages, actions et pensées de la catastrophe naturelle." *E-Spania: Revue interdisciplinaire d'études hispaniques médiévales et modernes* 12 (2011). May 29, 2012. <http://e-spania.revues.org/20760>.

Ribera, Juan Antonio. *El día de Lima. Proclamación Real, que de el nombre augusto del Supremo Señor D. Fernando el VI [...] hizo la muy noble, y leal Ciudad de los Reyes Lima: cabeza de la America Austral, fervorizada a influxo del zelo fiel, del cuydadoso empeño*. Lima: s.n., 1748.

Rodríguez de la Flor, Fernando. *Barroco. Representación e ideología en el mundo hispánico (1580–1680)*. Madrid: Cátedra, 2002.

Sainz de Valdivieso Torrejón, Miguel. *Parentación real, luctuosa pompa, suntuoso cenotafio que al augusto nombre y real memoria del serenisimo señor don Felipe V, Católico Rey de las Españas y Emperador de las Indias, mandó erigir el Excmo. Señor d. José Manso de Velasco*. Lima: Antonio Gutiérrez de Zavalos, 1748.

Salinas y Córdova, Buenaventura de. *Memorial de las historias del Nuevo Mundo Piru*. Ed. Warren L. Cook. Lima: Universidad Nacional Mayor de San Marcos, 1957.

San Lorenzo, Manuel de. *Teatro funesto de las reales exequias que a la Majestad de nuestro católico monarca el señor D. Luis Primero consagró la muy n[oble], leal, nombrada y gran ciudad de Granada*. Granada: Impreso en la imprenta de Andrés Sánchez, 1725.

Sánchez Jiménez, Antonio. *Lope pintado por sí mismo: mito e imagen del autor en la poesía de Lope de Vega*. Woodbridge: Tamesis, 2006.

Santander, José Antonio. *La lealtad satisfecha, el júbilo ensalzado, y gratos reconocimientos de la fidelidad conque expresso su sentimiento la ... Ciudad del Cuzco en las Exequias del ... S.D. Phelipe V*. Lima: en la Imprenta que està en la Plazuela del pie del Cerro, 1748.

Torrejón, Tomás de. *Parentación real, sentimiento público, luctuosa pompa, fúnebre solemnidad en las reales exequias del serenísimo señor don Luis I*. Lima: Imprenta de la calle de Palacio, 1725.

Valenzuela Márquez, Jaime. *Las liturgias del poder: celebraciones públicas y estrategias persuasivas en Chile colonial (1609–1709)*. Ediciones de la Dirección de Bibliotecas, Archivos y Museos, Centro de Investigaciones Diego Barrios Arana. Santiago: Lom Ediciones, 2001.

Valverde y Contreras, Vasco. *Oracion funebre en las honras que la ciudad del Cuzco celebro a la memoria de la Serenissima Reyna ... Doña Ysabel de Borbón*. Lima: Pedro de Cabrera, 1646.

Varela, Javier. *La muerte del rey: el ceremonial funerario de la monarquía española, 1500–1885*. Madrid: Turner, 1990.

Voltes Bou, Pedro. *Felipe V: fundador de la España contemporánea*. Madrid: Espasa-Calpe, 1991.

Walker, Charles F. *Shaky Colonialism: The 1746 Earthquake-Tsunami in Lima, Peru, and Its Long Aftermath*. Durham, NC: Duke University Press, 2008.

Chapter 13
The Imagery of Jerusalem in the Colonial City

Patricia Saldarriaga

In this chapter, I will examine the correlation between sacred and civic space and the extent to which sacred images had an impact on conceptual understanding and colonial architectural construction. My goal is to demonstrate that the imagery of Jerusalem directly influenced the way in which the conquistadors approached the New World. This imagery had already exerted an influence in Europe during the Crusades, the Middle Ages and the European Renaissance. For the purpose of the Counter Reformation, it was used in the colonial territory in architecture, literature and the arts to visualize ideal models based on the "City of Jerusalem" metaphor. I will also study the extent to which this imagery influenced the concept of identity. As a starting point, I will examine the writings of chroniclers such as *The Book of Prophecies* by Christopher Columbus, *The Truthful History of the Conquest of New Spain* by Bernal Díaz del Castillo, the *Natural and Moral History of the Indies* by José de Acosta and, among others, the text by Miguel Sánchez entitled *Image of the Virgin Mary, Mother of Guadalupe*.

One of the historical and cultural concerns that has remained latent for centuries, even millennia, is the concept of the end of time. At the end of the first millennium, the fear was based on explicit references to the "thousand years" mentioned in the Apocalypse, a period after which the forces of good would struggle against the forces of evil: "And when the thousand years are expired, Satan shall be loosed out of his prison, And shall go out to deceive the nations which are in the four quarters of the earth, Gog, and Magog, to gather them together to battle: the number of whom is as the sand of the sea" (Revelation 20:7–8). Concern for the end of time at the end of the first millennium was manifested in a clear proliferation of apocalyptic virgins, as these images were meant to relieve humanity's pain in the face of a grim future. This apocalyptic fear continued for the next thousand years and is still relevant even today. We only need to look at recent press to note the numerous references to the interpretation of the Mayan calendar, which indicated that the end of the world was supposed to occur in December 2012. These writers sought to inform the reader about various ways of interpreting the fatalism in the form of an ecological disaster and the planet's subsequent destruction. Umberto Eco and Carlo María

238   *The Transatlantic Hispanic Baroque*

Martini have classified this notion of the end of time as a cultural obsession, claiming that this concept is more common today in the twenty-first-century secular world than in the Christian world. According to Eco and Martini, the Christian world meditates on the end of the world, whereas "the secular world pretends to ignore it, but is fundamentally obsessed by it" (18).

The book that has most influenced the increase in this cultural obsession is the Book of Revelation (also known as the "Apocalypse"). However, it should be noted that the threat and fear discourse has always gone hand in hand with the imagery of salvation. Although our millennium is characterized by a kind of Manichean horror, the messianic and hopeful discourse is conveyed through the imagery of the city of New Jerusalem in the biblical text. It is a new city made possible by its very destruction: "And I saw a new heaven and a new earth: for the first heaven and the first earth were passed away; and there was no more sea. And I John saw the holy city, new Jerusalem, coming down from God out of heaven, prepared as a bride adorned for her husband" (Revelation 21:1–2).

After the first millennium, messianic discourse increased and emperors, kings, conquistadors, artists, architects and extremists became concerned about the world's and Jerusalem's salvation. Moreover, following the Muslim re-conquest of Jerusalem, two centuries of Crusades began. From its capture in 1099 until its final loss in 1244, the liberation of Jerusalem had been a constant preoccupation of our civilization. Even today, despite the conflict between Israel and Palestine, Jerusalem remains, with a few exceptions, the Holy City protected by Christians, Muslims and Jews.

The desire to reconquer Jerusalem and the city's imagery began to define the way in which the conquistadors and monarchs viewed themselves and their exploits. Even after the Kingdom of Jerusalem ceased to exist as such, the pretenders to the throne were still using the title of King of Jerusalem. This was the case with Henry II of Cyprus, Charles I of Naples (also known as Charles of Anjou) and thus the line of kings of the House of Austria and the House of Bourbon in Spain. When Philip II (1527–1598) married Mary I of England in 1554, Charles V ceded the Kingdom of Jerusalem to his son, and in his proclamation he included the title of "King of Jerusalem." This political event inspired Felipe de la Torre's comparison with David's abdication from the throne in favor of his son Solomon (Gonzalo Sánchez-Molero 743, De la Torre ff. 95v–96r). Furthermore, various modern interpretations claim that Philip II ordered the construction of El Escorial based on the architectural model of the Temple of Solomon (De la Cuadra Blanco, Gonzalo Sánchez-Molero, among others).

In his research on Tudor England and Philip II, Geoffrey Parker points out the messianic imagery inherited by Charles V, the Emperor of Habsburg, who was considered the long-awaited Messiah entering a city corresponding to Jerusalem (170). Imagery abounded in the form of prophecies, moral emblems,

The Imagery of Jerusalem in the Colonial City

such as emblem 34 by Sebastián de Covarrubias Orozco, paintings based on visions, and books (*Viaje de Turquía*, 1557, attributed to Andrés Laguna), which depicted the Habsburg Monarchy as a paradigm for Solomon. Parker asserts that this messianic propaganda about Charles V and Philip II did not necessarily originate from these Kings but was used for public consumption (174).

The main themes of the Apocalypse are the appearance of the apocalyptic woman (also known as the Virgin or Second Eve), the return of Christ, the Last Judgment, and the City of God: "And I saw a new heaven and a new earth" (21:1). "I saw the Holy City, the new Jerusalem, coming down out of heaven from God [...]" (21:2–3). "And he carried me away in the Spirit to a mountain great and high, and showed me the Holy City, Jerusalem, coming down out of heaven from God. It shone with the glory of God, and its brilliance was like that of a very precious jewel, like a jasper, clear as crystal." (21:10–11). The Book of Ezekiel (40–43) clarifies the connection between the temple and the city: "Son of man, this is the place of my throne and the place for the soles of my feet. This is where I will live among the Israelites forever" (43). As Marta Fernández explains: "This new Jerusalem, however, was not simply a city where a Temple was erected to worship God; rather, the entire city had become a Temple, while at the same time God was the Temple itself" (1013): "But I saw no temple in it, for the Lord God Almighty and the Lamb are its temple" (21:22).

Solomon's temple is discussed in 23 books of the Old Testament and 11 books of the New Testament, but the more detailed descriptions are in 3 Kings 6–8 and Ezekiel 40–42 and 46. Although Kings refers to the state of the temple during the era of David and Solomon, Ezekiel recounts the prophet's vision after the destruction of Solomon's Temple (Villalpando 10). It is important to note that in the Jewish tradition, Jerusalem is conceived of as a sacred place, as a Temple, a spiritual and physical center of the world. In Christian imagery, this city was considered the *umbilicus mundi* ("world's navel"), a place of pilgrimage associated with the divine.

The First Temple of this city was built by Solomon between 962–969 BCE. The temple was destroyed by the Babylonians in the year 517 (second construction). The city of Jerusalem was conquered by the Assyrians, the Babylonians, the Persians, the Macedonians, the Seleucids and the Hasmoneans. The Third Temple was built by Herod I the Great (73 BCE–4 BCE), but Pompey's Roman troops captured Jerusalem in 64 CE. Titus captured the city in 70 CE and further destroyed the Temple of Jerusalem. Hadrian then rebuilt and Romanized the city, renaming it Aelia Capitolina. The oldest images of the Temple that have been identified are engraved on coins of Bar Kochba, the Jewish leader who led a revolt against Emperor Hadrian in 132–135 CE (Rosenau 20).

The imagery of Jerusalem was a constant theme used by the Spanish Empire to justify and carry out the conquest. If we look at the primary source of the Columbian manuscripts, we can find numerous writings in which Christopher

240   *The Transatlantic Hispanic Baroque*

Columbus states that one of the purposes of his trips to the Indies is to recapture the city of Jerusalem, which was then in the hands of the Ottomans. Columbus' *Book of Prophecies*, in which the following paratext appears in the left-hand margin, is clear in this regard: "Prophecies compiled by Admiral Christopher Columbus for the Catholic Kings on the recapture of the city of Jerusalem and the discovery of the Indies." Other references to his desire to restore the city of Jerusalem are found in his diary (1492), the *Institución del mayorazgo* (1498), his last will and testament (1502), and his epistolary letters to Queen Isabella (1501), Pope Alexander VI (1502) and the Catholic Kings (1503) (Azcárate 369). Columbus believed he was predestined by God to conquer the Indies and therefore had a twofold purpose for his voyages: on the one hand, to use the gold found to restore Jerusalem for Christians and, on the other hand, to convert the Indians. As Bartosik-Vélez points out, Columbus—and not the Spanish Crown—was the first to promote the ideology of the Christian world empire during his voyages.

In *On the Wings of Time: Rome, the Incas, Spain and Peru*, Sabine MacCormack highlights Columbus' association of the Caribbean islands with Ophir, the place where King Solomon obtained gold and precious stones to build the Temple in Jerusalem. Moreover, several sixteenth-century exegeses, such as those by Benito Arias Montano and Las Casas, interpret these passages by identifying Ophir with Peruvian land (MacCormack 252). According to MacCormack, Montano's equating of Peru with Ophir, in the literal or historical sense, was an interpretation that was subsequently expanded upon and defended by other chroniclers such as Miguel Cabello Valvoa (1535–1608) and Fernando de Montesinos (1515–1582). Montesinos specifically refers to Peru's gold and silver, but also includes birds that Solomon may have brought to Ophir (Chapter 30).

Although the *Natural and Moral History of the Indies* by José de Acosta rejects the connection between gold/Peru/Ophir, the text does not completely depart from the association of Jerusalem with the New World. Quite the contrary; it reflects on the possibility that the conquest of the New World may be mentioned in the Bible: "And it seems a very reasonable supposition that there would be some mention in the Holy Scripture of a matter as great as the discovery and conversion to the Faith of Christ of the New World" (96).[1] If this historical event is mentioned in the Holy Scriptures, then, according to Acosta, the matter of the conquest and conquerors should have been dealt with in the form of a prophecy. The Jesuit Acosta finds a perfect parallel in the prophecy of Obadiah mentioned in the Old Testament, but he is somewhat cautious in his hermeneutical practice. According to this Hebrew Prophet, God reproached

---

[1]   This and all subsequent English translations of quotations are from José de Acosta, *Natural and Moral History of the Indies*, translated by Frances López-Morillas.

The Imagery of Jerusalem in the Colonial City 241

the inhabitants of Edom for the violence against the Jews in the Kingdom of Judea and warned them about the destruction of their city. This vision includes Jerusalem, which was destroyed and invaded.

Acosta begins with the following paragraph of this prophecy: "And the transmigration of this host of the children of Israel shall possess all the places of the Chanaanites even unto Sarepta and the transmigration of Jerusalem, that is, in Bosphorus, shall possess the cities of the south. And saviours shall come up into Mount Zion to judge the mount of Esau: and the kingdom shall be for the Lord" (95). Based on the interpretation of subsequent biblical translations, Obadiah's prophecy becomes a decisive justification: "There are some who say and affirm that a long time ago it was prophesied in the Holy Scripture that this New World would be converted to Christ, and by people of Spain" (95). Acosta reflects on a possible allegorical interpretation by questioning the Vulgate's geographical identification of these places in France and Spain—information which is not mentioned in the original version of the prophecy: "Since the word *Sepharad*, which Saint Jerome interprets as the Bosphorus or Strait and the Septuagint interprets as Euphrata, means Spain, some do not claim testimony from the ancients or any other convincing justification except that they believe it." (95). He even wondered about the possibility that Jerusalem might refer to the Church in a much broader way:

> Moreover, what need is there to interpret "the transmigration of Jerusalem into Sepharad" to mean the Spanish people unless we take Jerusalem spiritually and understand it to mean the Church? So "the Holy Spirit through the transmigration of Jerusalem that is in Sepharad" means the sons of the Holy Church who dwell in the ends of the earth or in the seaports; for this is what the word Sepharad means in Syriac, and this agrees well with our Spain, which according to the ancients is the last place on earth and is almost entirely surrounded by the sea. It would be possible to understand by "the cities of the south" these Indies, for most of this New World is toward the south and a large part of it faces the South Pole. (95–6)

However, Acosta makes clear that this is only one possible interpretation and states that "Whoever wishes to declare the prophecy of Abdias in this form should not be blamed" (96). With respect to the allegory, we can clearly see the connection between medieval thought and Acosta. The field of Patristics, especially based on the model of Juan Casiano (365–435), frequently uses biblical exegesis whereby a literal meaning and three figurative interpretations can be distinguished in texts. According to the literal meaning, Jerusalem is considered to be the historical capital of the Jewish people; in the allegorical sense, Jerusalem is the Church; but in the moral sense, Jerusalem would be the individual soul of the believer. However, in the anagogical sense, it refers to an eschatological interpretation in which Jerusalem becomes the heavenly

242   *The Transatlantic Hispanic Baroque*

city of God. Columbus had already applied this interpretation in his *Book of Prophecies* (2).

However, Acosta's *Natural and Moral History of the Indies* makes an obvious parallel between the Scriptures and the Indies. Many of its chapters conclude with a direct comparison between the nature of the Indies and divine ontology. The mineral wealth of the Indies and the method used to clean and purge silver, for example, is compared to divine doctrine and the process through which believers go in order to achieve purification (238). However, the clear motivation and justification for the foreign presence in the New World is the abundance of natural wealth:

> But it is a circumstance worthy of much consideration that the wisdom of our Eternal Lord has enriched the most remote parts of the world, inhabited by the most uncivilized people, and has placed there the greatest number of mines that ever existed, in order to invite men to seek out and possess those lands and coincidentally to communicate their religion and the worship of the true God to men who do not know it. Thus the prophecy of Isaiah has been fulfilled that the Church shall pass on to the right hand and to the left, which is, as Saint Augustine declares, the way the Gospel must be propagated, not only by those who preach it sincerely and with charity but also by those who proclaim it through temporal and human aims and means. Hence we see that the lands in the Indies that are richest in mines and wealth have been those most advanced in the Christian religion in our time; and thus the Lord takes advantage of our desires to serve his sovereign ends. (212)

The greater the wealth, the greater the dissemination of Christianity and the greater the justification for the conquest. It should be noted that no claim was made to the effect that Christianity brought moral or spiritual benefits to the Indies. The opposite is true: the Indies' wealth became the justification to fulfill the conquistadors' "desires" under the Lord's protection. If the goal was, among other things, to obtain riches for Jerusalem's conquest, then God provided them with these assets by enabling them to find, discover and conquer the Indies.

The Jesuit Acosta assigned a programmatic role to his own chronicle: "Let what I have said serve to make us understand how the Universal Lord and Omnipotent Author distributed his gifts and secrets and marvels through the globe that he created, for which he must be adored and glorified forever and ever, amen" (296). The interpretation of the *Natural and Moral History of the Indies* thus becomes an act similar to reciting a liturgical prayer, which concludes with the Hebrew word "amen." However, this prayer, whose aim is purification, almost justifies and even asks/begs for the destruction of the Indies, thereby leading to a spiritual conquest. Acosta compares the image of a corrupted Rome and Jerusalem with the pagan Indies:

> In other nations of Indians, such as those in Guatemala and the island and the New
> Kingdom of Granada, and the provinces of Chile and others that resembled the
> free communities of Spain, although there was a great multitude of superstitions
> and sacrifices, they could not be compared with Cuzco or Mexico, where Satan
> was in his Rome or Jerusalem, as it were, until he was cast out, much against his
> will. And in his place the holy cross was planted, and the kingdom of Jesus Christ
> occupied everything that the tyrant had usurped. (359)

The destruction and invasion of Jerusalem is compared here with the conquest of the New World. In *The Truthful History of the Conquest of New Spain*, Bernal Díaz del Castillo uses the image of Jerusalem only for apocalyptic comparisons and, in doing so, draws a parallel between the destruction of Tlatelolco and Jerusalem (91). In the same way that Satan was present in these cities, the Indies are represented with a strong emphasis on paganism. And if, according to the prophecy of Obadiah, Jerusalem was destroyed to allow the saviours to arrive, then both the conquistadors' presence in and destruction of the Indies would be completely justified. And if, as mentioned earlier, natural wealth is directly related to salvation, then the greater the natural wealth is, the greater the desire for expansion and evangelization. According to Jerónimo de Mendieta, non-converted Indians were considered to be evil pagans.

The Temple in Jerusalem and its apocalyptic association with the city of God transposed onto Earth served as a foundation and model for many visionary, literary, pictorial and/or architectural constructions, particularly during the Counter Reformation. However, it begs the question: why is it that, precisely during this period, the Temple of Solomon motif was so widely used in construction models? During its last session, number XXV of 1563, the Council of Trent had already declared that the veneration and exhibition of sacred images in temples and churches were mandatory. The arguments put forward in defense of these images, vaguely mentioned by the Council of Trent, originate in the former ecumenical councils who defended the images against the iconoclasts, particularly the Second Council of Nicaea, which vehemently defended the images made by Juan Damasceno. Moreover, ensuring that sacred images prevailed was connected with the idea of depicting God in imagery. Although iconoclasts rejected icons, since they supported a literal interpretation of the Scriptures and considered the inclusion of divine presence in images, the iconodulists argued in favor of divine representation in them (Manini and Saldarriaga 175–80). However, the only image considered to actually include divine presence is the Eucharist, since during transubstantiation, the wine and host literally become the blood and body of Christ. This was anathema to non-believers, since in sessions XII and XIII of the Council of Trent, all who were opposed to this belief would be accused of latria. However, the divine presence, once brought to the colonies, required a divine temple, a sacred space

244 *The Transatlantic Hispanic Baroque*

to safeguard it. Nothing could be more appropriate than the Temple of Solomon desired by the chroniclers and Philip II, announcing the New Jerusalem, a city full of hope for the renewal of the Church.

One of the most important texts on Baroque architecture is the treatise entitled *Ezechielem Explanationes* by the Córdoba Jesuit Juan Bautista Villalpando (1552–1608). This book, whose first volume was co-authored by Jerónimo de Prado between 1596 and 1604, not only includes a complete reconstruction of Solomon's temple, but is also an architectural, mathematical and theological theoretical treatise. It could also even be considered a treatise on optics, vision and knowledge acquisition. Most importantly, the Jesuit's treatise was written in the spirit of the Counter Reformation, and its reconstruction of the temple becomes an allegory for the reconstruction of the Church itself. Villalpando's reconstruction of Solomon's temple aims to visualize one of the most important metaphors that has survived over two millennia. The objective is to "visualize" the idea and imagery of Jerusalem in a concrete construction. Although the Córdoba Jesuit respects Vitruvius' principles regarding anthropomorphic architecture, Villalpando offers a different vision of the architect, since he not only based the design on nature, but, on the contrary, he presents a theological justification, as the design had sacred origins. However, there was resistance to Villalpando's text within the Jesuit order and the Church, as several Inquisitorial investigations questioned Villalpando's thesis. He was accused of heresy but subsequently found innocent. Within the Jesuit order, both Benito Arias Montano and Father Aquaviva opposed Villalpando's thesis (Villalpando 11).

The great significance of Villalpando's text lies in its attempt to reformulate the connection between architecture and the understanding of God. According to this Jesuit, understanding and visualizing architecture enables us to understand God. Moreover, like Saint John of Damascus, who suggested the incapacity to visualize divinity without sacred images, Villalpando asserts that only through understanding architecture can we understand God and represent the Church (Villalpando 109). The design proposed by Villalpando has divine authorship: it was God—not the profane architect—who designed the divine temple.

Another text that clearly identifies the colonial city with the imagery of Jerusalem is entitled *Imagen de la Virgen María, Madre de Dios de Guadalupe, milagrosamente aparecida en la ciudad de México. Celebrada en su Historia, con la profecía del capítulo doce del Apocalipsis* (Image of the Virgin Mary, Mother of Guadalupe, Miraculously Appeared in the City of Mexico. Celebrated in Her History with the Prophecy of Chapter Twelve of the Apocalypse), published in 1648 by the Jesuit Miguel Sánchez. This controversial text is of utmost relevance to Mexican religiosity, as it recounts the story for the first time of the Virgin of Guadalupe's apparition. The Virgin of Guadalupe imagery is developed methodically and, in doing so, explicitly identifies the City of Mexico with

The Imagery of Jerusalem in the Colonial City

Patmos of the Apocalypse. Moreover, Sánchez justifies the conquest in a similar way as the previously mentioned texts by Columbus and Acosta:

> This is the Image that along with the signs of Augustine, my Saint, I found on the island of Patmos in the possession of the Apostle and Evangelist Saint John, to whom I asked on my knees to give it to me and declared to him the reason and desire to celebrate with it the Virgin Mary, Mother of God in a miraculous image entitled Guadalupe, found in the City of Mexico, whose miracle, painting, insignias and restorations had been correctly copied. I said that if its Image represented the Church, also by the hand of the Virgin Mary the New World had been won and conquered and the head of the Church established in Mexico. (44–5)

The conquistadors' effort had paid off through the apparition of the Second Eve or Virgin of Guadalupe. Sánchez draws a perfect analogy with the Apocalypse, which Maza sums up thusly: "The John of Patmos is replaced by 3 Johns: Diego, Bernardino and Zumárraga; the apocalyptic woman is the Virgin of Guadalupe: San Juan, Juan Diego; San Miguel, Hernán Cortés; the dragon, idolatry; the wings, the Mexican wing; the city, the City of Mexico; the desert, the Tepeyac; the sun, the sun belt; the moon, the lagoons of Mexico; and the stars, the new Paradise" (77). This apocalyptic version by Sanchez thus justified the interpretation of Guadalupe associated with the myth of nation-building—a myth that had developed over the years. The City of Mexico was essentially destroyed, conquered and a new Mexican paradise was "established" where the Second Eve or the new Guadalupe imagery had appeared. This imagery served to allegorically represent the City of Mexico and subsequently America.

However, the association of the City of Mexico with Jerusalem is not unique to Sánchez. Many earlier texts make the same connection. Besides Columbus, one of the first to mention this association was fray Toribio de Benavente Motolinía:

> Oh, Mexico! So many mountains surround and crown you! Your fame will certainly spread now, since the Faith and Gospel of Jesus Christ shine in you. You were a master of sins before, but now you are a teacher of truth; you were in the shadows and darkness before, but now you offer the splendour of doctrine and Christianity. [...] You were then a Babylon full of confusion and wickedness; but now you are another Jerusalem, a mother of provinces and kingdoms! (Motolinía 201; cited in Gruzinski 241)

In his study entitled "The City as Temple," André Corboz presents a list of European cities that had been designed and identified with Jerusalem. Verona was given the name *Minor Hierusalem*. According to Saint Stephen, Bologna was the seat of the heavenly city; Pisa was called the Jerusalem of white

246   *The Transatlantic Hispanic Baroque*

marble; Milan replaced the former capital of Jerusalem with a New Jerusalem; Vatican City included the Sistine Chapel, whose sanctuary is identical to the Jerusalem Temple. At the entrance of the ancient Vatican Basilica, there were supposedly two columns from the Jerusalem Temple. Florence is represented as an apocalyptic Jerusalem and was to a certain extent protected even by the French, who left in 1439 (Ramírez et al. 17, 57–65). A connection can even be drawn between Hagia Sophia Church in Constantinople and the Temple of Solomon. Upon seeing the completed basilica, Emperor Constantine's famous words were: "Solomon, you have conquered" (Ramírez et al. 4).

Martha Fernández reminds us that since the *Ordenanzas de pobladores* (1573), the construction of Latin American cities included a checkerboard-style street design and a central square. As in the city of Jerusalem drawings, the temple or church occupied a focal point. With the arrival of the Spaniards, non-Catholic civic and divine space intermingled and formed the foundation for the Empire's Christian centrality. And it is precisely this centrality that approaches that of Jerusalem, as the checkerboard and depiction is the visualization of an ideal city and of an ideal order that evokes the celestial city.

There are many colonial constructions based on this model. According to Fernández, the conceptualization of Puebla de los Ángeles as Jerusalem begins when the cathedral was conceived as the actual temple of Jerusalem (1016). Interestingly, this parallel with Jerusalem and the construction of the city began when Antonio Tamariz de Carmona made the connection between the Kings of Spain and Solomon. Many legends about this city united the civic and sacred space. In the case of Puebla, angels descended from heaven to save sinners. The text by Diego Antonio Bermúdez de Castro is the most explicit in its connection with the Holy City:

> The Holy City of Jerusalem was presented to Saint John in his Revelation descending from heaven as a Bride adorned with all of the finery, wealth and perfections she was capable of, gladly awaiting her husband. It made her square-shaped figure even more pleasing to the eye, especially when, as decided by the One who carefully orders all things, an Angel carried a stick to measure the size of its area, the level of its walls and neatly arranged streets. That fortunate city was so similar to Puebla. Since those who measured its streets were the same kind of men who, by order of the Almighty, built the Holy Zion, one can easily deduce how beautiful this Angelic City will be with its well-designed streets, beautiful temples, rich houses and offices—all in a square-shaped figure. (Bermúdez de Castro 148)

In Puebla de los Ángeles, these angels descended from the sky to the earthly city.

We have already mentioned that beginning in 1573, after the enactment of laws in the Indies, the use of the checkerboard construction in cities became popular in the colonies. This design, which was studied by Ángel Rama, is a *reducción* that provides order in the new equivalent city of Jerusalem. The word *reducir* had multiple meanings. On the one hand, it implied "convinced and restored to better order" (Covarrubias 854) and, on the other hand, it meant "to conquer, pacify and dominate." It also implied "to convert to or convince of the knowledge of the True Religion" (*Diccionario* 534). In other words, colonial subjects are *reducido* to a civic space within which their actions needed to be limited.

In a study on the intersections of civic and political space in the provinces of Pasto and the Savanna of Bogotá between the sixteenth and eighteenth centuries, Cummins and Rappaport explain that until a space was *reducido* through architecture, it was planned in detail on maps on which the names of people were placed and determined how the city blocks were to be distributed. Both authors define urban space as the spatial application of a pre-written colonization discourse and thus claim that the subject's performance is shaped by this space. And it is precisely the intersection between civic and political/religious space that affected the subject's actions. As we see in Mendieta, prayer underwent a *reducción* linked to the body's space and disposition. The Indians worshiped their gods and spoke to them in squatting position, but now they had to pray on their knees anchored to the floor. Squatting position, which previously meant access to the divine and rest, now became associated with paganism in the new act of *reducción*. Similarly, if a non-baptized person attended a mass, he or she would have to sit at the back of the church and would have to leave the religious premises during transubstantiation (Cummins and Rappaport 183).

Various architectural constructions (literal or metaphorical) provided access to *reducciones*: doors, columns, ephemeral arches that were built for special occasions, architecture created using special techniques such as *trompe l'oeil* that conveyed imagery, or house facades and book covers. As Cummins and Rappaport point out, the terms "title page" and "frontispiece" were used interchangeably for book manuscripts in the sixteenth and seventeenth centuries, and this image suggested a spatial entrance that would transmit knowledge to the reader. According to these authors, the transfer either by means of a page or door places subjects in a state of liminal differentiation in time and space (183).

The *reducción* therefore aimed at a liminal identity process in which there was a before, an intermediary now (within a given *reducción*) and an after (promise of conquest). Whether or not one was Catholic determined whether or not one could access a given space, even after death. In other words, identity was limited and determined by the subject's performance within the architectural space. David A. Boruchoff presents an array of apocalyptic metaphors in his study on missionary projects in New Spain, in particular, the case of Solomon's "gate" as an entry point into the territories to be conquered. According to Boruchoff, discovering the occult upon opening the doors within the New Jerusalem would justify the conquest (5–9). However, the presence of the columns at the city's entrance *reducía* both the subject to be conquered and the conquerors themselves to a space marked by Jerusalem's imagery and the ambitions of the Christian world empire. Moreover, their identity as conquerors was associated with the presence of these columns, since they marked the space to be conquered. Although the monarchs were still considered Kings of Jerusalem even after the fall of the city, the conquistadors, through the Solomon metaphor, had a visual pretext to *reducir* the conquest to this space and identify themselves as such.

The importance of the city of Jerusalem has been studied very little within the broader cultural context of the Baroque, especially considering that Jerusalem had a great impact on the conceptualization of the Baroque in general. When we speak of Baroque architecture today, we almost immediately think of Solomonic columns, whose origin goes back to the Temple in Jerusalem. According to Ramírez, "no single element has represented the entire temple as effectively and persistently as the columns" (17). And the relevance of the columns can be seen in Rafael's work "The Healing of the Lame Man." Santiago Sebastián highlighted the fundamental role of Solomonic columns at the entrance of the Monastery of Huejotzingo, one of the first architectural constructions in the colonies (77–88). Entering the Franciscan space flanked by columns meant entering the Indian Jerusalem of Mendieta.

Both the writings by Vitruvius and studies by Alberti and Villalpando helped redefine the role of architecture, as divine order had to be evident in the earthly depiction. Much of baroque painting—the Blessed Virgin iconography, the scenes of the triumphal entrance of Christ and various versions of *The Church Militant and the Church Triumphant* by the Mexican Cristóbal de Villalpando (1649–1714)—include direct depictions of the city of Jerusalem. Saint Augustine's *City of God* served as a foundation for the construction of the monastery of Querétaro, Mexico. Sister María de Ágreda wrote *The Mystical City of God* and Sister Juana Inés de la Cruz in her verses recounted a competition between the celestial and earthly city.

Visualizing the colony with a religious substrate has produced many different interpretations, particularly regarding the notion of identity. Although the kings and emperors were identified with the title of King of Jerusalem and Solomon, the New Jerusalem and its inhabitants had to in some way evoke this metaphor of nostalgia for the Holy City. As clearly expressed by Larraín, a sociological discourse arose beginning in the 1980s which aimed to prove that Latin American identity is essentially Catholic (4)—an idea that has been corroborated by official documents and papal statements. During one of his five visits to the Basilica of Guadalupe, Jean Paul II's classic words "Mexico is ever faithful" give a clear indication of the Catholic essentialism with which Latin America is identified. Texts by Alberto Methol Ferré, Pedro Morandé and Bernardino Bravo-Lira (cited by Larraín) are signs of the ever-present Catholic essentialism in the discourse on identity. While Morandé affirms that Latin American identity developed through the indigenous world's contact with the Catholic religion and *reduce* Latin American culture to the oral substrate, Bravo Lira takes up the arguments and expands them to the legal discourse in order to prove that Latin America attaches greater importance to oral discourse. The written constitution therefore is not respected, which explains the military coups in these countries (Larraín 11).

The messianic designs brought to the colonies influenced the depiction of the city but did not eliminate local architectural foundations. On the contrary: as we have seen in the reductionist checkerboard design, the pre-existing civic space was adapted and served as the basis for the new ecclesiastical power. Consider, for example, the numerous constructions with Incan foundations that still exist in Cuzco. Although the colonizing project brought pre-established regulations from European culture with respect to the ideal city, they were represented based on an imperial vision imposed by a Catholic order in the New World territory. The constant negotiation of space went hand in hand with the development of identity. Colonial subjects and conquistadors therefore learned to identify themselves by playing their respective roles within the *reducción*.

Bibliography

Acosta, José de. *Historia natural y moral de las Indias.* Ed. José Alcina Franch. Madrid: Dastin, 2002.

———. *Natural and Moral History of the Indies.* Ed. Jane E. Mangan. Trans. Frances López-Morillas. Durham, NC: Duke University Press, 2002.

Azcárate, Juan Luis de León. "El *Libro de las profecías* (1504) de Cristóbal Colón: la Biblia y el descubrimiento de América." *Religión y Cultura* 53 (2007): 361–406.

Bartosik-Vélez, Elise. "The First Interpretations of the Columbian Enterprise." *Revista Canadiense de Estudios Hispánicos* 33.2 (Winter 2009): 317–34.

Bermúdez de Castro, Diego Antonio. *Theatro Angelopolitano o Historia de la cuidad de la Puebla.* Facsimile edition. Puebla: Junta de Mejoramiento Moral, Cívico y Material del Municipio de Puebla, 1985.

Boruchoff, David A. "New Spain, New England, and the New Jerusalem: The 'Translation' of Empire, Faith, and Learning (*translatio imperii, fidei ac scientiae*) in the Colonial Missionary Project." *Early American Literature* 43.1 (2008): 5–34.

Bravo Lira, Bernardino. "América y la Modernidad: de la Modernidad barroca e ilustrada a la Postmodernidad." *Jahrbuch für Geschichte, von Staat, Wirtschaft und Gesellschaft Lateinamerikas* 30 (1993): 409–433.

Colón, Cristóbal. *Libro de las profecías*. Ed. J. Fernández Valverde. Madrid: Alianza, 1992.

Covarrubias, Sebastián de. *Tesoro de la lengua castellana o española*. Madrid: Iberoamericana, 2005.

De la Cuadra Blanco, Juan Rafael. "El Escorial y el Templo de Salomón." *Anales de Arquitectura* (Valladolid) 7 (1996): 5–15.

Cummins, Tom and Joanne Rappaport. "The Reconfiguration of Civic and Sacred Space: Architecture, Image, and Writing in the Colonial Northern Andes." *Latin American Literary Review* 26.52 (July–December 1998): 174–200.

Damasus, John of. *On the Divine Images: Three Apologies against Those Who Attack the Divine Images*. Trans. D. Anderson. Crestwood, NY: St Vladimir's Seminary Press, 1980.

De la Torre, Felipe. *Institución de un Rey Cristiano*. Ed. R.W. Truman. Exeter: University of Exeter Press, 1979.

Díaz del Castillo, Bernal. *Historia verdadera de la conquista de la Nueva España*. Introduction by Felipe Castro Gutiérrez. Mexico, DF: Editores mexicanos unidos, S.A., 2005.

Diccionario de autoridades. Facsimile edition. 3 vols. Madrid: Gredos, 2002.

Eco, Umberto and Carlo María Martini. *En qué creen los que no creen. Un diálogo sobre la ética en el fin del mundo*. Trans. Carlos Gumpert Melgosa. Madrid: Temas de hoy, 2007.

Fernández, Martha. "La Jerusalén celeste. Imagen barroca de la ciudad novohispana." *Barroco Iberoamericano. Territorio, arte, espacio y sociedad*. 2 vols. Seville: Universidad Pablo de Olavide and Giralda, 2001. 2: 1211–28.

Gonzalo Sánchez-Molero, José Luis. "Los orígenes de la imagen salomónica del Real Monasterio de San Lorenzo del Escorial." *Literatura e imagen en El Escorial*. Coord. Francisco Javier Campos and Fernández de Sevilla. San Lorenzo de El Escorial: Real Centro Universitario Escorial-María Cristina, 1996. 721–50.

Gruzinski, Serge. *La ciudad de México: una historia*. Trans. Paula López Caballero. Mexico, DF: Fondo de Cultura Económica, 2004.

Larraín, Jorge. "Identidad latinoamericana: crítica del discurso esencialista católico." *Contra Corriente* 4.3 (Spring 2007): 1–28.

MacCormack, Sabine. *On the Wings of Time: Rome, the Incas, Spain, and Peru*. Princeton: Princeton University Press, 2007.

Manini, Emy and Patricia Saldarriaga. "Hacia la búsqueda del sentido en la representación: Juan Damasceno y Jacques Derrida." *Lienzo* 31 (2010): 175–202.

Maza, Francisco de la. *El guadalupismo mexicano*. Mexico, DF: Fondo de Cultura Económica, 1984.

Mendieta, Jerónimo de. *Historia eclesiástica indiana I y II*. 2 vols. Biblioteca de Autores Españoles 260–261. Madrid: Atlas, 1973.

Morandé, Pedro. *Cultura y modernización en América Latina*. Santiago: Pontificia Universidad Católica, 1984.

Motolinía, fray Toribio de Benavente. *Memoriales o libro de las cosas de la Nueva España*. Ed. Edmundo O'Gorman. Mexico, DF: Universidad Nacional Autónoma de México, 1971.

Parker, Geoffrey. "The Place of Tudor England in the Messianic Vision of Philip II of Spain: The Prothero Lecture." *Transactions of the Royal Historic Society*, 6th Series, 12 (2002): 167–221.

Rama, Ángel. *La ciudad letrada*. Hanover: Ediciones del Norte, 1984.

Ramírez, Antonio, André Corboz, René Taylor, Robert Jan Van Pelt and Antonio Martínez Ripoli. *Dios, arquitecto. Juan Bautista Villalpando y el Templo de Salomón*. Madrid: Siruela, 1991.

Rosenau, Helen. *Vision of the Temple: The Image of the Temple of Jerusalem in Judaism and Christianity*. London: Oresko Books, 1979.

Sagrada Biblia. Ed. Eloíno Nácar Fuster and Alberto Colunga. Madrid: Biblioteca de Autores Cristianos, 1985.

Sánchez, Miguel. *Imagen de la Virgen María, Madre de Dios de Guadalupe, milagrosamente aparecida en la Ciudad de México. Celebrada en su historia, con la profecía del capítulo doce del Apocalipsis*. Mexico, DF: Imprenta de la Viuda de Bernardo Calderón, 1648.

Sebastián, Santiago. "La significación salomónica del templo de Huejotzingo (México)." *Traza y Baza* 2 (1973): 77–88.

Villalpando, Juan Bautista. *Ezechielem Explanationes: A Sixteenth-Century Architectural Text*. Trans. Tessa Morrison. Lewiston, NY: Edwin Mellen Press, 2009.

PART IV
Neo-Baroque Approaches to Identity

Chapter 14

Elegies for a Homeland: A Baroque Chronicle, a Marxist Critique, and Conflicting Identities in Colonial Guatemala

W. George Lovell

They make strange bedfellows, very strange indeed. One is a baroque icon, his flowery chronicle epitomizing the period—its preferences, its prejudices, its predilections. The other is a creature of his age too, but born two and three-quarter centuries later, and of vastly different ideological mettle. Yet the dialogue between them, criollos both, cuts to the quick of the land they both loved, Guatemala.

Francisco Antonio de Fuentes y Guzmán (1642–1699). Severo Martínez Peláez (1925–1998). The *Recordación florida* and *La patria del criollo*: elegies both, written by offspring, respectively, of the capital of a colonial kingdom and its neo-colonial second city. How does one make sense of the relationship they struck, incongruities and all?

Making Acquaintance

I came to appreciate Fuentes y Guzmán when I began work on my doctoral dissertation. For it I chose to write about a little-known region of Guatemala, the Sierra de los Cuchumatanes, and to focus my investigations on what happened there under Spanish rule. Fuentes y Guzmán, I learned, had served the Crown as district governor of the Cuchumatanes in the 1670s, when he was in his early thirties and ruled the region with authoritarian zeal. His appointment allowed him to get to know the area well. Astute observations not only of the mores of indigenous locals, some of whose antics unleashed his wrath, but also the myriad attributes of locale, gifted him a wealth of knowledge that he drew upon when composing the *Recordación florida*, his self-proclaimed "historical discourse and material, military, and political exposition of the Kingdom of

256 *The Transatlantic Hispanic Baroque*

Guatemala."[1] Nowhere in this sprawling cornucopia does Fuentes y Guzmán reveal greater intimacy of the lay of the land than when discussing the Sierra de los Cuchumatanes, administered then as part of the Corregimiento of Totonicapán and Huehuetenango. I leaned heavily on what the chronicler had to say when reconstructing various aspects of the region's eventful, at times calamitous historical geography (Lovell, *Conquest*), and took delight in his quirky cartographic depiction of it (Figure 14.1).

Decades passed between my first encounter with Fuentes y Guzmán and my second, which arose after I became involved in a translation project—not that of the *Recordación florida*, which remains to be translated, but a formidable Marxist critique of Guatemala's colonial legacy, *La patria del criollo* (2009). Its author, Severo Martínez Peláez, introduces us to Fuentes y Guzmán in the opening pages of his work, not as a grown man in the service of King and country but a young boy terrified to find himself in the midst of an earthquake. It is a memorable opening passage:

> Catastrophe struck the city of Santiago de Guatemala on Saturday, February 18, 1651. At about one o'clock in the afternoon the ground rumbled and shook violently. Many buildings came tumbling down, and for more than a month thereafter, others that had suffered serious damage were leveled by subsequent tremors that continued night and day. Rich and poor alike, momentarily united in fear, jostled on the steps of convents, anxious to confess their sins. Above them, in towers that were beginning to topple, bells moaned, tolled by the earthquake's invisible hand.

> Mingling with the crowds thronging the patios was a boy named Francisco, who was destined never to forget his impressions of the day the earthquake struck. Forty years later he was to record the scene in a chronicle that, over time, would become famous: 'When I was but eight years old,' he wrote, 'I remember seeing hordes of people gathered in the atrium of San Francisco Church, lamenting their sins aloud.' (Martínez Peláez, *La patria del criollo: An Interpretation* 7–8)

When Martínez Peláez first made the acquaintance of Fuentes y Guzmán is not clear. In 1954, however, he fled for his life to Mexico, in the wake of an earthquake of a political sort—the overthrow in Guatemala of President Jacobo Arbenz Guzmán, whose agrarian and other socioeconomic reforms

---

[1] Emblematically baroque though its title may be, one can well understand how the subtitle of the *Recordación florida* ("Discurso historial y demonstración natural, material, militar y política del Reyno de Goathemala") would attract the interests of an intellectual of Marxist persuasion, or at least a scholar inclined to view the world through the lens of historical materialism. No one prior to Martínez Peláez saw in Fuentes y Guzmán such potential.

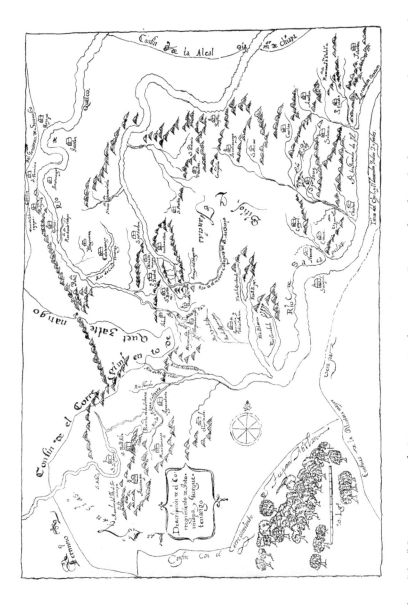

Figure 14.1 The "Corregimiento de Totonicapán y Huehuetenango," as rendered in the late seventeenth century by Francisco Antonio de Fuentes y Guzmán (private collection).

258   *The Transatlantic Hispanic Baroque*

Martínez Peláez supported. Heading into exile, he told Edeliberto Cifuentes years later, "I decided to take with me a 'piece of patria,' and what I considered most appropriate was Fuentes y Guzmán's *Recordación florida*" (108). Though *La patria del criollo* came to fruition in the decade that followed, its genesis is rooted in that flight from, and struggle against, imperialist intervention, for though Arbenz was toppled by dissident Guatemalan forces, his demise was plotted, funded, and assisted logistically by the US Central Intelligence Agency (Schlesinger and Kinzer).

What is it about the *Recordación florida* that exercised such an influence on Martínez Peláez? Was he alone in seeing in it something of unique worth, qualities that others failed to notice—or dismissed outright as pointless, pedantic, or irrelevant? What made Fuentes y Guzmán not only a source of voluminous information but also, in the hands of Martínez Peláez, turned him into a prominent, if not *the* principal protagonist in *La patria del criollo*?

Origins and Aspirations

Like many who live and write off the beaten track, Fuentes y Guzmán worked for the most part without recognition and in relative isolation. He was in his mid-thirties, already with important administrative duties to attend to, when the University of San Carlos was founded in Guatemala, and so never had the benefit of university training, much as he would have liked to. He studied as a youth at the Jesuit College of San Lucas, which José Mata Gavidia considers "the most important institution of higher education in the seventeenth century" (226). There he would have learned Latin, read the classics, and availed himself of whatever other expertise his teachers had to offer. Today, a library adjacent to the cathedral in the old colonial capital, known now as Antigua Guatemala, bears Fuentes y Guzmán's name, but in his time books were not readily available, though a printing press was established in Santiago by 1660, when he was still being schooled. Most of what he read upon graduation would have been in the form of documents that dealt with municipal affairs, for he assumed a post as *regidor* (alderman) on the *ayuntamiento* (city council) when he was a mere 18, and served on the body for 38 years. As *corregidor* of Totonicapán and Huehuetenango, and also, toward the end of his life, of Sonsonate, he would have familiarized himself with questions of regional government, in addition to following the constant bickering that went on between the city fathers of Santiago and members of the *Audiencia* (High Court) who represented Crown interests in Guatemala.

Fuentes y Guzmán we know to have written several other works besides the *Recordación florida*, but only one of them was published in his lifetime, *Fiestas reales* (1675), a poetic romance that celebrates the thirteenth birthday of Charles

II.[2] His motivation in penning the *Recordación florida* is rooted in his decades of service as a city councilor, for one of his jobs on the *ayuntamiento* was to function as its archivist, sifting through files in order to inform fellow members of council of the background to issues under discussion. Such dedication made Fuentes y Guzmán aware of repeated calls from the Crown for persons in the know to furnish it with information concerning the geography and governance of its colonies. While officials in other parts had long since complied, those in Guatemala had not. Fuentes y Guzmán considered himself well qualified to write in this capacity, and so he did, beginning his labors in the early 1680s, around his fortieth birthday. Some years later, he sent a copy of the first part of the *Recordación florida* to Spain in the hope of obtaining from the Council of the Indies royal sanction as its "official chronicler." He wrote directly to Charles II on April 23, 1687, by which time the youthful monarch of *Fiestas reales* was old enough to sit on the throne and rule of his own accord:

> My Lord: Having served the Crown, for twenty-seven years, as one of its officers in this far-flung Kingdom of Guatemala, I requested of one of Your ministers some time ago, in order to serve Your Majesty better, that I be honored by being named Chronicler of the Kingdom. The authority bestowed by said title would enable me to gain access to archives and release paperwork that I need to consult, thus allowing me to write a natural, military, and political history, the first part of which is already composed, and the second well-advanced.[3] (In Sáenz de Santa María xxxii–xxxiii)

Fuentes y Guzmán waited and waited, craving recognition. No reply from executive office, however, was forthcoming. He never heard back from Madrid about what he desired most. That did not deter him, however, from pushing ahead with his project, finishing a second part and planning a third, which his death pre-empted. In the end he produced a work of 929 manuscript pages. The earlier draft of the *Recordación florida* that Fuentes y Guzmán sent to Spain found its way into the holdings of the Biblioteca del Palacio Real, from which a two-volume edition was eventually printed in Madrid in 1882–1883. Not until

---

[2]   Sáenz de Santa María, to whom we owe insightful commentary about the life and work of Fuentes y Guzmán, describes *Fiestas reales* as a "cuaderno en cuarto que consta de diez y siete hojas impresas" (xxxvii). Another celebration in verse, *El milagro de la América*, an ode describing the cathedral of Santiago de Guatemala, has been lost, the fate also of Fuentes y Guzman's poetic rendering of the *Vida de Santa Teresa de Jesús*.

[3]   Though he had access to papers in *ayuntamiento* files, Fuentes y Guzmán complained that *audiencia* archives remained off limits to him, as was also the case with documents in the hands of the religious orders. Securing the title of "official chronicler" would have opened up these sources for consultation, so his pursuit of royal recognition in fact had a practical basis to it.

260 *The Transatlantic Hispanic Baroque*

1932–1933 was the *Recordación florida* published in its entirety, in Guatemala itself, based on the manuscript in the possession of the Archivo General de Centroamérica in Guatemala City.

The *Recordación florida* was not universally acclaimed by many who had occasion to peruse it in the course of preparing their own treatises on Guatemala. Fuentes y Guzmán's friend and contemporary, Francisco Vázquez, fails to acknowledge him in his work, even though Fuentes y Guzmán spoke highly of Vázquez's own *Crónica de la Provincia del Santísimo Nombre de Jesús* (1688), about which he was asked to furnish an opinion prior to its being printed. "Vázquez's work is admirable in all respects," he wrote, adding most revealingly: "And, because he is a native of the land of which he writes, more to be acclaimed by drumrolls" (in Martínez Peláez, *La patria del criollo: An Interpretation* 26). No reciprocal compliment was ever recorded. Nor were any kind words uttered by Francisco Ximénez in his *Historia de la Provincia de San Vicente y Chiapa* (1715–1720), the Dominican friar observing sarcastically "as for the *Recordación florida*, better to have called it 'a salad of mixed herbs,' because it more resembles something thrown together by an apothecary than the work of a historian" (cited in Sáenz de Santa María lxxiv). Though Domingo Juarros, author of *Compendio de Historia de la Ciudad de Guatemala* (1808–1818), considered him a "curious writer," he nonetheless recognized the importance of the *Recordación florida*, appreciating its attention to geographical and historical detail and lamenting that Fuentes y Guzmán's untimely demise meant "the loss of an intended third part of his history" (2: 16).

The first post-Independence writer of standing, Francisco de Paula García Peláez, chose to judge by omission, merely alluding in his *Memorias para la historia del antiguo reino de Guatemala* (1851–1852) to "a historian called Fuentes y Guzmán," whom he recognizes more as a municipal officer than a renowned chronicler (cited in Sáenz de Santa María lxxxv). José Milla was openly negative in his *Historia de la América Central* (1879), lambasting Juarros for taking at face value too much of what Fuentes y Guzmán has to say, especially his interpretation of indigenous documents, which Milla considered so shoddy as to feel obliged "not to place any trust in them" (1: vi). Most scathing of all was a contemporary of Milla's, Juan Gavarrete. In his "Advertencia sobre el autor de esta obra y su tercera parte," which Gavarrete wrote in 1875 and which forms part of the introductory material to the Guatemalan edition of *Recordación florida*, he berates Fuentes y Guzmán for being "little versed in indigenous languages, uncritical, disorganized, of depraved intent, and ignorant of the richness of the sources at hand," dismissing the chronicler as "a groveling, one-sided, pro-conquistador apologist" whose work, "a confused accumulation of exaggerated or unconnected associations," he considered as having "no other merit besides having saved for posterity notes and precious documents that, without it, would

Elegies for a Homeland 261

have been lost" (in Martínez Peláez, *La patria del criollo: An Interpretation* 29, 78).[4]

Martínez Peláez begs to differ, but does not resort to the same unflattering language in getting his point across; of Gavarrete he simply states "the liberal analyst failed to understand that every page of the *Recordación florida* is itself a precious document" (*La patria del criollo: An Interpretation* 78).[5] What did Martínez Peláez discern that others were so blind to?

Back Through the Looking Glass

Drawing on its contents time and again, Martínez Peláez states that he gave "priority attention" to the *Recordación florida* when composing *La patria del criollo* for three compelling reasons: "first, as a source of vastly different bits of historical data; second, as a personal account of an extremely complex social situation; and third, as a mirror of certain patterns of thought peculiar to colonial times" (*La patria del criollo: An Interpretation* 3). The third reason is the most pertinent for our purposes. Biography, Martínez Peláez makes clear, is not his goal: the "frequent references" made to "the life and times of Fuentes y Guzmán" are meant to be "illustrative," a strategic point of entry into "the very fabric of colonial life." After penetrating "that pattern of existence," the *Recordación florida* is moved to one side, "making room for other documents of historical worth." Fuentes y Guzmán, however, "takes his leave of us [...] only after we have become oriented to his world." Martínez Peláez also makes clear that his "analyses of Fuentes y Guzmán's frame of mind are not refutations of his views or attacks on him personally" but, rather, "explanations of the whys and the wherefores of his way of thinking" (*La patria del criollo: An Interpretation* 3–4). The values that matter most are group, not individual, in nature.

"Who exactly was this man?" Martínez Peláez asks. The answer, of course, must be contextual, and pertain to collective contingencies. Bloodline comes first. On his mother's side, Fuentes y Guzmán was of pedigree Spanish stock: his great-great-grandfather was none other than Bernal Díaz del Castillo, the veteran soldier who fought alongside Cortés in the conquest of Mexico and who, upon

---

[4] For Gavarrete in full flight, see his "Advertencia" in Fuentes y Guzmán (1: xx) and Sáenz de Santa María (lxxxv).

[5] The best evaluation of the chronicler's work is the astute, even-handed, and thoroughly researched contribution of Sáenz de Santa María, whose assiduous labors also include a second Spanish edition of the *Recordación florida*, published in Madrid in three volumes (230, 251, 259) between 1969 and 1972 as part of the series Biblioteca de Autores Españoles, under the title *Obras históricas de D. Francisco Antonio de Fuentes y Guzmán*. Megged also turns to Fuentes y Guzmán as a pertinent frame of reference in his study of the origins of criollo identity in Guatemala.

262 *The Transatlantic Hispanic Baroque*

settling in Guatemala after the battles were over, wrote the celebrated eyewitness account *Historia verdadera de la conquista de la Nueva España* (1632). His father's side of the family was also renowned, but no relation was held in such high regard as "mi Castillo." Fuentes y Guzmán brims with pride when he recalls "reading the original draft of the heroic and brave Captain [...] not only with curiosity but with eagerness, veneration, and affection," for the manuscript was safeguarded by "we, his descendents, with all due appreciation and in honor of his esteemed memory." Martínez Peláez (*La patria del criollo: An Interpretation* 10–11) emphasizes that Fuentes y Guzmán considered himself "not merely the offspring of conquerors but *an heir to the conquest*," a member of "an exclusive group" that "owned lands, used Indian labor to cultivate them, and occupied positions of authority" in colonial society. Above all else he belonged to a class of "criollos, as they call us," and identified himself as such.

What acts of allegiance did that entail, and what were some of the tensions, contradictions, and challenges that charged being so affiliated, designated, and self-identified?

The Criollo Conundrum

Martínez Peláez anchors the criollo consciousness of Fuentes y Guzmán and his ilk in their "belief in Hispanic superiority." He notes that the word "criollo," strictly defined, refers to "people in the Americas born of Spanish ancestry who were not the offspring of mixed unions or marriages" (*La patria del criollo: An Interpretation* 11).[6] Coined initially to refer "to the children of conquistadors and first-generation settlers," later on "the continuing influx of Spanish immigrants to the colonies lent new shades of meaning to the original term." Differences emerged "between a 'new' criollo and a criollo of 'old Indies' lineage because the descendants of the conquistadors did not want to place themselves on the same level as the children of newly arrived adventurers." Those belonging to the latter camp, meanwhile, "maintained that their status as new arrivals from Spain was worth more than ancestral ties," which did not go over well with the former, long-established criollos who "preferred to call themselves Spaniards whenever they had the chance, ignoring their birthplace and emphasizing their roots."

Martínez Peláez (*La patria del criollo: An Interpretation* 12) takes pains to point out, however, that criollo consciousness "involved far more than the mere question of nationalities." Foremost of all was "the belief that anyone of

---

[6] The word "criollo" is invariably translated as "creole," which in English can mean other things besides "people in the Americas born of Spanish ancestry." Though resorted to only rarely, the word "criollo" exists in English and may be used precisely to mean what it does in Spanish.

Spanish origin was superior to Indians and mestizos, or mixed bloods. This sense of superiority, which criollos attributed to their Spanish ancestry, was a fundamental part of their social awareness." But "Spanish origin" or "Spanish ancestry" was one thing; actually being born in Spain and coming to the New World as a "peninsular" was another, especially when it entailed being charged with a royal mission. Criollos, no matter to what extent they believed in "their much-touted superiority," never enjoyed "control over the reins of government," which relegated them to a "subordinate plane" and made them, as Martínez Peláez (*La patria del criollo: An Interpretation* 19) puts it, "a semi-dominant class." Certainly they were "offered rewards in terms of privileges and advantages," but nothing compared to what peninsular representatives of the Crown could count on in their "dominant position" in colonial society. Over time, criollo resentment resulted in "veiled modes of attack and defense" in the face of "anything or anybody Spanish." To appreciate "criollo ideology" and the "class dynamics" behind it, "we can turn to no better document than the *Recordación florida*," which Fuentes y Guzmán himself tells us he wrote out of "love [for] my *patria*, my homeland, which stirs me deeply" (in Martínez Peláez, *La patria del criollo: An Interpretation* 23).

What kind of a homeland did the chronicler have in mind when he so passionately put pen to paper?

For a Few, Not All

In the *Recordación florida*, the notion of a homeland, and the feelings it ignites, constitute "a lyrical song exalting the Kingdom of Guatemala," which "must be valued for what it is, regardless of the bonds of empire." The "mother country," therefore, is not what Fuentes y Guzmán venerates but, rather, "a new American homeland," one of exclusionary entitlement manifest "in the depths of emotion" that champion criollo interests. "Indians, of course," Martínez Peláez (*La patria del criollo: An Interpretation* 24) recognizes, "had their own homelands before they were conquered." The *Recordación florida*, however, envisions not a "patria de todos" but, instead, a "patria de pocos." Its thrust is about the creation of a "patria del criollo," the homeland of a privileged few, not all.

The homeland that Fuentes y Guzmán espoused, the one for which he was an avid proponent, and forever and lavishly praised, was one he never lived to see. It endures today, however, to the detriment not only of Guatemala's indigenous peoples, half the national population, but also that of *castas* or mixed bloods who, in varying degree, share with them the burden of exclusion.

264 *The Transatlantic Hispanic Baroque*

Sparrowhawks and Chickens

To sum up the hostility that developed between Spaniards and criollos, Martínez Peláez (*La patria del criollo: An Interpretation* 27) resorts to "a rather amusing and apposite refrain." It runs: "Gachupín con criollo, gavilán con pollo"—what the Spaniard is to the criollo, the sparrowhawk is to the chicken. The refrain "refers bluntly to the animosity between Spaniards and criollos, and implies that the former held a number of advantages over the latter," which were resented as much as they were longed for.

A half-century before it consumed Fuentes y Guzmán's attention, the adverse relationship was noticed and commented on by the English Dominican friar, Thomas Gage. During his sojourn in Guatemala, Gage (113, 122) observed that the two groups were "deadly enemies" who "never did agree," regarding one another with "spite and hatred." Contempt was so marked, Gage claimed, that were England to launch an invasion of the Spanish colonies, foreign forces would find support among disaffected criollos. The "English-American" writes:

> In all the Dominions of the King of Spain in America, there are two sorts of Spaniards more opposite one to another than in Europe the Spaniard is opposite to the French, or to the Hollander, or to the Portugal [sic]; to wit, they that are born in any parts of Spain and go thither, and they that are born there of Spanish parents, whom the Spaniards to distinguish them from themselves term criolio's [sic], signifying the Natives of that Country. This hatred is so great that I dare say nothing could be more advantageous than this to any other Nation that would conquer America. (Gage 20)

Gage, while serving in Guatemala as parish priest of Petapa, had no need to take sides. His watchful eye, however, captured not only peninsular haughtiness but also criollo truculence, pedantry, delusion, and sloth. Equally damning of both, he has some particularly sharp words to say about criollo character and disposition. "They have most cowardly spirits of war," he volunteers, "and though they will say they would fair see Spain, yet they dare not venture their lives at sea; they judge sleeping in a whole skin the best maxim for their creole spirits" (Gage 159). Gage captures criollo resentment with singular acumen when he writes "not only [...] are they kept from office but daily affronted by the Spaniards as incapable of any government, and termed half-Indians by them" (Gage 21).[7]

---

[7]   Megged notes that, by the late sixteenth century, the distinction in Guatemala between criollos and mixed bloods "was becoming increasingly vague," to such an extent that archival documents record the terms as synonymous, "mestizo o criollo" (424). Megged also notes, in relation to Church membership, "the mestizo origin of many of the creole novices," observing that peninsular Spaniards, according to Fuentes y Guzmán, considered them "of rough qualities and of crooked and indecent habits" (429). The insult was capped off by the

Elegies for a Homeland 265

An almost incredulous Martínez Peláez (*La patria del criollo: An Interpretation* 70) exclaims at this juncture "Considered, back then, as 'half Indians'"! He draws our attention immediately thereafter to the fact that "negative traits of criollo character contrasted with the positive attributes of Spanish immigrants, who for the most part were commercially minded." The daily round of criollos, on the other hand, "implied consumption without production, enjoyment without work, in short the life of a parasite. They even managed to despise the very people who kept them, hardly an attitude conducive to the emergence of a diligent, well-adjusted lot."

Martínez Peláez (*La patria del criollo: An Interpretation* 28–9) is at his critical best when discussing the split personality of criollos with respect to the "two Spains" that exercised such a hold on their lives and psyches. The principal cause of Fuentes y Guzmán's torment was the inability of later peninsular arrivals to hold their predecessors, the first conquerors, in the same high esteem as did criollos. In this key regard, the chronicler is worth listening to directly:

> They wish to cast aspersions on the very Spaniards themselves, however they may, decrying the most famous and heroic deeds of the conquerors, whose valor and gallantry they could not even begin to emulate. Because they can neither easily refute nor deny the illustrious and distinguished services rendered by conquerors in America, they judge that campaigns not undertaken in Africa and Europe do not merit credit or renown. Such is their arrogance that they condemn even the comfortable towns, which they found already established for occupation by them, without pausing to examine what those admirable and worthy men, who came in advance of us and were so superior to us, labored over with such diligence and lavished such care upon. (In Martínez Peláez, *La patria del criollo: An Interpretation* 31–2)

He refers to these naysayers as "advenedizos," a term that translates as "newcomers" or "outsiders" but that also carries the more derisory stigma of "upstarts." At a critical juncture in the dialogue, Martínez Peláez (*La patria del criollo: An Interpretation* 67) asks: "Why did Spaniards consider themselves to be above criollos?"

Fuentes y Guzmán was never able to answer that question satisfactorily. A suitable response eluded him especially when he compared the hazardous first years of the colony to "the lap of luxury in which we live and the sweet peace that we now enjoy," or when he recalled "those who won the land over for us and set everything up for our enjoyment." He goes so far as to assert that "everything we enjoy today is due to the industry, resolution, and hard work of those heroic

---

"creole novices" being referred to as "padres Indios" or "Indios e incapaces," derogatory in the extreme for any self-respecting criollo.

266 *The Transatlantic Hispanic Baroque*

Spaniards." How could these ungrateful "advenedizos," latecomers to the feast, fail to see for themselves how it was? "Nowadays they pay no attention whatsoever to the merits of those who served God and his Majesty the King, those who won this land so bountiful," the chronicler laments. "Those who now possess the land have forgotten all about these most noble men, superior to them in every way, and to whom they owe so much." He is left with no option but to conclude: "It is a grave affliction, perhaps even an incurable one, in my opinion, for a people to have a king who is so far away" (in Martínez Peláez, *La patria del criollo: An Interpretation* 30; Brading 310).

Might Fuentes y Guzmán's opinion be construed as one of the earliest articulations of criollo desires for independence?

The Reactionary Nature of *La patria del criollo*

When the *Recordación florida* was composed, Guatemala's independence from Spain was still a long way off. From his vantage point in the 1690s, Fuentes y Guzmán could not know that more than a century would pass before peninsular Spanish rule eventually gave way to criollo authority, in one guise or another. An even greater span of time, however, closer to two centuries, lay behind when he contemplated, and idealized, what was for him the defining moment in the forging of criollo identity: the Conquest. Martínez Peláez (*La patria del criollo: An Interpretation* 73) therefore concludes:

> [T]he concept of 'patria' that Fuentes y Guzmán conveys in the *Recordación florida* is a reactionary one. It is not driven by a vision of the future that revolves around development and change. On the contrary, it is a response to the threat of transformation implicit in imperial policy and in the arrival of Spanish newcomers. The overall tone of the *Recordación florida* is quite different from what we might expect of a work purporting to be a defense of, and elegy for, the homeland. Its narrative texture is one of nostalgia and sorrow, a lament. After we have finished reading it, this is the most enduring impression we are left with. It resonates with longing for the past, disapproval of the present, and fear of the future. Fuentes y Guzmán is obsessed with what might happen and how times have changed. Far from constituting some kind of affirmative speculation, his musings are somber and lugubrious, but nonetheless revealing.

The words of the chronicler echo with a valedictory ring. "In all the world," he moans, "there is no constancy, neither in the greatest thing, nor in the smallest." One beholds everywhere "the inconsistency of things, which are never manifest in true form." For Fuentes y Guzmán, "the principal defect of our time here on Earth is its lack of stability, which characterizes everything." He notes with regret that "in human affairs nothing is fixed or certain" (in Martínez Peláez, *La patria del criollo: An Interpretation* 73).[8]

The *Recordación florida*, then, as Martínez Peláez (*La patria del criollo: An Interpretation* 70) eloquently puts it, "truly is a 'recordación,' a remembrance, a process of focusing back in time, when things flourished, 'florida.'" Through the eyes of Fuentes y Guzmán, "we reflect on a prosperous and vibrant past, not the changing present, even less an uncertain future. His pessimism and his reactionary notion of a homeland, we must conclude, are the inevitable outcome of a profound sense of insecurity, one haunted by the ever-diminishing presence of a core of criollo families who were the true heirs of the Conquest."

When, at last, "the true heirs of the Conquest" found themselves in power, was the homeland they forged as reactionary as the one Fuentes y Guzmán dreamed of?

La patria del criollo as Colonial Guatemalan Reality

We noted earlier that, upon fleeing Guatemala for safe haven in Mexico after the fall of President Arbenz in 1954, Martínez Peláez took with him a "piece of patria" in the form of the *Recordación florida*. Only he understood his reasons for doing so, but among them must have been that, ideology and the passage of time apart, Martínez Peláez felt that he could identify with Fuentes y Guzmán in ways he knew he would be able to write about, years later, to penetrating effect. The two men, despite profound differences, shared common formative experiences that influenced how they came to view the world. Incidents that took place in childhood were of visceral import to both.

Like Fuentes y Guzmán, Martínez Peláez, much as he disowned it, hailed from resourceful criollo stock. In the late nineteenth century, his grandfather was among the many immigrants from Asturias in Spain who made their way to Latin America, ending up not in Argentina, Cuba, or Mexico, as was the case with most, but in Guatemala. There he had a son, Alfredo Martínez Rodríguez, who married into an "old criollo" family after he met Martínez Peláez's mother, Alicia Peláez Luna. Her parents were conspicuously well off, owning sizeable properties, a coffee farm on the Costa Cuca Pacific slope among them. As with Fuentes y Guzmán whenever his father took him, as a boy, to inspect the family estate, so too did Martínez Peláez relish such excursions into the Guatemalan

---

8   See Lovell and Lutz for further discussion of the family background and circumstances of Martínez Peláez, including his stormy relationship with his father and his never-ending grief for his mother, who committed suicide when he was six. These and other features of the professional as well as personal life of Martínez Peláez are examined in depth by the contributors to the volume edited by Peláez Almengor.

268 *The Transatlantic Hispanic Baroque*

countryside with his father, seeing first-hand the beauty of the land, marveling at its productive capacity, and being afforded a close look at rural life in general (20). It struck him repeatedly that it was Indians who did all the heavy lifting, and he recalled how uncomfortable he felt, coming of age, at hearing relatives and other landowners speak disrespectfully "about the social class that sustained them" (Asturias 36). The disconnect between what he observed, Indians toiling away endlessly, and what he had to listen to, complaints that Indians didn't work hard enough, was extreme.

His reading of the *Recordación florida* allowed Martínez Peláez (*La patria del criollo: An Interpretation* 8) to detect in Fuentes y Guzmán emotions not unlike those he himself felt when growing up, especially in relation to "the social class that sustained them"—Indians. How, in Fuentes y Guzmán's boyish eyes, criollos related to Indians registered on Martínez Peláez as being much the same as how they were treated in his day, centuries later. He continues:

> Indians, true enough, had to be kept in check and constantly reminded of their subordinate position—Francisco's parents and grandparents drummed that into him every day! Nonetheless, it was equally true that Indians would bring something good whenever they came to the house. He would see them almost daily in the hallway, pouring with sweat and panting as they swung from their backs bundles of firewood and sacks of grain. They brought vegetables, milk, and a brown sugar called *panela*, as well as many other fine things without which life would not have been half so sweet. Although the Indians brought much of the produce from afar, some of it they had grown themselves on the hacienda that belonged to young Francisco's parents. For this reason it was hard for him to understand his elders' admonishment that he should treat these barefoot, ragged, and sweat-drenched people with scorn.

Martínez Peláez (*La patria del criollo: An Interpretation* 9) draws his engagement to a close by commenting: "All this made for a great deal of inconsistency that was incomprehensible from a child's point of view."[9]

Seeing Guatemala "from a child's point of view," as at that moment did Fuentes y Guzmán, made a lasting impression on Martínez Peláez, not least because it was one with which he could identify, and indeed turned into an epiphany of sorts in *La patria del criollo*. His fundamental argument in the book is that Guatemala remains at heart a colonial society because conditions that arose centuries ago, when imperial Spain held sway, have endured. Economic circumstances that assure prosperity for a few and deprivation for the majority were neither altered by independence in 1821 nor, following almost half a

---

[9]   The conversation between Fuentes y Guzmán and Martínez Peláez that I highlight here is explored further by Carrillo in her erudite analysis.

century of conservative rule, by the liberal reforms of 1871, when policies pursued by President Justo Rufino Barrios transformed Guatemala into a "coffee republic" and only exacerbated already chronic geographies of inequality. The few in question, of course, are an elite group of criollos who assumed the role of governing Guatemala without the bloody confrontations experienced elsewhere in Spanish America; the majority, for the most part, are indigenous Mayas, whose impoverishment and exploitation are shared by many mixed-race Guatemalans. In an assertive closing passage, Martínez Peláez insists:

> What needs to be stressed is the survival of colonial characteristics long after colonial rule has ended. It is especially important not to be deluded by the rhetoric of Liberal ideology, for the truth is that *the coffee dictatorships were the full and radical realization of criollo notions of homeland*. Criollos created the concept of nationhood and established Guatemalan identity ... Most importantly, it was neither Spanish blood nor Spanish skin color that determined membership of the criollo class or defined that class as a compact entity. What mattered most was the ability to acquire land and exploit servile labor. (*La patria del criollo: An Interpretation* 278–9)

Martínez Peláez (*La patria* 424) emphasizes his point not by recourse to archival sources or published literature but by drawing upon, no doubt recalling Fuentes y Guzmán, a boyhood memory. It involves a scene he witnessed one day in his native Quetzaltenango, where he noticed gangs of Indians tied together on a city street, rounded up prior to being trucked or marched to the coast as forced labor, "with groups of women following behind the men at a short distance," trying to keep them in sight. "Even as children," he writes, "we knew they came from highland towns and were heading off in silence, bound together and led under escort, to work on the coffee plantations of the Costa Cuca."

The last word, with all due respect to Fuentes y Guzmán, must be extended to the man who breathed new life into the *Recordación florida* by making it the centerpiece of *La patria del criollo*, extracting from a Baroque chronicle the raw material from which a Marxist critique was wrought. "A sad colonial scene," comments Martínez Peláez, "that we saw with our very own eyes, half-way through the twentieth century."

Bibliography

Asturias, José Enrique. "Historia de un historiador." *La patria del criollo: tres décadas después*. Ed. Oscar Peláez Almengor. Guatemala: Editorial Universitaria de la Universidad de San Carlos de Guatemala, 2000. 31–59

270   *The Transatlantic Hispanic Baroque*

Brading, David. *The First America: The Spanish Monarchy, Creole Patriots, and the Liberal State, 1492–1867*. Cambridge: Cambridge University Press, 1991.

Carrillo, Ana Lorena. *Árboles de historias: configuraciones del pasado en Severo Martínez y Luis Cardoza y Aragón*. Guatemala: Ediciones del Pensativo, 2009.

Cifuentes, Edeliberto. "José Severo Martínez Peláez: Una vida hecha obra de arte." *La patria del criollo: tres décadas después*. Ed. Oscar Peláez Almengor. Guatemala: Editorial Universitaria de la Universidad de San Carlos de Guatemala. 2000. 89–132.

Díaz del Castillo, Bernal. *Historia verdadera de la conquista de la Nueva España*. Mexico, DF: Editorial Porrúa. 1970.

Fuentes y Guzmán, Francisco Antonio de. *Historia de Guatemala o Recordación florida: discurso historial, natural, material, militar y político del reino de Goathemala*. 2 vols. Edited and introduced by Justo Zaragoza. Madrid: Luis Navarro, 1882–1883.

———. *Recordación florida: discurso historial y demonstración natural, material, militar y política del reyno de Guatemala*. 3 vols. Biblioteca Goathemala, vols 6–8. Edited and introduced by J. Antonio Villacorta, Ramon A. Salazar and Sinforoso Aguilar. Guatemala: Sociedad de Geografía e Historia de Guatemala, 1932–1933.

———. *Obras históricas de D. Francisco Antonio de Fuentes y Guzmán*. 3 vols. Biblioteca de Autores Españoles 230, 251, 259. Edited and introduced by Carmelo Sáenz de Santa María. Madrid: Ediciones Atlas, 1969–1972.

Gage, Thomas. *A Survey of the Spanish West-Indies: Being a Journal of Three Thousand and Three Hundred Miles on the Continent of America*. London: Thomas Horne, 1702.

———. *The English-American: A New Survey of the West Indies, 1648*. Edited and introduced by A.P. Newton. London: George Routledge and Sons, 1928.

García Peláez, Francisco de Paula. *Memorias para la historia del antiguo reino de Guatemala*. 3 vols. Guatemala: Tipografía Nacional, 1943.

Gavarrete, Juan. "Advertencia sobre el autor de esta obra y su tercera parte." *Recordación florida: discurso historial y demonstración natural, material, militar y política del reyno de Guatemala*. 3 vols. Biblioteca Goathemala, vols 6–8. Edited and introduced by J. Antonio Villacorta, Ramon A. Salazar and Sinforoso Aguilar. Guatemala: Sociedad de Geografía e Historia de Guatemala, 1932–1933. 1: xix–xx.

Juarros, Domingo. *Compendio de la historia de la ciudad de Guatemala*. 2 vols. Guatemala: Tipografía Nacional, 1937.

Lovell, W. George. *Conquest and Survival in Colonial Guatemala: A Historical Geography of the Cuchumatán Highlands, 1500–1821*. 3rd edition. Montreal, QC and Kingston, ON: McGill-Queen's University Press, 2005.

————, and Christopher H. Lutz. *Historia sin máscara: vida y obra de Severo Martínez Peláez*. Guatemala: Centro de Estudios Urbanos y Regionales and Facultad Latinoamericana de Ciencias Sociales, 2009.

Martínez Peláez, Severo. *La patria del criollo: ensayo de interpretación de la realidad colonial guatemalteca*. Mexico, DF: Fondo de Cultura Económica, 1998.

————. *La Patria del Criollo: An Interpretation of Colonial Guatemala*. Translated by Susan M. Neve and W. George Lovell. Edited and introduced by W. George Lovell and Christopher H. Lutz. Durham, NC: Duke University Press, 2009.

Mata Gavidia, José. *Anotaciones de historia patria centroamericana*. Guatemala: Cultura Centroamericana, 1953.

Megged, Amos. "The Rise of Creole Identity in Early Colonial Guatemala: Differential Patterns in Town and Countryside." *Social History* 17.3 (1992): 421–40.

Milla, José. *Historia de la América Central*. 2 vols. Guatemala: Establecimiento Tipográfico "El Progreso," 1879–1882.

Peláez Almengor, Oscar, ed. *La patria del criollo: tres décadas después*. Guatemala: Editorial Universitaria de la Universidad de San Carlos, 2000.

Sáenz de Santa María, Carmelo. "Estudio preliminar." *Obras históricas de D. Francisco Antonio de Fuentes y Guzmán*. 3 vols. Biblioteca de Autores Españoles 230, 251, 259. Edited and introduced by Carmelo Sáenz de Santa María. Madrid: Ediciones Atlas, 1969–1972. 1: v–lxxxii.

————. "El siglo XVII en el reino de Guatemala, a través de su cronista don Francisco Antonio de Fuentes y Guzmán." *Anuario de Estudios Americanos* 38 (1971): 153–64.

Schlesinger, Stephen and Stephen Kinzer. *Bitter Fruit: The Story of the American Coup in Guatemala*. Cambridge, MA: Harvard University Press, 2005.

Vázquez, Francisco. *Crónica de la Provincia del Santísimo Nombre de Jesús de Guatemala*. 4 vols. 2nd edition. Biblioteca Goathemala, vols 14–17. Guatemala: Sociedad de Geografía de Historia. 1937–1944.

Ximénez, Francisco. *Historia de la Provincia de San Vicente de Chiapa y Guatemala*. 3 vols. Biblioteca Goathemala, vols 1–3. Guatemala: Sociedad de Geografía e Historia, 1930.

Chapter 15

Neo-Baroque Catholic Evangelism in Post-Secular Mexico

Kristin Norget

Stage 1 (Basilica de Guadalupe, Mexico City, July 31, 2002): On his fifth and final visit to Mexico, Pope John Paul II canonizes Juan Diego Cuauhtlatoatzin (the Náhuatl name appearing on all Vatican publicity)—the Indian man to whom the Virgin of Guadalupe, Mexico's patron saint, is said to have appeared in 1531.[1] The canonization, taking place at the Basilica of the Virgin of Guadalupe on the famous hill of Tepeyac, makes Juan Diego the first indigenous saint in the Americas. The following day, on August 1, the Pope beatifies two Indian (Zapotec) peasant men, Juan Bautista and Jacinto de los Angeles, from the Zapotec town of San Francisco Cajonos located in Oaxaca, one of the most indigenous and socially and politically marginal states in the country.[2] Both Juan Diego's canonization ceremony and that of the two *Mártires de Cajonos* (as the Church called them) include the active participation of indigenous persons and elements—music, dress, dance, healing rites, even incense—of apparently indigenous origin. They are broadcast live to millions via the national television channels, and in Mexico City to the thousands filling the central city plaza or *zócalo* where masses of people watch the event on a giant screen (see Villamil). The ceremonies provoke much media coverage and commentary, both celebratory (the canonization makes Mexico home of the first indigenous saint in Latin America) and critical (left-leaning intellectuals in officially secular Mexico still love to hate the Church). The Church also promotes the rites widely on its website, including the homilies of John Paul II.

Stage 2 (Basilica de Guadalupe, Mexico City, December 12, 2012): The Feast day of the Virgin of Guadalupe, the object of one of the most important pilgrimages of Latin America. Inside the Basilica, television stars of the country's

---

[1]   Juan Diego's was John Paul's 464th canonization as Pope. The Virgin's shrine at Tepeyac is now the center of the world's largest pilgrimage, attracting roughly 15 million pilgrims annually; in 2011, 7 million arrived to the Sanctuary between December 9–12.

[2]   Beatification is the third of the four steps in the path toward canonization. Once beatified, a person is referred to as a "Beato" or "Blessed."

274   *The Transatlantic Hispanic Baroque*

biggest television channel, Televisa, croon "Las Mañanitas" (the traditional Mexican birthday song) to the Virgin's image on the altar, beside which stands a huge Mexican flag. Television cameras on articulated arms swing over the lucky attendees who found seats on the Basilica's main floor. Behind them, a steady stream of devotees, many of them holding images of the Virgin above their heads, is herded through the building by officious volunteers. While the very formal mass progresses, sometimes barely audible to the crowd, Church representatives and Mexico's pious, elite classes sit in the balcony above; at the close of the mass they receive communion directly from clergy seated among them. Outside a thick human blanket covers the plaza, spreading into the streets nearby and the other centuries-old chapels and temples that align the square. Crowds of pilgrims from all parts of Mexico and sometimes beyond have set up encampments of tents or just sleeping bags towards the rear of the plaza; elsewhere an anthropologist beholds itinerant salespeople, tightrope walkers, troupes of Conchero[3] and other indigenous dancers and musicians, traditional healers with herbs, incense and conch shells; police officers; European tourists, and television camera crews.

Stage 3 (St Peter's Basilica, the Vatican, December 13, 2012): "Creole Mass"[4], dedicated to the Virgin of Guadalupe on the occasion of the Bicentennial of the Independence of the countries of Latin America and the Caribbean. During the mass, which is transmitted by television channels across the world, the Virgin is heralded as the as "Emperatriz de las Américas y el Caribe." John Paul's successor Pope Benedict XVI, now 86 years old and visibly frail, blesses people as he moves across the lush carpet on a mobile cart, accompanied by men in white bow ties and gloves. Youth bearing flags that represent all the Latin American nations parade across the nave of the Vatican Basilica, coming to stand alongside the Virgin's image on the altar. In the words of the bishop-commentator, the ceremony evokes the Church's desire for "[u]n proyecto de paz para Americalatina. Un compromiso de desarollo, de velar a los mas pobres." On this Vatican stage the Virgin does not belong to just Mexico but is re-signified formally as the patroness of all the ("indigenous") America, and the Caribbean. Thus, "La Morenita," the brown-skinned Guadalupe, "la estrella de evangelización" (as the commentator calls her), is conscripted to perform extra signifying labor as

---

3   Concheros are largely urban Mexicans (the movement began in Mexico City) who don "traditional" Indian dress to participate in ancient Aztec dances, accompanied by drummers and others playing traditional instruments; many repudiate Catholicism and have learned classical Náhuatl. See Rostas; González Torres.

4   Composed by the Argentinians Ariel Ramirez and Félix Luna in 1964 (during Vatican II), the *Misa Criolla*, which combined Spanish text with Andean instruments, melodies and rhythms, was one of the first non-Latin Masses. It was the first time that Benedict XVI had ever presided over this mass.

Neo-Baroque Catholic Evangelism in Post-Secular Mexico 275

the icon of African-origin or indigenous Others in the Caribbean beyond Latin America—Catholics for whom the Church pledges a particular mission. During the mass, the Pope announces, to enthusiastic applause by those in attendance, his plans to travel to Cuba and Mexico the following spring.

***

Each of the above scenes, enacted on distinct stages, can be taken as richly layered examples of the institutional Roman Catholic Church's current baroque evangelizing campaign. Manifest in a particular way in Latin America, this campaign originated in a multi-pronged general backlash to the reforms unleashed by the Second Vatican Council that had moved toward a putting of perspective of theology and decentralization of Church authority. In Mexico, an overwhelmingly Catholic country,[5] these performances have become "inculturated" or indigenized in a manner that both reflects the Vatican's general concern to recognize and celebrate non-European, "local" cultures, and to counteract the evangelizing assault of other Christian churches that, as in other Latin American countries, have successfully lured millions of indigenous away from Catholic affiliation. Yet the rites must also be understood as referencing one another: they are plays within other plays, spaces within other spaces, fragments that must be understood as signifying a coherent whole. Chock-full of complexity, chaos, and contradiction, multi-textual, but also embellished with hyperbole, unctuous emotionalism and sensationalism, they are grounded in an older baroque cultural system but are open, even messianic, absorbing new signs and symbols in a quest to evoke "states of transcendence that amplify viewer's experience of the illusion" (Ndalianis 20).

This chapter is based on field research over more than the last 20 years in Mexico (especially the state of Oaxaca) on popular religious practice and culture, social movements, progressive and conservative political currents within the Catholic Church, and more recent work on the Church's increasing recourse to media (television and Internet) in its evangelizing strategies, as focused on the celebration of the Feast day of the Virgin of Guadalupe in Mexico City. Thinking about the festival performance of the Virgin of Guadalupe in relation to literature on globalization, religion and media, the aesthetics and politics of culture and, more lately, on ideas of the baroque, has led me to fix on the neo-baroque as a fertile interpretive frame for elucidating key aspects of important political transformations underway both within the Church and in the manner in which religion and politics are intertwined in contemporary, twenty-first-century Mexico.

---

5   Mexico has the largest population of Catholics in the world behind Brazil. Of its estimated 102 million residents, 80 percent are Catholic.

276 *The Transatlantic Hispanic Baroque*

I argue that the purposeful, Church-sponsored neo-baroque, syncretic spectacles described above—rites aimed simultaneously at local audiences in Mexico and an international public viewing the event on television, the Internet, or through other visual media—demonstrate a conscious manipulation of images as mediations of Vatican power in Mexico and beyond (Norget, "Popes, Saints"). Indeed, the Church's eager embracing of television and new media technologies has expanded the possibilities for the *spectacular* effects of current Church evangelization strategies as they engage audiences in new ways and through now a multiplicity of platforms, surfaces, and spaces—material, digital, and imaginary. At the same time, Mexico's largest media conglomerates, Televisa and TVAzteca, jostle with each other over rights to air aspects of these public celebrations, only too conscious of the power of such Catholic ritual performances as means of legitimation and of bending the minds and hearts of the masses.

Mexico is known for the salience of such rituals in the everyday perpetuation of national identity and culture, including the high participation in the country in the rites of traditional Catholicism (Lomnitz, *Deep Mexico*; De la Torre). The pervasive organization of individual and collective life around Catholic rituals can be seen in the size of traditional cults and the majority devotion to Catholic symbols, such as the Virgin of Guadalupe at the national level, or of saints and virgins at the local level. Ritual practices surrounding saint cults, including pilgrimages, are still important performances of regional and national identity.

Awareness of the neo-baroque as a more encompassing aesthetic or "structure of feeling" (Williams, Ch. 9), however, demands an evaluation of the Church-sponsored ceremonies described above in the larger frame of the cultural dynamics of globalization. For these ritual performances are also part of a scale-making project (Tsing), concerned with collapsing distances of time and space in enactments of *localization*—here, the adaptation of universal doctrine and liturgy to the specificities of local cultural contexts (Norget, "Popes, Saints"). They illustrate the Church's mode of managing one of its central concerns: its self-affirmation as a unified global faith-community in today's world, in which the numerical force of Catholicism is no longer centered in Western Europe. This reality requires it to direct and assure the allegiance of potentially fragmenting particularities of local, peripheral Catholicisms—whether in places far from Rome (Mexico, Oaxaca) or close (Mexicans or other Latin Americans in Rome, etc.) at the same time as dramatizing a coherence and universalism (Norget, "Popes, Saints"). In keeping with the neo-baroque logic of the institutional Roman Catholic Church's contemporary project of a "new evangelization," also marking the ceremonies is a marked polycentrism: no longer centered in the Vatican nor aimed mainly at European audiences, these rites are part of a repertoire of practices that acknowledge the non-European, local cultures far from Rome, while signifying these as authentically *Catholic*.

Neo-Baroque Catholic Evangelism in Post-Secular Mexico 277

Thus, today's performances are singularly *neo-baroque*—much wider and more expansive in their terms of cultural reference, now multiple in the technologies and modes through which they are expressed and received, and emerging from fundamentally changed social and cultural conditions (Ndalianis 2).

Thus, although an officially secular country, the legitimation of the right of rule in Mexico relies on a convergence of baroque political and religious ritual—rites aimed, on the one hand, at an assertion of transcendent Truth and on the other, at the making of moral citizens. Indeed, it is precisely its "capacity to encompass coexisting and contrary associations" that makes the baroque useful for thinking about and describing such contradictions (Parkinson Zamora 134)—in a globalized, "post-secular" world, it is a political aesthetic *par excellence*. In such public performances in Mexico we behold a *mise-en-scène* of baroque sensibility: extravagant spectacle, sentimentality, illusionism, multi-temporality, allegory, "ethnic" hybridization, and other complexity accompany a potent admixture of nationalism and sacred devotion. I suggest that such legitimation strategies are part of a "new order" of Catholic Church governmentality, one that can settle quite comfortably within the complex neo-baroque folds of Mexican society and culture.

More generally, this chapter builds on the work of theorists who have underlined the Baroque as a productive frame of cultural analysis (e.g. Maravall; Buci-Glucksmann; Egginton), and in particular to recent work which argues that formal features of this current transhistorical aesthetic, especially as related to pivotal, changed social and economic factors unfolding over roughly the last three decades, are worth examining more carefully (Ndalianis; Calabrese; Deleuze). As Ndalianis explains, the baroque is its own complex system: not frozen or canonized as a style, it can be seen to travel through time, manifesting itself at significant historical junctures, moving through "new metamorphic states and cultural contexts" (7). Compared with post-modernism, the neo-baroque engages with particular historical and cultural contexts such as those of Latin America; in this way it distinguishes itself from most theoretical postcolonialisms (Parkinson Zamora 130). This power to illuminate cultural contextual specificity, emerges, as Maravall contends, from a particular kind of historical situation, that of social crisis and change (Ndalianis 14).

In today's Mexico, the neo-baroque encompasses the chaotic mixedness, dynamism, discordances and cultural hybridity evident throughout "postmodern" Mexico City (Monsiváis; Parkinson Zamora). As a more self-conscious political aesthetic "from below," it may also be seen in the evocative, sensually immediate neo-baroque paintings of Rigoberto A. Gonzalez that depict the gut-wrenching violence surrounding Mexico's drug trade, or even in the striking self-representational icons, graffiti, or narratives of contemporary movements like the EZLN (Ejercito Zapatista de Liberación Nacional) or the APPO (Asamblea Popular de los Pueblos de Oaxaca) (Norget,"Popes, Saints").

278   *The Transatlantic Hispanic Baroque*

But manifest in public arenas as a political or ideological instrument deployed "from above," one whose effects are now augmented by new mediatic forms, the neo-baroque captures the complexity of and preoccupation with a performative-spectacular artifice that works to paper over and reconcile—as if they are held in mystical abeyance—the glaring contradictions, violence, and disparities roiling the society from which it arises and which it shapes.

The Contemporary Neo-Baroque Roman Catholic Church

What I refer to as the "neo-baroque" Catholic Church is the outcome of the evolution of Church theology and doctrine over roughly the past century, and especially since the Second Vatican Council (1962–1965), which initiated a sea change in the Church's sense of itself in the contemporary world. The *aggiornamiento*, or updating of the Roman Catholic Church, represented by Vatican II and set in motion by John XXIII heralded finally the Church's engagement with the constitutional principle of religious freedom, and the separation of church and state. Historical-critical methodologies were the fruit of the emergence of a historical consciousness and the retrieval of a wider Catholic tradition. An openness to modernity was marked by a break with an authoritarian form of governance and the shift toward diverse expressions of Catholicism within a world-church. Post-conciliar reforms instated a new centripetal dynamic in theology and praxis as these were adapted to local and national conditions, partly through a new emphasis given to local churches and national conferences of bishops. An important concept born through this process was that of inculturation—"the process of adapting (without compromise) the Gospel and the Christian life to an individual [non-Christian] culture" (McBrien 1242)—which pointed to the Church's desires for a more dialogic interaction with "Other" cultural communities in the context of evangelization and missionization.

In Latin America, liberation theology pushed further Vatican II's decentralizing and relativizing thrust. Liberation theologians' Church of the Poor challenged the customary boundary between secular and sacred spheres, encouraging the insertion of clergy into the struggles and suffering of their communities, especially the impoverished and marginalized, including indigenous populations. This new paradigm of Church implicitly relocated the moral and authentic heart of Catholicism from the institution to the people and their historical, everyday struggles against the official forces of oppression (Napolitano and Norget). In places with a high native population such as southern Mexico, Indigenous Theology and the "Indigenous Pastoral" (*Pastoral Indígena*), which encouraged the marrying of Catholic doctrine and liturgy with indigenous languages, rites and senses of the sacred, represented progressivists' ideal of the inculturation of the faith (Norget, "Knowing").

Over time, however, the progressive theological principles born from Vatican II and which inspired certain dynamic clergy all over Latin America, including Mexico, engendered divisions within the ranks of the Church with regard to views of the Church's proper role in Mexican society. From the beginning of his papacy in 1978, for example, Pope John Paul II made efforts to restore the authority and moral doctrines of the pre-Vatican II era. Such a philosophy shaped his speeches during his many visits to Mexico, where on more than one occasion he openly denounced liberation theology. Since John Paul II's pontificate, in fact, the theme of the Roman Catholic Church's global rhetoric aimed at reinvigorating Catholics' faith has been that of a "new evangelization"—a serious re-engagement with Catholic scripture and doctrine that emphasizes unity, solidarity, and homogeneity. The Pope's efforts to reign in Catholic doctrine were a response to the push toward "vernacular" interpretations of Catholic identity and doctrine unleashed in the wake of Vatican II. Within this effort at a reinvigoration and standardization of Catholic faith, liberation theology and indigenous theology are regarded as threatening this call for a return to the pillars of doctrine. At the same time that progressivists can be seen to push the relativism that the concept implies to its limits, conservatives have seized upon the notion of inculturation for the sake of courting local cultures. Thus, today a much diluted version of "indigenous theology" is touted by the conservative (i.e. Vatican-aligned) leadership of the Mexican Bishops Council (CEM) as the central theme of pastoral ("evangelization") plans that are seen as leading toward a new rapprochement and engagement with indigenous peoples.

Within the wider campaign of the New Evangelization, the last four decades at least, the Holy See has deployed an array of strategies—for example, closer papal control over the nomination of bishops, the fostering of new conservative, transnational, lay ecclesial movements (e.g. Opus Dei, the Charismatic Catholic Renewal, Legionaries of Christ),[6] and an upsurge, especially outside of Europe, in the number of beatifications and canonizations—"saint-making"—and a spectacularization of certain Church events (e.g. the Pope's international tours, canonizations, Catholic World Youth Days) as means of maintaining its social and moral authority and global presence. Backlash reforms, beginning during the papacy of John Paul II, are thriving in similar and even new forms under Benedict XVI. José Casanova has referred to these as part of a "re-Romanization" of world Catholicism and an internationalization of Rome (i.e. the Vatican)

---

[6]   Opus Dei, the reactionary clandestine political and theological organization originating in Franco's Spain, and the ultra-conservative Legionaries of Christ, for example, were openly supported by John Paul II, and have been strongly promoted by Benedict XVI.

280   *The Transatlantic Hispanic Baroque*

itself (Casanova, "Globalizing"; see also Jenkins).[7] In the context of the rapidly expanding populations of Catholics in Africa, Asia, and Latin America, this new economy of sanctity (Napolitano and Norget) also shows a quite baroque preoccupation with place-making images as mediations of institutional Catholic Church identity and power.

Thus, a renewed emphasis in the Vatican's current public performances on relics, images, emotional excess, and spectacle rehearse a late-medieval, baroque style of Christendom when the Church was focused on a "rhetoric of immediacy" (Morgan 65)—that is, techniques for eliciting from believers emotional and sensational reactions, and converting their engagement with the sacred into an arguably more visual and Church-dependent experience. Indeed, Casanova ("Globalizing"; "Religion") argues that from the middle of the nineteenth century to today, one can track the emergence of the transnational characteristics of medieval Christendom that had nearly disappeared or weakened in the early modern era: papal supremacy and centralization and internationalization of the Church government, the convocation of ecumenical councils, transnational religious cadres, missionary activity; transnational schools, centers of learning and international networks; shrines as centers of pilgrimage and international encounters; transnational religious movements such as the Charismatic Catholic Renewal (Csordas).

These aesthetics of current Vatican practice hark back to the nature of piety during the baroque era of the seventeenth century, the onset of which coincided with the defensive campaigns of the triumphal Roman Catholic Church of the Counter-Reformation. As encapsulated by the Council of Trent (1545–1563) and the Holy Inquisition, the Counter-Reformation was infused with a fresh zeal for the faith in the face of a perceived decadent Europe, and the appearance of a distinctly more actively authoritarian and controlling Church obsessed with control and a kind of rationalization of the faith. Following Council of Trent reforms, in line with a new "pedagogy of the sacred" (Gruzinski, *Images*), clergy in New Spain began to eagerly promote saint cults, colorful images, extravagant and lush demonstrations of wealth and beauty in churches, the recitation in unison of prayers and doctrine, and feast day celebrations (Taylor 48–9).[8] These "externals" of faith were part of the crystallization of a distinctly *baroque* Catholicism that "stressed the pathos rather than the ethos of religion" (Taylor 48).

---

[7]   Casanova observes that this has been combined with an increasing centralization of Churches at the national level ("Globalizing" 135).

[8]   In 1563, in the Council of Trent's 25th and last session, the medieval doctrines of purgatory, the invocation of saints and the veneration of relics were re-avowed, as was the efficacy of indulgences as dispensed by the Church, although not without some caveats (and despite harsh opposition by reformist bishops).

Today, a preoccupation with the centralization of the neo-baroque Church is seen in a new focus on the personage and image of the Pope as the embodiment of Vatican authority.[9] The renewed Vatican fixation on saints and saint-making can also be seen as part of this fomenting of emotional connection with larger, more encompassing community or religious regime. In fact, a notable post-Vatican II shift in institutional Church teachings has moved the focus of devotion from Christ to the invocation of the saints. Saints here are regarded as means of swaying God's sympathy by calling on their example, marking a change in the influence on the "subjective dispositions" of worshippers (Morgan 142). During the papacy of John Paul II and continuing under Benedict XVI, saint-making has become more and more common. As I have discussed elsewhere (Norget, "Popes, Saints"), the current upsurge in canonizations and beatifications forms part of a "war of images" (Gruzinski, *Images*) and a localizing praxis of emplacement deployed to maintain peripheral populations (i.e. vis-à-vis Rome) within the Catholic Church's paternalistic fold of social and moral authority and influence, at the same time as the institution is seen to remain seemingly open to local diverse cultures and realities.

Pope John Paul II beatified more martyrs and canonized more saints than all his twentieth-century predecessors combined—including Mother Teresa and, two months after Juan Diego was made a saint, the founder of the conservative movement Opus Dei, Josemaría Escrivá de Balaguer. The canonization of Escrivá, beatified a mere 17 years after his death, was one of the first to be processed after John Paul II reformed the church's Code of Canon Law in 1983, which streamlined the process of sainthood.[10] Mexico has seen a special intensity in the Church's rate of beatifications and canonizations, especially in the present decade: in 2001, 25 Mexican martyrs of the Cristero Revolution from the state of Jalisco were beatified, then again, in 2005, this time by Pope Benedict, 13 more. Benedict has decentralized beatifications, now allowing the ceremony to take place in the country where the martyrs lived, thus allowing for such carefully programmed performances of a localization of the faith to be experienced by home-grown audiences (Norget, "Popes, Saints").[11]

---

[9]   Casanova identifies the papacy as the transnational core of the Church's new "regime" in the new global system, as expressed in widely disseminated papal encyclicals dealing with secular issues in addition to Catholic faith, the pope's increasingly active and vocal role in international politics, and his public visibility as the supreme moral watchdog and defender of universal human rights and the sacred dignity of the human person ("Globalizing" 122).

[10]   These reforms effectively expedited the labor-intensive, highly bureaucratic process. For example, John Paul eliminated the so-called "devil's advocate" position from the investigating process. This person's job was to attack the evidence in favor of canonization (CBC News 2011).

[11]   The ceremony took place in Guadalajara, Mexico. The martyrs—three priests and ten lay people—were killed during religious persecutions in Mexico during the 1920s. Such

282 *The Transatlantic Hispanic Baroque*

The emotionally evocative, material accent in the Church's new evangelization strategy is exemplified by the preoccupation with saintly relics and their recruitment in the project of localization. Months after John Paul II was beatified in 2011 by his successor Benedict XVI in Rome, his relics (a glass vial containing the Pope's blood, a wax effigy of John Paul, and various personal objects: his mitre, some shoes and other clothing) were first displayed at the Basilica of Guadalupe, then for the next four months travelled to over a hundred different cities and towns throughout Mexico. Like the national tours of entertainment stars or prominent politicians, each stage of the journey was a regularly featured segment on the local and national television news.

As papal blood and body (i.e. the pontiff's relics) are enlisted, in rather sensational fashion, to feed national and local faith in Mexico, on other occasions the "localization" of universal Catholic faith draws thirstily on the flavours and inflections of local cultures, including indigenousness. The canonization ceremony of Juan Diego and beatification of the Martyrs of Cajonos illustrate the particular way indigenous culture is incorporated into the Church's new evangelization. To illustrate, virtually all elements of the ceremony's "native" character—the participants' dress, the dancing, the traditional instruments and music, the indigenous *limpia* or cleansing—had been scripted, the creative addition of Italian Archbishop Piero Marini, since 1987 the official Master of Pontifical Liturgical Celebrations at the Holy See (and head of the Office for the Liturgical Celebrations of the Supreme Pontiff), which organizes all liturgies celebrated by the Pope, including canonizations and beatifications. Promoting "a progressive liturgical vision of worship that is dynamic, participatory, and shaped by local culture" (Allen 62), Marini had adopted the most aesthetically appealing aspects of native culture, with little concern over their origins. The result was a complex collation of Catholic liturgical staples with "authentic" native folkloric elements whose "ethnic" signification was emblematic and nonspecific—all within an explicitly official Catholic frame. The ceremony was thus conspicuously "inculturated,"[12] an apparent celebration of indigenous culture, yet one in which the troubling Otherness of that culture had been thoroughly tamed (Norget, "Popes, Saints").

---

group canonizations and beatifications are becoming more common. In 2007, Benedict set a Church record by approving the beatification of 498 Spanish Martyrs, priests murdered at the hands of Republicans during the Spanish civil war.

[12] As Allen notes, John Paul II developed the teachings of Vatican II that recognized the "truth and grace" of other religions; yet the former Pope espoused the view "that God, through the person of the Holy Spirit, 'inspires' at least some elements of other religions" (Allen, "Inculturation at Papal Masses")—a position that implies the Catholic "Truth" still trumps any other.

A Mediatic Church

Such developments in the Catholic Church's "pedagogy of the sacred" that have augmented its visual and emotional appeal have also opened the door for a more ready collusion between mediatization and evangelization. In the last decade especially, the Church in Latin America has attempted to reinforce its evangelization strategies through coverage and promotion of its teachings, events and activities on the Internet, television, video, radio, and other media forms (e.g. newspaper advertisements, posters, billboards, and comic books) (Zires, "Los mitos"; "Nuevas imágenes").

In Mexico, approximately 15 percent of Mexicans remain illiterate—a figure rising to roughly 30 percent in indigenous communities. This situation makes television in the country a powerful medium of communication. Roughly 87 percent of the national population had access to television in their homes in 1990 (Brown and Sighal); a figure that has undoubtedly grown since then. While the proportion of the national population that regular accesses the Internet still remains smaller, this situation too is quickly transforming. Meanwhile, Televisa and TVAzteca, the biggest national channels, regularly promote Church-sponsored events, or devote hours of coverage to religious spectacles like the recent tour of the effigy and relics of the late Pope John-Paul II discussed above (Indexmundi). Catholic agencies and companies (e.g. Guadalupe Communicaciones, the Pontifical Mission Societies) have arisen over the past years, and busily produce documentaries, films, and videos for various television channels, and for the Archdiocese of Mexico for broadcast on its website. Multimedia channels such as MonteMaría Television, Galavisión, and EWTN-Televisión Católica, all based in Mexico City, transmit coverage of such ceremonies and other Catholic programming throughout Mexico, Latin America, and internationally.

In the Virgin of Guadalupe's feast day celebration that I witnessed in Mexico City in December 2011, television cameras were positioned in the best, most strategic spots in the Basilica, often obstructing the view of members of the live audience. During Pope Benedict XVI's recent first visit (March 2012) to Guanajuato, Mexico, over a dozen television cameras covered every aspect of his celebration of Mass. In short, it is easy to see that it is not just evangelical Christian Churches in the country that are exploiting media for evangelization purposes.

Far beyond straightforward efforts at spreading the (Catholic) Word, these televised Catholic ritual spectacles are also aimed at a different kind of engagement of Catholic viewers. I witnessed a rehearsal of the visual spectacularity of this evangelistic aesthetic in December of 2012, at the celebration of the Virgin of Guadalupe festival in Mexico City. Inside the Basilica the solemnity of official liturgy mixed with, yet clearly dominated, the color and creative spontaneity of popular devotion. In coverage of the mass on the largest television channels

284   *The Transatlantic Hispanic Baroque*

(Televisa and TV-Azteca) this dynamic was accentuated with a careful inter-collation of images from both "inside" and "outside," drawing on the spirit of sacrifice, self-abnegation and passionate devotion—and even raw, periodic unruliness—of popular practices into the frame of the Church's carefully regulated, elaborate liturgy within the Basilica.

In this light, we can begin to recognize canonizations/beatifications and Church-sponsored saint celebrations as multi-faceted political rituals, orchestrating a multitude of sentiments in a solemn yet sensationally forceful display of Vatican presence. With the help of the media, these events, multi-sited or translocal but also multi-temporal in their referents—Oaxaca, Mexico, Rome; the past, the present, the [ideal] future—may reach the same, and new, audiences, engaging them in novel ways. Thus, while the mass dedicated to the Virgin in Mexico City moves back and forth between carefully selected and manipulated scenes within and outside of the Basilica de Guadalupe (e.g. visibly fatigued pilgrims approaching the Basilica on their knees; images of the crowd in the plaza outside, including close-ups of people weeping with devotion—all accompanied by the angelic voices of the boys' choir on the altar), imagery and comments accompanying the Virgin's other mass in St Peter's Basilica shift fluidly between Rome and the Americas (this mass is covered by Galavisión, a channel also owned by Televisa).

Additionally, in a manner "abjuring diachronic history" (Parkinson Zamora 130), hagiographies of the Virgin and Juan Diego are narrated in the coverage of both masses as self-evident historic "facts," images from the saints' (constructed) pasts interspersed with live images from the masses. Similarly, pre-recorded coverage of soap opera and other stars of Televisa or Azteca who are dressed in "folkloric" (Indian) garb and singing melodramatically before the Virgin's image (seemingly, quite strikingly, as if to a lover) serves as the "warm-up" act for the (live) coverage of the mass itself, thereby blurring the two separate events into one. References to the Virgin heard in the songs or in the sentimental discourses of the event's television commentators name her "La Morena," "Mi Madre Querida," "Mi Cariño," "Mi Salvadora"; this register of passionate, maternal/romantic affect underlines the event's ornate pathos, an apotheosis of a primordial, *pure*, unquestioning devotion free of the taint of worldly events or related worries or cynicism that these usually connote elsewhere in the media or in the public sphere.

At the same time in the rites one can observe the rationalizing, didactic thrust so characteristic of the Church's "new" evangelization: For example, with the help of his co-host, a heavily made-up, telegenic Mexican television personality, the Bishop-commentator of the St Peter's Basilica mass explains the roles and functions of the various positions in each ranks in the ecclesiastic hierarchy as he might the positions of players on a football field, making the Church less mysterious and more comprehensible to viewers. During close-up shots of members of the congregation receiving communion, the Bishop gushes his enthusiasm that media has been incorporated into the service so that the ceremony may reach even people who cannot leave their homes: "During service people are free to kneel and so can participate in the mass—like any Sunday—even though they are elsewhere," and thereby become "one pilgrim more!" (*un peregrino más*).

An intimacy and immediacy were being conjured here, yet also an exclusion. For the Church was in charge, and during its earnest explanations a certain idealized mode of Catholic piety was being encouraged and imparted. As the Church had the power to exclude certain devotees from the Basilica to witness the actual mass, so too certain kinds of Catholics did not "belong" in the implied audience of reference within the coverage of the local-international mass in St Peter's Basilica. Indeed, these masses were pieces in a larger project of Catholic subject-making that has extensions outside of what are ostensibly the official confines of the institutional Church.

Conclusion

In their multi-temporal and multi-sited character, a fixation on the vibrant details of "ethnic" and other cultural signification, visual theatricality, sensorial allure, and other details of spectacle encompassed within an explicitly formal and elaborate liturgical frame, the Roman Catholic Church's contemporary evangelization rites are well equipped for all-out "shock-and-awe" assault meant to impact on Catholic believers in new ways that shape their senses of themselves as both Catholics and as Mexicans.

This aesthetic is reminiscent of the defensive posture of the seventeenth-century baroque Catholic Church which, similar to today, used its powerful aesthetic of baroque triumphalism to represent itself as a bastion of a morality and universal Truth in the face of post-Reformation challenges to its religious hegemony. Today, at this point in the twenty-first century, the Church is undergoing a radical revisionism propelled by Rome, intended to rein in the significant "progressive" transformations (e.g. theological pluralism and relativism, trends toward a decentralization of authority) initiated by Vatican II. This can be seen, for instance, in the particular way that "culture" is managed within the Church, and the techniques and technologies the Church deploys for the communication and material, sensory localization and emplacement of faith.

The illusion mentioned earlier of an inert indigenousness within performances of the Church's "new evangelization" underlies a particular allegorical narrative that makes clear the terms of legibility of the expressions of indigeneity appearing in many of the rites I have described. The Zapotec Martyrs of Cajonos of Oaxaca, for example, were beatified for their role, in

286   *The Transatlantic Hispanic Baroque*

1700, in disclosing to local Catholic officials the "idolatrous" practices of some of their neighbors, a deed for which they were subsequently lynched by their fellow townsfolk—that is, their kin. With their beatification the Martyrs were re-signified as authentic products *and* defenders of the true, live, word of God. The original violence of the colonial project itself, the violence enacted on the bodies of the Martyrs, and then on their fellows accused of their murder (who were tried and then cruelly killed by the Spanish) become sublimated, enfolded into a moral Christian teleology. Beatified, the Martyrs become newly remade indigenous Catholic subjects, different from other (non-Catholic) indigenous and different from other Catholics, and yet members of the same single timeless global Catholic public (Norget, "Popes, Saints"). In this Church narrative the terms and dynamic of the Conquest are summarily whitewashed: instead of colonization and its accompanying arm of evangelization marking a cultural rupture, a site of oppression, the Church has fashioned itself as the eternal mother that can save Latin America, especially its most historically marginalized and oppressed.

Similar efforts to appropriate and control elements of popular or indigenous culture smacking of an independent creative spirit or other agendas are evident in the live celebration and in television coverage of the Virgin of Guadalupe's feast day centered in the Virgin's Basilica in Mexico City, and in coverage of the mass in St Peter's Basilica in Rome. In Mexico City, the Church's Basilica-focused celebration can be seen to claim the popular aspects of the feast day in the plaza (showing its own hybridized "baroque-from-below")—the massive throngs of pilgrims, encampments, dance troupes; the cacophony of noise; the brash commercialism in the market stalls or *tiainguis* that align the plaza selling statuettes, t-shirts, globes and so on bearing the Virgin's image—as reflections of a kind of primordial and authentic Catholic devotion enacted on an extension of the Basilica's stage, while recognizing that it is unable to discipline or control completely the boisterous, disorderly aspects of the popular celebration.

Meanwhile, the Vatican ceremony is a "creole" one, explicitly ethnically marked, apparently referring to Latin America, and yet a highly idealized and homogenized version of the continent. Thus, this ceremony privileges a folkloric, generic Latin America: indigenous, black, colorful and spicy; quaint, innocent, gentle, naïve. Cultural asymmetries loom large in this performance, most obviously given by the clear paternalistic dialectic repeatedly expressed between Mexico (City) and Rome (the Vatican), a site with its own resonances of Empire. These rites demonstrate several boundary transversals: national borders, "ethnic" categories and, as mentioned earlier, conventional temporal categories. Like other inculturated ceremonies I have discussed in this chapter, this "creole" rite also encompasses the classical theological dialectic between transcendence and immanence intrinsic to Roman Catholic doctrine and to the Church's very identity: the Church presents itself as timeless and omnipotent, capable of being at once everywhere—transcendent, omnipresent—and of being in *specific* locations, acknowledging, *representing* local(ity), cultural contexts and histories. Responding perhaps to the *horror vacui* given by constant news and images presenting an external world rent by violence, poverty and hunger, and the ills of feminism, homosexuality and the erosion of the traditional family, and general spiritual and moral bankruptcy, in these ceremonies every space—auditory, visual, emotional—is filled.

We must remember that current baroque strategies of the Catholic Church are profoundly different from former ones, shaped in part by multimedia interests and new digital technology that have expanded the possibilities for evangelization and the boundaries of the imaginaries of individual Catholics. As Ndalianis notes, today's neo-baroque involves the visual, the auditory and the textual in forms connotative of the dynamism of seventeenth-century baroque form, but that dynamism is expressed today in technologically and culturally different ways (4). In Mexico, the collusion of mass media channels and Church in the transmission of certain prominent rituals such as canonizations and saint celebrations allows for an even more controlled, forceful programmatic presentation of the Church's intended message. At the same time, the post-secular Mexican state can draw on the Church's continued power and moral authority by identifying itself, now quite unapologetically, with certain aspects of the Church's evangelizing agenda.

At the same time, following Victor Turner's well-known writings concerning the liminal properties of ritual, I believe that in their visual and sentimental extravagance we can see such events as collaborating in the creation of an ideal, subjunctive reality; a proposition for another order—whether in Mexico or in the world at large—in which (a Vatican-directed) Catholic morality is restored to its former hegemony and thereby forming the central cohering thread in the social and cultural fabric of formerly Catholic nations. Lomnitz has discussed the particular historicity of contemporary Mexico (one felt most acutely during the seemingly endless economic "crisis" characterizing the 1980s) as being one of "present saturation" ("Times" 134)—a kind of suspension in time or by paralysis induced in people by the interruption of the relevance of learned past expectations (such as those of hard work being rewarded by some—even if chronically insufficient—remuneration), and the erosion of hope in the future. Lomnitz explains that anxiety and insecurity produced by such a situation require a kind of way of bridging private hopes and the reality narrated elsewhere in the public domain of a futility in efforts to control the nation's (or one's own) fate. It is this sense of present saturation—a particular kind of pervasive collective sensibility characterized by a profoundly felt insecurity, frustration and seeming hopelessness—that I believe can highlight the significance of the Catholic Church's deeply enchanting neo-baroque spectacles.

288   *The Transatlantic Hispanic Baroque*

Present-day Mexico is dominated by images and messages of the mounting horrors of narco-violence, environmental destruction, political Machiavellianism and corruption at all levels of government, chronic inflation and economic uncertainty—all of which only serve to further erode the classic post-revolutionary nationalist narratives of modernity that promised (universal) "progress" as inevitable: whereas it seems that hope can no longer be rightly pinned to customary secular discourses of nationalism, in today's context the possibility for messianic redemption is alive and well in hybrid, sacred figures like the Virgin of Guadalupe, and in other saints and *beatos* like Juan Diego, the Martyrs of Cajonos—and even in non-indigenous yet eminently popular saints such as the Martyrs of the Cristero War, or even, though in a less localized fashion, by new saint-in-the-making, Pope John Paul II. Couched in impressive neo-baroque ritual guise—elaborate, carefully coordinated simulacra of a concerted Catholic Church reality—these saints become mediating symbols for the projection and negotiation of social concerns and problems that cannot be addressed elsewhere. (As Bishop Enrique Glennie, Rector of the Basilica of Guadalupe, underlined during a television broadcast of the Mexico City celebration of the Virgin's mass, "La Virgen está en cualquier casa mexicana"). Thus, during the celebration, "La Guadalupana" becomes a lightning rod of the nation's current fears; she is the consummate martyr, an allegory of sacrifice on the national stage of the Basilica, which itself is transported via television and other media onto several other stages, into other imaginaries. The discourses that erupt around the brown Virgin's celebration are those that underscore her transcendent, nurturing, healing role, and the centrality of the Catholic Church as a key harmonizing agent for Mexican society—organic to Mexican society and culture, and the necessary, nay, perhaps the only, salve for all ills. She is, in short, the future itself.

Bibliography

Allen Jr, John L. "Inculturation at Papal Masses; Maciel gets Front-Row Seat; Next, Poland and St Faustina." *National Catholic Reporter* 1.50 (August 2002). May 13, 2013. <http://www.nationalcatholicreporter.org/word/pfw0809.htm>.

———. *All the Pope's Men: The Inside Story of How the Vatican Really Thinks.* New York: Doubleday, 2004.

Brown, William J., and Arvind Sighal. "Ethical Dilemmas of Prosocial Television." *Communication Quarterley* 38.3 (1990): 268–80.

Buci-Glucksmann, Christine. *Baroque Reason: The Aesthetics of Modernity.* Trans. Patrick Camiller. London: Sage, 1994.

Calabrese, Omar. *Neo-Baroque: A Sign of the Times.* Princeton: Princeton University Press, 1992.

Casanova, José. "Globalizing Catholicism and the Return to a 'Universal' Church." *Transnational Religion and Fading States.* Ed. Suzanne Hoeber Rudolph and James Piscatori. Boulder, CO: Westview, 1997. 121–43.

———. "Religion, the New Millennium, and Globalization." *Sociology of Religion* 62 (2001): 415–41.

Csordas, Thomas. "Global Religion and the Reenchantment of the World: The Case of the Charismatic Catholic Renewal." *Anthropological Theory* 7 (2007): 295–314.

De la Torre, Renée. "Religión y cultura de masas. La lucha por el monopolio de la religiosidad contemporánea." *Revista Comunicación y Sociedad* 27 (1996): 161–98.

Deleuze, Gilles. *The Fold: Liebnitz and the Baroque.* Minneapolis, MN: University of Minnesota Press, 1992.

Egginton, William. *The Theatre of Truth: The Ideology of (Neo)Baroque Aesthetics.* Stanford, CA: Stanford University Press, 2010.

González Torres, Yolotl. *Danza tu palabra: la danza de los concheros.* Mexico, DF: Plaza y Valdés, 2005.

Gruzinski, Serge. *Images at War: Mexico from Columbus to Blade Runner (1492–2019).* Trans. Heather MacLean. Durham, NC: Duke University Press, 2001.

———. *The Mestizo Mind: The Intellectual Dynamics of Colonization and Globalization.* Trans. Deke Dusinberre. New York: Routledge, 2002.

Hernandez, Danya P. "Artist Rigoberto A. Gonzalez Paints Mexico Drug Violence Baroque-Style." *Borderzine: Reporting Across Fronteras.* April 22, 2011. September 20, 2012. <http://borderzine.com/2011/04/artist-rigoberto-a-gonzalez-paints-mexico-drug-violence-baroque-style>.

Indexmundi. "Mexico Literacy." July 8, 2012. <http://www.indexmundi.com/mexico/literacy.html>.

Jenkins, Philip. *The Next Christendom: The Coming of Global Christianity.* Revised and expanded edition. New York, NY: Oxford University Press, 2007.

Lomnitz, Claudio. *Exits from the Labyrinth: Culture and Ideology in the Mexican National Space.* Berkeley: University of California Press, 1992.

———. *Deep Mexico, Silent Mexico: An Anthropology of Nationalism.* Minneapolis, MN: University of Minnesota Press, 2001.

———. "Times of Crisis: Historicity, Sacrifice, and the Spectacle of Debacle in Mexico City." *Public Culture* 15.1 (2003): 127–47.

Maravall, José Antonio. *Culture of the Baroque: Analysis of a Historical Structure.* Minneapolis, MN: University of Minnesota Press, 1986.

McBrien, Richard P. *Catholicism.* New York: Harper Collins, 1994.

Monsiváis, Carlos. "The Neobaroque and Popular Culture." Trans. James Ramey. *Publications of the Modern Languages Association* 124.1 (2009): 118–88.

Morgan, David. *Visual Piety: A History and Theory of Popular Religious Images.* Berkeley: University of California Press, 1998.

Napolitano, Valentina and Kristin Norget. "Introduction. Economies of Sanctity: The Translocal Roman Catholic Church in Latin America." *Postscripts* 5.3 (2009): 251–64.

Ndalianis, Angela. *Neo-Baroque Aesthetics and Contemporary Entertainment.* Cambridge: MIT Press, 2004.

Norget, Kristin. "'Knowing Where We Enter': Indigenous Theology and the Catholic Church in Oaxaca, México." *Resurgent Voice in Latin America: Indigenous Peoples, Political Mobilization, and Religious Change.* Ed. Edward Cleary and Tim Steigenga. New Brunswick, NJ: Rutgers University Press, 2004. 154–86.

———. *Days of Death, Days of Life: Ritual in the Popular Culture of Oaxaca.* New York: Columbia University Press, 2006.

———. "Popes, Saints, *Beato* Bones and other Images at War: Religious Mediation and the Translocal Roman Catholic Church." *Postscripts* 5.3 (2009): 337–64.

———. "Ché, Stalin and the Virgin of Guadalupe: New Aesthetics of Popular Protest in Mexico." Paper presented at the Annual Meeting of the American Anthropological Association, New Orleans (November 17–21, 2010).

Parkinson Zamora, Lois "New World Baroque, Neobaroque, Brut Barroco: Latin American Postcolonialisms." *Publication of the Modern Languages Association* 124.1 (January 2009): 127–42.

Rostas, Susana. *Carrying the Word: The Concheros Dance in Mexico City.* Boulder, CO: University of Colorado Press, 2009.

Taylor, William B. *Magistrates of the Sacred: Priests and Parishioners in Eighteenth-Century Mexico.* Stanford, CA: Stanford University Press, 1996.

Tsing, Anna. *Friction: An Ethnography of Global Connection.* Princeton: Princeton University Press, 2005.

Villamil, Jenaro. "Medios electrónicos volvieron a promover el papacentrismo." *La Jornada*, August 2, 2002.

Williams, Raymond. *Marxism and Literature.* Marxist Introductions Series. London and New York: Oxford University Press, 1977.

Zires, Margarita. "Los mitos de la Virgen de Guadalupe, su proceso de construcción y reinterpretación en el México pasado y contemporáneo."*Mexican Studies/ Estudios Mexicanos* 10.2 (1994): 281–313.

———. "Nuevas imágenes guadalupanas. Diferentes límites del decir guadalupano en México y Estados Unidos." *Comunicación y Sociedad* 38 (2002): 59–76.

Chapter 16

La Fiesta de Santo Tomás as a Technology of Culture: Memory, Carnival, and Syncretism in the Modern Guatemalan Identity

Anabel Quan-Haase and Kim Martin

Introduction

La Fiesta de Santo Tomás of Chichicastenango, Guatemala, represents an opportunity to study two aspects of the emergence of the Hispanic Baroque: first, it allows for an examination of the ways that different forms of representation reflect modes of domination. We employ Bakhtin's theory of the carnivalesque to examine how the fiesta portrays, questions, and reverses power struggles stemming from Guatemala's colonial reality, hacienda work relations, and immigration that continue to shape Guatemalan modern identity. The second aspect of the Hispanic Baroque that La Fiesta de Santo Tomás allows us to trace and assess is the process of syncretism and cultural parallelism between various social and ethnic groups in modern Guatemala. This chapter will argue that the festival serves as a technology of culture, as it embodies and perpetuates past traditions and belief systems that continue to co-exist during the festival in a modern city.

Of great importance to the understanding of the Hispanic Baroque has been the theorizing around how cultural diversity emerges from the coming together of the pre-Columbian world with the Spanish colonial cultural, political, and religious system in what is referred to as the First Transatlantic Culture. Despite the fact that "the concepts and ideology of the conquistadores were the mold in which Indian concepts and ideas were reshaped" (Hawkins 23), the diverse and varied reality that the Spaniards encountered in the Atlantic world created a complex and unpredictable cultural system. We employ the example of Chichicastenango as a means to further question how the process of syncretism takes place and to show its continued relevance in modern Guatemala as a means for identity formation, expression, and contention.

292 *The Transatlantic Hispanic Baroque*

The Hispanic Baroque has often been misrepresented by historians and anthropologists because it lacked the adequate technologies to represent its own voice. Compared to the historiography of Europe or North America, there are few written texts, maps, or even government documents that act as witness to the changes that occurred during the colonial era (Hawkins 40). Quoting Robert Carmack, Lovell writes in *Conquest and Survival in Colonial Guatemala* about how "highland Guatemala is a region particularly rich in documentary source material, and abjectly poor in bibliographic organization and reconstructive syntheses" (7). This shows that most of the sources that exist provide only limited insight into the historical, social, and cultural processes of this region. There are two reasons for this lack of accessibility to the Hispanic Baroque culture, in particular from the perspective of the Maya. The first is power relations, as friars or others in a position of religious or political power often wrote about an indigenous culture that they did not participate in, and perhaps also did not understand. Second is the lack of tools that were available through which local culture could be recorded, systematized, analyzed, and preserved.

One set of tools that has been largely overlooked is the expression of lasting customs and power relations in festivals as a technology of culture. It is perhaps a stretch to refer to a festival as a technology, but it is argued in this chapter that the metaphor of the "technology of culture" (Suárez) provides a research tool to investigate how various cultural elements have come together and their social, historical, and political value. Shea tells us that Guatemalan festivals are "an important source of information, as most of the economic and social activities of a community are integrated into the festival" (38). As technologies of culture, these festivals are rich sources of information about the encoding in dance, music, dress, and social practice. Culture is understood here as "a mechanism of adaptation, and as a set of technologies that allows for the visualization of the complexity that human life keeps creating" (Suárez 35).

The study of how memory, the carnival, and syncretism all shape the modern Guatemalan identity cannot be undertaken without careful consideration of how various cultural, religious, and social practices come together. Suarez has emphasized how the emerging of the First Transatlantic Culture "has to take into account both the American and the European dimension of the phenomenon, and, above all, must describe the results of the encounter of these two regions over time" (Suárez 35). The time component is often neglected in studies of syncretism and will be at the forefront of this investigation. Similarly, Lovell reflects on how nothing about the modern state of Guatemala is post-colonial: "How Guatemala operates, how its resources are appropriated, exploited, and profited from, how its ethnic groups relate and coexist in a troubled nation state, how its Maya peoples (those of the Cuchumatán highlands a dozen or so among 20) endured assaults on their land and their lives in the nineteenth and twentieth centuries to sustain a presence in the twenty-first—these elemental

Memory, Carnival, and Syncretism in the Modern Guatemalan Identity   293

characteristics register full only when viewed in colonial perspective" (Lovell 199). Don Severo, a Guatemalan historian, writes "Colonial reality is our everyday reality" (Lovell 199). Thus, in order to understand the meaning of the Fiesta de Santo Tomás, it is necessary to look at phenomena as they unfold in modern Guatemala with a clear understanding of the complex history that gives meaning to these events.

Chichicastenango

Chichicastenango is a medium-sized town of about 120,000 inhabitants in the highlands of Guatemala.[1] The city itself is located in the *departamento* of Quiché at an altitude of 6,500 feet, high in the Sierra Madre mountain range. The Quiché and the Cakchiquel[2] had been involved in rigorous fighting over this territory as it was a central trading point between various indigenous groups. As a result of the existing rivalry, both indigenous groups were defeated by the Spaniards with the help of the Aztecs around the 1520s (Shea 3). Chichicastenango was then re-settled as a town serving primarily the political interests of the Spaniards. The town is also known as the village of Santo Tomás and it was run by Dominican missionaries from the 1530s onwards.

Chichicastenango has great relevance to the Quiché and the Cakchiquel because the sacred book, the Popol Vuh, was discovered in this area. The Popol Vuh is central to the Mayan cosmovision because it narrates the origins of the human species. This book was originally translated by Francisco Ximénez, a friar, and provides insight into the pre-Columbian[3] belief system of the Maya.

The large majority of inhabitants of Chichicastenango are of Quiché origins, with also a percentage of Ladino population. Ladinos live primarily in the city of Chichicastenango and the indigenous population is spread in the surrounding areas. About 55 to 65 percent of Guatemala's population is indigenous, second in size only to Bolivia's in all of Latin America. The distinction between indigenous groups, such as Quiché, Cakchiquel, etc., and Ladino is primarily based on ethnic backgrounds and self-identification. Despite the large indigenous population, Ladinos have ruled the government in Guatemala since the early nineteenth century.[4]

---

[1]   Census information in Guatemala is very inaccurate; therefore the population estimate is imprecise. This results from problems with conducting the census in these areas.

[2]   There exists some variation in the spelling, such as Kaqchikeles.

[3]   We define the pre-Columbian era as all periods in the history and prehistory of the Americas that precedes any significant European influence. Related terms are pre-colonial Americas.

[4]   Shea discusses the social and political ramifications of the distinction between Maya and Ladino. She writes: "Most Guatemalans have a mix of Mayan and Spanish book to

294 *The Transatlantic Hispanic Baroque*

Because of its rich cultural heritage, Chichicastenango has received considerable interest from anthropologists, primarily in the 1930s and 1940s. The town can be described as a typical colonial settlement with cobblestone streets, stucco-white houses, a central plaza with two churches, a town hall (*municipalidad*), and marketplace. Chichicastenango has become known nationally and internationally because of its large, diverse, and colorful market, which takes place on Thursdays, Sundays, and holidays. Its layout follows the traditional composition with the plaza at the center, surrounded by the Catholic church (la Iglesia de Santo Tomás) on the south west side, the town hall next to the church on the west side, the church (la Iglesia Capilla) on the opposite side of the plaza (south east), and the museum on the south (Shea 25).

The Marketplace

The marketplace in Chichicastenango is the heart of the town and was established adjacent to the ancient Cakchiquel temple as is the case in many towns established during the colonial era (see Hutson). Unlike other colonial marketplaces, which are confined to a specific geographic area, the market in Chichicastenango has gradually expanded, occupying different places near the central plaza and the Iglesia de Santo Tomás. Part of the market now takes place directly on the front steps of the church as well as in areas on the boundaries of the central plaza, such as the sidewalks and streets (Shea 25). The expansion of this market from a small square at the center of town to a sprawling space in which the Mayan merchants take over the traditionally Ladino area must not go unnoticed.

According to Smith, the first constitution of Guatemala (as part of the Central American union) established equality for all and eradicated the special standing accorded Indians in the Spanish colonial systems as part of the larger project of integrating Guatemala (77). Specifically, Article 12 of the Constitution of 1824 established that all citizens and habitants of the republic, without distinction, were subject to the same rights and privileges as determined by law. The new constitution stated: "Todos los ciudadanos y habitantes de la República, sin distinción alguna, estarán sometidos a lo mismo orden de procedimientos y de juicios que determinan las leyes (Art. 143)" (Moreno 49). This shows that since Guatemala became independent from Spain and developed its own constitution in 1824, all inhabitants were awarded equal standing. Nonetheless, the reality of Guatemala is one where Ladinos (and those of European descent) continued to

---

varying degrees, with some pure Mayas and a minority of pure-blooded Spanish at either end of the spectrum. So those who consider themselves Maya may have the same racial characteristics as those who do not" (1).

Memory, Carnival, and Syncretism in the Modern Guatemalan Identity 295

hold power, often at the expense of indigenous groups. This is delineated in how the city and market place are organized and utilized by various social groups.

At the market a wide range of products are sold including fruits, vegetables, meats, clothing (including traditional clothing such as huipiles, cortes, and fajas), and masks (Shea 25). The market is particularly well known for displaying colorful and elaborate textiles. The importance of trade for merchants from the areas surrounding Chichicastenango has existed for some time, but as global travel becomes more popular, products such as textiles (clothing, blankets, and tablecloths) and masks are specifically created with the international tourist in mind. In this sense, globalization has had a direct impact on the marketplace, and visitors to the town can leave with a mask of a Spanish Conquistador or a piece of hand-weaved clothing without having ever witnessed the festival in which these items play such an important role.

The market is generally crowded as people rely on it for buying their food twice a week, with a mix of locals and people from the surrounding areas arriving to both sell and buy products. Visitors from Guatemala city (the capital) and tourists also come to visit the market (Shea 25). During the festivals, however, the market becomes particularly crowded, as these are important religious and cultural celebrations that draw a large crowd.

Many aspects of the marketplace in Chichicastenango are incredibly well-organized, taking into consideration the large number of vendors/merchants that come to sell their products from near and far. The vendor stands are set up in long lines, allowing visitors to easily navigate them without creating bottlenecks or chaos. The designated days and spaces where the market takes place provide for the people of Chichicastenango a continuation of these practices over time.

The central plaza has historically played an important role in Europe as well as in the Americas. Mikhail Bakhtin studied the importance of what he termed the "carnival square" when he looked at festivals in Renaissance France (see Bakhtin). The central section of a town, usually cited for public use, was, for Bakhtin, the "symbol of communal performance" (255). Everyone who uses the central square takes on a social role that they are expected to play. Ladinos, who traditionally inhabit the downtown core, step aside on market days to allow the Mayan population to take over and sell their goods. Even the steps of the church are used by vendors when the central plaza can no longer contain them. This organization of the central plaza changes during Fiesta time. The social and religious order, and even reality itself, is suspended and replaced with a tradition in which everyone plays a different role, knowing full well that normalcy will prevail in just a few days' time.

296 *The Transatlantic Hispanic Baroque*

La Fiesta de Santo Tomás

La Fiesta de Santo Tomás takes place annually in the week before Christmas. This is the most important Christian celebration in Chichicastenango because it is in honor of Santo Tomás, the patron saint of the church and city. The celebration takes place in parallel to many of the traditional European Christmas markets. Even though some resemblance exists between the two kinds of events (outdoor event, market place, selling of food and goods, participation of local and non-local visitors), La Fiesta de Santo Tomás has some unique elements that emerge from the coming together of pre-Columbian and colonial beliefs, practices, and customs.[5]

The market is set up several days before Christmas, and is accompanied by such spectacle as music, dance, adornment, and fireworks. As on traditional market days, the plaza space is taken over and the vendors sprawl onto the sidewalks and the streets surrounding the central square. Even the steps of the Iglesia de Santo Tomás are adorned with images of the Virgin Mary or of patron saints not only by groups of citizens of the town, but also by people from neighboring villages (Coester 97). The fiesta of Santo Tomás is a transnational social field that brings together those living in Chichicastenango, inhabitants of the villages around Chichicastenango, people from the city, tourists, and migrant workers who return home for the holidays (Basch et al.; Burrell).

At the center of the celebration is the Baile de la Conquista (or Dance of the Conquest). The men who play the roles of the conquistadors are dressed in traditional costumes; brightly colored and representing historical figures such as Hernán Cortés de Monroy y Pizarro, Pedro de Alvarado y Contreras, and Bernal Díaz del Castillo (Coester 97). Burrell describes how the "dancers wear elaborate costumes representing the ornate clothing of the Spanish invaders and white-faced, blue-eyed masks with blond hair" (Burrell 26). In the context of the fiesta, the Baile de la Conquista is a means of greeting local and non-local groups who bring with them religious icons from nearby towns and cities as they arrive to the plaza. Prior to the arrival of the religious icons, the conquistadors enter the town to the sounds of pipes and drums, dancing through the streets until they reach "an old fashioned house with a large corral quite near the church" (Coester 98). When they are told that a group is approaching with an image, the conquistadors stand at attention at the steps of the Iglesia de Santo Tomás. The two groups then acknowledge each other and the man who has been selected to carry the icon steps forward and sets a burning pile of wood on the altar. This group then walks through the smoke towards two acolytes from the church who

---

[5] The town of Todos los Santos, Cuchumatanes has a similar festivity that takes place yearly early in December. Burrell describes this festivity in detail and the coming together of various elements.

have come out to greet the effigy. The guardians, the men who are releasing the image, fire off guns outside the church and present their icon, which is then taken inside (Coester 98).

In her article on fiesta customs in Todos Santos, Guatemala, Burrell notes the importance of nostalgia in festivals like the Baile de la Conquista. The "power of nostalgia," she writes, is essential for "pursuing continued community identity and belonging" (27). Although Burrell's focus is on migrant workers who come home to celebrate traditional practices, the power of nostalgia on the minds of Guatemalans who have never left their country must not be ignored. By recreating the arrival of the Spanish, those indigenous to Guatemala have an opportunity to mock the systems that have been put in place to control them (e.g. haciendas, civil hierarchies, religion, and more recently drug cartels) without any repercussions (Burrell 26). The treatment at the hands of various authorities since the arrival of the Spaniards links Guatemala's indigenous people together in memory just as the plaza in front of Santo Tomás links them in space.

Hutcheson, when he speaks of dances similar to the Baile de la Conquista in their development and scope, states that:

> The performances must thus be seen as acts of restoration and return, memory works whose iterative presence in the public space each year links personal experience with the past and with communal aspiration, the concrete desire to bring them out again. Through dance the past is made present again, and becomes available once more for participants and onlookers alike. (869)

Brandes notes that the traditional fiesta has "its own body of specialized information about the relationship among political and social entities" (quoted in Rodríguez 39).

There is an interesting mix of Mayan and Christian elements in this traditional fiesta. The richly decorated clothes with which they adorn their images, the ceremonial pageant around the town and the music that accompanies them were all customary in pre-Columbian fiestas (Early 187). Friedel, Schele, and Parker note the importance of dance to the people of Guatemala: "Dance was a central component of social, religious, and political endeavors for the Maya. Kings danced, nobles danced, the people danced—and together they created the community" (Friedel et al. 292). These types of festivals were hardly unique to the Maya, however. Spanish and other mainland European countries celebrated their own fiestas which included mock-battles, dances, and pageants involving Royal Entries to various towns. When they came to the Americas, the Catholic celebrations, like Saints Days, continued to be a part of the cultural calendar and often involved a historical scene like the Baile de la Conquista. Harris states that, because these festivals are theatre works rather than simple historical re-enactments, they "represent the past in order to comment on the present, often

298 *The Transatlantic Hispanic Baroque*

interrogating it in startling ways" (Harris 19). Both the Mayans and the Spanish had historical traditions that allowed them to celebrate the fiesta without feeling threatened by each other.

The social order is not the only arrangement that is suspended during the Fiesta de Santo Tomás. Religion is the understood reason for this celebration, which, for the Ladino community, is a Christian service in celebration of a patron saint. The presentation of effigies to Santo Tomás, the donation of money, the lighting of candles dedicated to the miracles of Santo Tomás, and the prayers to the saint himself, all take place during this celebration. The Ladino population separate themselves from the festivities, and although they do not leave the town, they are only present for the rest of the festival as spectators. This separation is in social, economic, and ethnic distance. Ladinos have made no attempt to join the festivities in any way and their involvement is merely as outside observers. The lack of involvement of Ladinos in the festivities of Chichicastenango is a good indication that the Ladino and Mayan world continue to exist, to a large extent, in parallel. There is little willingness on part of Ladinos to get involved, reach out, and even obtain a minimal understanding of the meaning of these cultural, religious practices.

Many of the ways that Mayans traditionally celebrate their religion are not understood by the Catholics in power. As Coester found out on an expedition to Chichicastenango in the 1930s, the Mayan traditions of shooting guns and of burning gum on the church steps were allowed to continue because it was assumed that these acts had no longer meaning. When Coester asked a local church Father why these rituals were allowed, he received the reply "Well, they like to burn the gum. They don't know why they do it, so I don't interfere" (Coester 98). This attitude allows the dominant groups to assume that the customs of the Mayans are harmless and unimportant. In doing so, it creates a convenient method for the Ladino population to negotiate over both space and historical representation with the Mayans; if they do not believe that the Mayan traditions have any importance, they do not mind giving them the power over both of these situations for the duration of the festival.

Early notes that the Mayans initiated the syncretistic process with the Spanish because they believed after the conquest that their gods had failed them. During the colonial period, the Catholic saints were incorporated into the Mayan system of belief as gods of the Spaniards, and the physical churches may have taken the place of caves that the Mayans believed were the dwellings of their gods (Early 190). Regardless of their apparent observation of the Catholic religion, indigenous people continue to uphold their own traditions: the Fiesta de Santo Tomás is one example of this. The traditionally Christian celebration (a Saints Day) is used in Chichicastenango as a smokescreen for both pagan elements and the inversion of authority. All sectors of society are placated with the knowledge that, after the festival, all will return to normal.

The Mayans are completely in charge of the celebration; they provide the money, create the music, provide the entertainment and sell the goods to those participating in the festival.[6] This transition of the use of space from the Ladinos to the Mayans creates with it an inversion of power much like that referred to by Bakhtin. Not only are the Mayans in charge of the days' events, they are also profiting financially by selling their goods to visitors, and, indeed, even to the Ladinos themselves.

The suspension of reality that takes place during the Fiesta is accompanied by what Bakhtin calls a "free and familiar contact among people" (Bakhtin 251). Bakhtin's theories on the carnivalesque have been used elsewhere by anthropologists to highlight the importance of festivals and the marketplace in the Colonial Americas (Hutson 130). As elsewhere, many elements of the carnivalesque are present at the Fiesta de Santo Tomás. Everyone becomes a part of the celebration, and individuals, such as those participating in the Baile de la Conquista or those on the various stages that surround the main square, have a different relationship to each other than they would have on a non-fiesta day. This free and familiar attitude, according to Bakhtin, does not simply apply to the relationships between people, but to everything in general: "Carnival brings together, unifies, weds and combines the sacred with the profane, the lofty with the low, the great with the insignificant, the wise with the stupid" (Bakhtin 251).

Space is not the only negotiation that is taking place during this festival. The representation of memory and history are also being worked out in ways that the two cultures see fit. The origins of the Baile de la Conquista reflect the power relations between indigenous people and European conquerors. The dance becomes a means of expressing the subjugation and exploitation. By the 1980s the dance continues to serve political and social forms of expression. Carrescia and Bossen show how low-paid workers are highly dependent on plantation owners, in terms of obtaining wages. The dance serves as an expression of these hierarchies and how low-paid workers were exploited and mistreated. Since many migrant workers no longer work in the plantations, but have immigrated to the United States (often illegally) the meaning of the representations in the dance have changed over time.

Identity in Modern Guatemala: The Emergence of Parallel Cultures

A central theme in the Hispanic Baroque literature has been the theorizing of the coming together of the pre-Columbian world with the Spanish colonial cultural system in what is referred to as the First Transatlantic Culture. A major

---

[6]   Burrell explains how in the past there existed a direct dependence between the festival and the money obtained from plantation owners to be able to afford the costs. This has radically changed since migrant workers in the US send money back to Guatemala that helps fund these festivals (23, 26).

challenge in this area of investigation is the existence of multiple terms (e.g. transculturation, syncretism, hybridity, mestizaje) for describing the process of acculturation as well as the large number of theoretical accounts (e.g., periphery/center; hybridity) that have been proposed for explaining how it unfolds. We employ the example of La Fiesta de Santo Tomás in Chichicastenango as a means to further question how the process of the coming together of such diverse and complex cultural systems takes place and its continued relevance in modern Guatemala as a means for understanding the processes of identity formation and expression.

Recent theorizing about modern colonialism in terms of the geopolitical theories of center/periphery only captures some elements of how the First Transatlantic Culture emerged. Wallerstein has proposed to investigate the role of the Americas/Caribbean in the world system in terms of distinctions between center/periphery. After 1898, US imperialism has relegated the Americas/Caribbean to the periphery of the economic, cultural, and social system. Within this system of analysis, Chichicastenango and the Fiesta de Santo Tomás are located at the very periphery of the political and social order. The theory of center/periphery only provides a limited understanding because many residents from Chichicastenango have immigrated to the US, leading toward a steady flow of information, goods, and resources from the center to the periphery.[7] As a result of new migratory patterns, it is often argued that applying a perspective that examines "borders, borderland, and *fronteras*," as proposed by Mignolo, provides a much more relevant analysis of the reality of modern colonialism (see Gabilondo).

In our investigation we take an approach that continues the line of thinking put forward in theories of regionalism and localism. At the center of these theories is the tension that exists between local cultures, customs, and practices, and the overpowering forces of globalization (Melo). Our focus is not directly on the negotiation of these tensions, but rather on the local practices that continue to exist despite the impact of globalization. We acknowledge though that globalization and large-scale immigration have an impact not only on the customs and practices taking place in Chichicastenango themselves, but also in how these are given meaning by the various social groups involved. The festival, and its feeling of being "autóctono"[8] (belonging to the authentic celebrations of the pre-Columbian Mayan culture), may suggest that Guatemala, and Chichicastenango in particular, continue to exist at the fringe. This is misleading, however, because Guatemala is part of a complex web of immigration, where

---

[7]   See for example Mignolo, who states that "I conceive of the [world] system in terms of internal and external borders rather than centers, semiperipheries, and peripheries" (33).

[8]   The term "autóctonas" refers to authentic, stemming from another era.

Memory, Carnival, and Syncretism in the Modern Guatemalan Identity 301

a large percentage of Guatemalans live in the US, Mexico, or other parts of Central and South America.

The fact that little evidence remains as to the nature of pre-Columbian lifestyle makes it difficult, if not impossible, to analyze the extent to which practices and forms of expression that qualify as purely "autóctonas" continue to persist in the current cultural system. Hawkins argues that most analysis of the survival of pre-Columbian practices is merely "inferential reasoning underlying much of what is claimed about preconquest Mayan cultures and society" (Hawkins 40). Therefore, we do not attempt to classify elements in the Fiesta de Santo Tomás and the Baile de la Conquista as either falling into the category of "autóctono" or as foreign (brought to Mesoamerica by the Spaniards), because there is no true way to classify cultural elements such as customs or celebrations. Instead, we attempt to discern the function that these festivities continue to have in the current cultural system.

Our analysis follows the line of thinking put forward by García Canclini in *Hybrid Cultures*, where it is argued that culture in Latin America is expressed as "multitemporal heterogeneity" (2–3) revealing elements from pre-Columbian America, colonial America, and modern "influences" stemming from the US dominance in the Americas/Caribbean and globalization. This hybridity consists of reuniting traditional belief systems, cultures, and traditions with new information and communication technologies, Western clothing, and modern modes of transportation. With little apparent friction or tension, hybridity occurs during the Fiesta de Santo Tomás as the old and the new co-exist, the roles of domination are reversed, and all members of the community participate in parallel worlds and spheres.[9] The parallelism emerges from disparate points of departure. Indigenous groups are active participants and shape the events, while the Ladinos are relegated to the role of observers. We concur with García Canclini that hybridity is not a phenomenon that is unique to border towns, but rather it is a central feature of all Latin American cultural existence.

The concept of hybridity has been explored in depth, but there remains work to be done on presenting the argument in terms of a localized study. In the following section we want to take the concept of hybridity a step further and hope to offer a more theoretical model of the processes underlying the unfolding of hybridity over time. The process of hybridity is revealed at three different levels in the Fiesta de Santo Tomás, allowing for an exploration of the current cultural system.

---

[9]   The lack of friction and tension does not refer to the historical struggles and socio-political problems that have resurfaced over and over again in the bloody history of Guatemala. Rather it refers to the co-existence of these cultural elements in the festivities themselves.

302   *The Transatlantic Hispanic Baroque*

First, modernity is part of the reality that becomes suspended in the moment of the fiesta. Guatemala is part of a global system of production, exploitation, and immigration. In the majority of indigenous families, at least one member has legally or illegally immigrated to the US to work and provide for their family (Burrell). This has provided a direct connection between the periphery of the Americas/Caribbean and the centers of power. While Guatemala continues to be marginalized, the flow of information has made it a part of the global networked society.

Nonetheless, during the Fiesta de Santo Tomás and the Baile de la Conquista old protocols, norms, beliefs, and customs are revived, without much questioning. Tradition takes over and becomes perpetuated. While modernity is never made irrelevant by these traditions, there are moments in time when the current cultural system takes over in importance.

The second process of hybridity is the appropriation of identity and cultural forms that take place during the fiesta. The Baile de la Conquista is a good example of how various elements fuse to form cultural expression. The Baile itself is a relic from pre-Columbian traditions of dance as a form of celebration. The pictorial images that remain of Mayan tradition show ornate clothing as a means of spiritual enlightenment. While the performance may be a reincarnation of pre-Columbian forms of expression, the masks and costumes are colonial creations allowing the Mayans to negotiate their space by denouncing and re-appropriating the Spanish identity. By incorporating Spanish elements, new forms of cultural expression emerge, suggesting a merger of various elements. The lack of participation, engagement, and interest of the Ladino population, however, suggests that the festival continues to be a Mayan event that exists in parallel to the mainstream Ladino world. These two spheres have not integrated in the festival into a fully "communal performance" (see Bakhtin), but rather one remains as the performer (Mayans) and the other as the spectator (Ladinos).

The third process shows that modernity and tradition can work in parallel with each other. This is best exemplified in the music, which plays a central role during the fiesta but is perhaps one of the most difficult elements to analyze. The music is loud to the extent of being perceived as unbearable, but provides the right kind of backdrop for this celebration. There is never a single genre or type of music performed, but rather different styles clash against each other in a cloud of noise. There is always marimba, the traditional instrument performed. But simultaneously, pop-music is blasting from several speakers. This music can consist of Latin American salsa, rumba, and merengue and can also include hits from the North American, Latin American/Caribbean, and European pop-music industry. Despite the different styles of music not fitting with one another, they are often set-up in direct proximity, further increasing the noise level, but also making it difficult to distinguish between the two genres. Perhaps it is the noise level, and emerging chaos, that gives the participants in the festival a feeling of elation and celebration. On a more symbolic level, it shows yet again how these various cultural elements, which are in diametric opposition to each other, can work in parallel without raising much concern or disturbance to those directly participating in the festival.

We conclude this section by agreeing with many previous writers that the process of hybridity is not a simple one. In accord with Hawkins, we "argue against simple notions of cultural syncretism, cultural separatism, or pre-Hispanic cultural continuity among the Indians by suggesting that many of the unique and un-Spanish aspects of Indian culture are an inverse creation of the overlord culture brought to America by Spaniards" (Hawkins 23). Magaloni Kerpel, in her careful analysis of images created shortly after the conquest, suggests that "Esta expressión pictórica no es, sin embargo, la suma de dos tradiciones, un sincretismo simple que reduce todo a la apropriación de patrones y modelos visuales" (30). It is not simply a merging, fusing, or coming together of the two cultures that is occurring. Neither can it be understood as a simple process of domination, as Kerpel explains: "No es tampoco producto o resultado del proceso de colonización y dominación, aunque está marcado por ello." But quite to the contrary, there is agency involved in the creation of the new customs, belief systems, and forms of expression, as Magaloni Kerpel concludes: "Es resultado del esfuerzo creativo indígena por tener una respuesta histórica funcional frente a la realidad de la conquista. Es la formulación de un nuevo discurso visual, apropriado para la recién comenzada era cósmica cristiana, pero emanado y enraizado en la milenaria tradición mesoamericana de respresentación visual y simbólica de hechos históricos" (30). The festival is a visual and symbolic representation of historical events, power struggles, and identity embedded in a pre-Columbian belief system.

Technologies of Culture

The Fiesta de Santo Tomás—including the Baile de la Conquista, the market, and the religious festivities—has continued as a cultural tradition long after Guatemala has become a nation-state and has left behind its colonial roots (Lovell). This tradition has survived despite many other currents, influences, and cultural, political, and social forces. If we understand that the Fiesta helps to inform the Hispanic Baroque as a cultural system, and that it is part of the conflicting processes of identity formation, then it can be identified as a technology of culture. It demonstrates that despite the attempt during the conquest to provide a mold with which to "annex" all of the Americas/ Carribbean, this process was far from straightforward and predictable. What La Fiesta de Santo Tomás demonstrates first and foremost is that the pre-Columbian culture around the region of Chichicastenango has shown a high

304   *The Transatlantic Hispanic Baroque*

level of resilience and continues to exist in parallel to mainstream Ladino culture. Many of the practices described in the Fiesta de Santo Tomás are clearly not a result of the conquest itself. These practices are a direct expression of pre-Columbian beliefs as they encounter and merge with a new social and religious order. It is exactly this continuation that creates cultural diversity. It is the practice of ancient patterns of behaviour, dances, music, and costume. This practice is accompanied with complex mythological beliefs. These beliefs are deeply engrained in the indigenous identity and as such, even if expressed in new ways and in new social contexts, are a continuation of a past era.

The importance of the Fiesta de Santo Tomás as a technology of culture can only be understood in the context of Guatemalan's historiography (Lovell). In our introduction we argued that there are few written texts, maps, or even government documents that document the historical process of adaptation taking place during the colonial era. In particular, the Mayan voice is absent in these representations of the historiography of Guatemala. We argue that the Fiesta de Santo Tomás functions as a technology of culture by showing the complex interweaving of pre-Columbian culture with a new reality of colonization, globalization, and immigration. It is in this juxtaposition that the Mayan voice is made visible. As Hutson has demonstrated, it is during the fiesta when the carnivalesque occurs, that the "real self" is expressed (Hutson 140). This is the moment where many elements of the process of adaptation are revealed. The festival serves as a means for those involved to make sense of their history and redefine their identity both vis-à-vis the festival itself as well as in relation to other cultural forms of expression. In his final section, Hutson notes that the aspects of the carnivalesque help the marketplace to emerge as a "site of struggle." However, we might argue the opposite: at Chichicastenango the marketplace, and more specifically the Fiesta de Santo Tomás, seems to be an unspoken negotiation over space and memory that allows a temporary suspension of reality to take place. Various cultures continue to exist in parallel with each other, integrating elements from various sources as needed to question, interpret, and rewrite history.

Bibliography

Bakhtin, Mikhail. "Carnival and the Carnivalesque." *Cultural Theory and Popular Culture: A Reader*. Ed. John Storey. 3rd edition. Athens, GA: University of Georgia Press, 1998. 250–59.

Basch, Linda, Nina Glick Schiller and Christina Szanton Blanc. *Nations Unbound: Transnational Projects, Postcolonial Predicaments, and Deterritorialized Nation-States*. Amsterdam: Gordon and Breach, 1994.

Burrell, Jennifer L. "Migration and the Transnationalization of Fiesta Customs in Todos Santos Cuchumatán, Guatemala." *Latin American Perspectives* 32.5 (2005): 12–32.

Coester, Aldred. "The 'Danza de los conquistadores' at Chichicastenango." *Hispania* 24.1 (1941): 95–100.

Early, John. D. "Some Ethnographic Implications of an Ethnohistorical Perspective of the Civil-Religious Hierarchy among the Highland Maya." *Ethnohistory* 30.4 (1983): 185–202.

Friedel, David, Linda Schele and Joy Parker. *Maya Cosmos: Three Thousand Years on the Shaman's Path.* New York: William Morrow, 1993.

Gabilondo, Joseba. "Spanish, Second Language of the Internet? The Hispanic Web, Subaltern-Hybrid Cultures, and the Neo-Liberal Lettered City." *Revista Canadiense de Estudios Hispánicos* 31.1 (2006): 107–128.

García Canclini, Néstor. *Hybrid Cultures: Strategies for Entering and Leaving Modernity.* Trans. Christopher L. Chiappari and Silvia L. López. Foreword by Renato Rosaldo. Minneapolis, MN: University of Minnesota Press, 1995.

Harris, Max. *Aztecs, Moors, and Christians: Festivals of Reconquest in Mexico and Spain.* Austin, TX: University of Texas Press, 2000.

Hawkins, John. *Inverse Images: The Meaning of Culture, Ethnicity, and Family in Postcolonial Guatemala.* Albuquerque, NM: University of New Mexico Press, 1984.

Hutcheson, Maury. "Memory, Mimesis, and Narrative in the K'iche' Mayan Serpent Dance of Joyabaj, Guatemala." *Comparative Studies in Society and History* 51.4 (2009): 865–95.

Hutson, Scott R. "Carnival and Contestation in the Aztec Marketplace." *Dialectical Anthropology* 25 (2000): 123–49.

Lovell, George W. *Conquest and Survival in Colonial Guatemala: A Historical Geography of the Cuchumatán Highlands, 1500–1821.* 3rd ed. Montreal, QC and Kingston, ON: McGill-Queen's University Press. 2005.

Magaloni Kerpel, Diana. "Imágenes de la conquista de México en los códices del siglo XVI. Una lectura su contenido simbólico." *Anales del Instituto de Investigaciones Estéticas* 25.82 (2003): 5–45.

Melo, Jorge Orlando. "Contra la identidad." *El Malpensante* 74 (2006): 85–94.

Mignolo, Walter. *Local Histories/Global Designs: Coloniality, Subaltern Knowledges, and Border Thinking.* Princeton: Princeton University Press, 2000.

Moreno, Laudelino. *Historia de la relaciones interestatuales de Centroamerica.* Madrid: Compañía Ibero-americana de Publicaciones, 1928.

Rodríguez, Sylvia. "Fiesta Time and Plaza Space: Resistance and Accommodation in a Tourist Town." *The Journal of American Folklore* 111.439 (1998): 39–56.

Shea, Maureen E. *Culture and Customs of Guatemala.* Westport, CT: Greenwood Press, 2001.

Smith, Carol A, ed. *Guatemalan Indians and the State, 1540 to 1988.* Austin, TX: University of Texas Press, 1992.

Suárez, Juan Luis. *The Hispanic Baroque.* SSHRC Application form. 2007.

Index

acculturation 104, 300
Acosta, José de, Jesuit 237, 240–2, 245
Natural and Moral History of the Indies 237, 240–2
advenedizos (newcomers) 265–6
Ágreda, Sister María de 132, 248
Aguilar Piñal, Francisco, 97
Agustín, Miguel, friar 41
Alba, Duke of 137
alférez real (standard bearer) 174 see *paseo del pendón*
Alfonso VI of Portugal 137
Allo Manero, María Adelaida 222
Alonso, Dámaso 164
Altamirano, Francisco 162
Álvarez de Toledo, Gabriel 220
Amirrol, Hafiz 206
Amsterdam 198, 200
ancien régime 129, 187
Anderson, Benedict 5
Andreasen, Robin 39
Anne, Queen of Austria, death of 174
Anzaldúa, Gloria 6
Apocalypse 237–9, 244–6, 247
Árbenz Guzmán, Jacobo 256–7, 267
Ardemans, Teodoro, architect 209–13, 215
Declaración y extensión sobre las Ordenanzas de Madrid (1719)
Fluencia de la tierra y curso subterráneo de las aguas (1724)
Arias Montano, Benito, Jesuit 240, 244
Aragon/Aragonese 57, 63, 134, 144, 181, 193, 196n8
Argaiz, Gregorio de, Benedictine friar 140
Argan, Carlo 207
Aristotle/Aristotelianism 37, 155n9, 158, 209

asiento de negros (slave trade monopoly) 195
Asturias 101, 140, 144, 267
Atlantic world 198, 291
Atran, Scott 36–7
Auersperg, Count of 135
Austin, Katherine A. 10
Austria, House of 133, 134–6, 138, 141, 174, 238
Avendaño, Fernando de, mestizo priest 42, 48–9
Azanza López, José Javier 222

Balbuena, Bernardo de, Creole and author 179
Grandeza mexicana (1604)
Bakhtin, Mikhail 291, 295, 299, 302
Baños de Velasco, Juan 141
Barcelona 102
Bar-Yam, Yaneer 3
Baroque 13, 9–11
alterity and essentialism 49–50
architecture of the 248–9
and "baroque-from-below" 286
and the Counter Reformation 81, 101
and identity construction 75–6
metropolitan cities of 172–3, 182–3
modalities of race, 36, 39–40
Spanish elements of 105, 122–3
and spectacle 172–5
"product of imperial mass civilizations" 207
See also Hispanic Baroque; Neo-Baroque
Bartosik-Vélez, Elise 240
Bataillon, Marcel 97n3
Bautista Villalpando, Juan, Jesuit 244
Ezechielem Explanationes (1596–1604)

308 *The Transatlantic Hispanic Baroque*

Benavente Motolinía, Toribio de, 245
Benedict XVI, Pope, 274, 279, 281–3
Benjamin, Walter 206
Bermúdez de Castro, Diego Antonio 246
Bertelli, Sergio 220
Blackstone, William 7, 27, 19, 28–30
    Commentaries 27
    Rights of Persons 31
Bochart, Samuel 142
Bodin, Jean 65–6, 187, 190
Boethius, Anicius Manlius Severinus 17,
    18–20, 22–4, 26, 28–30
Bonet Correa, Antonio 211, 212
Book of Revelation *See* Apocalypse
Borja, Francisco de, Jesuit 156
    Brief Treaty of how to Preach the Holy
    Gospel (1555) 156
Borja, Juan de, President of the Audiencia
    of Santa Fe, 78, 79, 82
Borromeo, Carlo, Cardinal (Naples) 104,
    108
Bottineau, Yves 210, 214, 215
Bourbon, House of 6, 198, 213, 220–22,
    229, 238
Braganza, House of 134, 137
Braudel, Fernand 207
Bravo Lira, Bernardino 248, 249
Buenos Aires 179
bullfights 64, 98, 173, 174, 175
Burrell, Jennifer L. 296–7, 299n6

Cabello Valvoa, Miguel 240
cabildos (municipal governments) 174, 180
Cádiz, 192, 195, 196, 198–200
Cakchiquel, indigenous group 293, 294
Calancha, Antonio de la (priest) 178
    Crónica moralizada del orden de San
    Agustín en el Perú (1638) 178
Calvo, Thomas 231
Cañete, Marquis of 172
Cañizares-Esguerra, Jorge 38–9n4
Cano, Juan 198
Cantabria/Cantabrians 140–2
Capuchins 102, 121
Carmack, Robert 292

Carmelites 119, 121
Cartagena 159
    festivities for Carnival in 175
Cassanova, Jose 279, 280n7
"castas" (mixed bloods) 263
Castile 5–6, 56, 57, 63, 64, 101–6, 134,
    137, 138n12, 139–40, 175, 181,
    187–91, 193–5, 200
    aristocracy of 139
    Courts of 137
Catalonia and Catalans 5, 63n26, 99, 101,
    105, 188n1, 189, 193
Catholic Church 277–8, 280, 287, 288
    clergy, Roman Catholic 102–4, 107,
    109–10, 114–15
    contemporary baroque strategies of 287
    Catholic Reformation 115
Catholic world 69, 115, 119
Catholicism, 77, 81–5, 96–7, 101–2, 104,
    113, 116–8, 276, 278–9
    faith in 276, 281, 282, 285
    ligueur families 120
    pre-Baroque 104
    piety 85, 96, 101, 103, 109, 244, 280,
    285
        inward and public 82n7
    Tridentine 102, 115–16, 122
    See also Baroque; Catholic Church,
    Counter Reformation
Ceán Bermúdez, Juan Agustín 215
centre/periphery 176, 183, 188, 300, 302
Certeau, Michel de 205
Cervantes de Salazar, Francisco, humanist
    178
    Crónica de la Nueva España (1564)
Christian, William Jr 101
Charismatic Catholic Renewal (Csordas)
    280
Charles II 8, 129–30, 132–3, 137–8, 140,
    175, 208–10, 219, 220
Charles III 212, 213
Charles V 67, 96n2, 116, 131–2, 138, 238,
    239
Chichicastenango 11, 291–6, 298, 300,
    303–4

Index

Chile 172, 243
Churriguera, José Benito 209–11
   Churrigueresque style 215
Cisneros, Diego, doctor 181
   Sitio, naturaleza y propiedades de la
      ciudad de México (1618)
Cobo, Bernabé, Jesuit 181, 183
   Historia de la fundación de Lima
      (1639)
Coester, Aldred, 298
cognitive linguistics 152–3
colonialism 76, 77, 277, 300
Columbus, Christopher 237, 239–40, 242,
   245
   The Book of Prophecies 237
composiciones (inventories of foreigners) 194
conceptual metaphor 153, 163
Corboz, André 245
corporeal metaphor 154
Corpus Christi, feast of and processions
   100, 102–3, 174
Correcha, Miguel, *corregidor*, murder of
   85–7
Cortés, Jerónimo, humanist 40, 42, 43, 46
   El non plus ultra del lunario (1594) 401
Cortés, Martín rebellion 175
costumbrismo 182
Council of Trent (1545–1563) 96, 101–2,
   243, 280
Counter Reformation 96, 978, 101–2, 108,
   100
   and the Baroque in Spain 98
   liturgies of 176
   and "New Catholicism" 102
   and reformist clergy 115
   and universal saints 108
   see also Baroque; Catholic Church;
      Catholicism; Council of Trent
Covarrubias Orozco, Sebastián 238–9
Coyaima 7, 75–89
   and Baroque Catholicism 84
   Hispanic Baroque, integration into 86,
      89
   legal identity of 81
   religious faith, dubious 82

   see also Pijao
Creoles and creolism 6, 8, 262n6, 264–5,
   274, 286
   Elite 194, 229
   Metropolis 172–83
   terminology of 176–7
"criollo", definition and lineage of 262; *see*
   also Creole and creolism
Critical Race Theory 49
Cruz, Sister Juana Ines de la 248
Cueva, Juan de la 179
Cummins, Tom 247
Cutter, Charles 76
Cuzco 179, 222, 226, 249
   Celebration of Ferdinand VI 226–9
   La lealtad satisfecha (1748) publication
      in 226–7

Da Sommaia, Costanza 61
Da Sommaia, Girolamo, Florentine student
   and patrician 58–70
   and *confradía de Aragón* 63
   diary 59, 62–3, 67, 68
   family background 601
   immersion in Spanish culture and
      letters 68
   intellectual and social circles 64–5
   and life writing 62
   and Medici Florence 59–60, 68–9
   reading habits 65–8
   Seneca and Stoicism, influence of 62–3
Deleuze, Gilles 206
Della Porta, Giambattista 43–7
Descartes/Cartesianism 19, 49–50
Díaz del Castillo, Bernal 237, 243, 261–2,
   296
   The Truthful History of the Conquest of
      New Spain (1632) 262
Dodds, Jerrilynn D. 208
Domínguez Ortiz, Antonio, 96, 190
Dorantes de Carranza, Baltasar 178
Dubois, Claude-Gilbert 3

Echeverría, Bolívar 9–10
Eco, Umberto 237–8

310   *The Transatlantic Hispanic Baroque*

Eire, Carlos M. 99
El Callao (fort) 162, 222, 226
Elliott, John H. 69n38, 111
encomenderos 78, 79, 180
Enlightenment 3, 9, 109, 183
Erasmus 95, 97
Escardo, Juan Bautista, Jesuit 155n11, 158
   Rhetorica christiana (1647) 158
Escobar, Jesús 207, 208
Escrivá de Balaguer, Josemaría 281 *See*
   Opus Dei
essentialism 4–5, 7, 77, 248–9
   constructionist 35–41, 43, 49, 50

Fayard, Janine 108
Ferdinand I of Aragon 61
Ferdinand II of Aragon 101
Ferdinand III 141
Ferdinand IV 220, 222–3, 226–32
Feijoo, Benito Jerónimo 47, 105,
   139–40n16
Fernández, Martha 239, 246
Fernández Albaladejo, Pablo, 219
First Transatlantic Culture, 291, 292
Flanders *see* Low Countries
Foucault, Michel 40
France/French 46, 65, 97, 107, 109, 113–5,
   117, 118, 120–123, 131, 133, 135
Franco, Alonso, Creole Dominican 181
Frías Salazar, Antonio de 113, 144
Frye Jacobson, Matthew 49
Fuentes y Guzmán, Francisco Antonio de,
   corregidor and author 255
   Biography and official roles 258–9
   on "criollo" and Peninsular tensions 262–6
   Recordación florida 258
      Drafting of 259–60
      Concept of "patria" in 266–8
      Fiestas reales (1675) 258–9
   See also criollo; Martín Peláez, Severo
Funeral ceremonial and rituals 9, 151, 160,
   161, 174, 179, 220–22, 226

Gage, Thomas, renounced Dominican 179,
   264

Galenism 209
Galindo, Juan, *corregidor* of the Coyaima 83
Gallego, Isidro, Jesuit 151–2, 159–63
gachupín 177, 178, 264
García, Alexandre, jurist 137–8
García Canclini, Néstor 6, 30–31
García, Esteban, Augustinian 181
Garofalo, Emanuela 222
Genoa/Genoese 56, 58, 70, 189–90,
   190–3, 197, 198, 200
Germany/Germans 42, 64, 95, 103, 106,
   109, 132, 134, 136
Glennie, Bishop Enrique 288
globalization 4, 10, 176, 275–7, 295, 300,
   301, 304
Gómez de Mora, Juan 209, 214–16
González Dávila, Gil, Jesuit historian 53,
   56, 58, 64
González, Tirso, Jesuit 109, 162
González, Rigoberto A., painter 277
Gracián, Baltasar, Jesuit 163
   Oráculo manual
Granada 110, 220, 243
Grenz, Stanley J. 19
Guamán Poma de Ayala, Felipe 182
   Nueva crónica y buen gobierno (1615)
Guatemala 11, 175, 177, 243, 256, 259,
   260, 262, 264, 267–9, 291–6, 299
   1824 Constitution of 294
Guicciardini, family 61–5

Habsburgs *see* Austria, House of
Halbwachs, Maurice 206
Hanseatic cities 190, 198
Hawkins, John 303
Henry IV 113
Hermant, Héloïse, 139
Herrera, Pablo 160
Herrerian architectural style 210, 211
Herzog, Tamar 57n9, 191, 200
Hispanic Baroque, 13, 67, 11, 86, 89, 291,
   299, 303
   "first global cultural formation" 2
   and identity formation 75–7
   see also Baroque; Neo-Baroque

Index 311

Hispanic empire 2, 4, 8, 11, 58, 69
Hispanism 144
    Austro-Hispanism 133, 141
    "Hispanophilia" 118, 120, 123
Hobbes, Thomas 17, 21–6, 28, 31, 32
    Leviathan 21, 22, 31
Holy Office, 83, 105, 106
Hooghe, Romeyn de, Dutch engraver 132
Hutcheson, Maury 297
Hutson, Scott R. 304
hybridity 300–303
hybridization 6, 277, 286
    non-hybrid communities 7
    and identity-based practices 11

Iberian Atlantic 35, 189, 194
Ignatius of Loyola 121, 154, 173
imperialism/empire, 6, 55–6, 76, 130–32,
    135–6, 138, 140, 142–4, 188, 207,
    222, 249, 258, 266, 300
    and imperial capitals 207, 288
    See also Hispanic Empire
Incas 175, 182, 222, 227, 229
Indians (Americas) 41, 46, 80–84, 174,
    227, 229–31, 263–6
Indies 171–2, 174, 176, 178, 180, 182, 192,
    194–6, 198, 240–243, 246, 262
indios naturales 230–231
Inquisition, 64, 66n32, 83, 96, 102–3,
    105–7, 110, 280
    in Baroque Spain 102, 105
Isabella, Queen 101, 240
Italy/Italians 56, 59, 65–6, 6970, 95, 97,
    100, 102–7, 117, 118, 210
    Spain's cultural impact on 109

Jansenism 95, 104
Jarque, Antonio, Jesuit 158
    The Christian Orator (1660) 158
Jerusalem 9, 172, 177, 182, 237–41, 243–6,
    247
    imagery of 239
    Kingdom of 238
    Puebla de los Ángeles, connections with
    246

Temple in 243
Jesuits 103–4, 108–10, 119–21, 129,
    134–5, 138, 143, 151–7, 173, 176,
    183, 227, 230, 140, 252, 244, 258
    expulsion from Spain (1767) 110
    Provincial Congregation 162
    Ratio studiorum 157
    Spiritual Exercises 157
John of Austria 138–41, 144
John IV of Portugal 134
Johnson, Mark 153, 154
John XXIII, Pope 278
John Paul II, Pope 273
Juana, Inés de la Cruz 248
jueces conservadores (judges concerned with
    contraband) 199, 199n11 [Cádiz]
Junta de Regencia (Regency Council) 135

Kaup, Monika 10, 76
Kerpel, Magaloni 303
Kubler, George 176, 210, 214

Ladinos 77, 84–7, 293–5, 298–9, 301–2,
    304
Lakoff, George 153, 154
Lapide, Cornelio A., Jesuit 158
Larkin, Brian 82n7
Latour, Bruno 35
Leddy Phelan, John 76
Leibniz, Gottfried Wilhelm 206
León Pinelo, Antonio de 179
    Paraíso en el Nuevo Mundo (1656) 179
Leopold I 132, 135, 138
Lima 8, 39, 152, 152, 160–62, 1725, 179,
    181–3, 206, 222
    as Baroque metropolis 178–9, 224
    celebrations for Ferdinand VI 230–32
    commemoration of Philip V 223–7
    competition with Cuzco 226–31
    earthquake in (1746) 162, 223–5
    funerary practices 222
    proclamation of Charles II in (1666)
    175
    see also Cuzco, St Rose of Lima
Lisbon 134, 138

312   *The Transatlantic Hispanic Baroque*

Treaty of (1668) 136
Lomnitz, Claudio 287
López de Corella, Alonso, 38, 39–40
López de Velasco, Juan, geographer 177
Lovell, George W. 292–3
Louis XIV of France 118, 131–3, 135–8
Low Countries 8, 57, 67, 113, 115–21, 122,
     134, 135, 137, 175, 189–90, 191
Luca, Carlo Antonio de 24

MacCormack, Sabine 240
Machado, Antonio, poet 109
Madrid, Court of 135, 136, 196–7
     and Baroque architects 210–15
     ceremonial capital of the Spanish
         monarchy 208
     imperial ideology, lack of 208–9
Maeztu, Ramiro de 96n2
Maravall, José Antonio 2, 75, 97, 98, 207,
     277
     La cultura del barroco (1980) 97
La Margarita del cielo: Santa Margarita de
     Crotona (play) 174
Mariana, Juan de 121
Mariana of Austria, Regent and Queen 129,
     135, 138, 220
Marini, Piero, Archbishop 282
Martín González, Juan José 212
Martínez Peláez, Severo 255
     On Francisco Antonio de Fuentes y
         Guzmán 255–6, 258, 261
     on criollo consciousness 262–7
     La patria del criollo 255–6, 258,
         261–9
     see also criollo; Fuentes y Guzmán,
         Francisco Antonio de; Guatemala
Martini, Carlo María 237–8
Mary, Queen of Scots 115
Maya 237, 269, 292–4, 297–9, 301–2, 304
Mayans, Gregorio 105
Medina de las Torres, Duke of 133, 137
Megged, Amos 264n7
Mendieta, Jerónimo de 243, 247, 248
Menéndez Pidal, Ramón 96n2
metropolis, etymology of 171n1

mestizo 7, 9, 39, 42, 48–9, 80, 88, 177, 263,
     264n7
Mestre, Antonio 95, 97, 99, 100, 219
Mexican Bishops Council (CEM) 279
Mexico, 89, 11, 172–8, 179, 182–3, 194,
     261, 273–8
     cathedrals in 178n3
     illiteracy in 283
     national television channels in 283
     see also Neo-Baroque
Mexico City 9, 244, 245, 273, 274, 284,
     286, 288–9
Mitchell, Don 207
Molinos, Miguel de, theologian
     (1628–1696) 109
modernism/modernity 2, 45, 9, 10, 26, 37,
     40, 42, 183, 213, 277–8, 288, 291,
     302
Montesinos, Fernando de 240
Montoliu, Pedro 206
Morán, Jacinto, Jesuit 161
Morandé, Pedro 248–9
"mulattoes" 173–5

nacionista 139–140n16
Natagaima 78, 80, 81, 85
Ndalianis, Angela 277
Neo-Baroque 1, 10–11, 273, 276–9, 281
     performance of 277
     and syncretic spectacles 276
     use of ethnic cultural significations 285,
     286–9
     see also Baroque; Hispanic Baroque
Nestor, Patriarch of Constantinople 19,
     20, 21
New Jerusalem, image of 238–9, 244,
     246–8
     and messianism 238
New Spain 56, 76, 82n7, 159n16, 171–3,
     177, 179, 181, 280
     and civic spaces 247–8
New World 10, 41, 46–7, 76, 171, 177, 181,
     200, 240–3, 263
Nithard, Everardo, Jesuit 129, 135, 138,
     139–40, 237, 243, 247

No está el cielo seguro de ladrones (play) 174
Nueva Granada 75, 77, 82, 159
Nueva Planta 219
Nuevo Baztán 211
Núñez de Castro, Alfonso 141
Núñez de Haro, Alonso, Archbishop of
    Mexico 151n1

Oaxaca 11, 273, 275–6, 284, 285
Ochoa Brun, Miguel Ángel 131
Olavide, Pablo de 107
Olivares, Count Duke of 133, 176, 180
Oña, Pedro de 226
Ophir, equated with Peru 240
Opus Dei 279, 281
orality 152n3, 155
Ortega y Gasset, José 153n6
Osorio, Alejandro 221, 225
Ottoman Empire 114, 198, 240

Palafox, Juan de 180
Pan-Hispanism *see* Hispanism
Panich, Lee M. 77
Pardo Tomás, José, 106
Paredes, Joseph de, Jesuit 227
Paredes y Flores, Mariana de Jesús, funeral
    oration for 160
Parker, Geoffrey 238
Parkinson Zamora, Lois 76
Parra, Andres, *teniente* 87
paseo del pendón (procession of the
    standard) 174
"Pastoral Indígena" 278–9
Peace of Aachen/Aix-la-Chapelle, Treaty of
    (1668) 136, 138
Peace of the Pyrenees (1659) 130, 134
Peace of Westphalia (1648), 132, 190
Pellicer, Joseph de 142-4
    Prefación de la Monarchía de los Godos
        (1671)
Peralta y Barnuevo, Pedro ("*Doctor oceano*")
    183, 224, 224n6
    Lima fundada o conquista del Perú
        (1732) 224
Pérez-Magallón, Jesús 3, 105

periphery *See* centre/periphery
Perry, William 17
Peru, 89, 42, 56, 67, 172, 176-9, 182-3, 220,
    222-8, 230-232, 240, 260
    as synecdoche of Hispanic Empire 225
    Viceroyalty of 178
Philip I 138
Philip II 66, 70n40, 101, 105, 113, 116,
    123, 174-5, 177, 193, 207, 219,
    238-9, 244
Philip III 159, 171
Philip IV 131-2, 134, 136, 138, 173, 219
Philip V 105, 209-10, 219, 222, 227
    funerals and obsequies for 219, 222,
        223, 225-8, 231-2
Pike, Burton 205
Pijao 75, 77–80, 86, 88, 89
    see also Coyaima
Pizarro, Francisco 222
Poggio, Eleonora 194
Portugal 5, 56, 131, 133–8, 176, 194
Potosí 174, 179, 225
Pouncey, Lorene 222
Prado, Jerónimo de, Jesuit 244
prágmatica de los lutos (funeral regulations)
    220
pre-Columbian era 291, 293, 296, 300, 302,
    304
    definition of 293n3
    surviving practices 297
Protestantism/Protestants 109, 114–16,
    122, 200
providentialism 179, 180, 221
    urban 173, 177, 183
    debates on 180–81
Pyrrhonism 142

Quiché 293
Quietism 109
Quito 151, 159-62

R. de la Flor, Fernando 23, 152n3, 221
race 5, 7, 8, 11, 357, 39–41, 43, 49-50
    biological definition of 36

314 *The Transatlantic Hispanic Baroque*

typological and geographical concepts
of 39
Ramírez, Alonso 171
Infortunios de Alonso Ramírez (1690)
171
Ramírez, Antonio 248
Ramos del Manzano, Francisco 140
Rappaport, Joanne 247
reducción 247
Renaissance 23, 176, 177, 208, 211, 237,
295
resguardo (reserves) 75, 78, 80–81, 83, 87,
88
Rey Fajardo, José del 159n16
Reyes, Alfonso 179
Riaz de los Mozos, Mónica 222
Ribero, Pedro de 210
Ringrose, David R. 207
Río Barredo, María José el 208
Robertson, Jamie 76-7
Roche, Daniel 187
Rodriguez, Lína 152n3
Rodríguez Castelo, Hernán 160, 162
Root, Michael 7, 36, 49
Rojas, Alonso 151, 159
Rome 106, 134, 176, 207, 222, 242–3, 276,
279, 281-2, 284, 285–6
Rufino Barrios, Justo, president 269

St Augustine 48, 151, 242, 245, 248
St Franciso Solano 273
St John of Damascus 244
St Juan Diego, 273, 274, 281-2, 284, 288
canonization of 273
St Martín de Porres 173
St Rose of Lima 161, 173
St Stephen 245–6
St Teresa of Ávila 109
St Toribio de Mogrovejo 173
Sainz de Valivieso Torrejón, Miguel 224,
225–6
Santa Maria della Vittoria 109
Salamanca, 7, 55, 59, 176, 178, 222
University of 55-70

appeal to Italian humanist culture
59
elite imperial identity of 58
and *estudiantes extranjeros* 56, 58,
69
as Spanish "imperial space" 58, 69
Irish students and colleges 578
see also Da Sommaia, Girolamo
Salazar, Eugenio de, member of the Council
of the Indies 176
Salinas y Córdoba, Buenaventura de,
Franciscan 182, 183, 224
*Memorial de las Historias del Nuevo
Mundo: Perú* (1630)
Salvatierra, Count of 182
Sánchez, Miguel, Jesuit 237
*Imagen de la Virgen María, Madre de
Dios de Guadalupe* (1648) 244
Sandoval, Alonso de 41–2
Santander, José Antonio 228
Sebastián, Santiago 248
Second Vatican Council (1962-1965) 275,
278, 279, 281–2
Seneca, influence on "national politics" 142
Severo, Don 293
Sierra de los Cuchumatanes 256
Sigüenza y Góngora, Carlos 171
Skinner, Quentin 24
slavery/slaves 21, 35n.1, 41, 79, 175, 176
Smit, Bonaventura De 106
Smith, Carol A. 294
Solórzano Pereira, Juan de 180
Política indiana (1647)
Solomon's Temple 238, 239, 243, 244
See also New Jerusalem
Spain 2, 8, 42, 46, 50, 58-62, 68-70, 95-101,
106-110, 241, 243, 259, 262–6,
268, 279, 294
and Catholicism 114, 117, 119, 121
funeral rituals, standardization of
221
Crowns of 140
and foreigners 187–8, 192–4

Index

hegemony and imperium of 56, 60n17, 61-2, 67, 75, 176, 122-23, 130–31, 189-90
identity restoration of 139-40
and leadership 116
metropolises and urbanity of 175–8
and military defeat 195
residence and naturalization in 191–6
Spanish monarchy 34, 68, 10, 56–9, 63, 116–17, 123, 130-131, 136, 171, 181, 187–8, 190, 195, 198, 208, 221, 227
reform and renewal of 117
Stelluti, Francesco, 45, 46n6
Suárez, Juan Luis 24
sub-Saharan Africa 35–6, 41–2, 46
Superunda, Count of 230
syncretism 11, 276, 291, 292, 298, 300, 303

Tamariz de Carmona, Antonio 246
Tapié, Victor-Lucien 105
Taylor, Charles 19
Tenochtitlan 178
Thirty Years' War 132
Tlatelolco, destruction of 243
Túpac Amaru II, rebellion of (1780) 232
Torquemada, Juan de 412
Torres, Felipe de la 238
Tovar Martín, Virginia 209
Treaty of Utrecht 219
Turner, Victor 287

United Provinces *see* Low Countries

Valenzuela, Pedro de 134
Valenzuela Márquez, Jaime 221

Vatican 273–6, 279–80, 281
Vatican II *see* Second Vatican Council
Vázquez, Francisco 260
Crónica de la Provincia del Santísimo Nombre de Jesús (1688) 260
Vázquez de Espinosa, Antonio, 180
Compendio y descripción de las Indias occidentales (1630)
Verdú Ruiz, Matilde, 215
Vico, Giambattista 153
Victoria, Tomás Luis de, composer 103
Vienna, Court of 135
Villalobos, Arias de 179
Villalpando, Cristóbal de, painter 248
The Church Militant and the Church Triumphant
Viñas Mey, Carmelo, 197
Vitelleschi, Mutio, Jesuit 161
Virgin of Guadalupe 11, 173, 244, 273–4, 276, 283, 286, 288
Virgin Mary 122, 173, 237, 244-5, 296
ceremonials associated with 173
Spanish devotion to 122

Wachtendonck, Hendrick de 116
Wade, Peter 35, 50
Wallerstein, Immanuel 300
War of Devolution 136
Watteville, Baron de, Spanish ambassador 131
Whorf, Benjamin Lee 152n4
Wölfflin, Heinrich 1

Yoon, Carol Kaesuk 37n2

Zapotec Martyrs of Cajonos, Oaxaca 285-6

Lightning Source UK Ltd.
Milton Keynes UK
UKHW020955141022
410458UK00004B/60